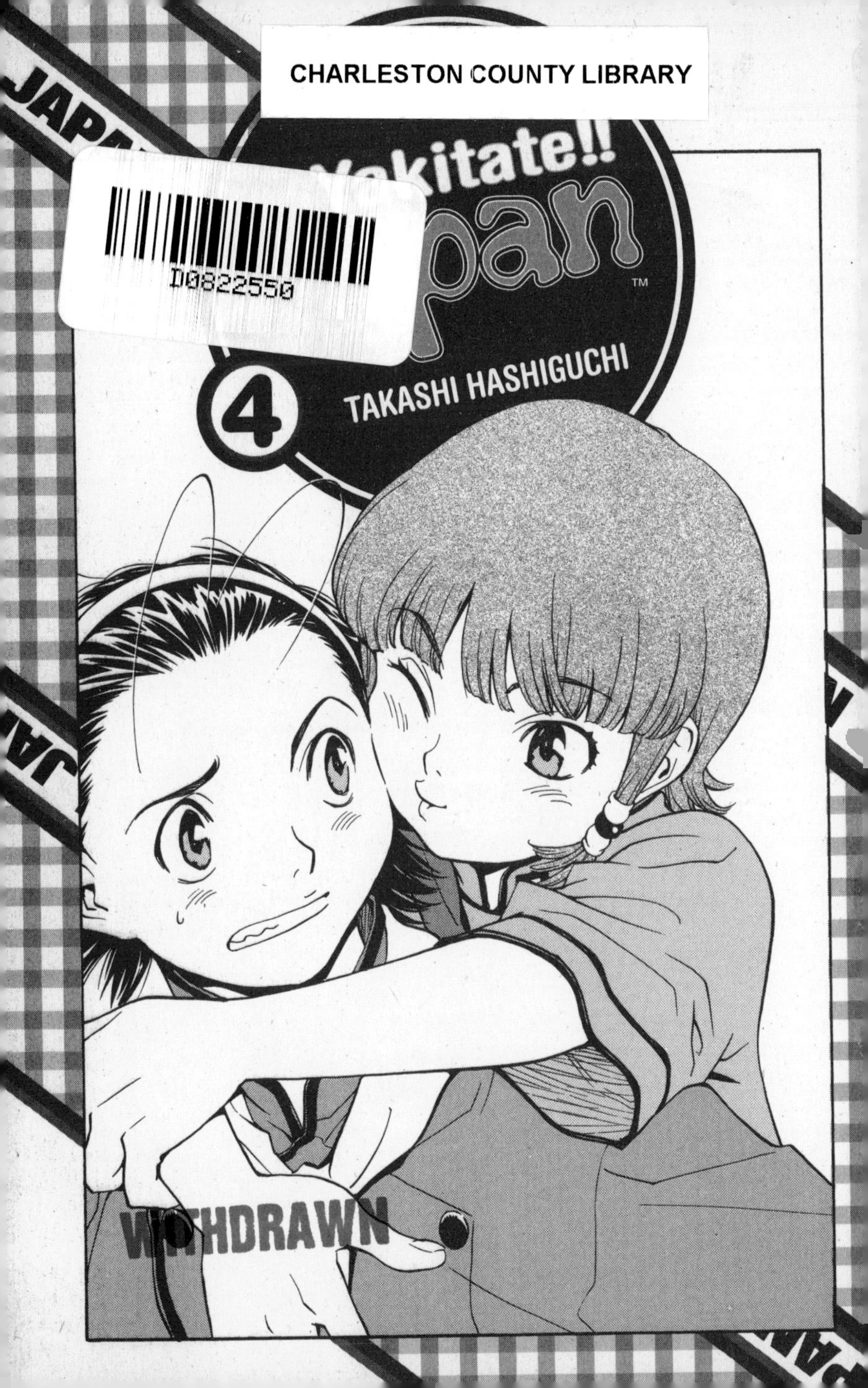
kitate!!
pan
™
4
TAKASHI HASHIGUCHI
JAPAN

YAKITATE!! JAPAN
4
VIZ Media Edition

★The Story Thus Far★

Kazuma Azuma is a young baker obsessed with creating an original bread, or "Ja-pan," that will come to symbolize his nation. Using the "Hands of the Sun," warm hands that are well-suited to making bread dough, Kazuma has a good shot at accomplishing his lofty goal!

Tsukino Azusagawa, scion of Japan's number one bakery chain, Pantasia, spotted his talent at a store competition and hired him to boost sales at the store's South Tokyo Branch. The knowledgeable Kawachi, Kazuma's rival and sometimes friend, was hired at the same time.

Now, the two young bakers are fighting to win the annual Rookie Tournament within the Pantasia Group. Although the two passed through the first preliminary without trouble, Azuma had a difficult time in the second preliminary after making a near-disastrous ingredient choice. He somehow managed to clear that hurdle by employing the super-sophisticated "Ultra C" technique, then passed the second preliminary along with Kawachi.

However, the assignment in the Main Competition is melon bread, a recipe Kazuma has struggled with in the past…What is he going to do?!

CONTENTS

Research Assistance: Koichi Uchimura
(Bakery Consultant).

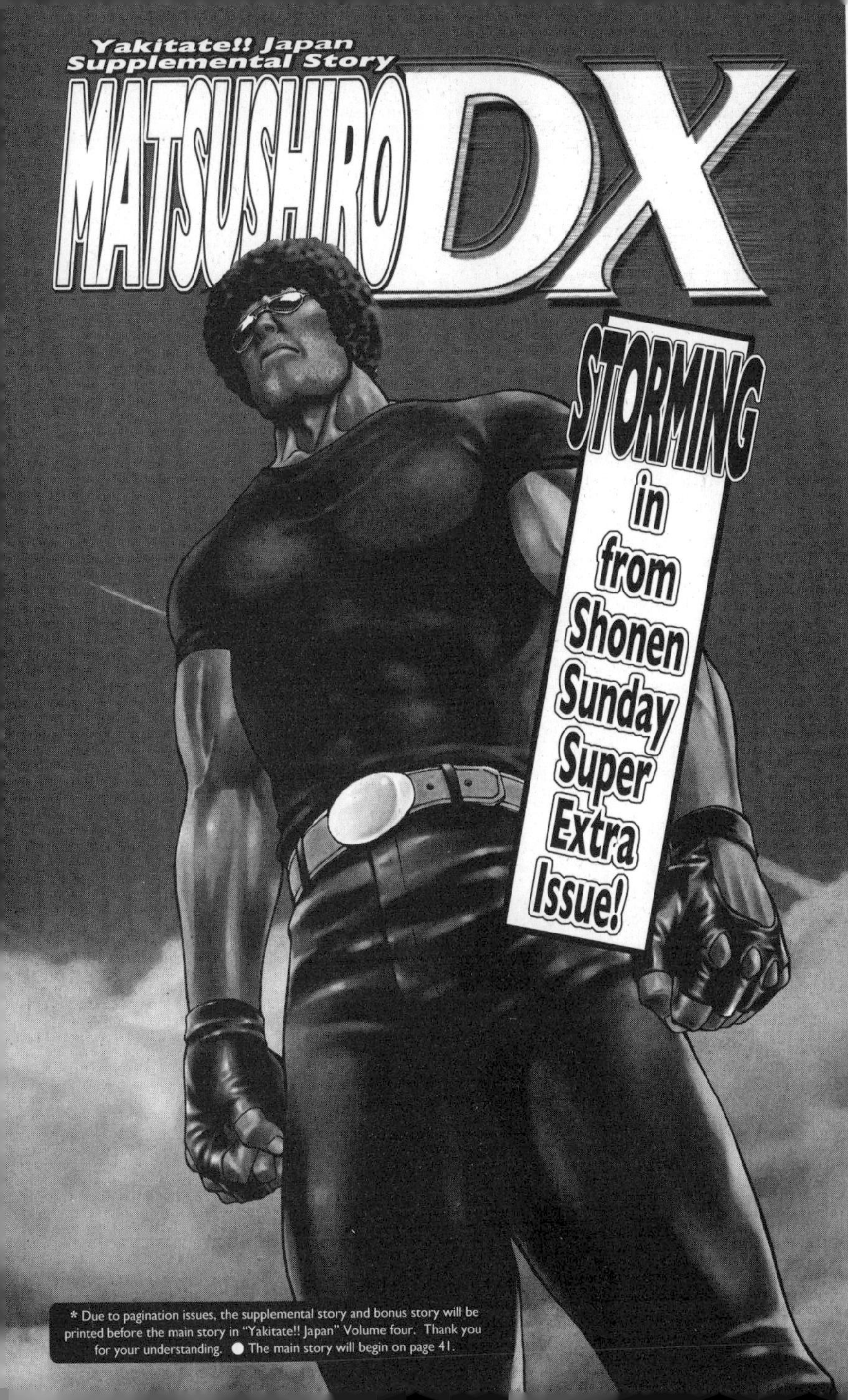
Yakitate!! Japan
Supplemental Story
MATSUSHIRO DX
STORMING in from Shonen Sunday Super Extra Issue!

* Due to pagination issues, the supplemental story and bonus story will be printed before the main story in "Yakitate!! Japan" Volume four. Thank you for your understanding. ● The main story will begin on page 41.

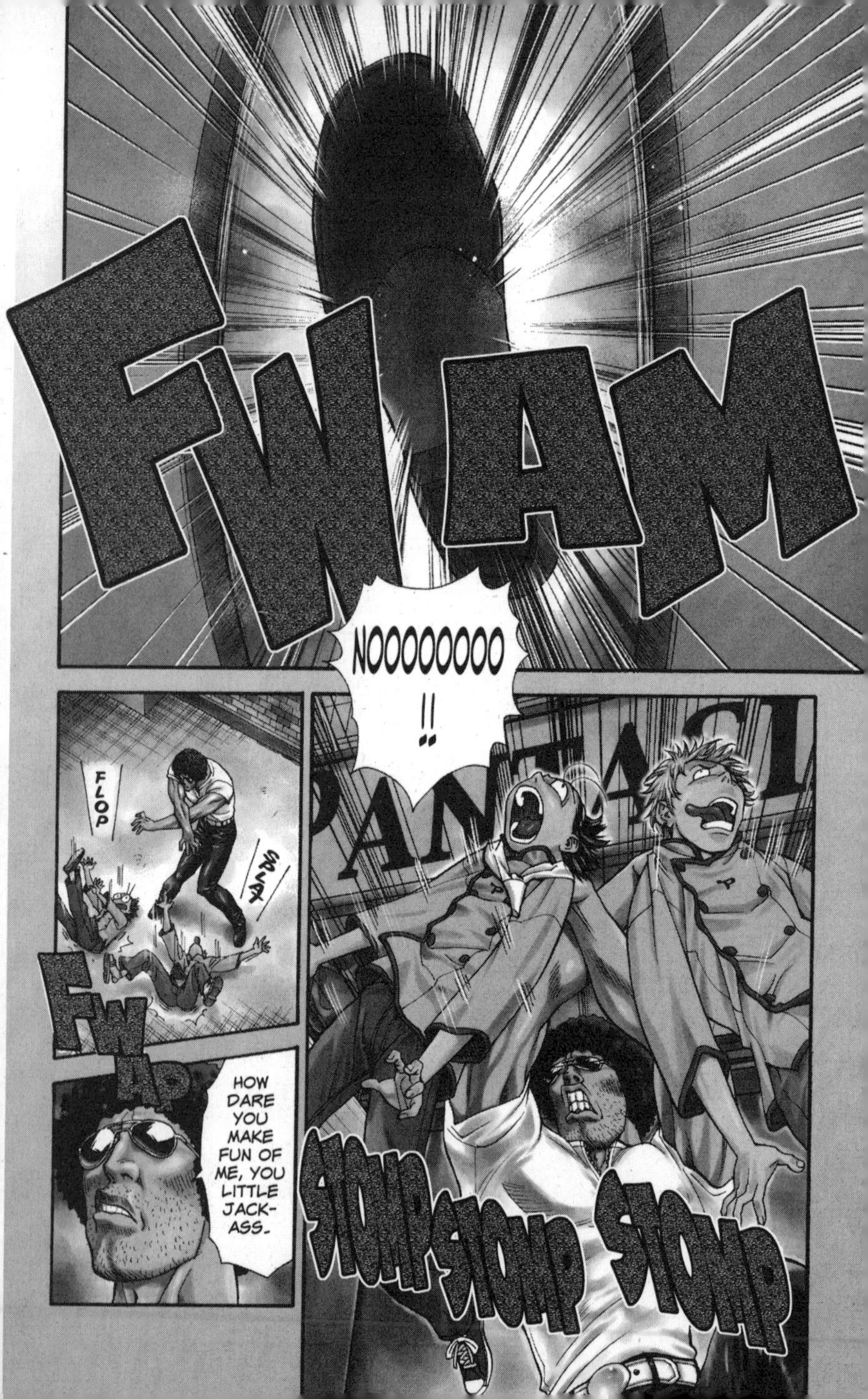
FWAM
NOOOOOOO !!
STOMP STOMP STOMP
FLOP
FWAP
HOW DARE YOU MAKE FUN OF ME, YOU LITTLE JACK-ASS.

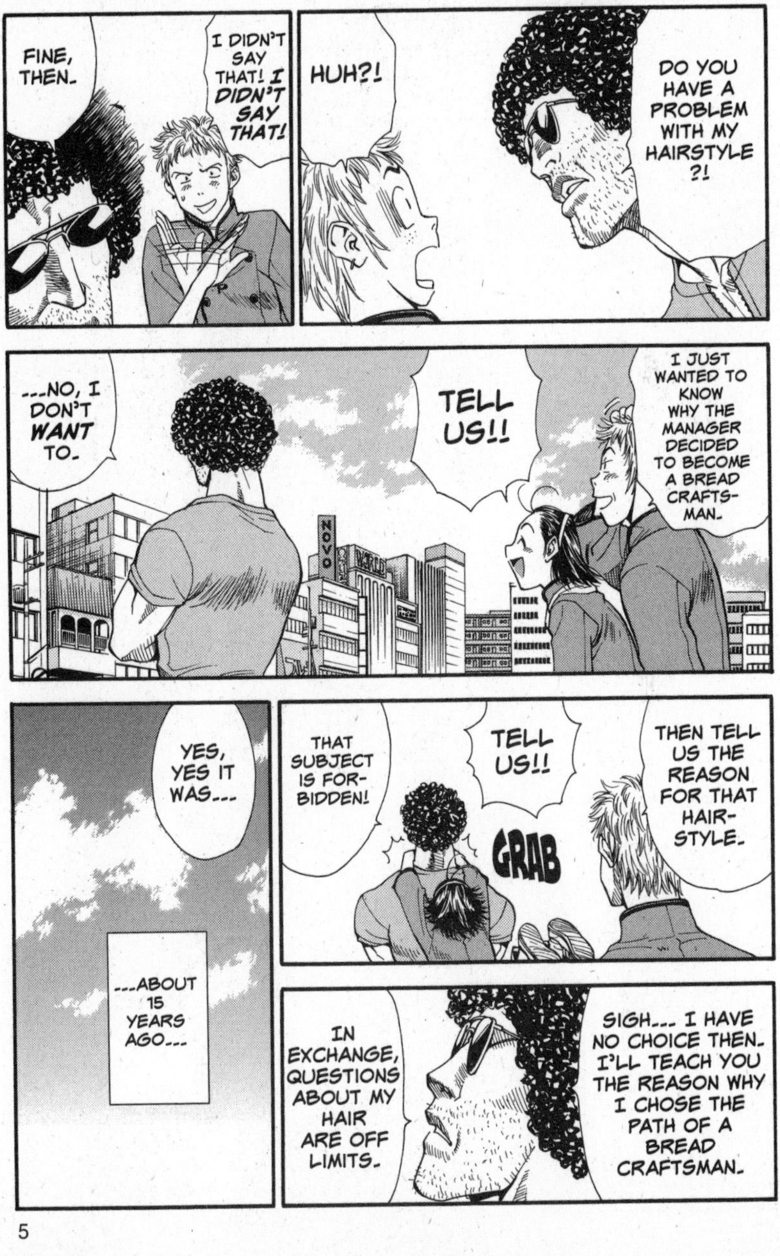
DO YOU HAVE A PROBLEM WITH MY HAIRSTYLE ?!
HUH?!
I DIDN'T SAY THAT! *I DIDN'T SAY THAT!*
FINE, THEN.
I JUST WANTED TO KNOW WHY THE MANAGER DECIDED TO BECOME A BREAD CRAFTS-MAN.
TELL US!!
...NO, I DON'T *WANT* TO.
THEN TELL US THE REASON FOR THAT HAIR-STYLE.
TELL US!!
GRAB
THAT SUBJECT IS FOR-BIDDEN!
SIGH... I HAVE NO CHOICE THEN. I'LL TEACH YOU THE REASON WHY I CHOSE THE PATH OF A BREAD CRAFTSMAN.
IN EXCHANGE, QUESTIONS ABOUT MY HAIR ARE OFF LIMITS.
YES, YES IT WAS...
...ABOUT 15 YEARS AGO...

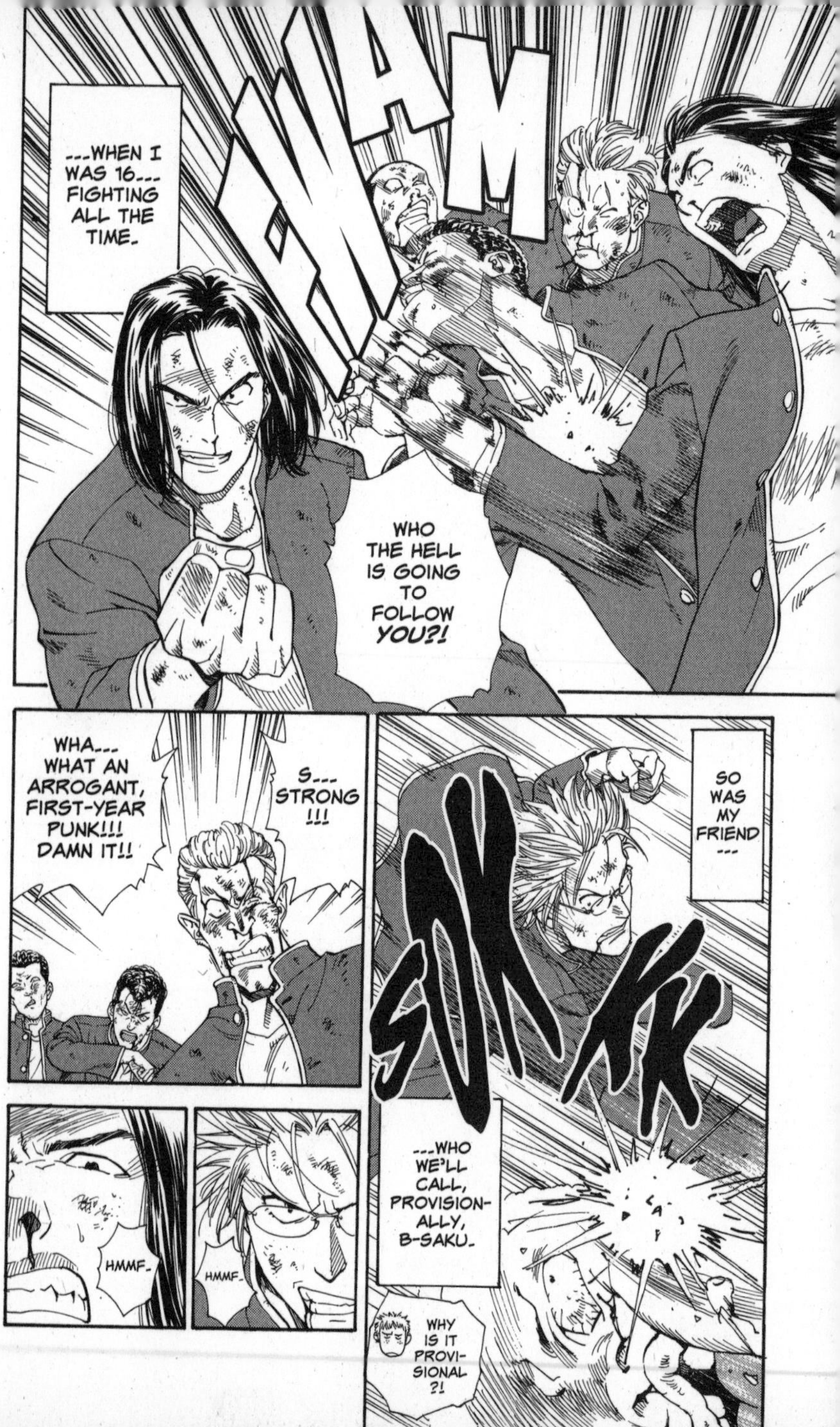
WHAM
---WHEN I WAS 16--- FIGHTING ALL THE TIME.
WHO THE HELL IS GOING TO FOLLOW YOU?!
SO WAS MY FRIEND---
SOKKK
---WHO WE'LL CALL, PROVISIONALLY, B-SAKU.
WHY IS IT PROVISIONAL?!
S--- STRONG!!!
WHA--- WHAT AN ARROGANT, FIRST-YEAR PUNK!!! DAMN IT!!
HMMF.
HMMF.

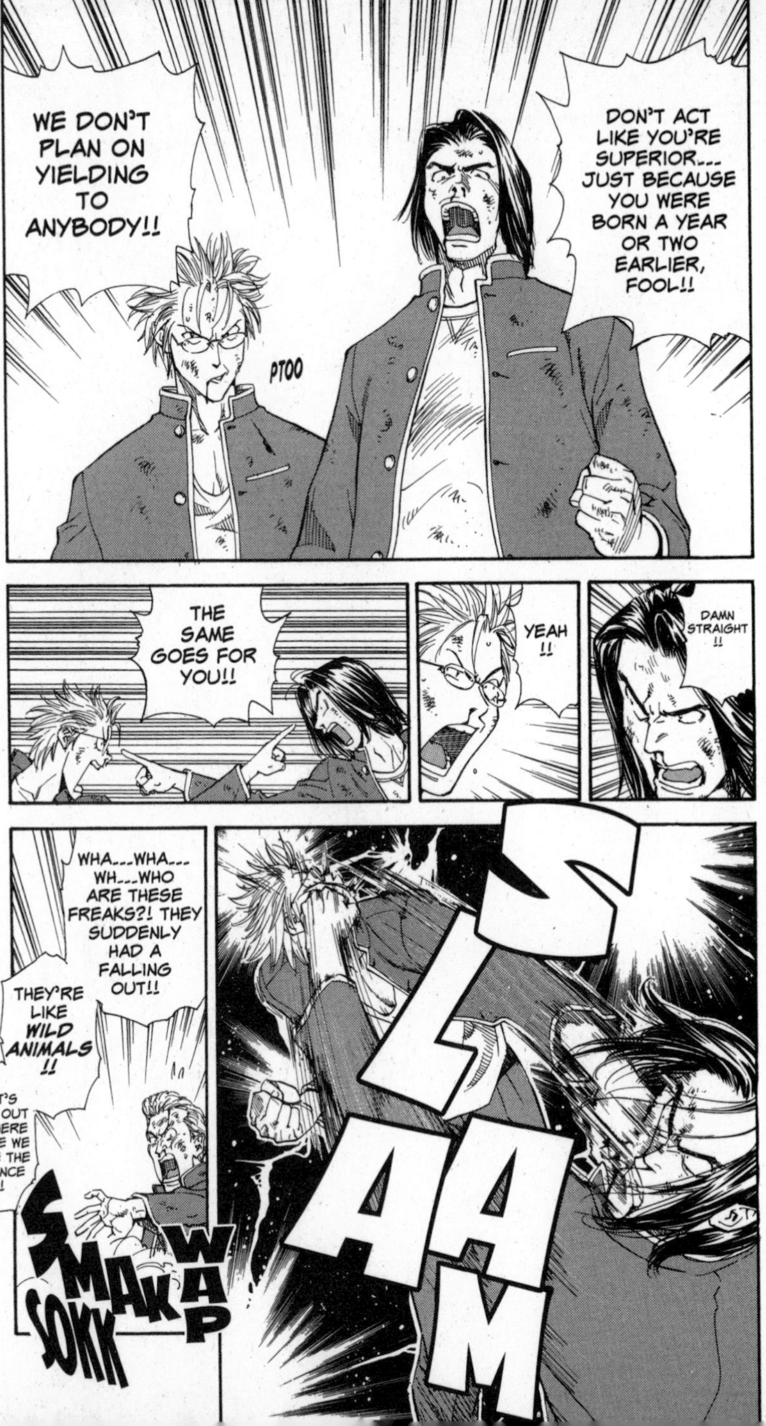
DON'T ACT LIKE YOU'RE SUPERIOR... JUST BECAUSE YOU WERE BORN A YEAR OR TWO EARLIER, FOOL!!
WE DON'T PLAN ON YIELDING TO ANYBODY!!
PTOO
DAMN STRAIGHT!!
YEAH!!
THE SAME GOES FOR YOU!!
SLAAM
WHA...WHA... WH...WHO ARE THESE FREAKS?! THEY SUDDENLY HAD A FALLING OUT!!
THEY'RE LIKE *WILD ANIMALS*!!
LET'S GET OUT OF HERE WHILE WE HAVE THE CHANCE!!
WAP
SMAK
SOKK

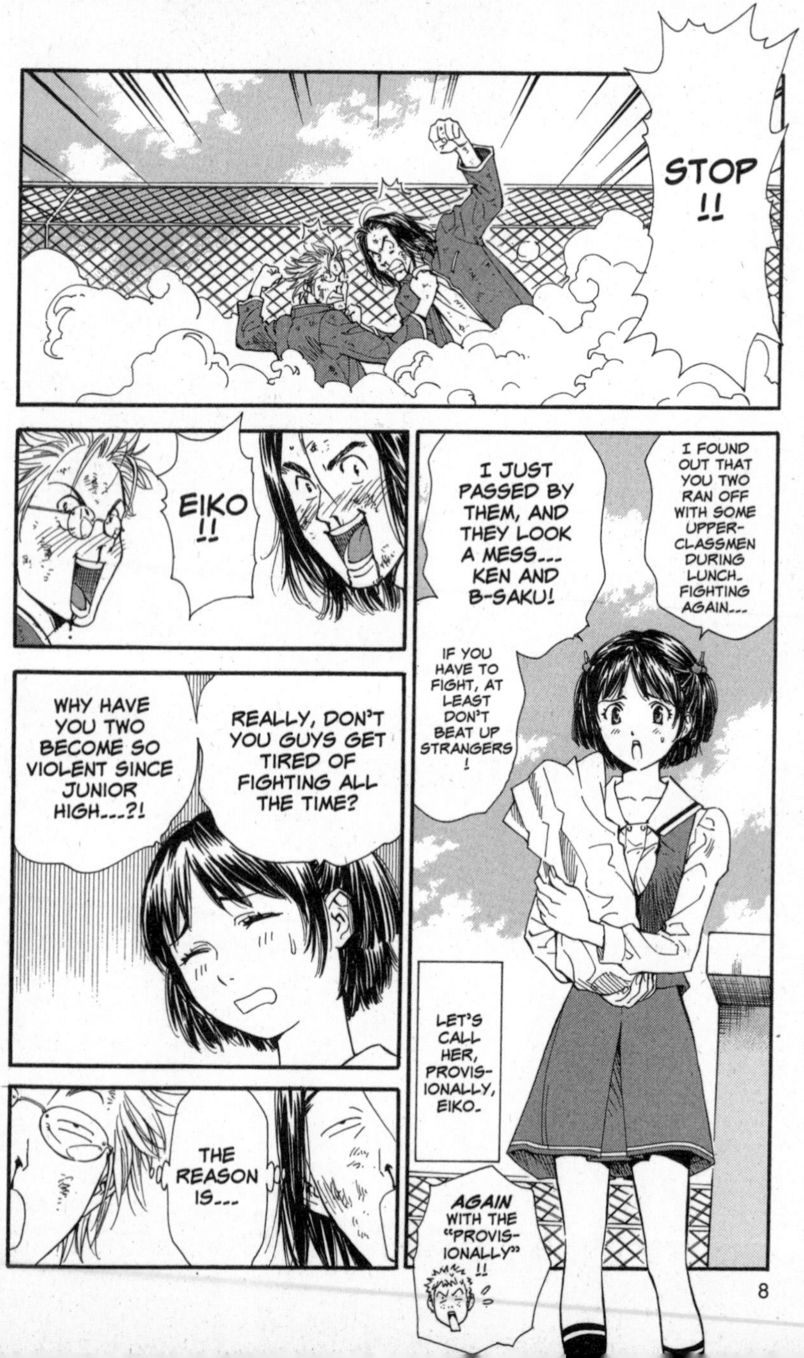
STOP !!
I FOUND OUT THAT YOU TWO RAN OFF WITH SOME UPPER-CLASSMEN DURING LUNCH. FIGHTING AGAIN...
I JUST PASSED BY THEM, AND THEY LOOK A MESS... KEN AND B-SAKU!
IF YOU HAVE TO FIGHT, AT LEAST DON'T BEAT UP STRANGERS!
LET'S CALL HER, PROVISIONALLY, EIKO.
AGAIN WITH THE "PROVISIONALLY" !!
EIKO !!
REALLY, DON'T YOU GUYS GET TIRED OF FIGHTING ALL THE TIME?
WHY HAVE YOU TWO BECOME SO VIOLENT SINCE JUNIOR HIGH...?!
THE REASON IS...

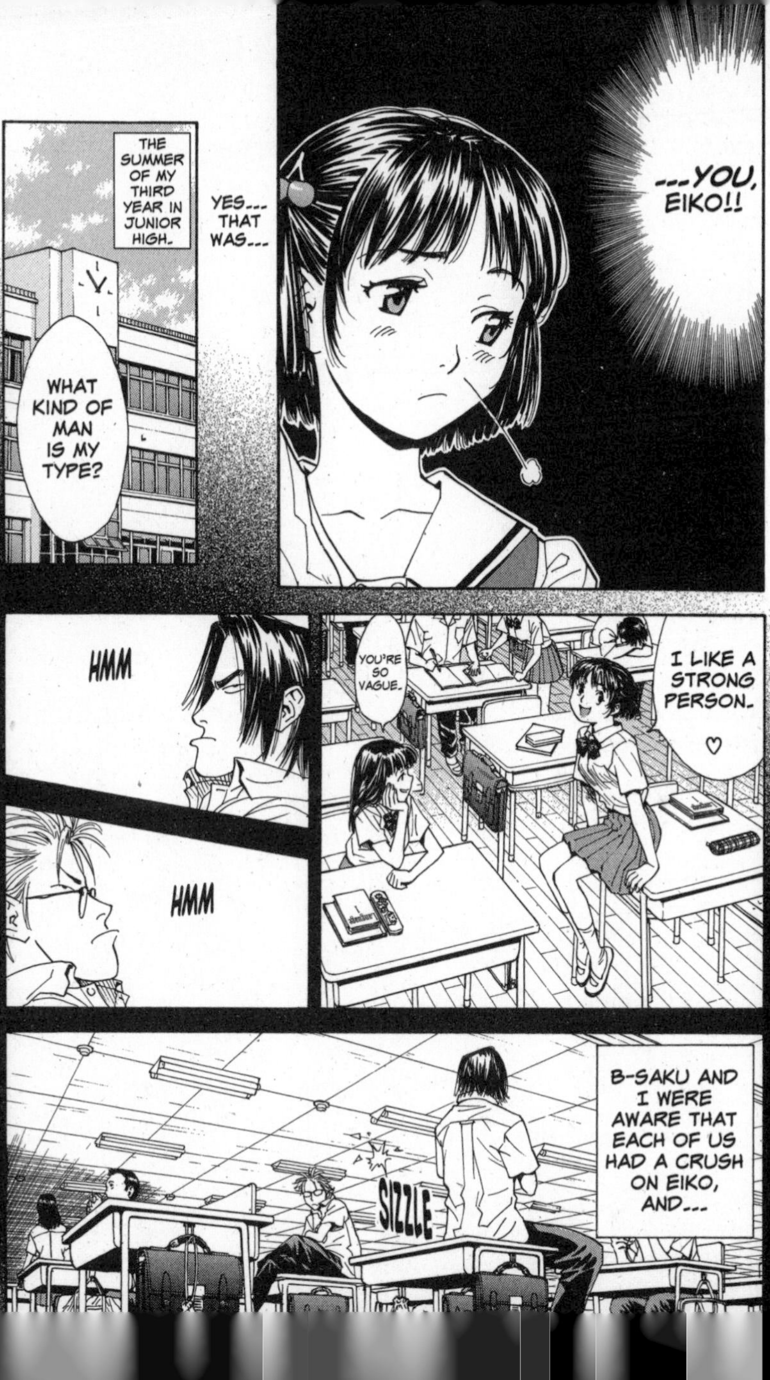
---YOU, EIKO!!
YES... THAT WAS...
THE SUMMER OF MY THIRD YEAR IN JUNIOR HIGH.
WHAT KIND OF MAN IS MY TYPE?
I LIKE A STRONG PERSON. ♡
YOU'RE SO VAGUE.
HMM
HMM
B-SAKU AND I WERE AWARE THAT EACH OF US HAD A CRUSH ON EIKO, AND...
SIZZLE

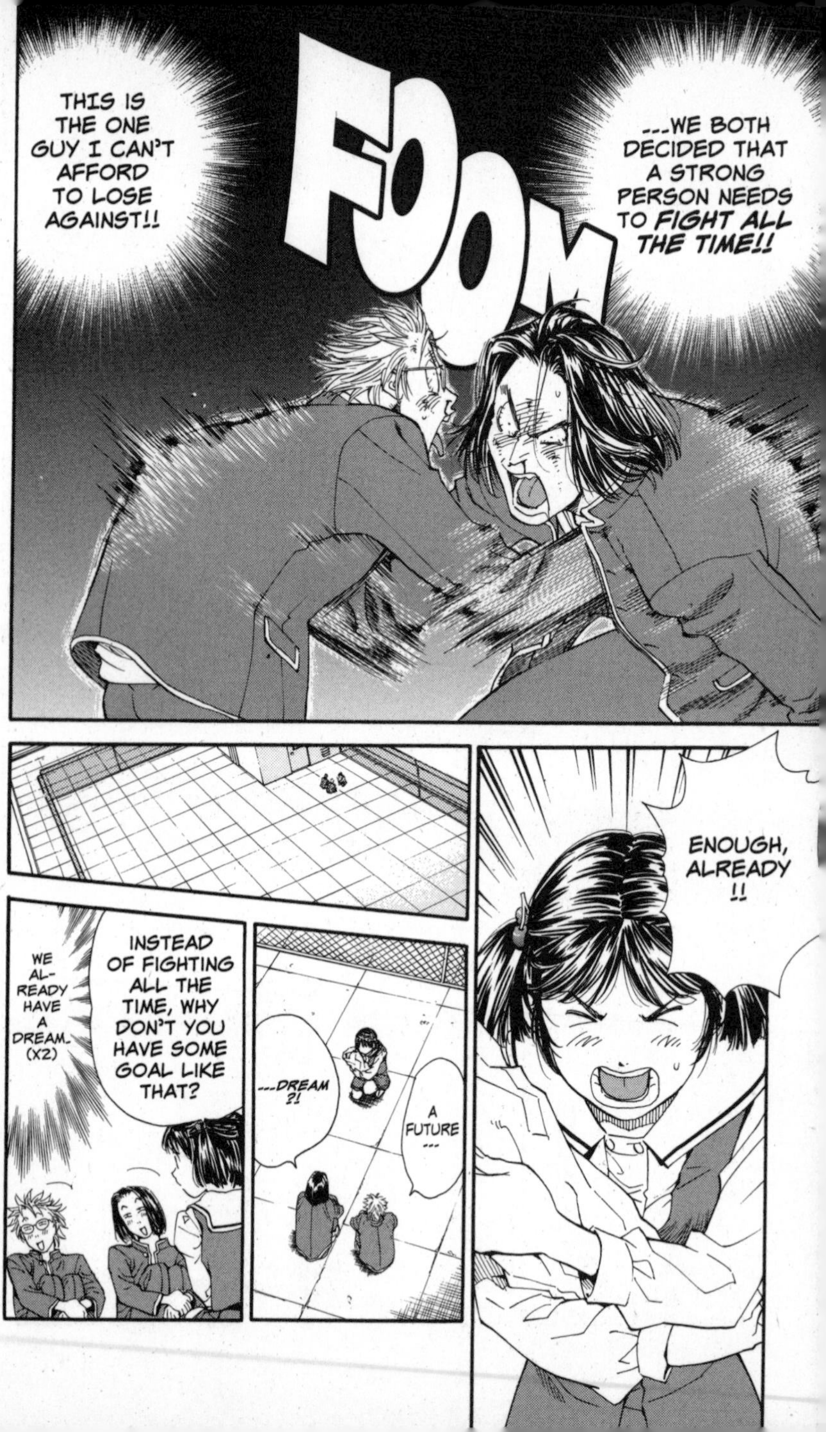
---WE BOTH DECIDED THAT A STRONG PERSON NEEDS TO *FIGHT ALL THE TIME!!*
FOOM
THIS IS THE ONE GUY I CAN'T AFFORD TO LOSE AGAINST!!
ENOUGH, ALREADY!!
A FUTURE ---
---DREAM ?!
INSTEAD OF FIGHTING ALL THE TIME, WHY DON'T YOU HAVE SOME GOAL LIKE THAT?
WE AL-READY HAVE A DREAM. (X2)

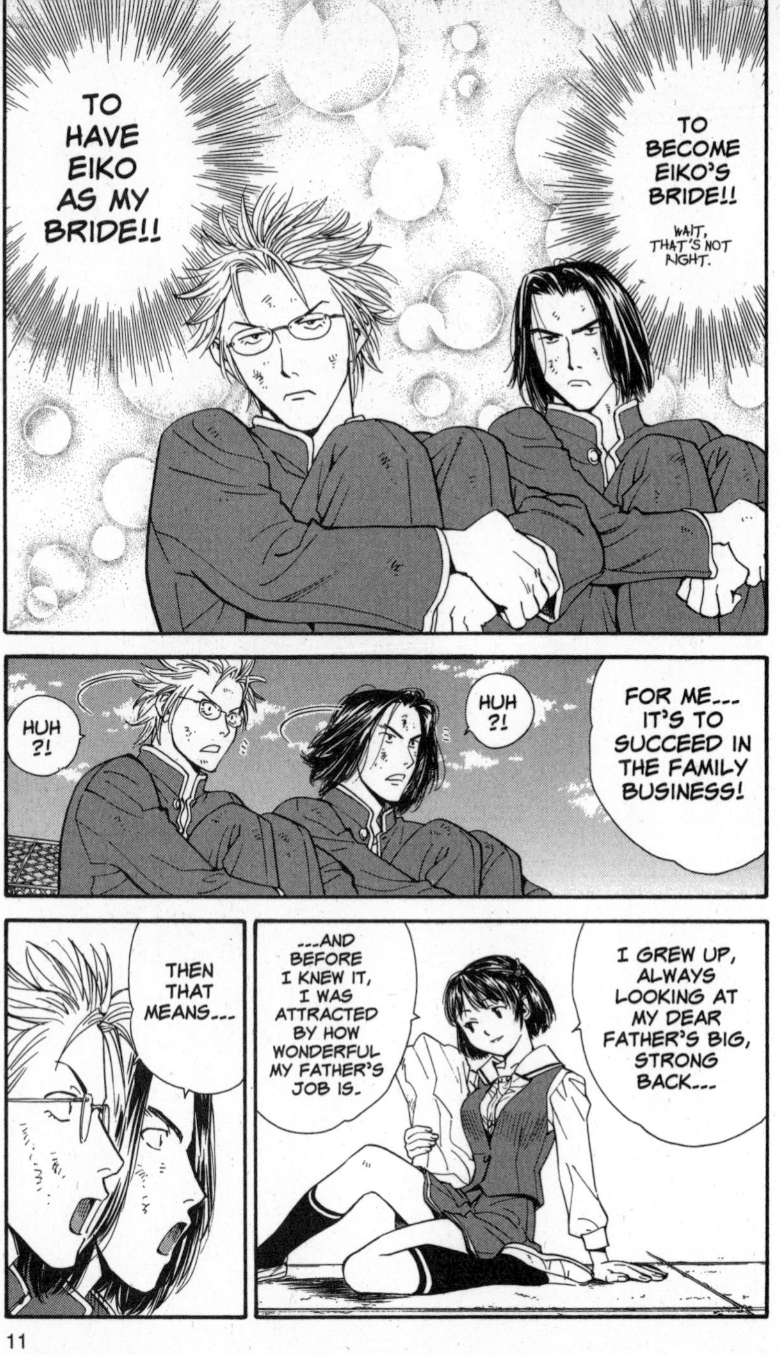
TO BECOME EIKO'S BRIDE!!
WAIT, THAT'S NOT RIGHT.
TO HAVE EIKO AS MY BRIDE!!
FOR ME... IT'S TO SUCCEED IN THE FAMILY BUSINESS!
HUH ?!
HUH ?!
I GREW UP, ALWAYS LOOKING AT MY DEAR FATHER'S BIG, STRONG BACK...
...AND BEFORE I KNEW IT, I WAS ATTRACTED BY HOW WONDERFUL MY FATHER'S JOB IS.
THEN THAT MEANS...

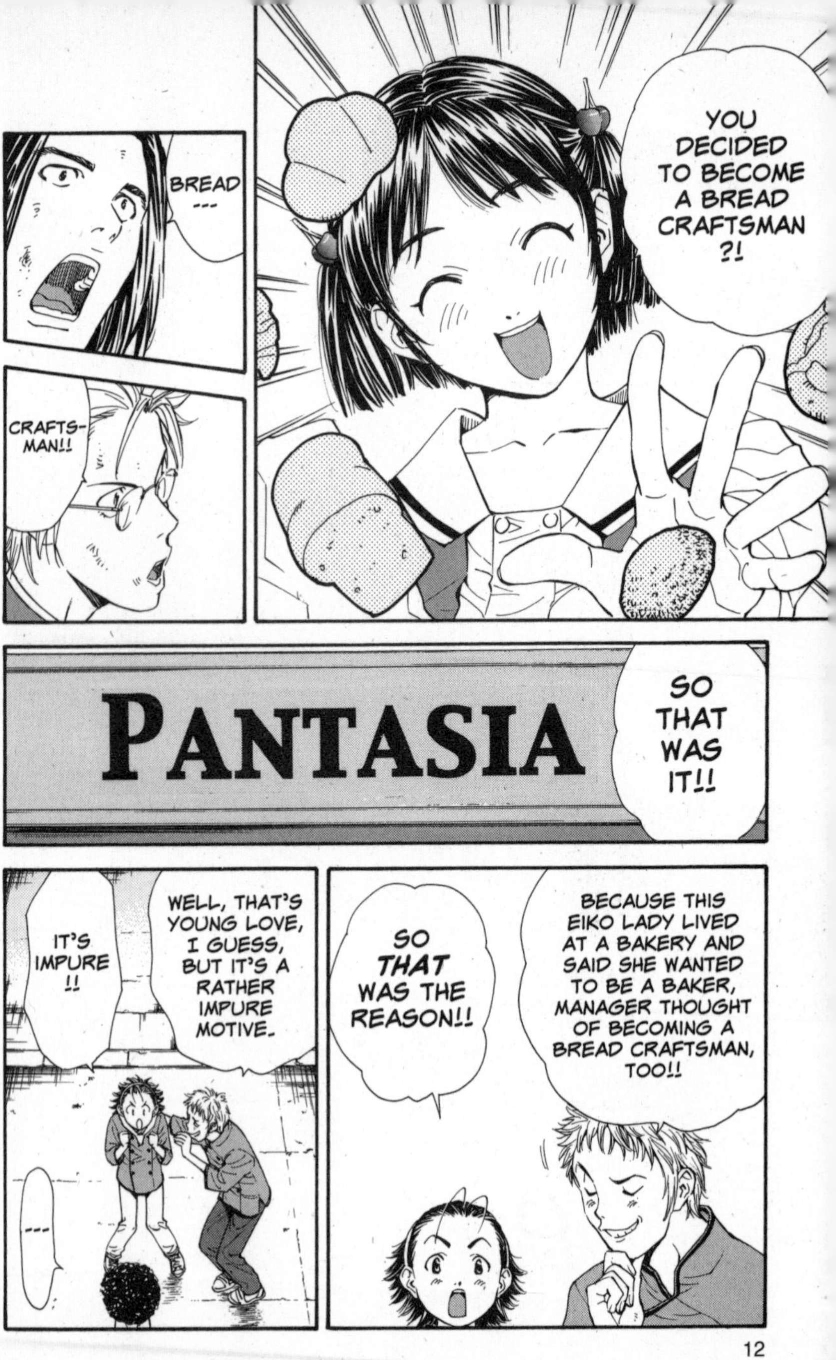
YOU DECIDED TO BECOME A BREAD CRAFTSMAN ?!
BREAD ---
CRAFTS-MAN!!
PANTASIA
SO THAT WAS IT!!
BECAUSE THIS EIKO LADY LIVED AT A BAKERY AND SAID SHE WANTED TO BE A BAKER, MANAGER THOUGHT OF BECOMING A BREAD CRAFTSMAN, TOO!!
SO *THAT* WAS THE REASON!!
WELL, THAT'S YOUNG LOVE, I GUESS, BUT IT'S A RATHER IMPURE MOTIVE.
IT'S IMPURE !!

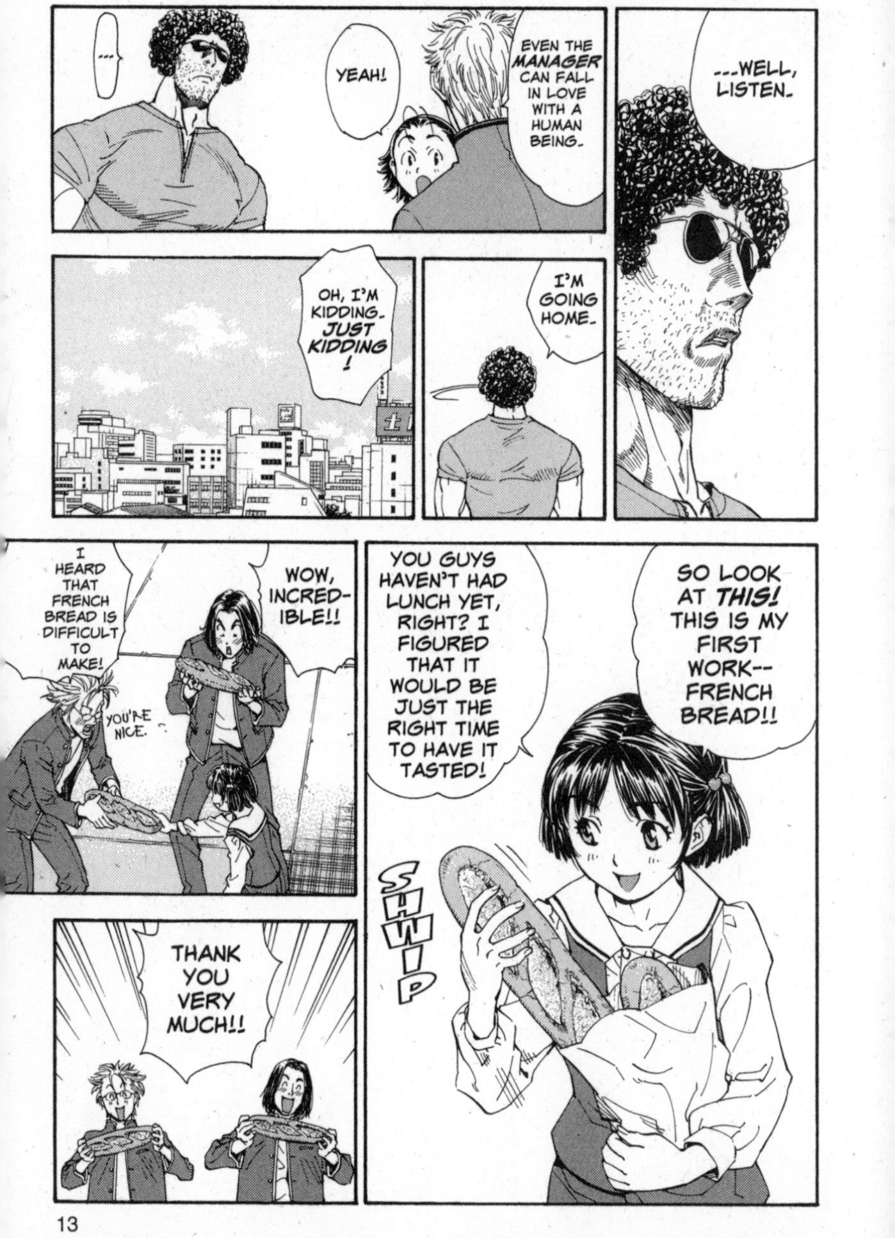
---WELL, LISTEN.
EVEN THE MANAGER CAN FALL IN LOVE WITH A HUMAN BEING.
YEAH!
...
I'M GOING HOME.
OH, I'M KIDDING. JUST KIDDING!
SO LOOK AT THIS! THIS IS MY FIRST WORK-- FRENCH BREAD!!
YOU GUYS HAVEN'T HAD LUNCH YET, RIGHT? I FIGURED THAT IT WOULD BE JUST THE RIGHT TIME TO HAVE IT TASTED!
SHWIP
WOW, INCREDIBLE!!
I HEARD THAT FRENCH BREAD IS DIFFICULT TO MAKE!
YOU'RE NICE.
THANK YOU VERY MUCH!!

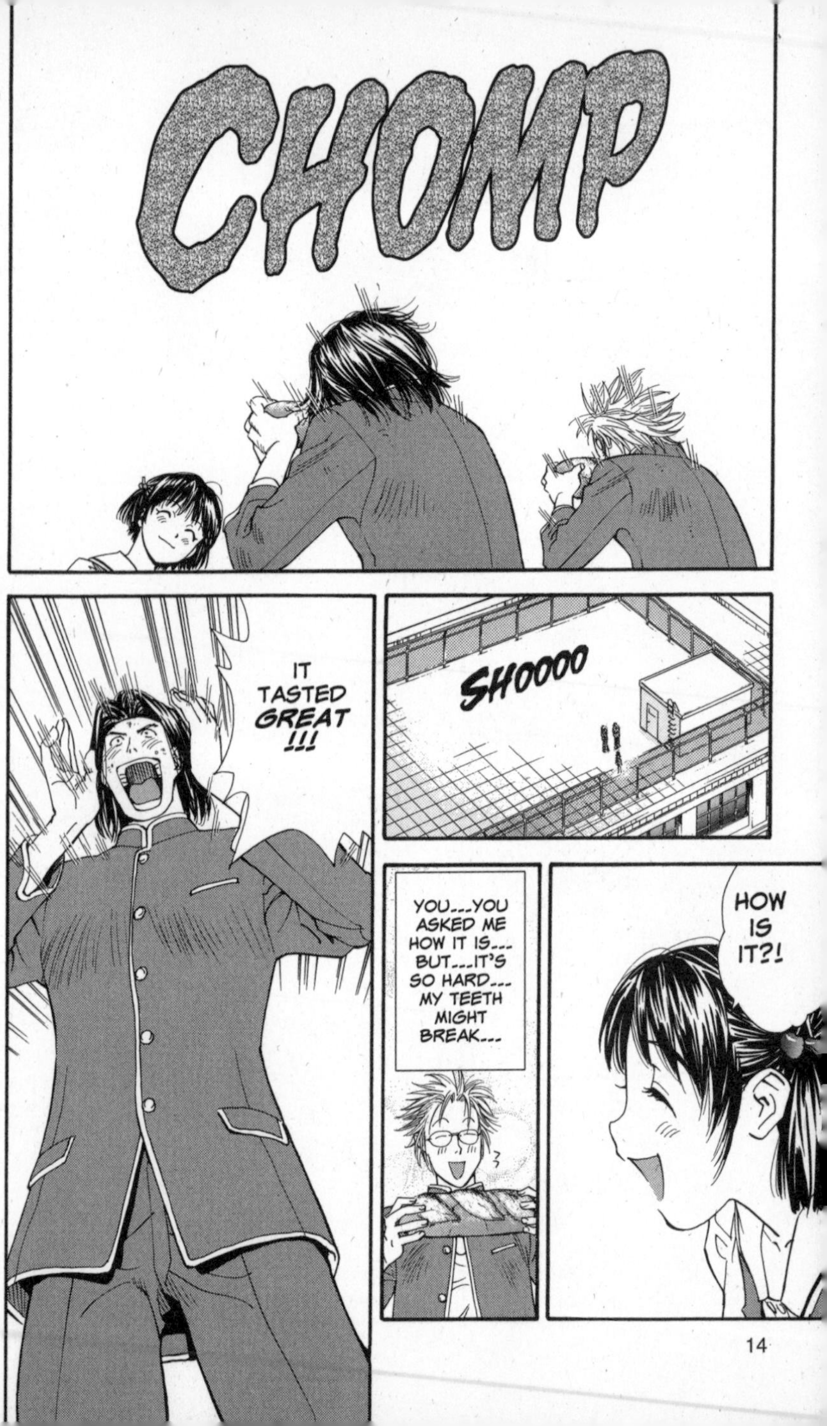
CHOMP
SHOOOO
HOW IS IT?!
YOU...YOU ASKED ME HOW IT IS... BUT...IT'S SO HARD... MY TEETH MIGHT BREAK...
IT TASTED GREAT!!!

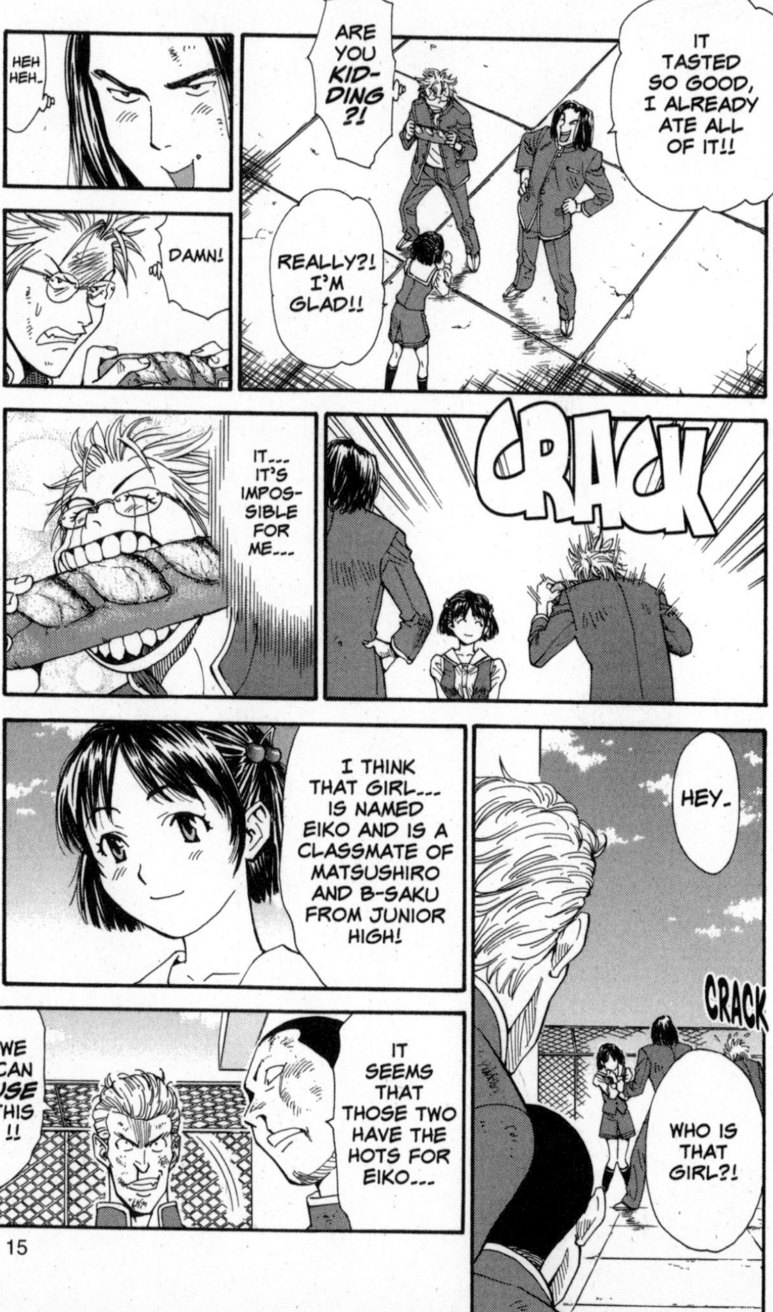
IT TASTED SO GOOD, I ALREADY ATE ALL OF IT!!
ARE YOU KIDDING?!
REALLY?! I'M GLAD!!
HEH HEH..
DAMN!
CRACK
IT... IT'S IMPOSSIBLE FOR ME...
HEY.
CRACK
WHO IS THAT GIRL?!
I THINK THAT GIRL... IS NAMED EIKO AND IS A CLASSMATE OF MATSUSHIRO AND B-SAKU FROM JUNIOR HIGH!
IT SEEMS THAT THOSE TWO HAVE THE HOTS FOR EIKO...
WE CAN USE THIS!!

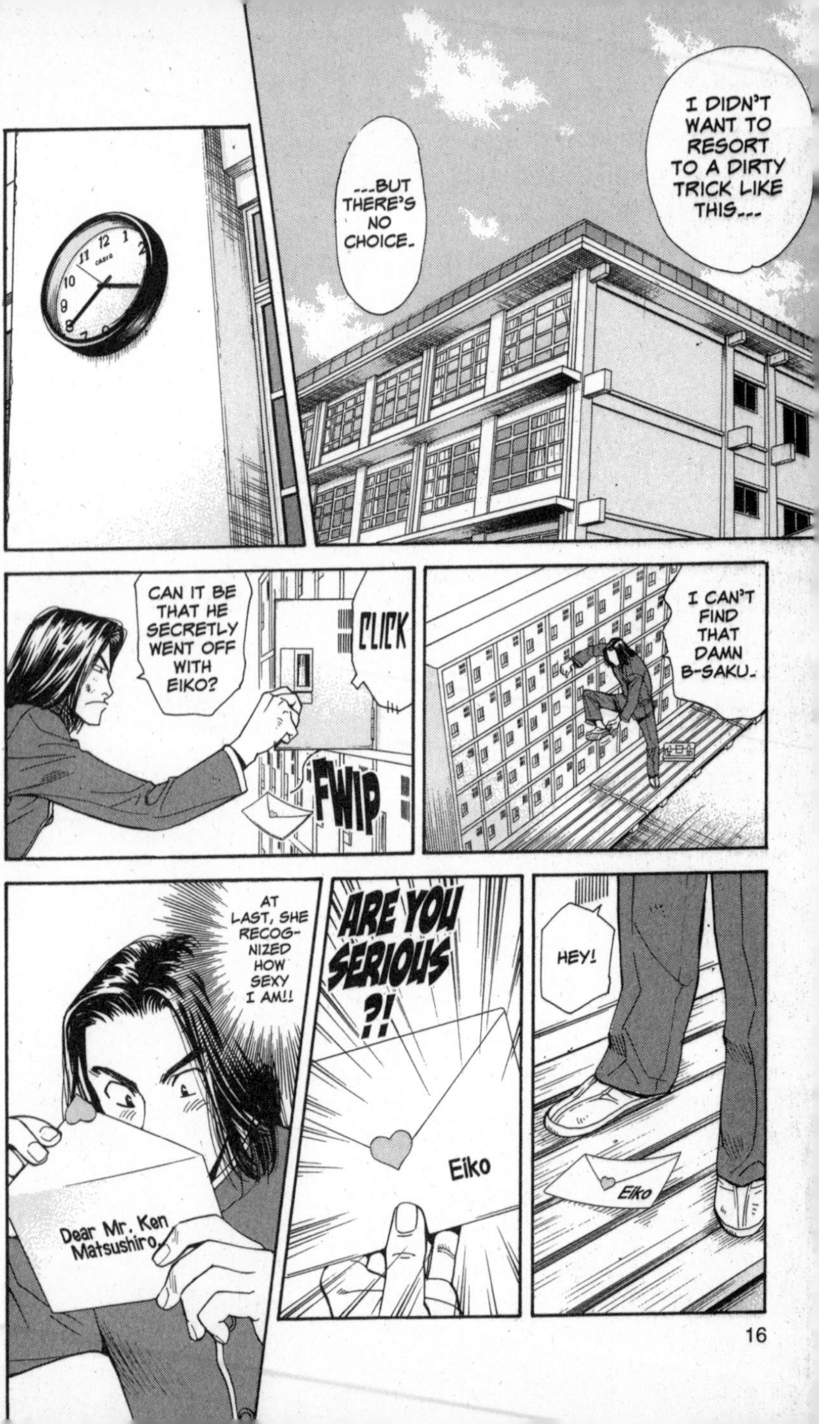
I DIDN'T WANT TO RESORT TO A DIRTY TRICK LIKE THIS...
...BUT THERE'S NO CHOICE.
I CAN'T FIND THAT DAMN B-SAKU.
CAN IT BE THAT HE SECRETLY WENT OFF WITH EIKO?
CLICK
FWIP
HEY!
Eiko
ARE YOU SERIOUS?!
Eiko
AT LAST, SHE RECOGNIZED HOW SEXY I AM!!
Dear Mr. Ken Matsushiro,

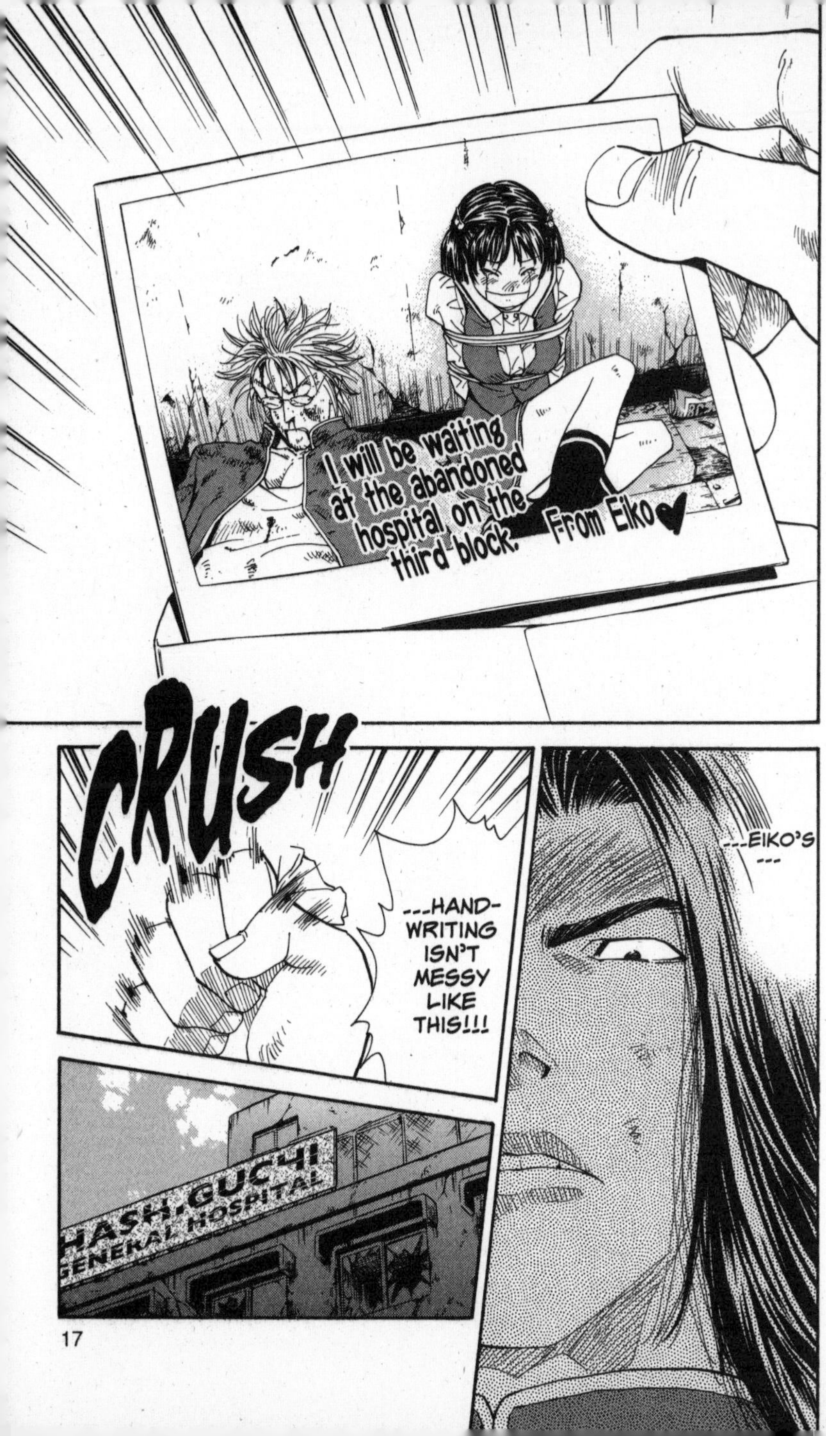

I will be waiting at the abandoned hospital on the third block. From Eiko♥
---EIKO'S ---
CRUSH
---HAND-WRITING ISN'T MESSY LIKE THIS!!!
HASH-GUCHI GENERAL HOSPITAL

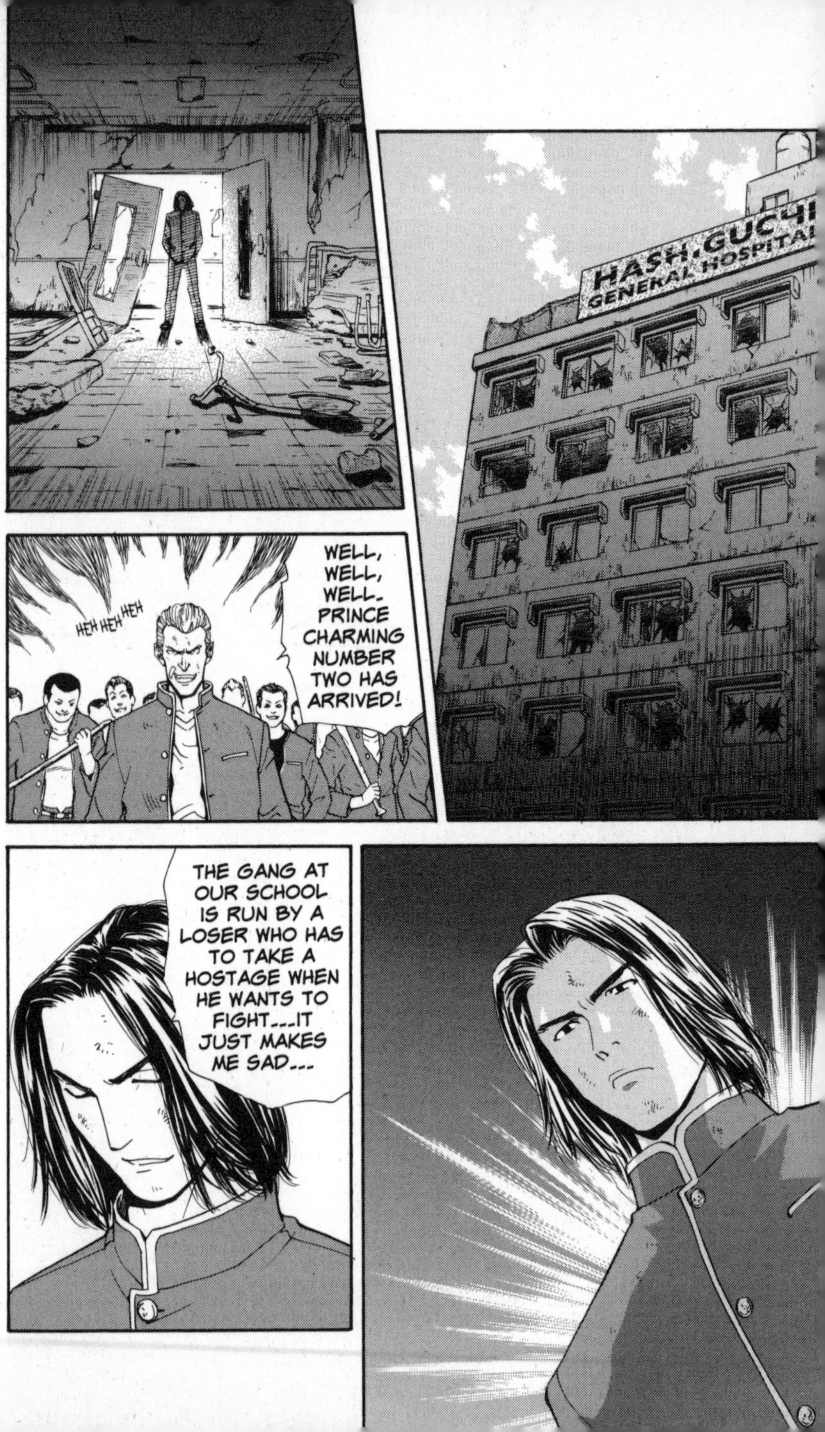
HASHIGUCHI
GENERAL HOSPITAL
HEH HEH HEH
WELL, WELL, WELL. PRINCE CHARMING NUMBER TWO HAS ARRIVED!
THE GANG AT OUR SCHOOL IS RUN BY A LOSER WHO HAS TO TAKE A HOSTAGE WHEN HE WANTS TO FIGHT...IT JUST MAKES ME SAD...

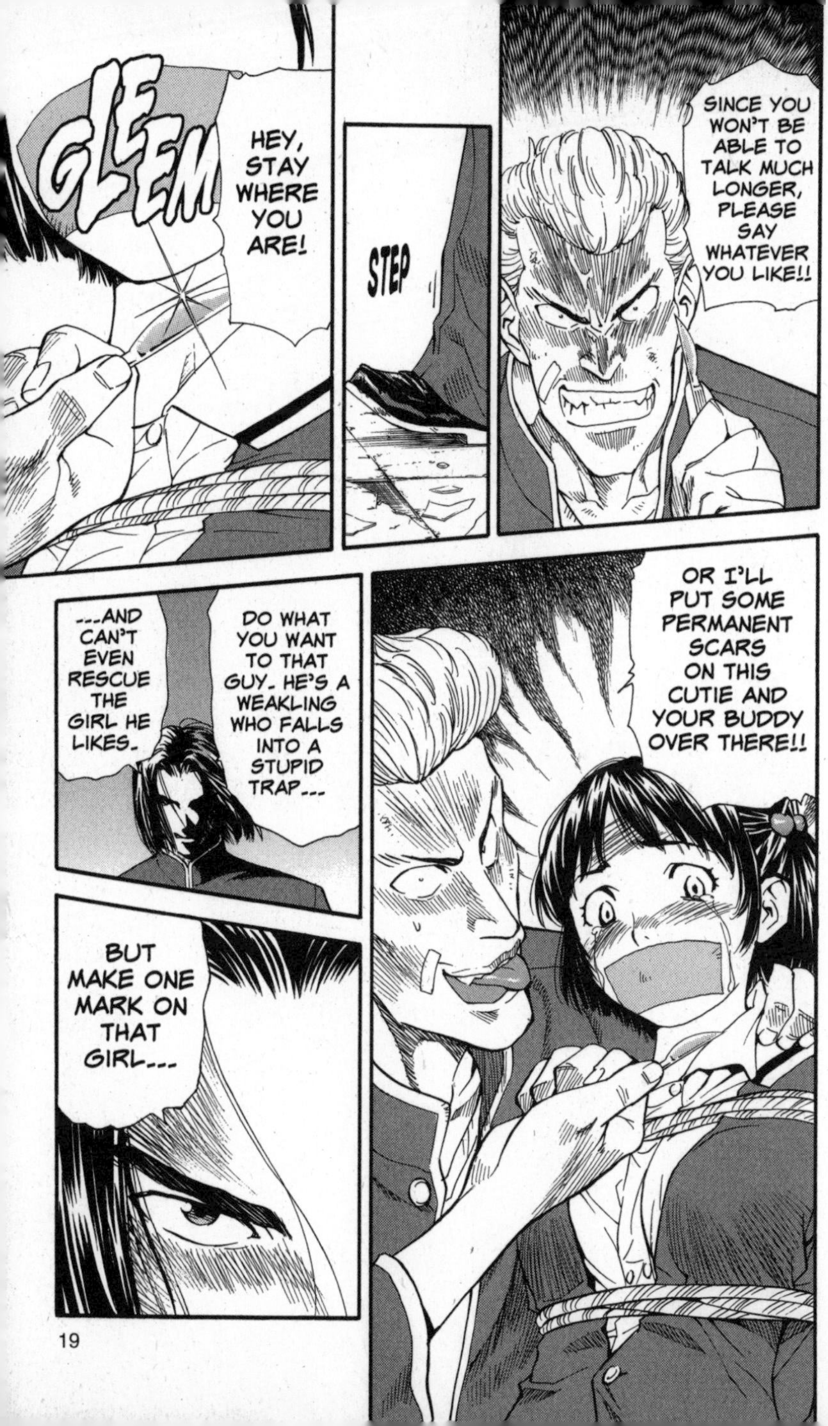
SINCE YOU WON'T BE ABLE TO TALK MUCH LONGER, PLEASE SAY WHATEVER YOU LIKE!!
STEP
GLEEM
HEY, STAY WHERE YOU ARE!
OR I'LL PUT SOME PERMANENT SCARS ON THIS CUTIE AND YOUR BUDDY OVER THERE!!
DO WHAT YOU WANT TO THAT GUY. HE'S A WEAKLING WHO FALLS INTO A STUPID TRAP...
...AND CAN'T EVEN RESCUE THE GIRL HE LIKES.
BUT MAKE ONE MARK ON THAT GIRL...

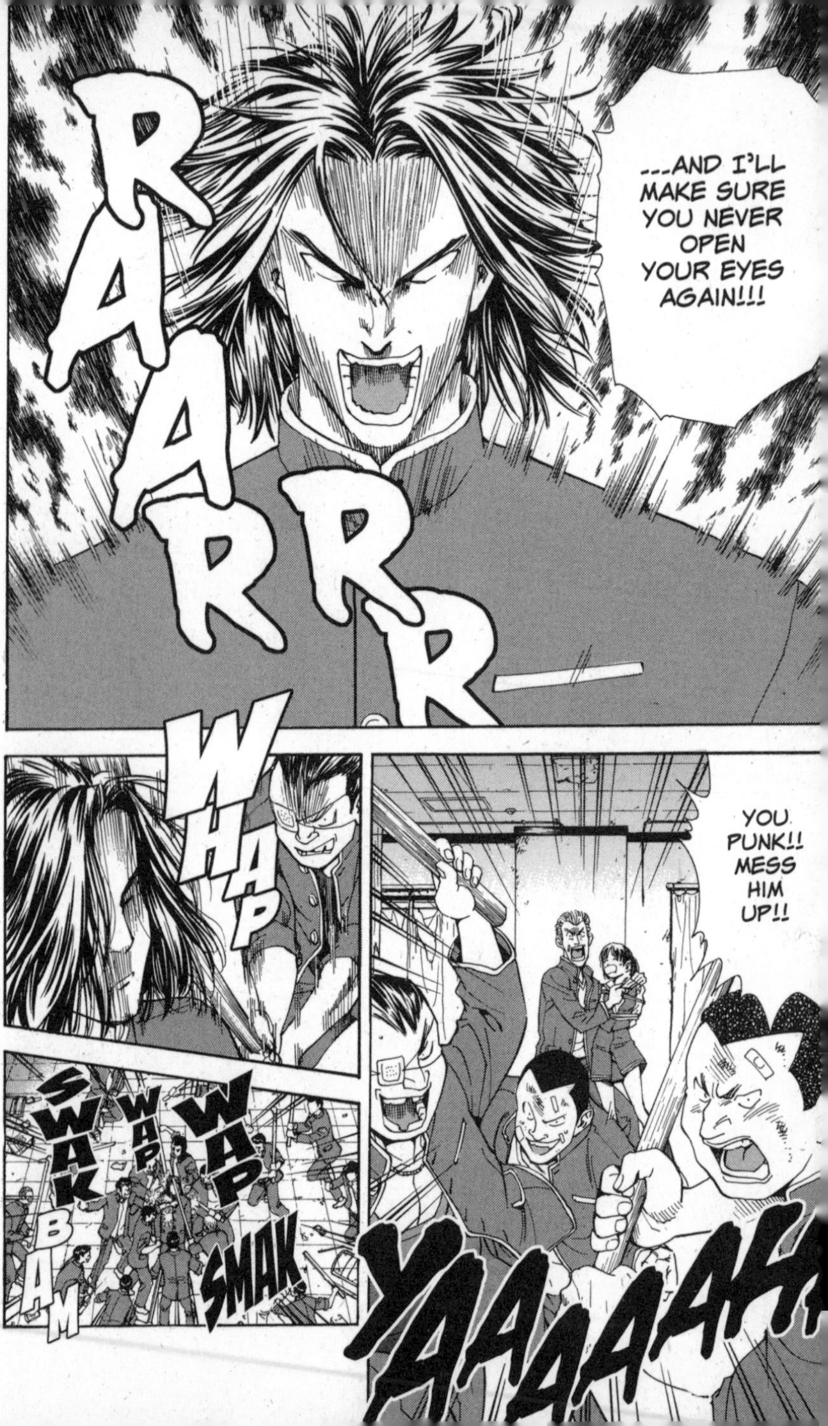

---AND I'LL MAKE SURE YOU NEVER OPEN YOUR EYES AGAIN!!!
RAARRR-
YOU PUNK!! MESS HIM UP!!
YAAAAAH
WHAP
WAP
WAP
SWAK
SMAK
BAM

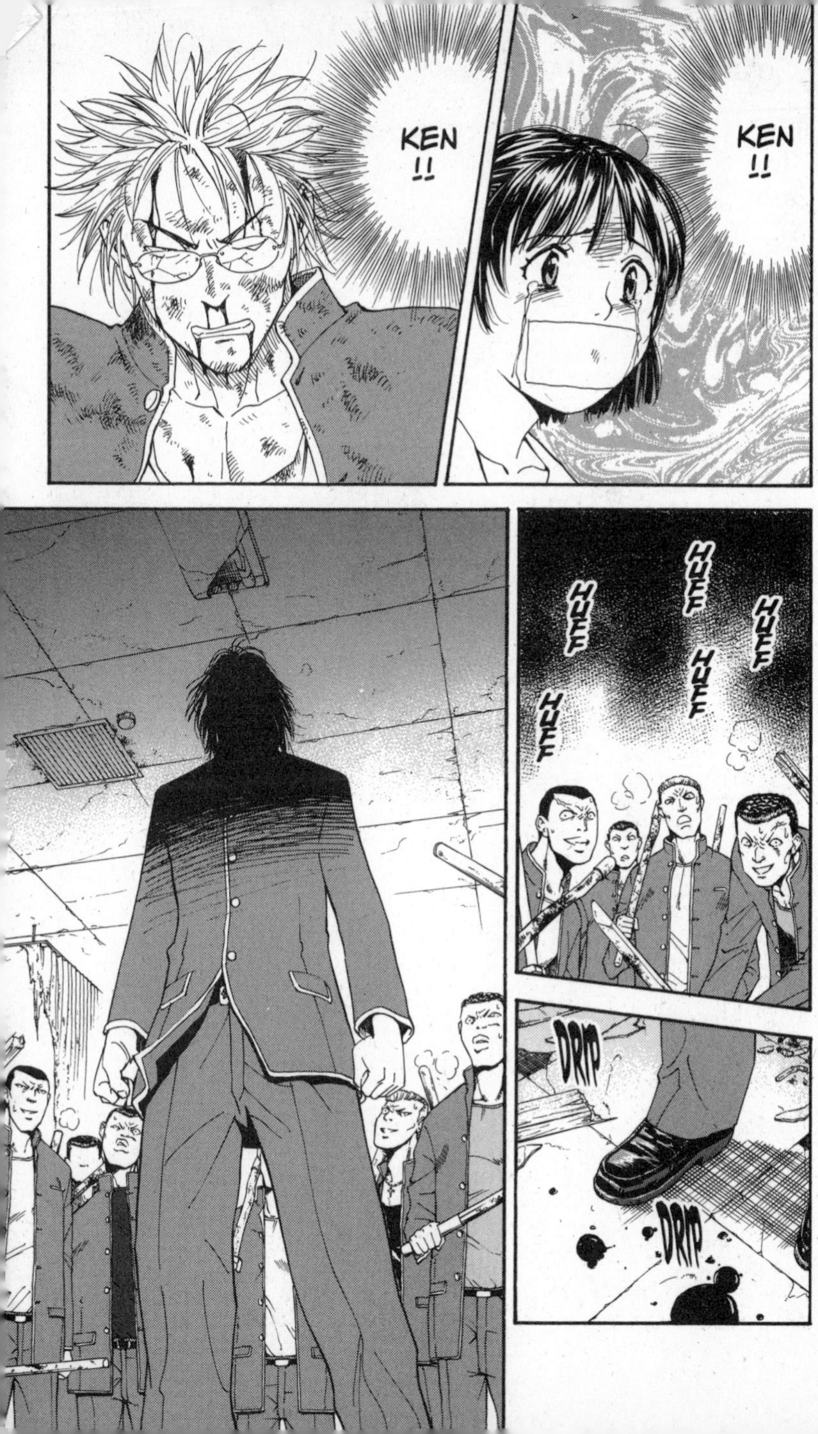
KEN !!
KEN !!
HUFF HUFF HUFF HUFF
DRIP
DRIP

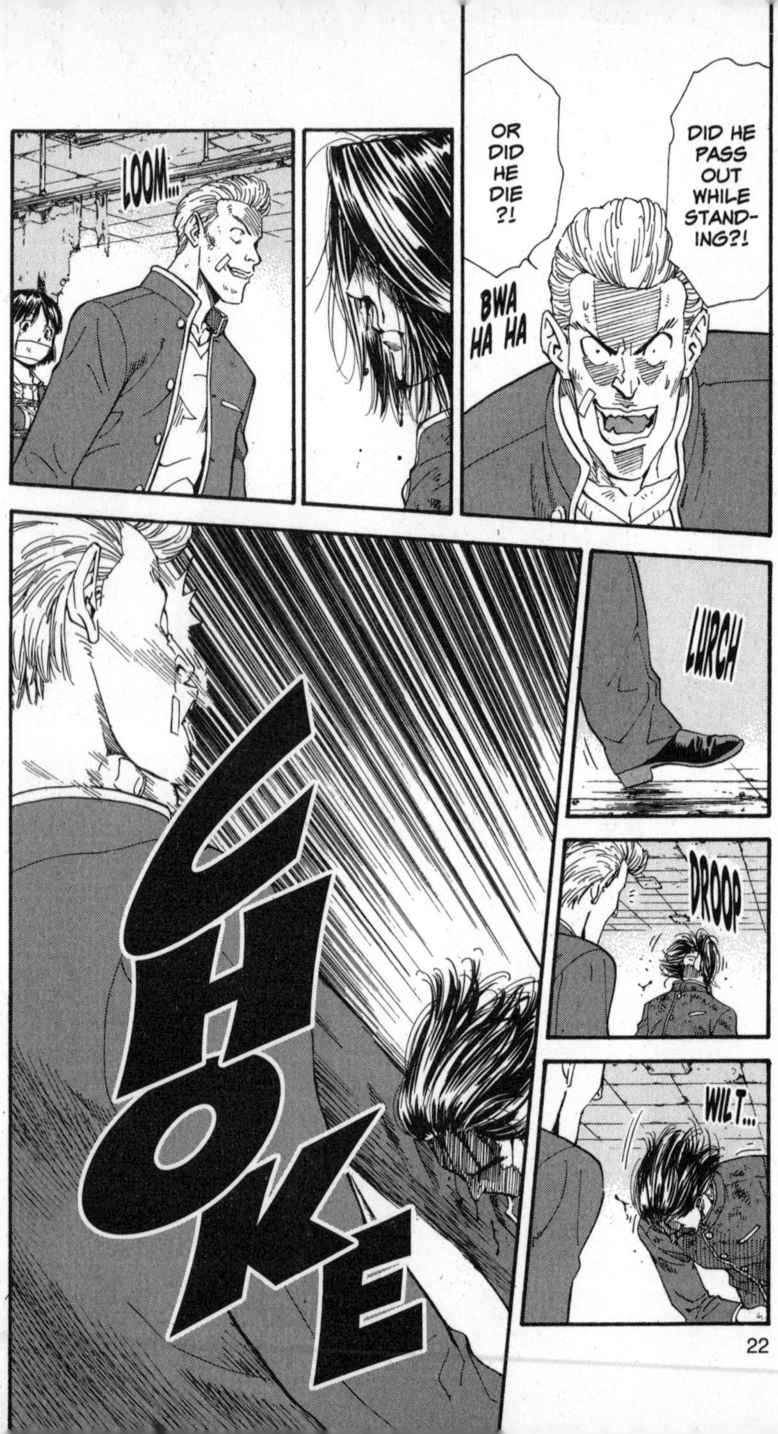
DID HE PASS OUT WHILE STANDING?!
OR DID HE DIE ?!
BWA HA HA
LOOM...
LURCH
DROOP
WILT...
CHOKE

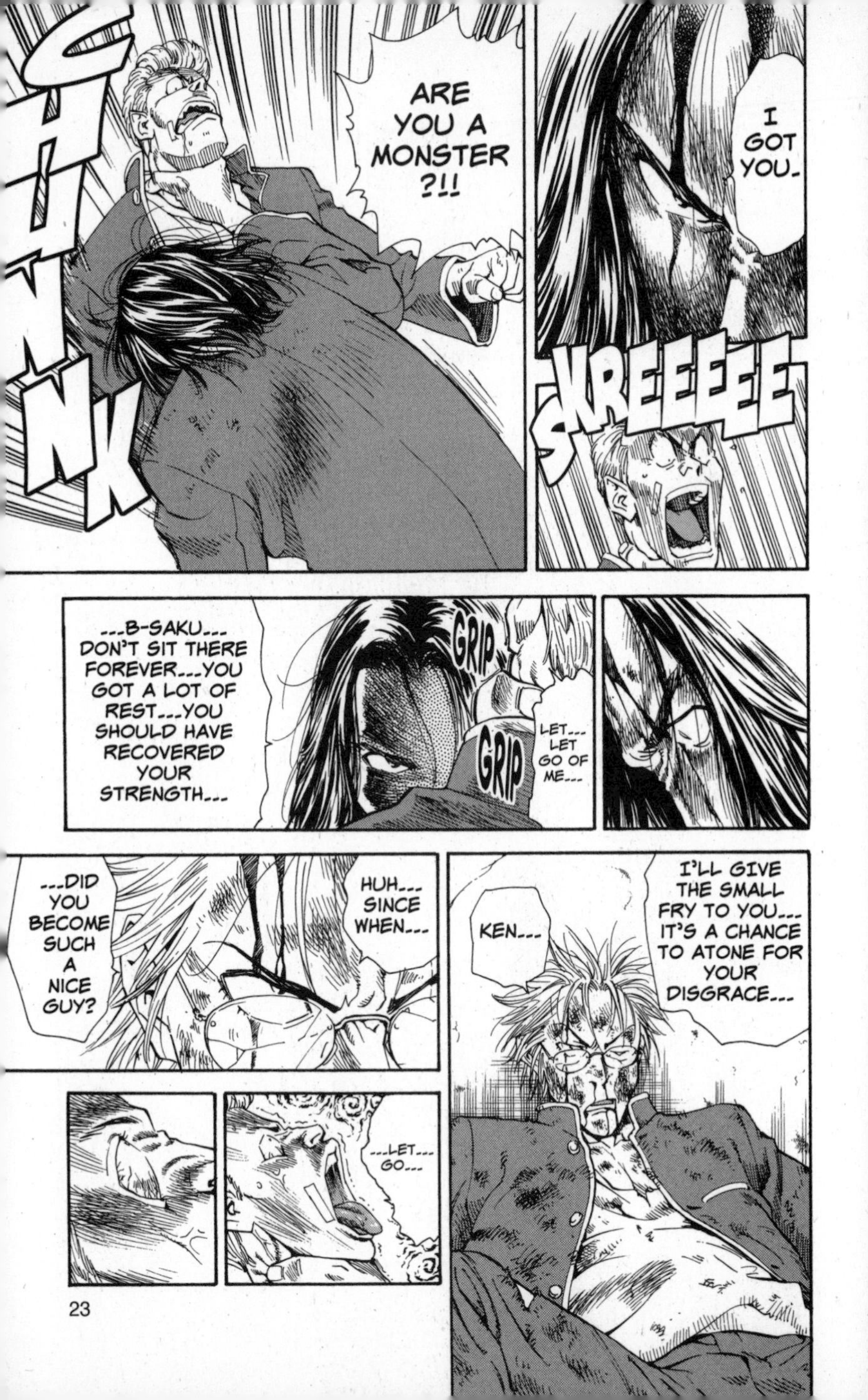
I GOT YOU.
SKREEEEE
CHUNK
ARE YOU A MONSTER ?!!
GRIP
GRIP
LET... LET GO OF ME...
...B-SAKU... DON'T SIT THERE FOREVER...YOU GOT A LOT OF REST...YOU SHOULD HAVE RECOVERED YOUR STRENGTH...
I'LL GIVE THE SMALL FRY TO YOU... IT'S A CHANCE TO ATONE FOR YOUR DISGRACE...
KEN...
HUH... SINCE WHEN...
...DID YOU BECOME SUCH A NICE GUY?
...LET... GO...

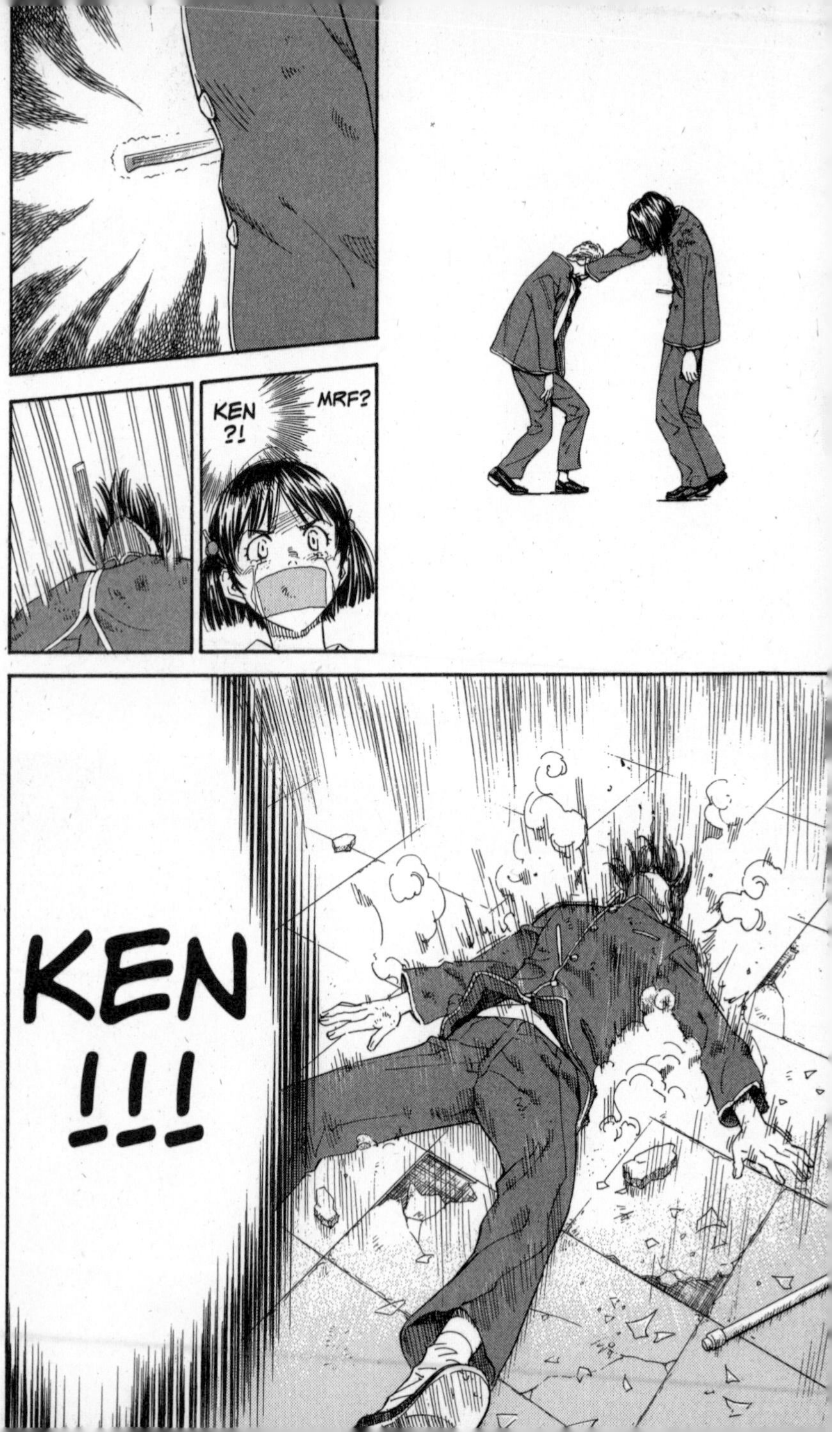
MRF?
KEN ?!
KEN !!!

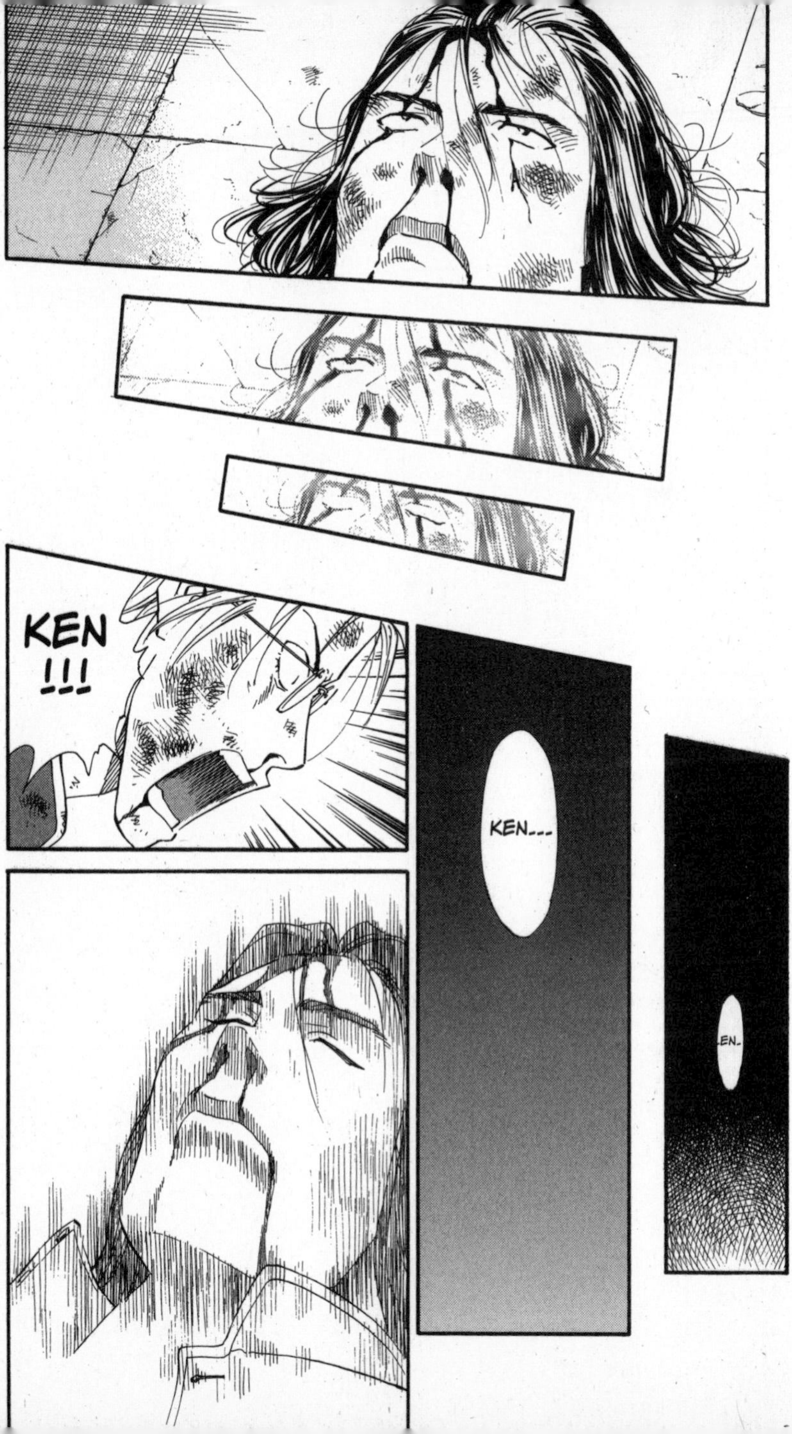
EN...
KEN...
KEN !!!

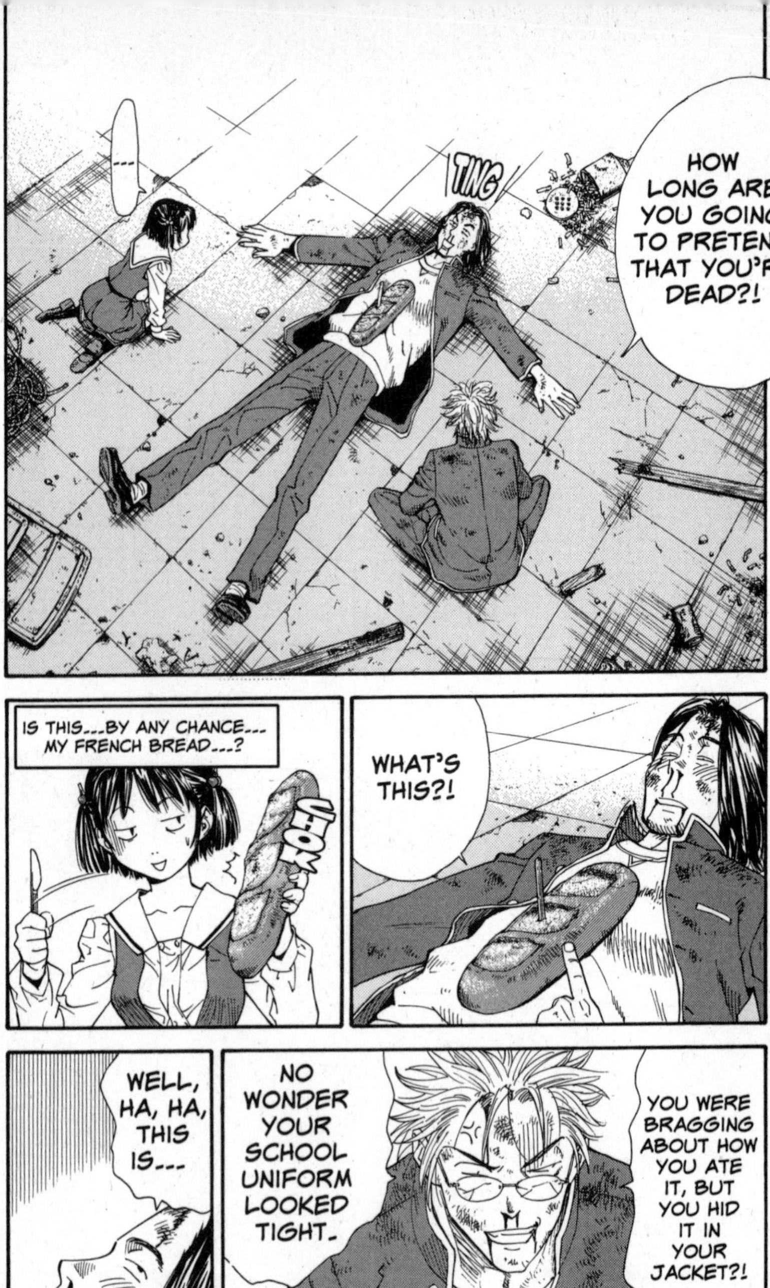
HOW LONG ARE YOU GOING TO PRETEND THAT YOU'RE DEAD?!
TING
...
WHAT'S THIS?!
IS THIS...BY ANY CHANCE... MY FRENCH BREAD...?
YOU WERE BRAGGING ABOUT HOW YOU ATE IT, BUT YOU HID IT IN YOUR JACKET?!
NO WONDER YOUR SCHOOL UNIFORM LOOKED TIGHT.
WELL, HA, HA, THIS IS...

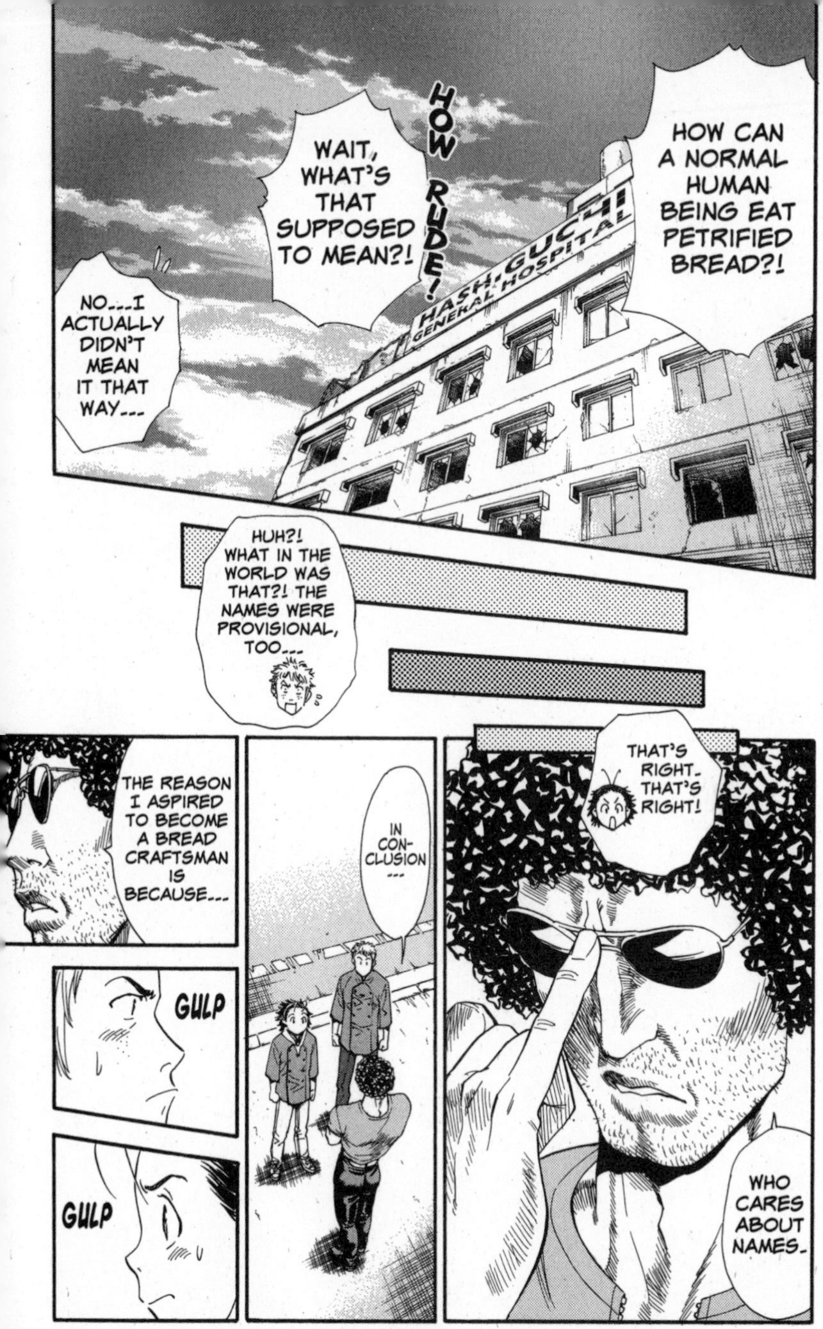
HOW CAN A NORMAL HUMAN BEING EAT PETRIFIED BREAD?!
HOW RUDE!
HASHIGUCHI GENERAL HOSPITAL
WAIT, WHAT'S THAT SUPPOSED TO MEAN?!
NO...I ACTUALLY DIDN'T MEAN IT THAT WAY...
HUH?! WHAT IN THE WORLD WAS THAT?! THE NAMES WERE PROVISIONAL, TOO...
THAT'S RIGHT. THAT'S RIGHT!
WHO CARES ABOUT NAMES.
IN CON- CLUSION ...
THE REASON I ASPIRED TO BECOME A BREAD CRAFTSMAN IS BECAUSE...
GULP
GULP

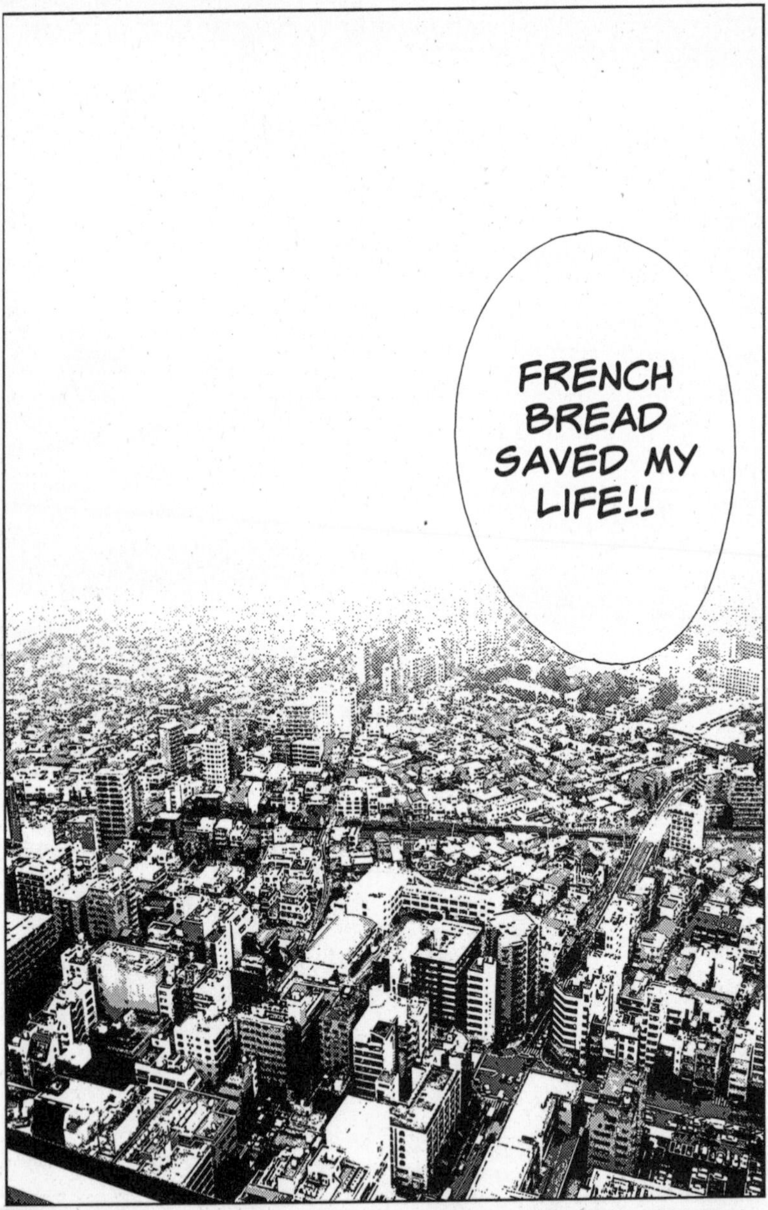
FRENCH BREAD SAVED MY LIFE!!

Yakitate!! Japan Supplemental Story: Matsushiro DX—The End

BONUS♥

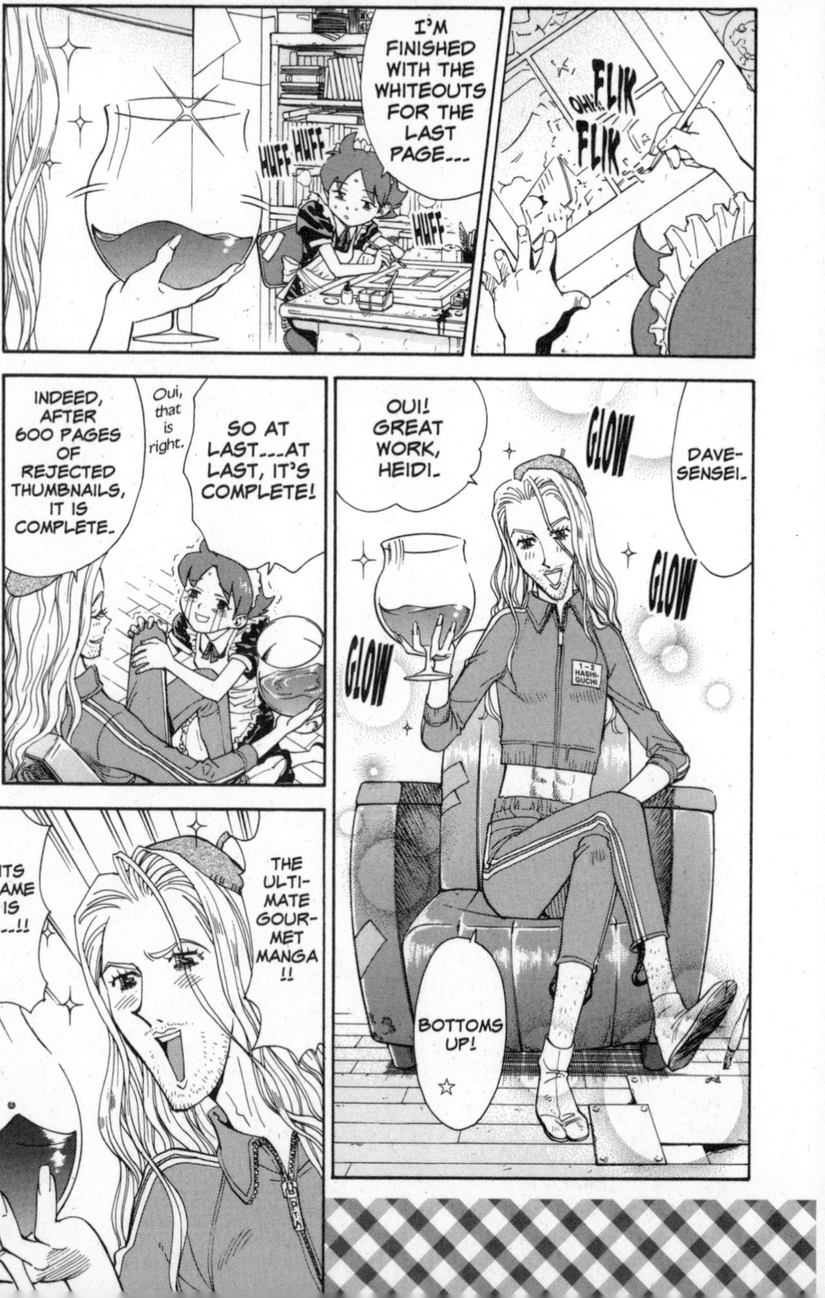
OH!!
FLIK
FLIK
I'M FINISHED WITH THE WHITEOUTS FOR THE LAST PAGE...
HUFF HUFF
HUFF
DAVE-SENSEI...
OUI! GREAT WORK, HEIDI...
GLOW
GLOW
GLOW
BOTTOMS UP! ☆
SO AT LAST...AT LAST, IT'S COMPLETE!
Oui, that is right.
INDEED, AFTER 600 PAGES OF REJECTED THUMBNAILS, IT IS COMPLETE...
THE ULTIMATE GOURMET MANGA!!
ITS NAME IS ...!!

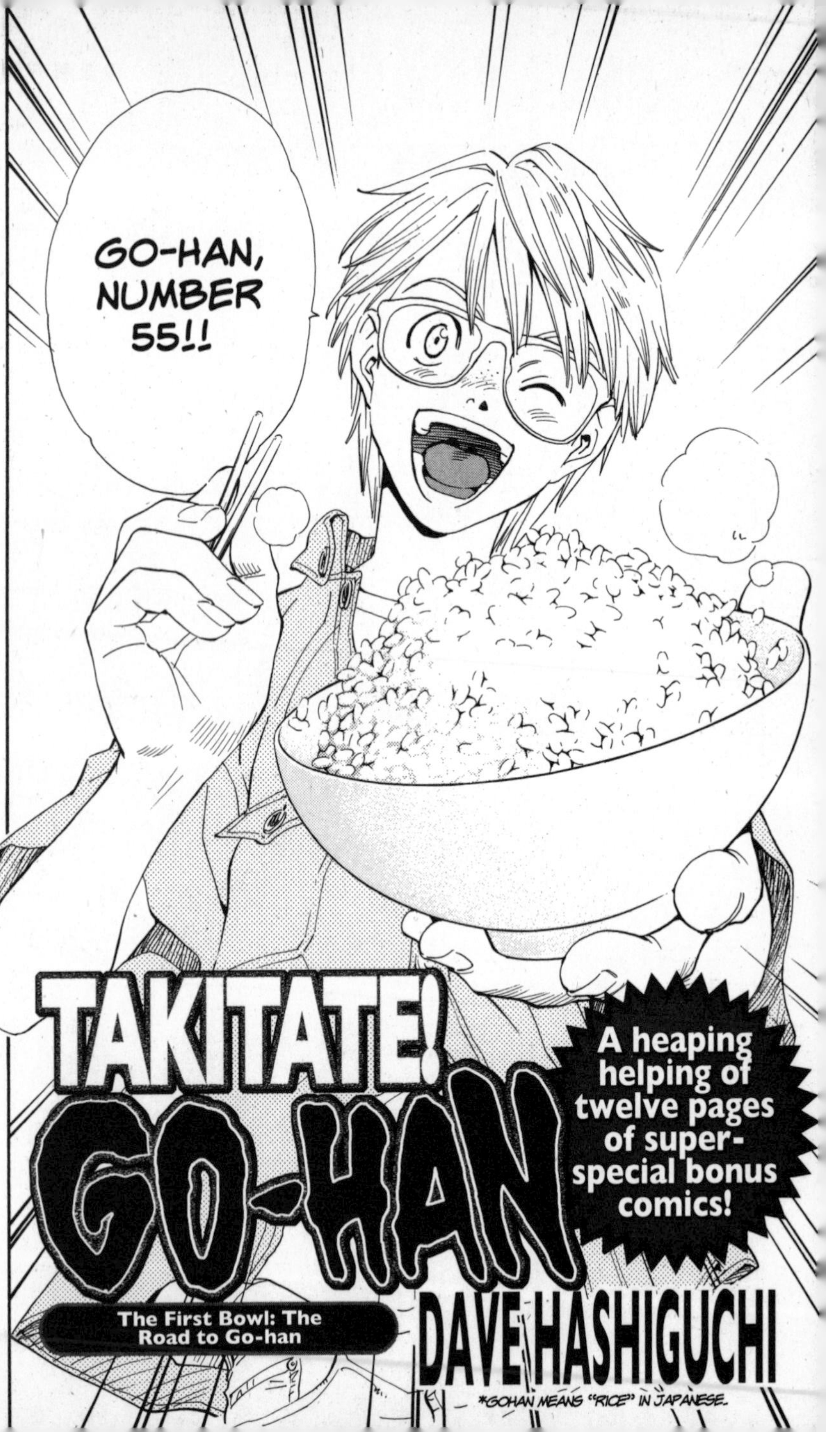
GO-HAN, NUMBER 55!!
TAKITATE! GO-HAN
A heaping helping of twelve pages of super-special bonus comics!
The First Bowl: The Road to Go-han
DAVE HASHIGUCHI
*GOHAN MEANS "RICE" IN JAPANESE.

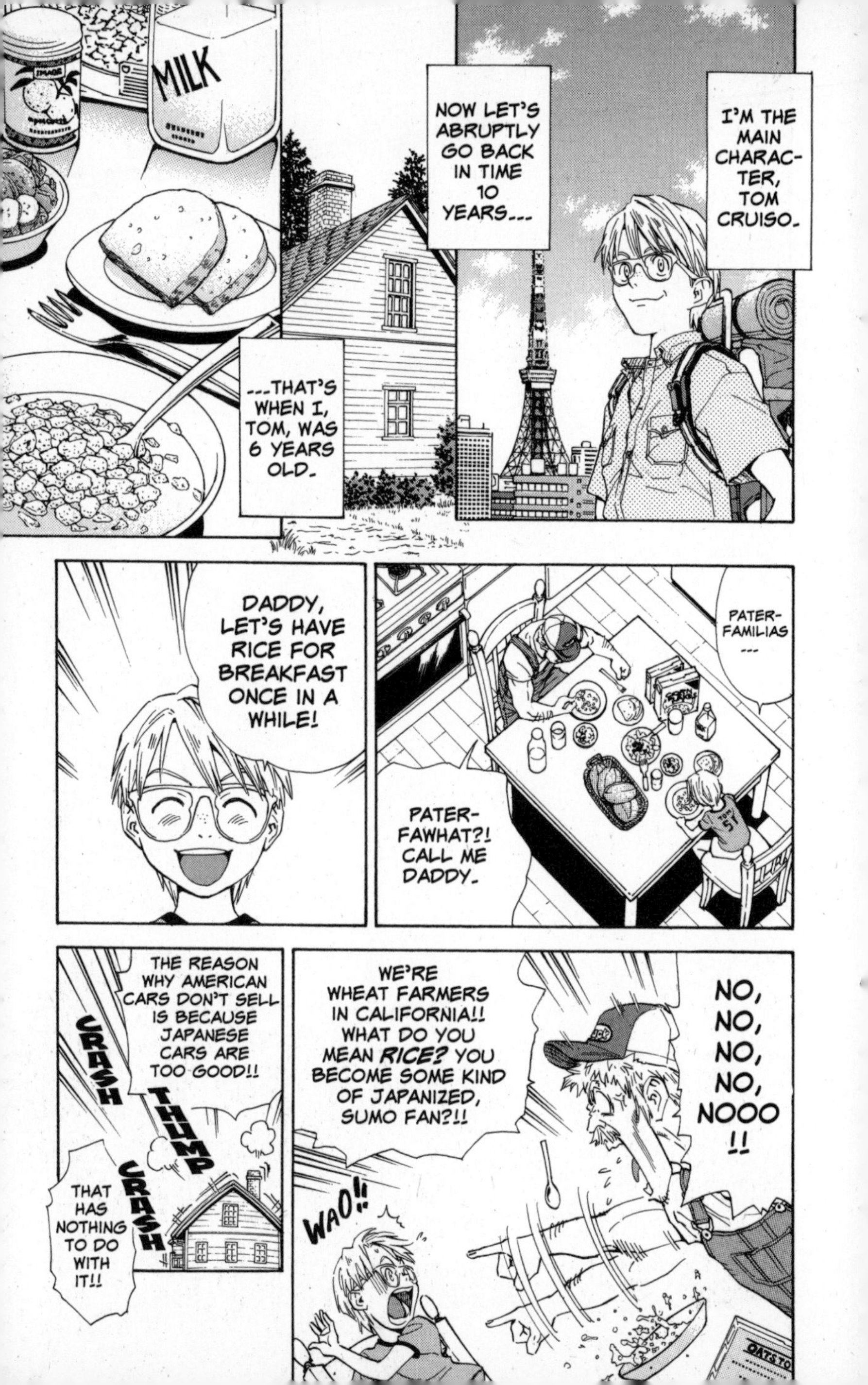
I'M THE MAIN CHARACTER, TOM CRUISO.
NOW LET'S ABRUPTLY GO BACK IN TIME 10 YEARS...
...THAT'S WHEN I, TOM, WAS 6 YEARS OLD.
MILK
PATER-FAMILIAS...
PATER-FAWHAT?! CALL ME DADDY.
DADDY, LET'S HAVE RICE FOR BREAKFAST ONCE IN A WHILE!
NO, NO, NO, NO, NOOO!!
WE'RE WHEAT FARMERS IN CALIFORNIA!! WHAT DO YOU MEAN *RICE?* YOU BECOME SOME KIND OF JAPANIZED, SUMO FAN?!!
WAO!!
THE REASON WHY AMERICAN CARS DON'T SELL IS BECAUSE JAPANESE CARS ARE TOO GOOD!!
CRASH
THUMP
CRASH
THAT HAS NOTHING TO DO WITH IT!!

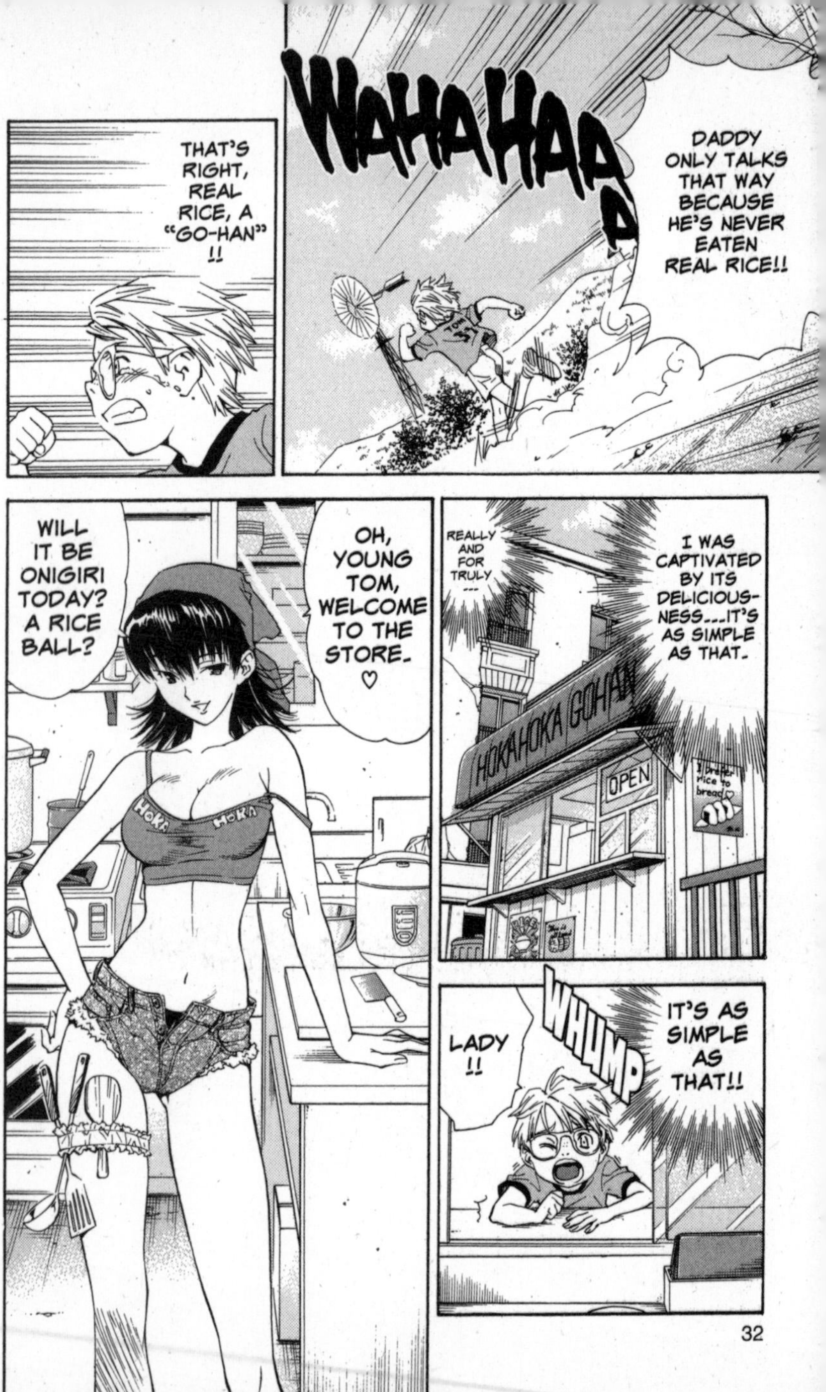
WAHAHAHAA
DADDY ONLY TALKS THAT WAY BECAUSE HE'S NEVER EATEN REAL RICE!!
THAT'S RIGHT, REAL RICE, A "GO-HAN" !!
REALLY AND FOR TRULY...
I WAS CAPTIVATED BY ITS DELICIOUS-NESS...IT'S AS SIMPLE AS THAT.
HOKAHOKA GOHAN
OPEN
I prefer rice to bread♡
IT'S AS SIMPLE AS THAT!!
WHUMP
LADY !!
OH, YOUNG TOM, WELCOME TO THE STORE. ♡
WILL IT BE ONIGIRI TODAY? A RICE BALL?

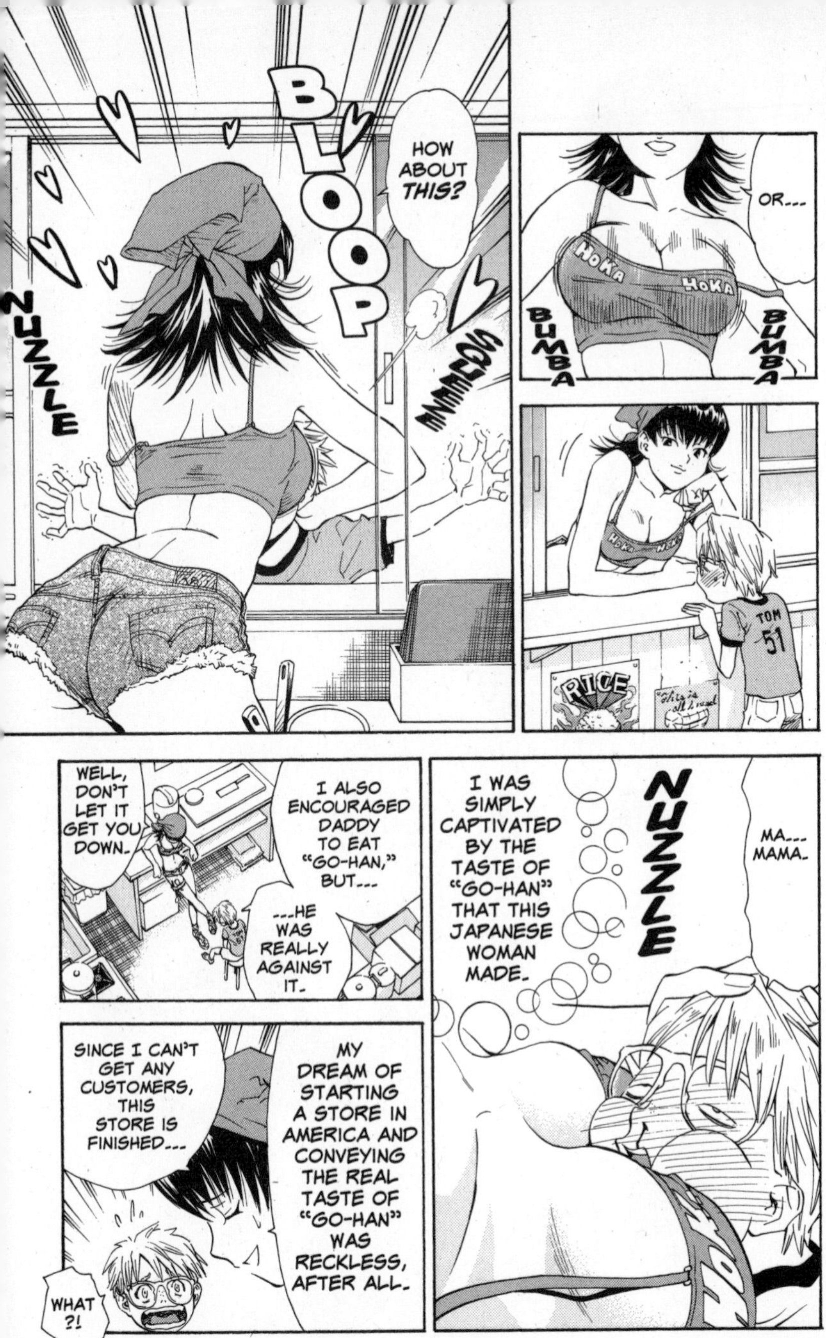
OR...
HOKA HOKA
BUMBA BUMBA
HOKA HOKA
TOM 51
RICE
HOW ABOUT THIS?
BLOOP
SQUEEEE
NUZZLE
MA... MAMA.
NUZZLE
I WAS SIMPLY CAPTIVATED BY THE TASTE OF "GO-HAN" THAT THIS JAPANESE WOMAN MADE.
I ALSO ENCOURAGED DADDY TO EAT "GO-HAN," BUT...
...HE WAS REALLY AGAINST IT.
WELL, DON'T LET IT GET YOU DOWN.
MY DREAM OF STARTING A STORE IN AMERICA AND CONVEYING THE REAL TASTE OF "GO-HAN" WAS RECKLESS, AFTER ALL.
SINCE I CAN'T GET ANY CUSTOMERS, THIS STORE IS FINISHED...
WHAT?!

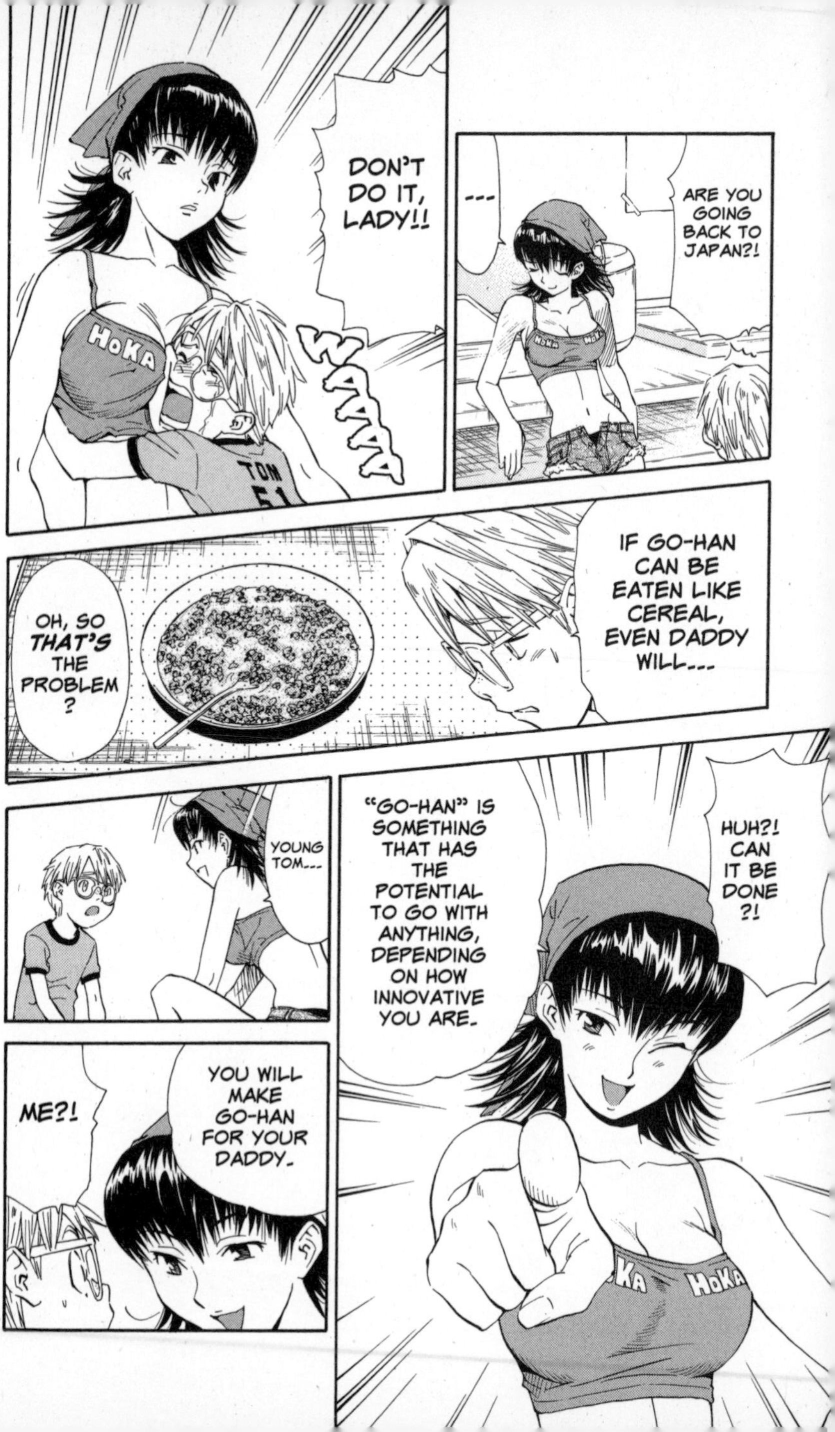
ARE YOU GOING BACK TO JAPAN?!
...
DON'T DO IT, LADY!!
IF GO-HAN CAN BE EATEN LIKE CEREAL, EVEN DADDY WILL...
OH, SO *THAT'S* THE PROBLEM?
HUH?! CAN IT BE DONE?!
"GO-HAN" IS SOMETHING THAT HAS THE POTENTIAL TO GO WITH ANYTHING, DEPENDING ON HOW INNOVATIVE YOU ARE.
YOUNG TOM...
YOU WILL MAKE GO-HAN FOR YOUR DADDY.
ME?!

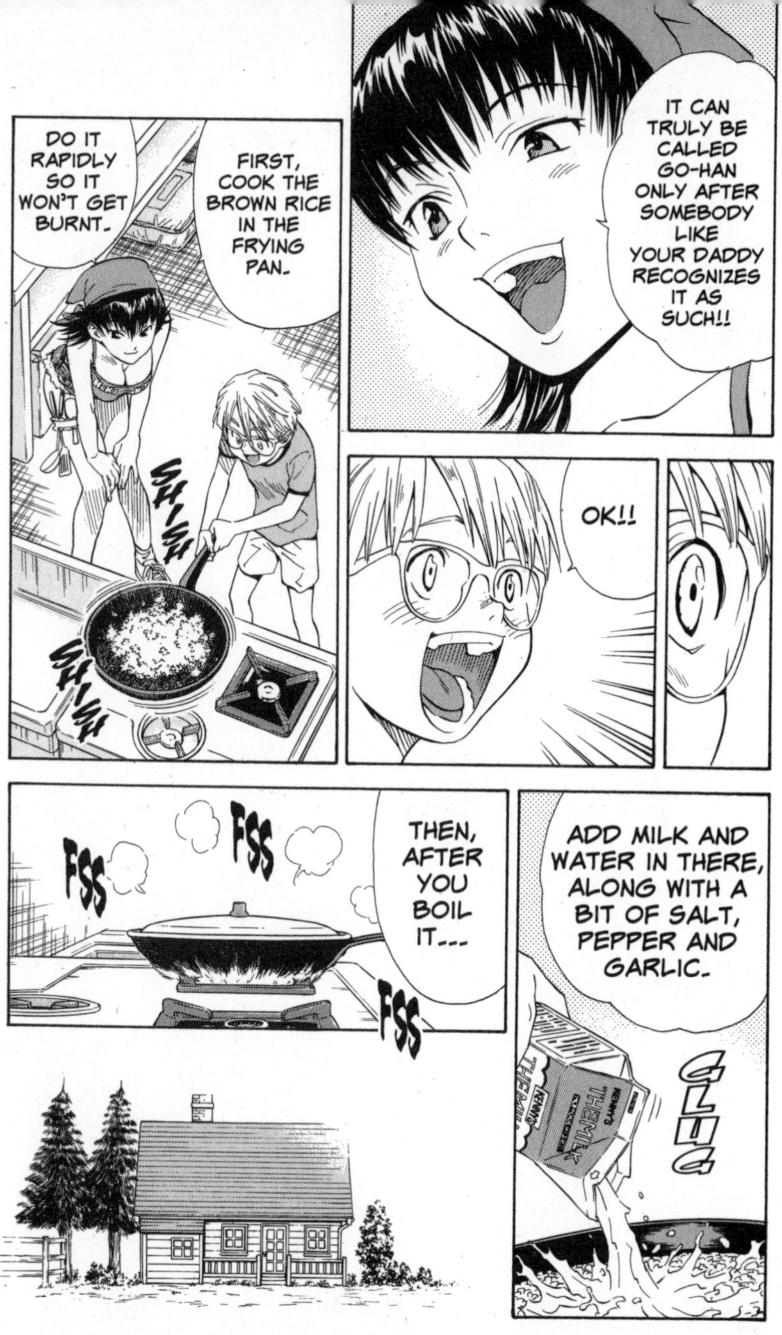
IT CAN TRULY BE CALLED GO-HAN ONLY AFTER SOMEBODY LIKE YOUR DADDY RECOGNIZES IT AS SUCH!!
OK!!
FIRST, COOK THE BROWN RICE IN THE FRYING PAN.
DO IT RAPIDLY SO IT WON'T GET BURNT.
SHISH
SHISH
ADD MILK AND WATER IN THERE, ALONG WITH A BIT OF SALT, PEPPER AND GARLIC.
GLUG
THEN, AFTER YOU BOIL IT...
FSS
FSS
FSS

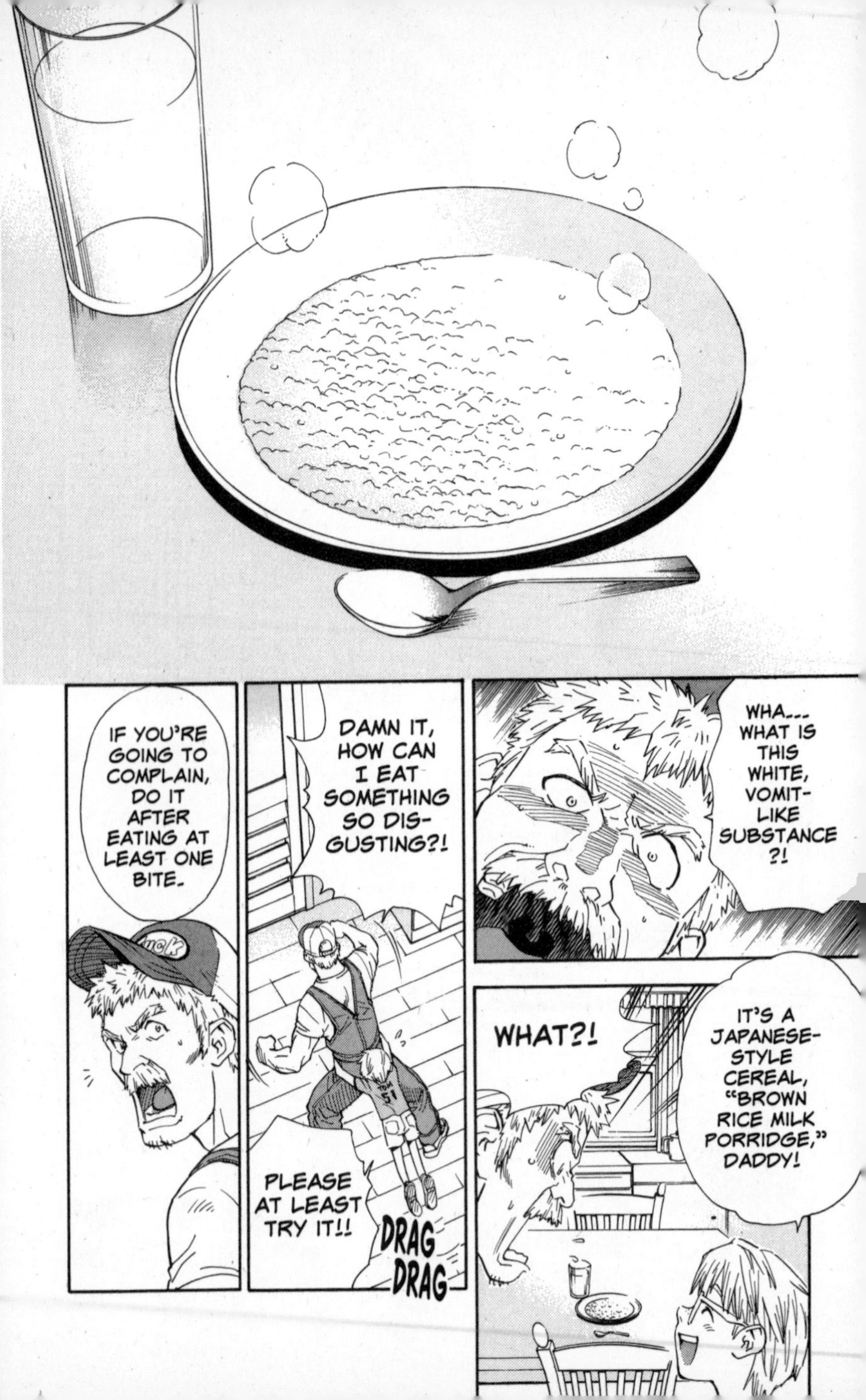
WHA... WHAT IS THIS WHITE, VOMIT-LIKE SUBSTANCE?!
IT'S A JAPANESE-STYLE CEREAL, "BROWN RICE MILK PORRIDGE," DADDY!
WHAT?!
DAMN IT, HOW CAN I EAT SOMETHING SO DIS-GUSTING?!
PLEASE AT LEAST TRY IT!!
DRAG DRAG
IF YOU'RE GOING TO COMPLAIN, DO IT AFTER EATING AT LEAST ONE BITE.

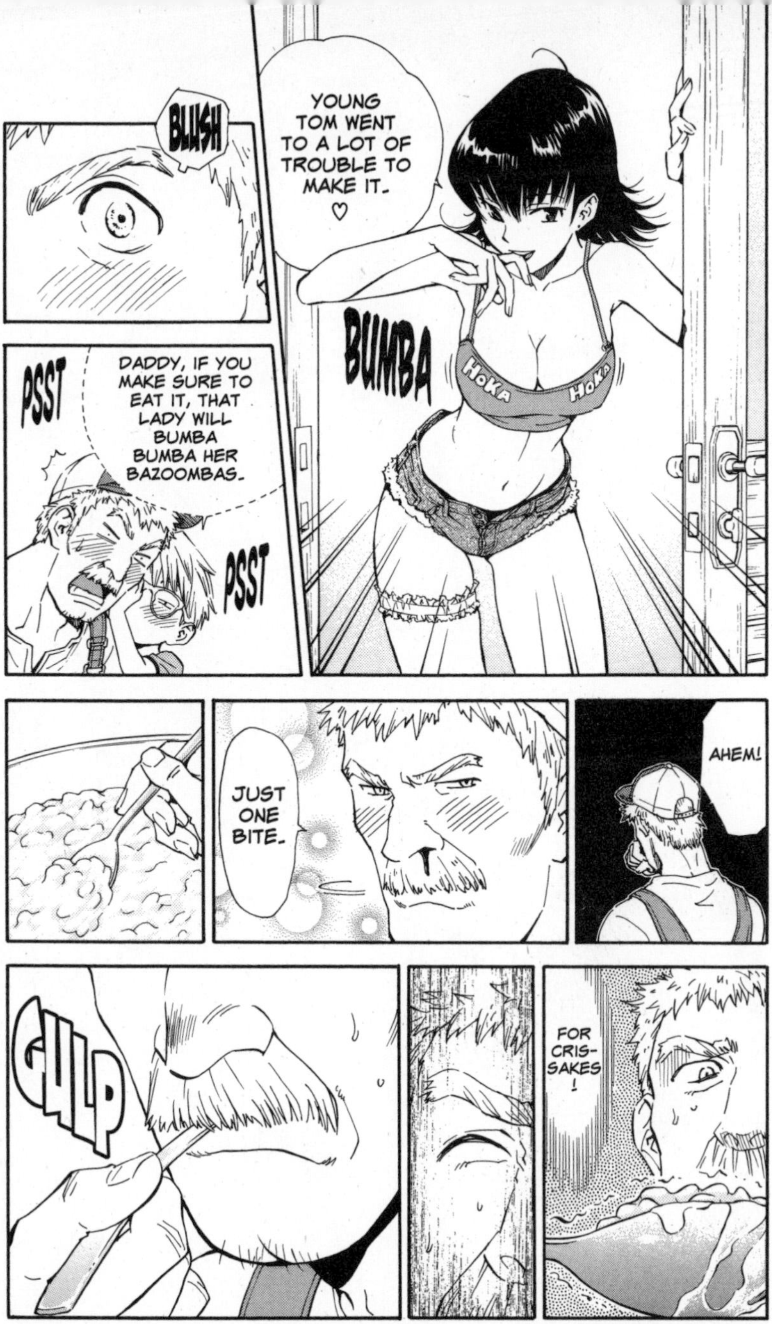
YOUNG TOM WENT TO A LOT OF TROUBLE TO MAKE IT. ♡
BUMBA
BLUSH
PSST
DADDY, IF YOU MAKE SURE TO EAT IT, THAT LADY WILL BUMBA BUMBA HER BAZOOMBAS.
PSST
AHEM!
JUST ONE BITE.
FOR CRIS-SAKES!
GULP

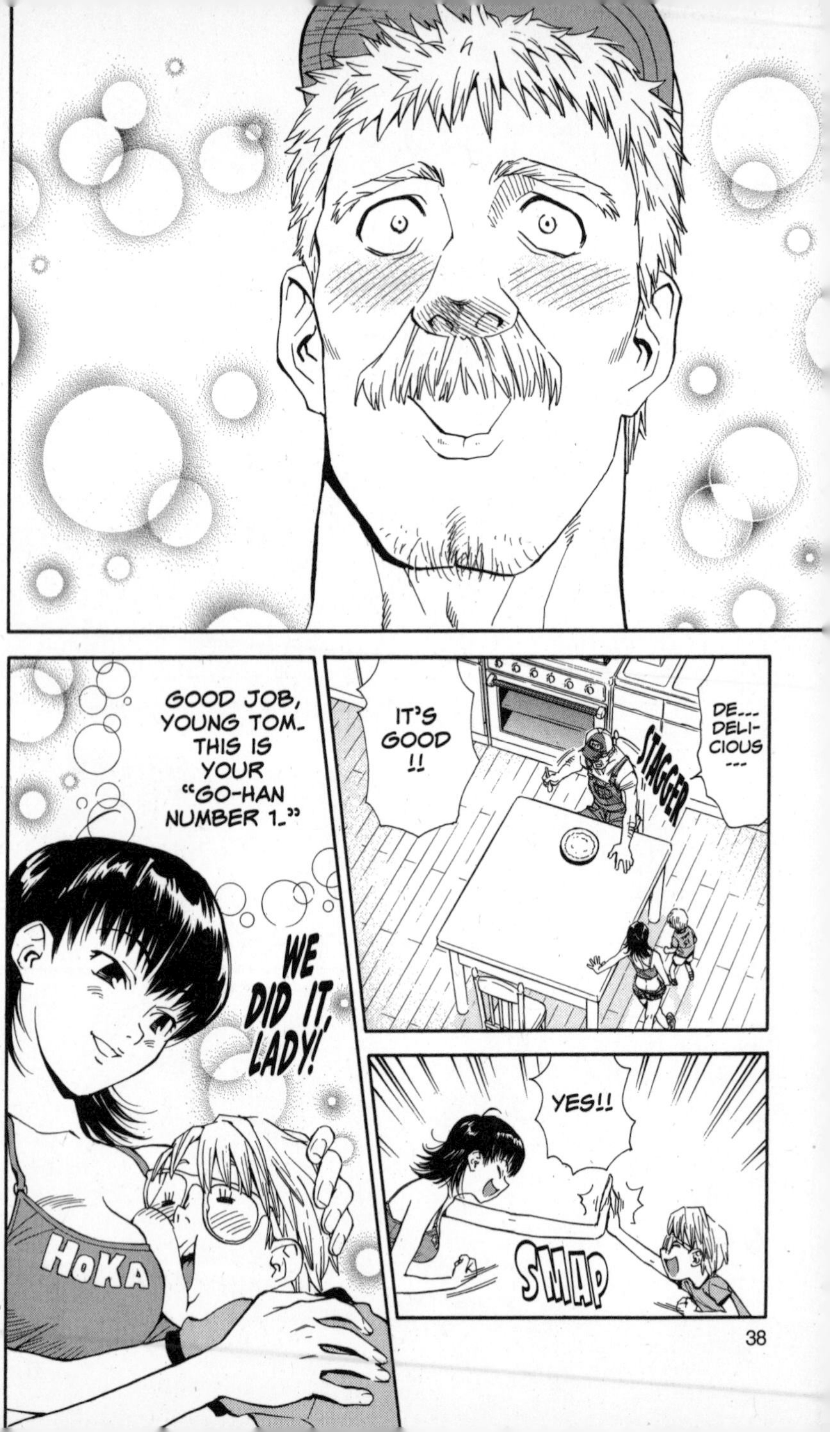
DE... DELICIOUS...
STAGGER
IT'S GOOD!!
YES!!
SMAP
GOOD JOB, YOUNG TOM. THIS IS YOUR "GO-HAN NUMBER 1."
WE DID IT, LADY!
HoKA

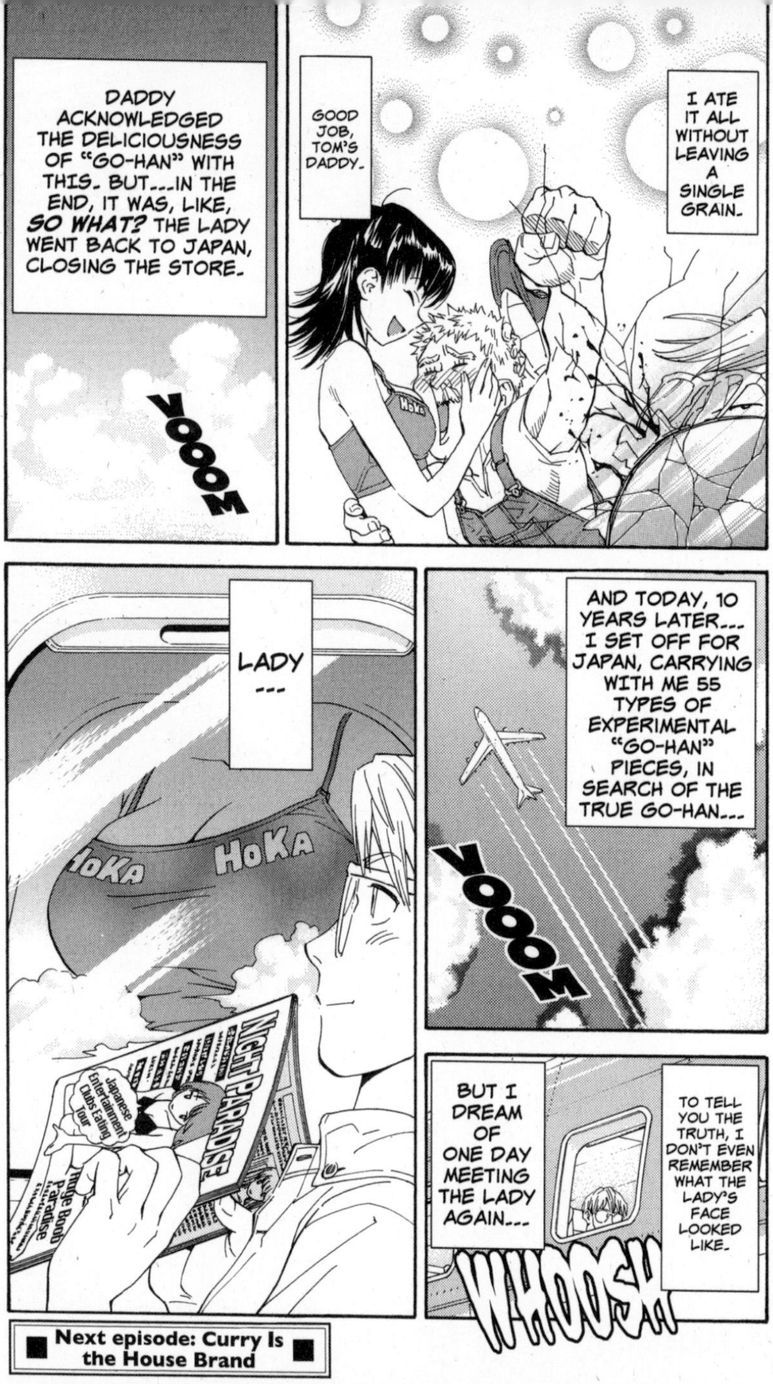
I ATE IT ALL WITHOUT LEAVING A SINGLE GRAIN.
GOOD JOB, TOM'S DADDY.
DADDY ACKNOWLEDGED THE DELICIOUSNESS OF "GO-HAN" WITH THIS. BUT...IN THE END, IT WAS, LIKE, *SO WHAT?* THE LADY WENT BACK TO JAPAN, CLOSING THE STORE.
VOOOM
AND TODAY, 10 YEARS LATER... I SET OFF FOR JAPAN, CARRYING WITH ME 55 TYPES OF EXPERIMENTAL "GO-HAN" PIECES, IN SEARCH OF THE TRUE GO-HAN...
VOOOM
TO TELL YOU THE TRUTH, I DON'T EVEN REMEMBER WHAT THE LADY'S FACE LOOKED LIKE.
BUT I DREAM OF ONE DAY MEETING THE LADY AGAIN...
WHOOSH
LADY...
HoKa
HoKa
NIGHT PARADISE
Japanese Entertainment Clubs Eating Tour
Fringe Book Paradise

■ Next episode: Curry Is the House Brand ■

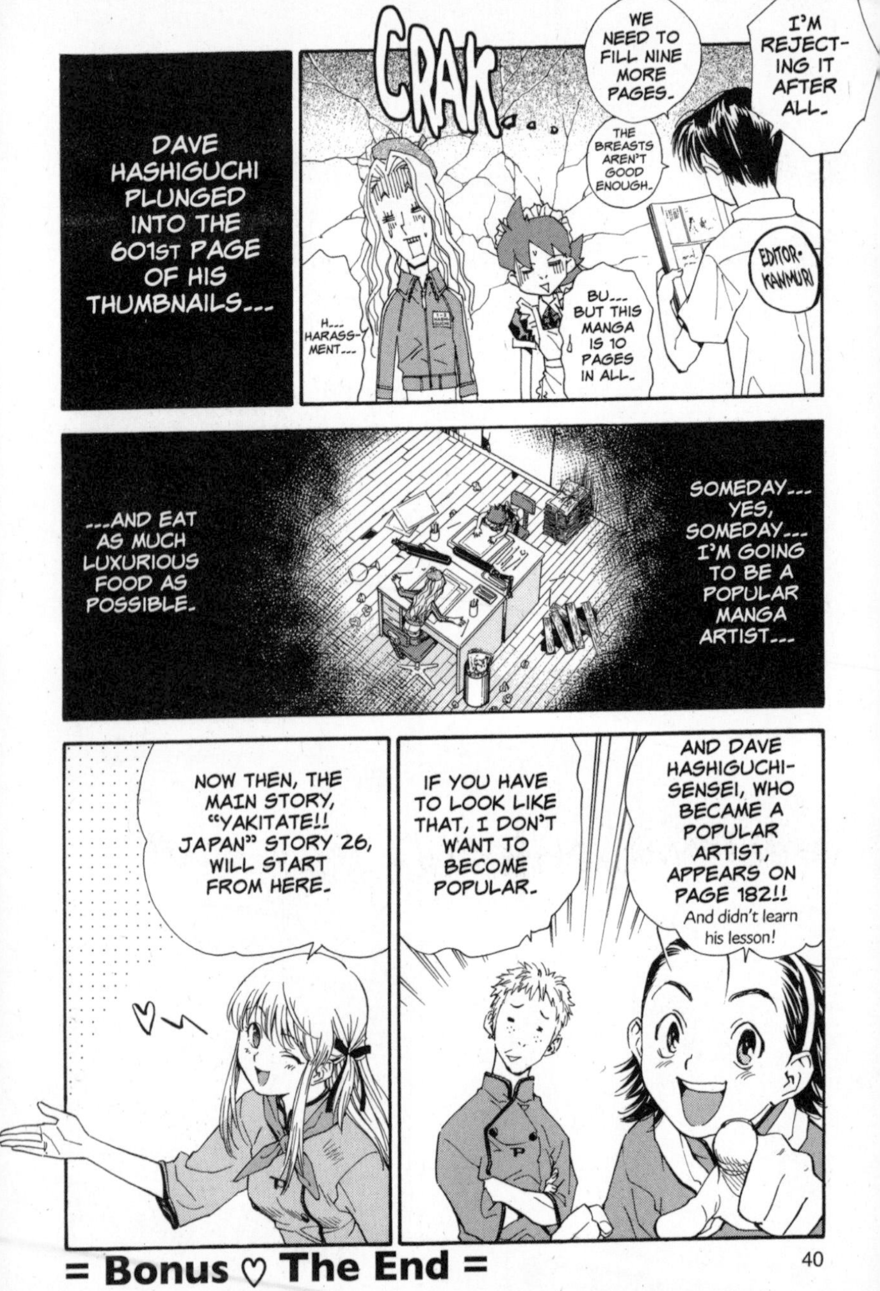
I'M REJECTING IT AFTER ALL.
WE NEED TO FILL NINE MORE PAGES.
CRAK
THE BREASTS AREN'T GOOD ENOUGH.
EDITOR: KANMURI
BU... BUT THIS MANGA IS 10 PAGES IN ALL.
H... HARASSMENT...
DAVE HASHIGUCHI PLUNGED INTO THE 601ST PAGE OF HIS THUMBNAILS...
SOMEDAY... YES, SOMEDAY... I'M GOING TO BE A POPULAR MANGA ARTIST...
...AND EAT AS MUCH LUXURIOUS FOOD AS POSSIBLE.
AND DAVE HASHIGUCHI-SENSEI, WHO BECAME A POPULAR ARTIST, APPEARS ON PAGE 182!!
And didn't learn his lesson!
IF YOU HAVE TO LOOK LIKE THAT, I DON'T WANT TO BECOME POPULAR.
NOW THEN, THE MAIN STORY, "YAKITATE!! JAPAN" STORY 26, WILL START FROM HERE.

= Bonus ♡ The End =

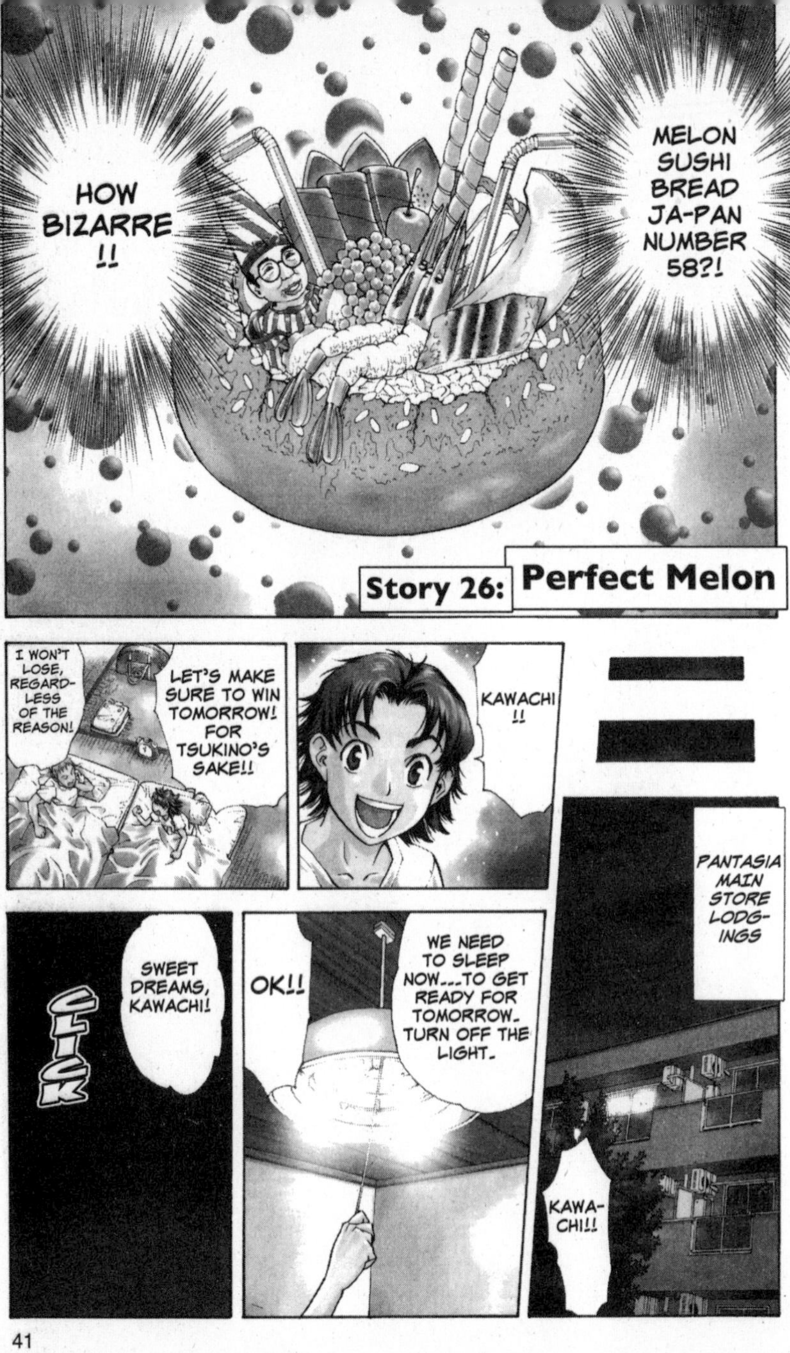
MELON SUSHI BREAD JA-PAN NUMBER 58?!
HOW BIZARRE !!
Story 26: Perfect Melon
PANTASIA MAIN STORE LODGINGS
KAWA-CHI!!
KAWACHI !!
LET'S MAKE SURE TO WIN TOMORROW! FOR TSUKINO'S SAKE!!
I WON'T LOSE, REGARDLESS OF THE REASON!
WE NEED TO SLEEP NOW... TO GET READY FOR TOMORROW. TURN OFF THE LIGHT.
OK!!
SWEET DREAMS, KAWACHI!
CLICK

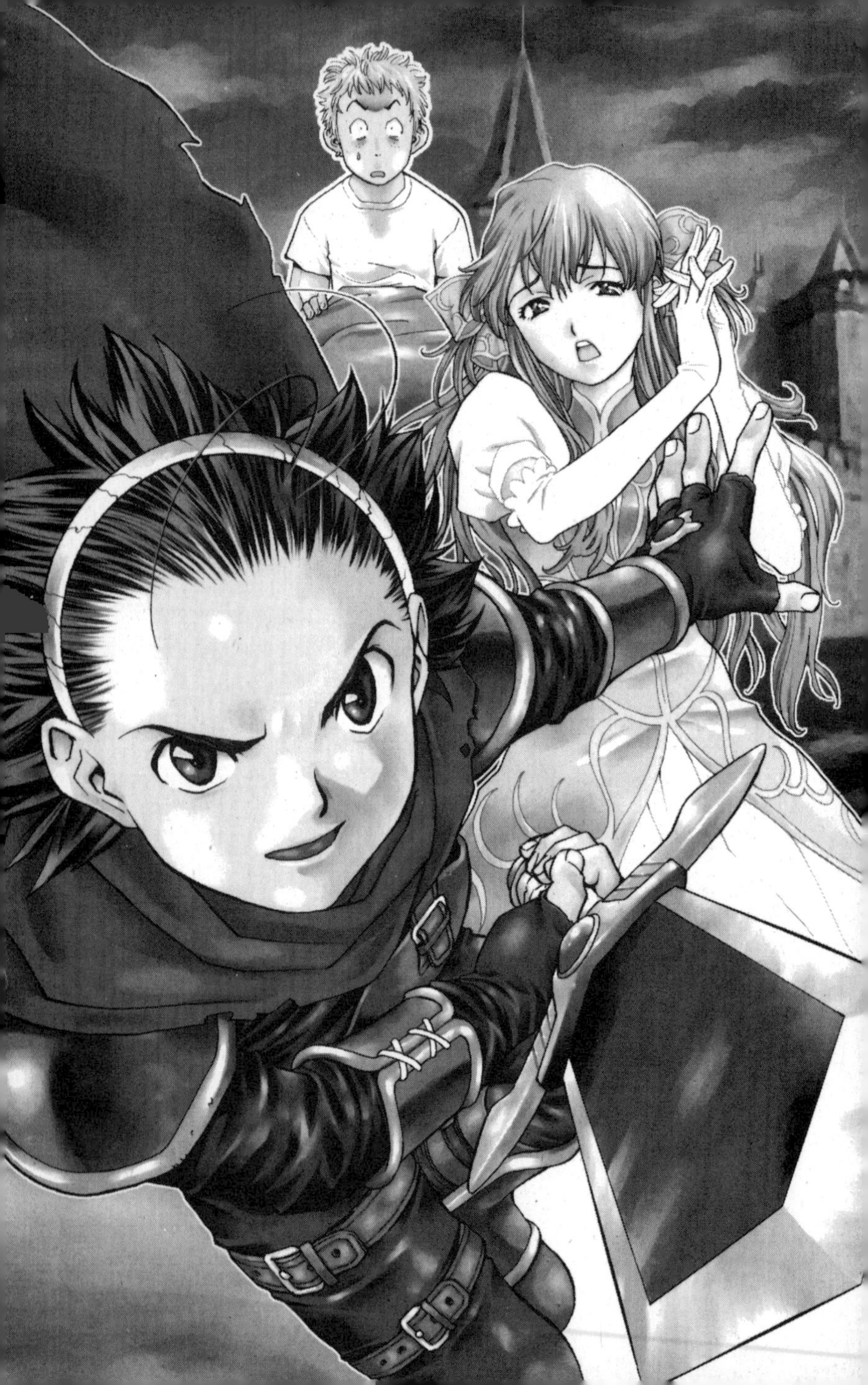

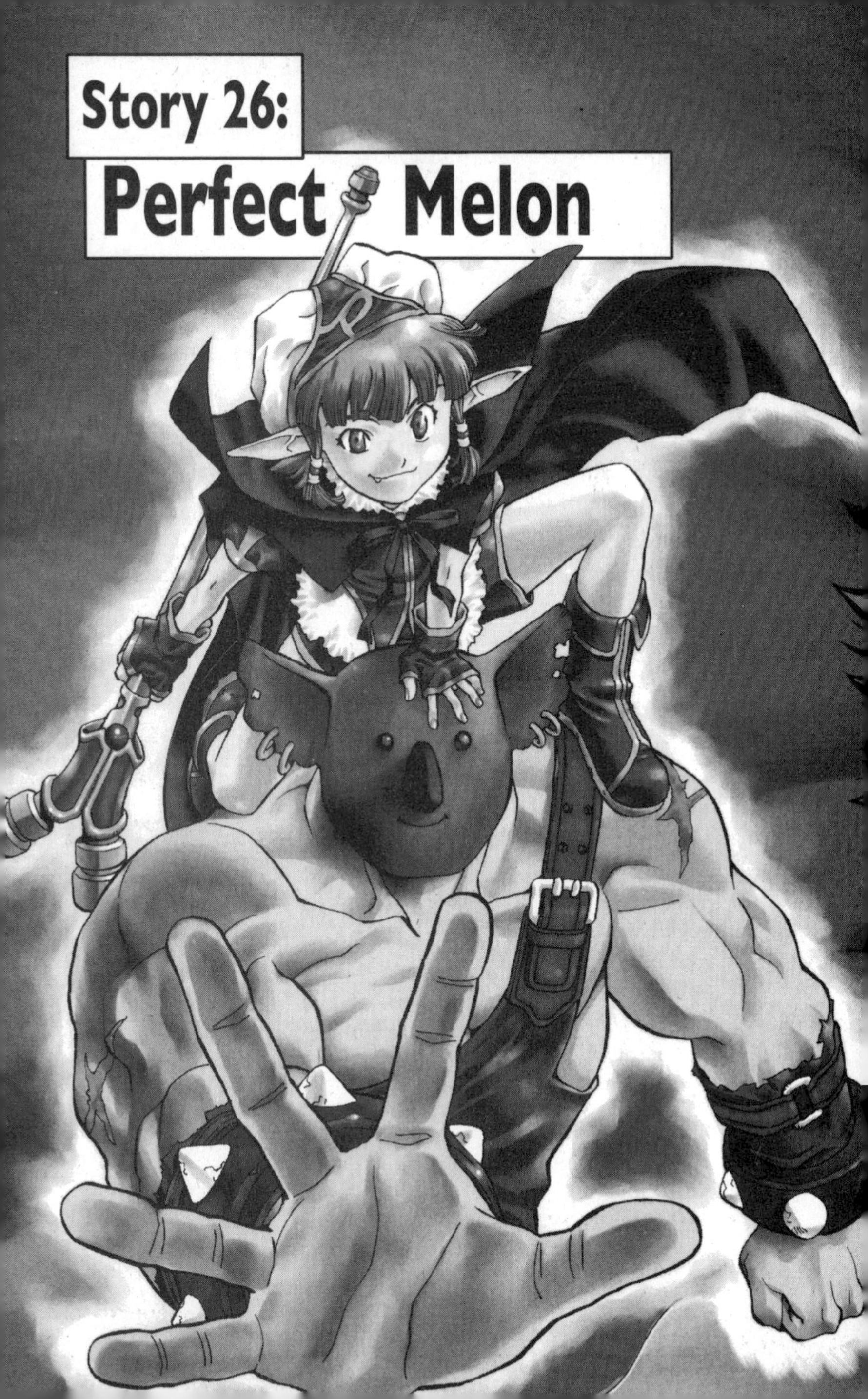
Story 26:
Perfect Melon

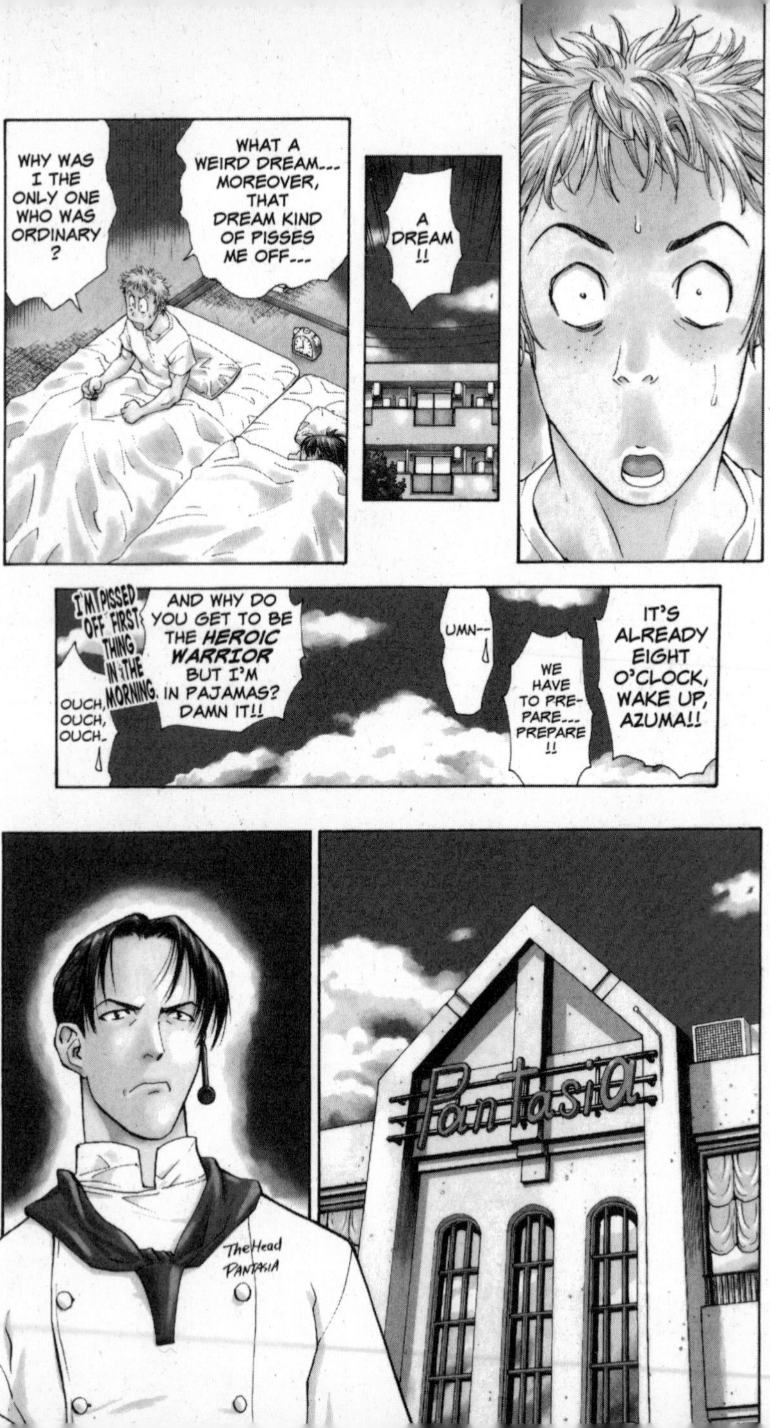
A DREAM!!
WHAT A WEIRD DREAM... MOREOVER, THAT DREAM KIND OF PISSES ME OFF...
WHY WAS I THE ONLY ONE WHO WAS ORDINARY?
IT'S ALREADY EIGHT O'CLOCK, WAKE UP, AZUMA!!
WE HAVE TO PRE-PARE... PREPARE!!
UMN--
AND WHY DO YOU GET TO BE THE HEROIC WARRIOR BUT I'M IN PAJAMAS? DAMN IT!!
I'M PISSED OFF FIRST THING IN THE MORNING.
OUCH, OUCH, OUCH...
Pantasia
The Head PANTASIA

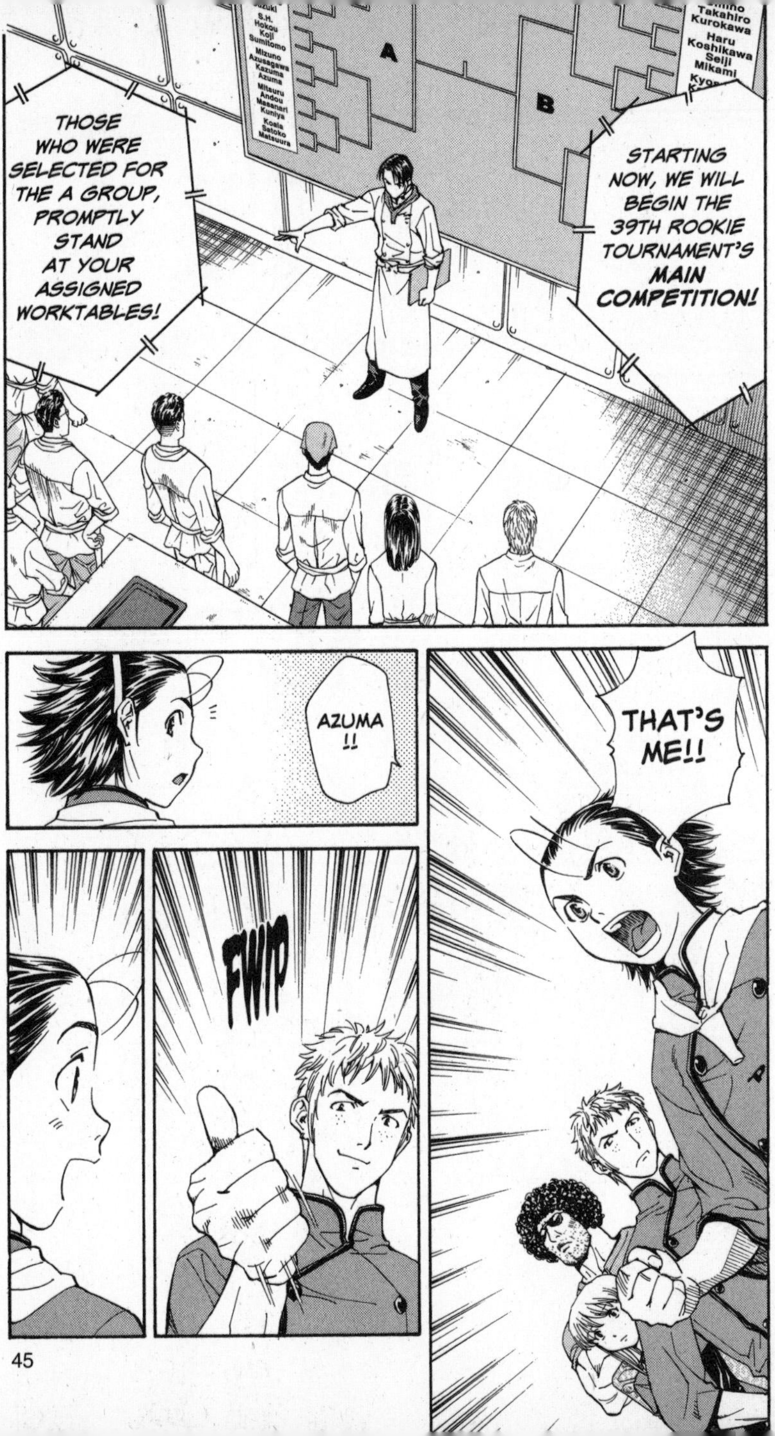
STARTING NOW, WE WILL BEGIN THE 39TH ROOKIE TOURNAMENT'S MAIN COMPETITION!
THOSE WHO WERE SELECTED FOR THE A GROUP, PROMPTLY STAND AT YOUR ASSIGNED WORKTABLES!
A
B
THAT'S ME!!
AZUMA!!
FWIP

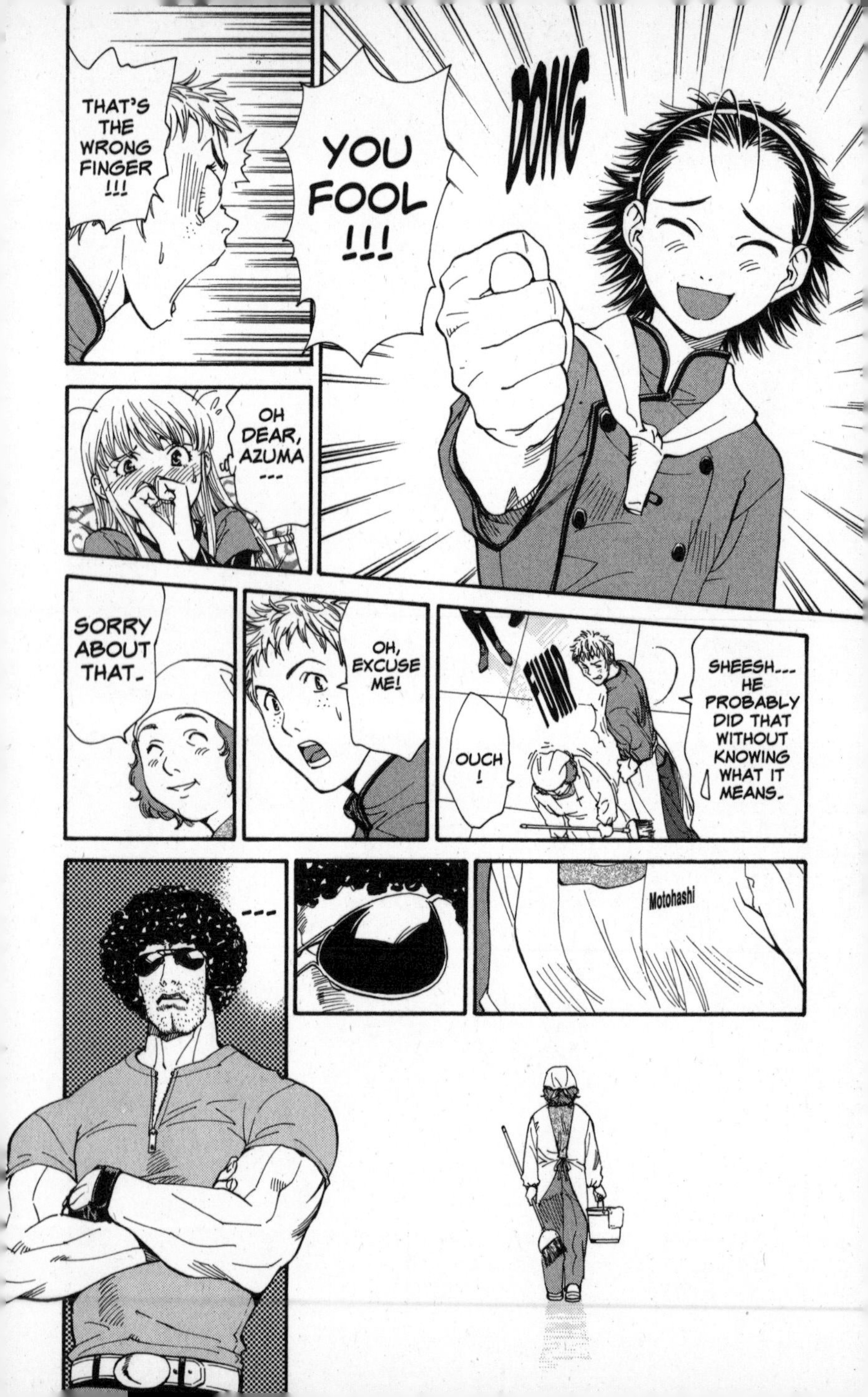
DONG
YOU FOOL!!!
THAT'S THE WRONG FINGER!!!
OH DEAR, AZUMA...
SHEESH... HE PROBABLY DID THAT WITHOUT KNOWING WHAT IT MEANS.
OUCH!
OH, EXCUSE ME!
SORRY ABOUT THAT.
Motohashi
...

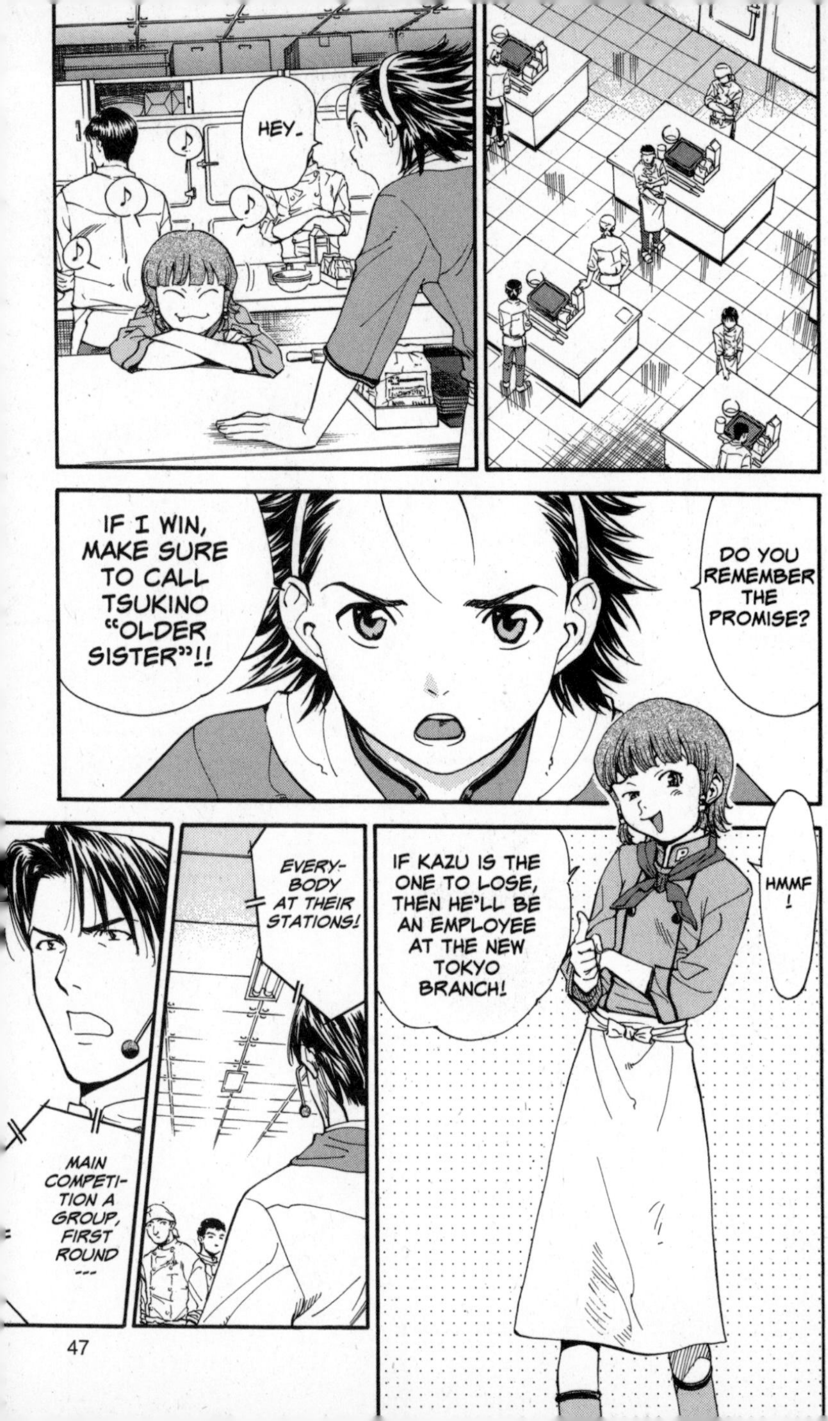
HEY.
DO YOU REMEMBER THE PROMISE?
IF I WIN, MAKE SURE TO CALL TSUKINO "OLDER SISTER"!!
HMMF!
IF KAZU IS THE ONE TO LOSE, THEN HE'LL BE AN EMPLOYEE AT THE NEW TOKYO BRANCH!
EVERYBODY AT THEIR STATIONS!
MAIN COMPETITION A GROUP, FIRST ROUND ---

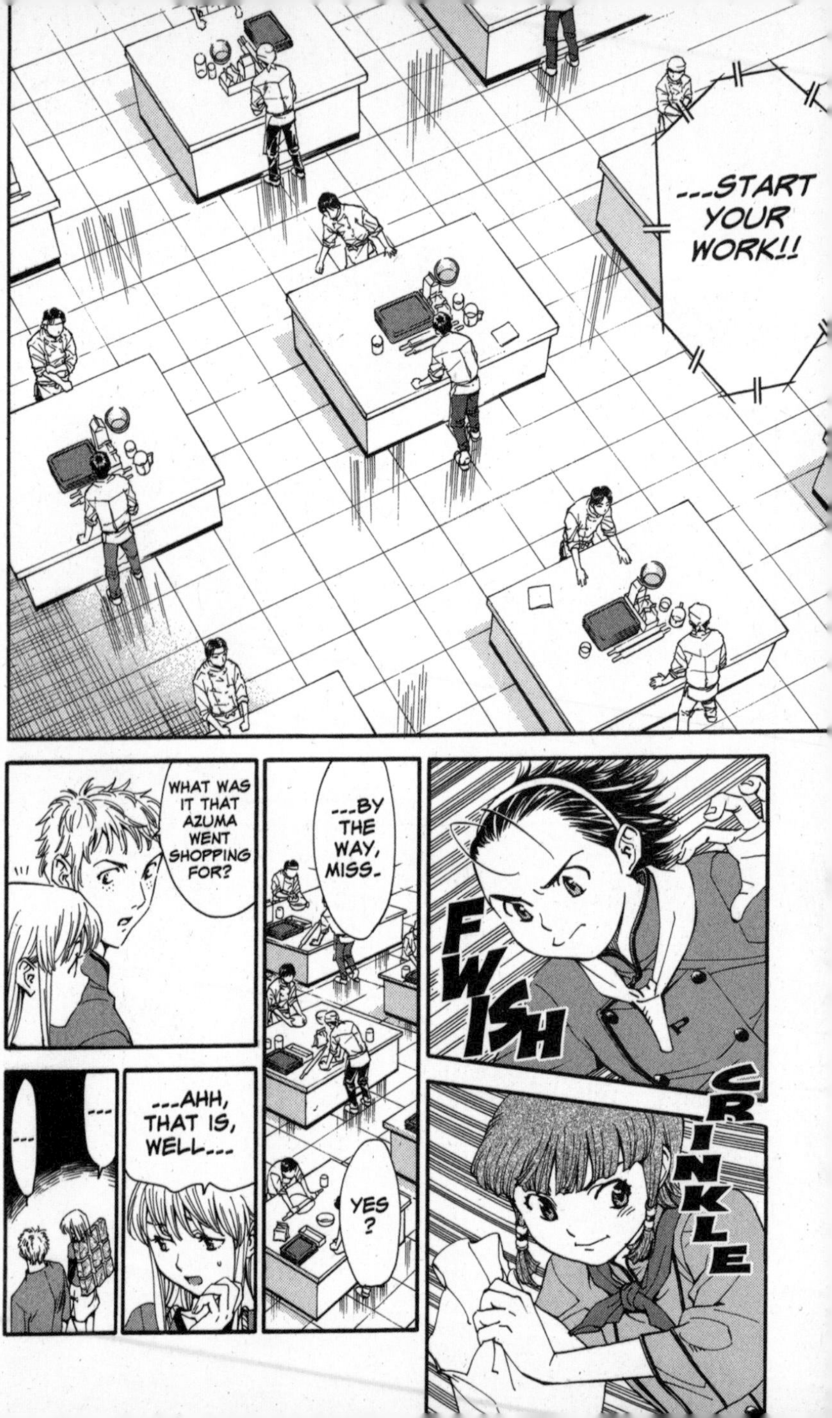
---START YOUR WORK!!
FWISH
---BY THE WAY, MISS.
WHAT WAS IT THAT AZUMA WENT SHOPPING FOR?
!!
YES?
---AHH, THAT IS, WELL---

CRINKLE

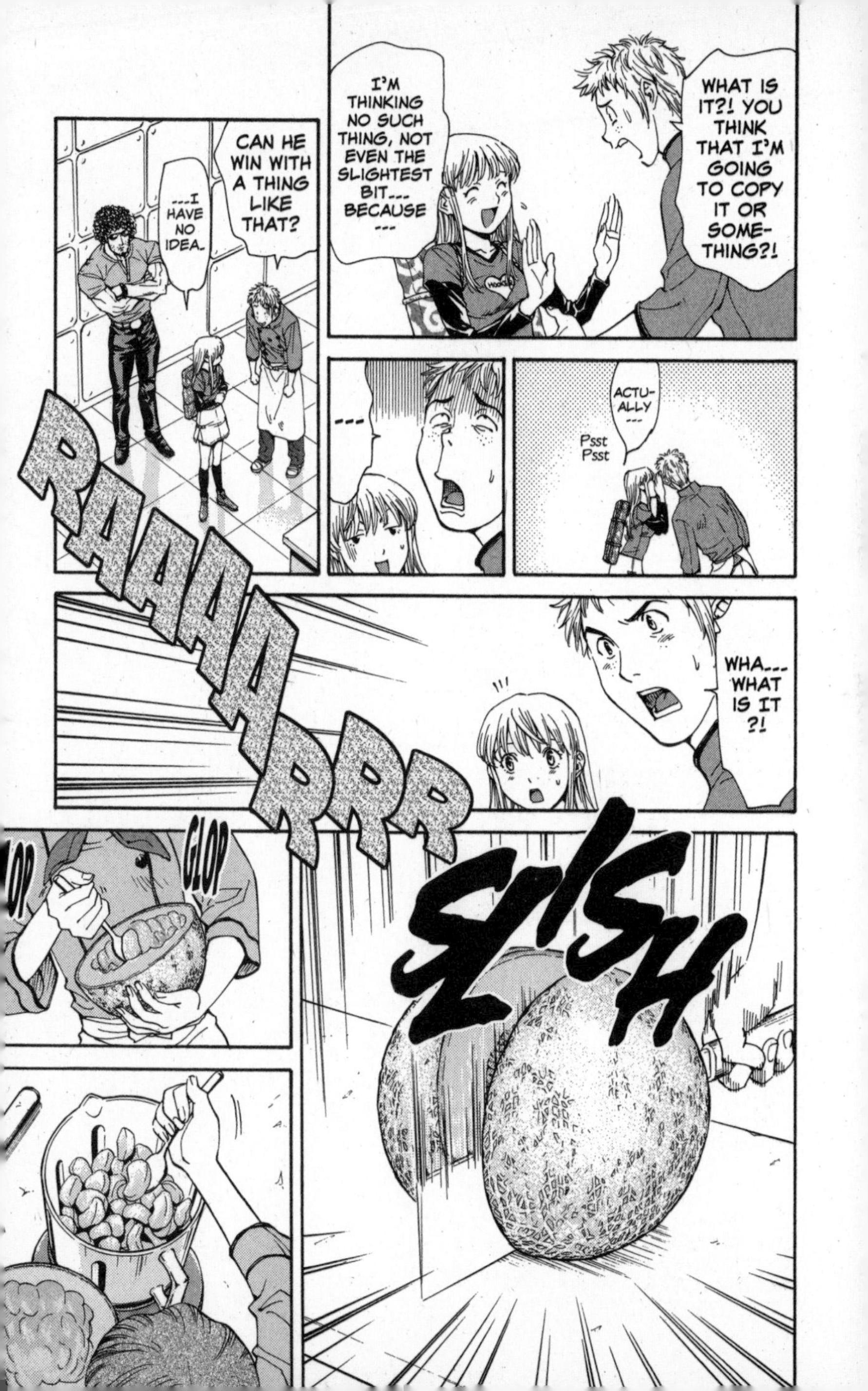
WHAT IS IT?! YOU THINK THAT I'M GOING TO COPY IT OR SOME-THING?!
I'M THINKING NO SUCH THING, NOT EVEN THE SLIGHTEST BIT... BECAUSE ...
ACTU-ALLY ...
Psst Psst
...
CAN HE WIN WITH A THING LIKE THAT?
...I HAVE NO IDEA.
RAAAAARRRR
WHA... WHAT IS IT ?!
SLISH
GLOP

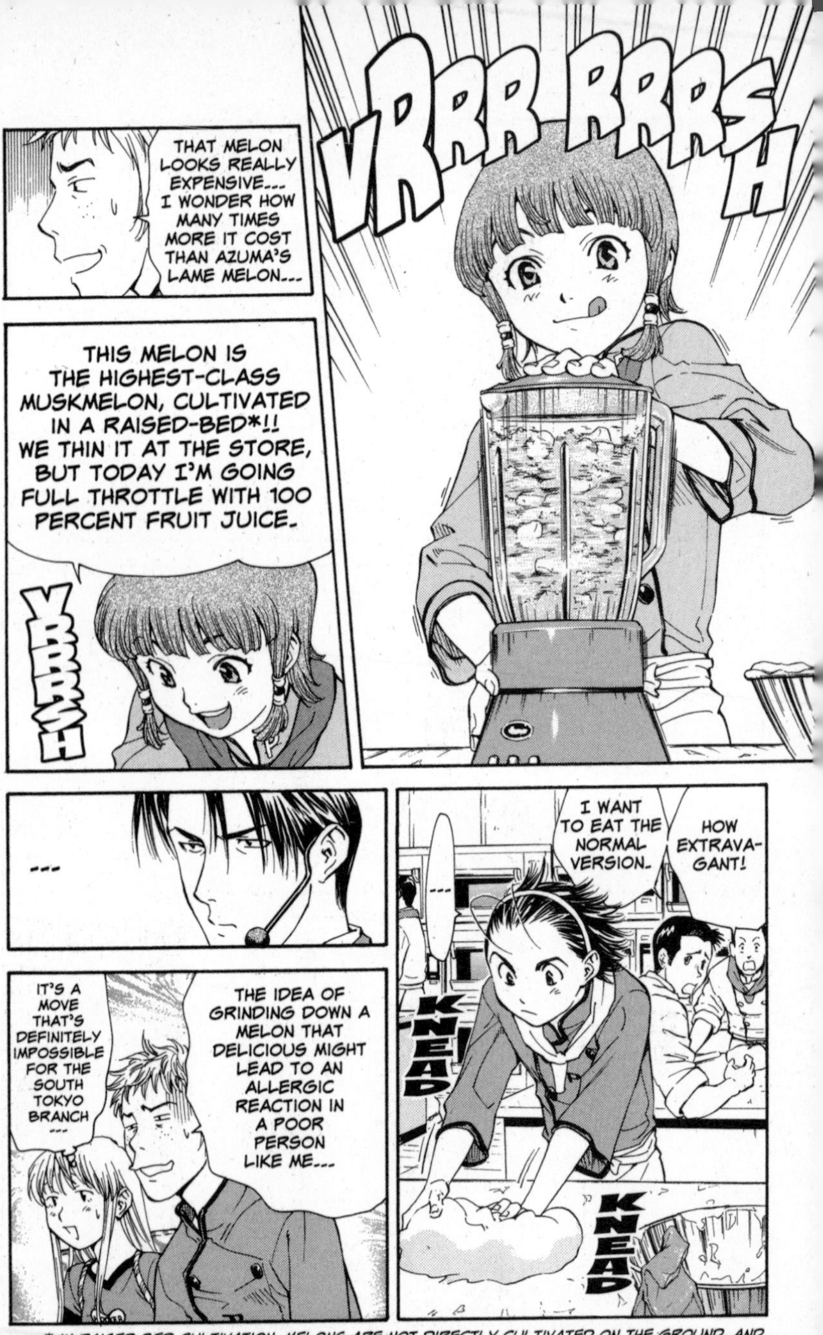
VRRR RRRSH
THAT MELON LOOKS REALLY EXPENSIVE... I WONDER HOW MANY TIMES MORE IT COST THAN AZUMA'S LAME MELON...
THIS MELON IS THE HIGHEST-CLASS MUSKMELON, CULTIVATED IN A RAISED-BED*!! WE THIN IT AT THE STORE, BUT TODAY I'M GOING FULL THROTTLE WITH 100 PERCENT FRUIT JUICE.
VRRRSH
HOW EXTRAVA-GANT!
I WANT TO EAT THE NORMAL VERSION.
...
KNEAD
KNEAD
...
THE IDEA OF GRINDING DOWN A MELON THAT DELICIOUS MIGHT LEAD TO AN ALLERGIC REACTION IN A POOR PERSON LIKE ME...
IT'S A MOVE THAT'S DEFINITELY IMPOSSIBLE FOR THE SOUTH TOKYO BRANCH...

* IN RAISED-BED CULTIVATION, MELONS ARE NOT DIRECTLY CULTIVATED ON THE GROUND, AND DIRT, WATER AND FERTILIZER ARE ADJUSTED TO FIT EACH MELON. IT IS GROWN BY SPENDING LOTS OF TIME AND EFFORT, LIKE YOU WOULD MAKING LOVE TO A WOMAN IN A TWIN BED.

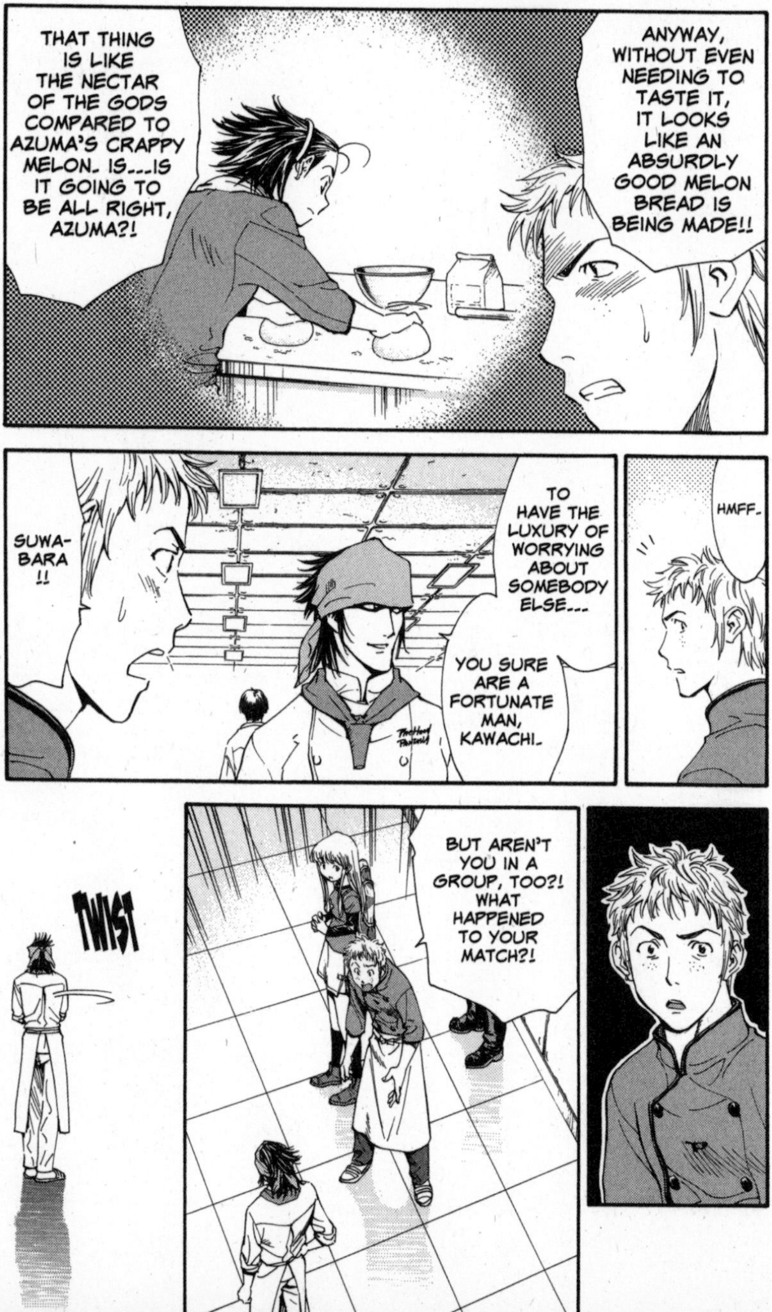
ANYWAY, WITHOUT EVEN NEEDING TO TASTE IT, IT LOOKS LIKE AN ABSURDLY GOOD MELON BREAD IS BEING MADE!!
THAT THING IS LIKE THE NECTAR OF THE GODS COMPARED TO AZUMA'S CRAPPY MELON. IS...IS IT GOING TO BE ALL RIGHT, AZUMA?!
HMFF.
TO HAVE THE LUXURY OF WORRYING ABOUT SOMEBODY ELSE...
YOU SURE ARE A FORTUNATE MAN, KAWACHI.
SUWA-BARA!!
BUT AREN'T YOU IN A GROUP, TOO?! WHAT HAPPENED TO YOUR MATCH?!
TWIST

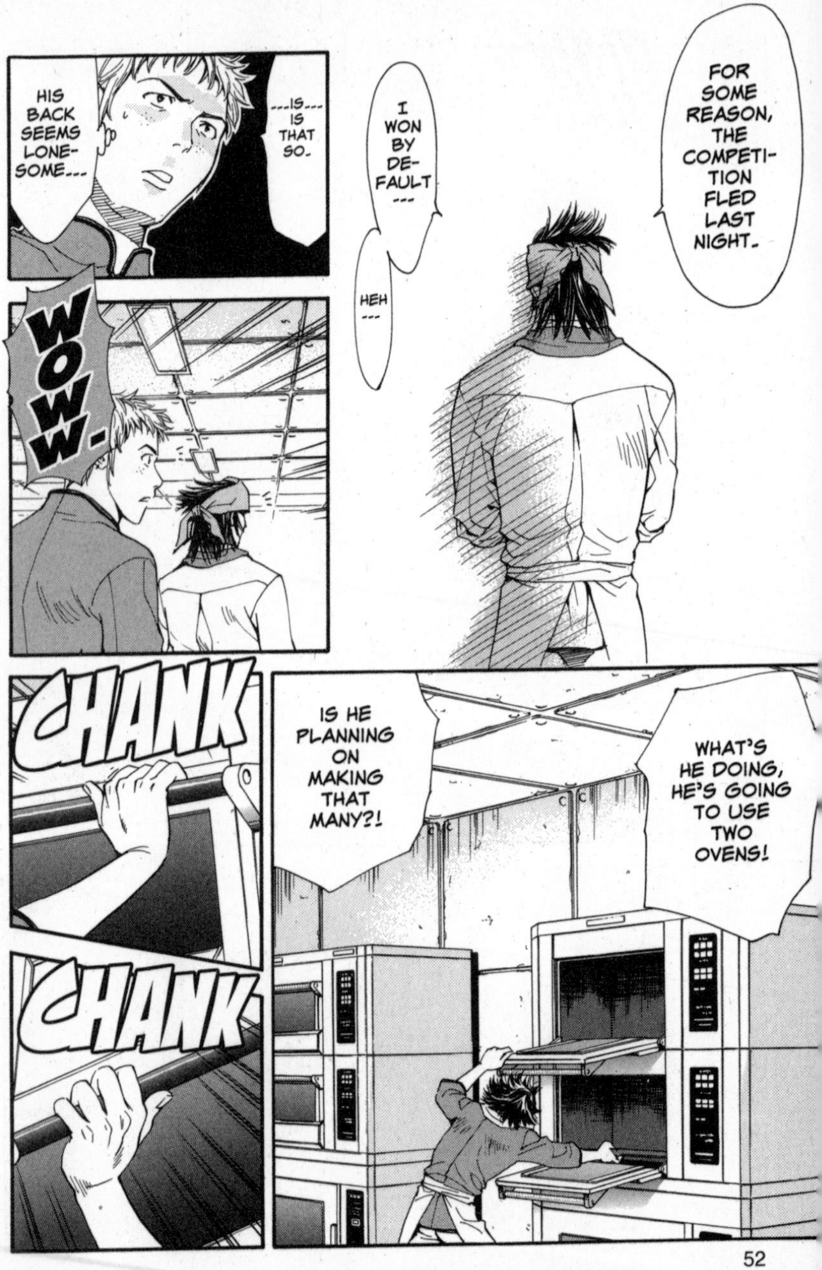
FOR SOME REASON, THE COMPETITION FLED LAST NIGHT.
I WON BY DEFAULT...
HEH...
...IS... IS THAT SO.
HIS BACK SEEMS LONESOME...
WOWW.
WHAT'S HE DOING, HE'S GOING TO USE TWO OVENS!
IS HE PLANNING ON MAKING THAT MANY?!
CHANK
CHANK

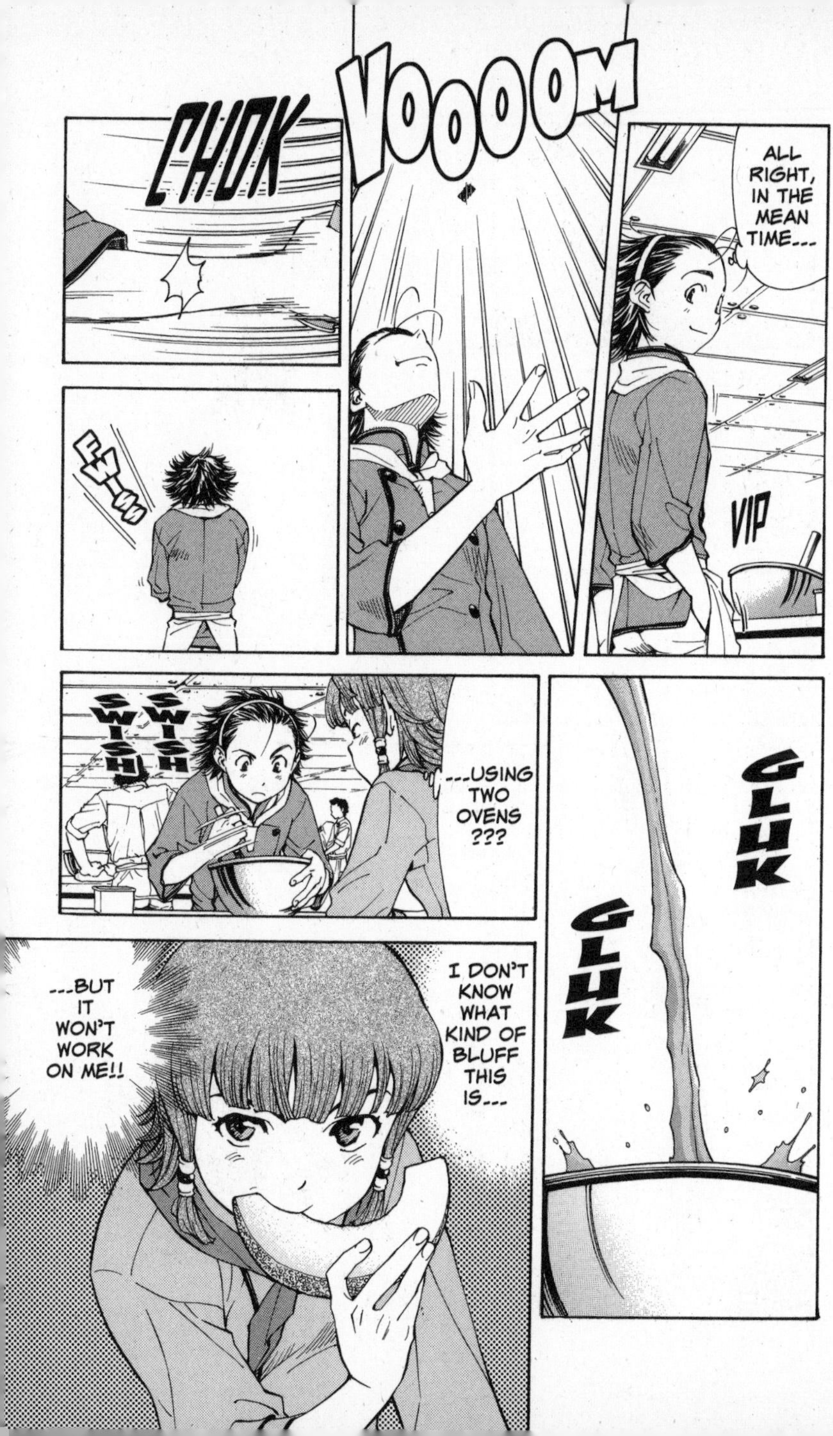
ALL RIGHT, IN THE MEAN TIME...
VIP
VOOOOM
CHOK
FWISH
GLUK
GLUK
...USING TWO OVENS???
SWISH
SWISH
I DON'T KNOW WHAT KIND OF BLUFF THIS IS...
...BUT IT WON'T WORK ON ME!!

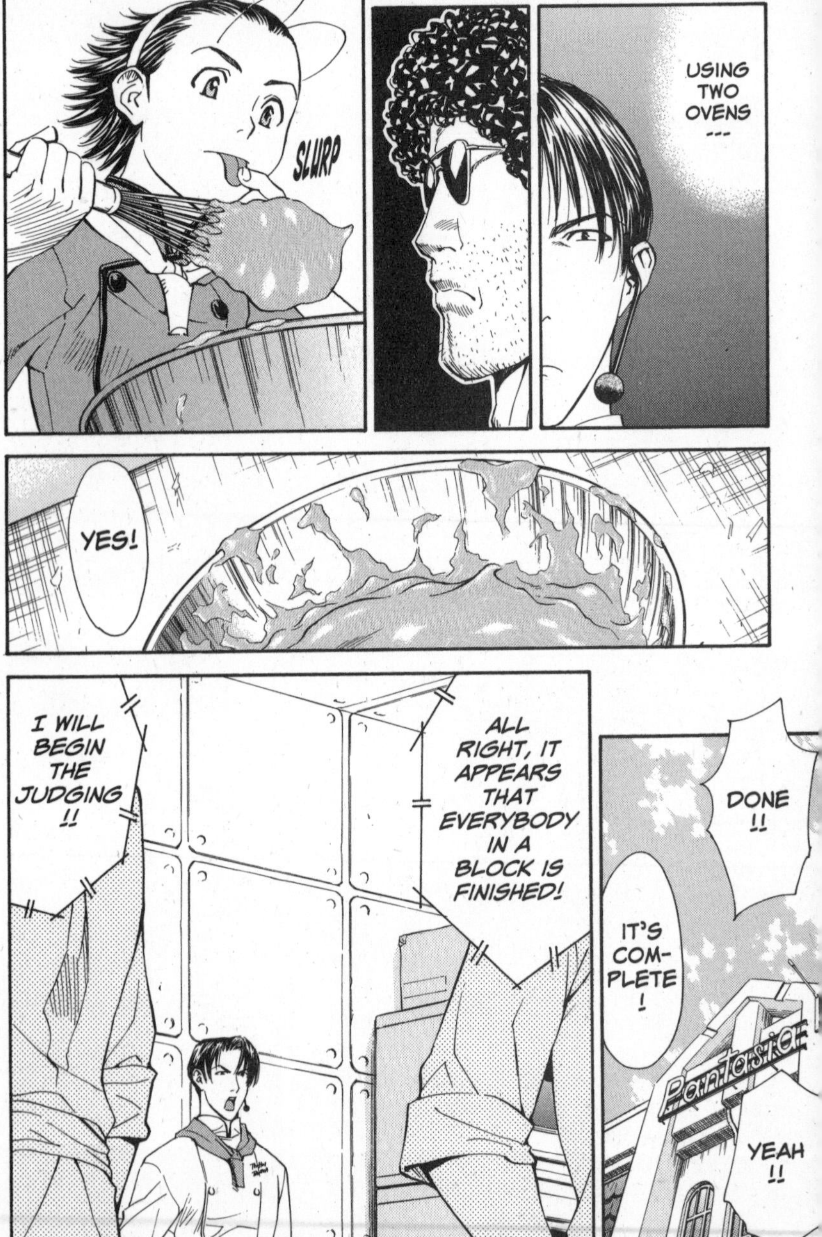
USING TWO OVENS ---
SLURP
YES!
DONE!!
IT'S COMPLETE!
Pantasia
YEAH!!
ALL RIGHT, IT APPEARS THAT EVERYBODY IN A BLOCK IS FINISHED!
I WILL BEGIN THE JUDGING!!

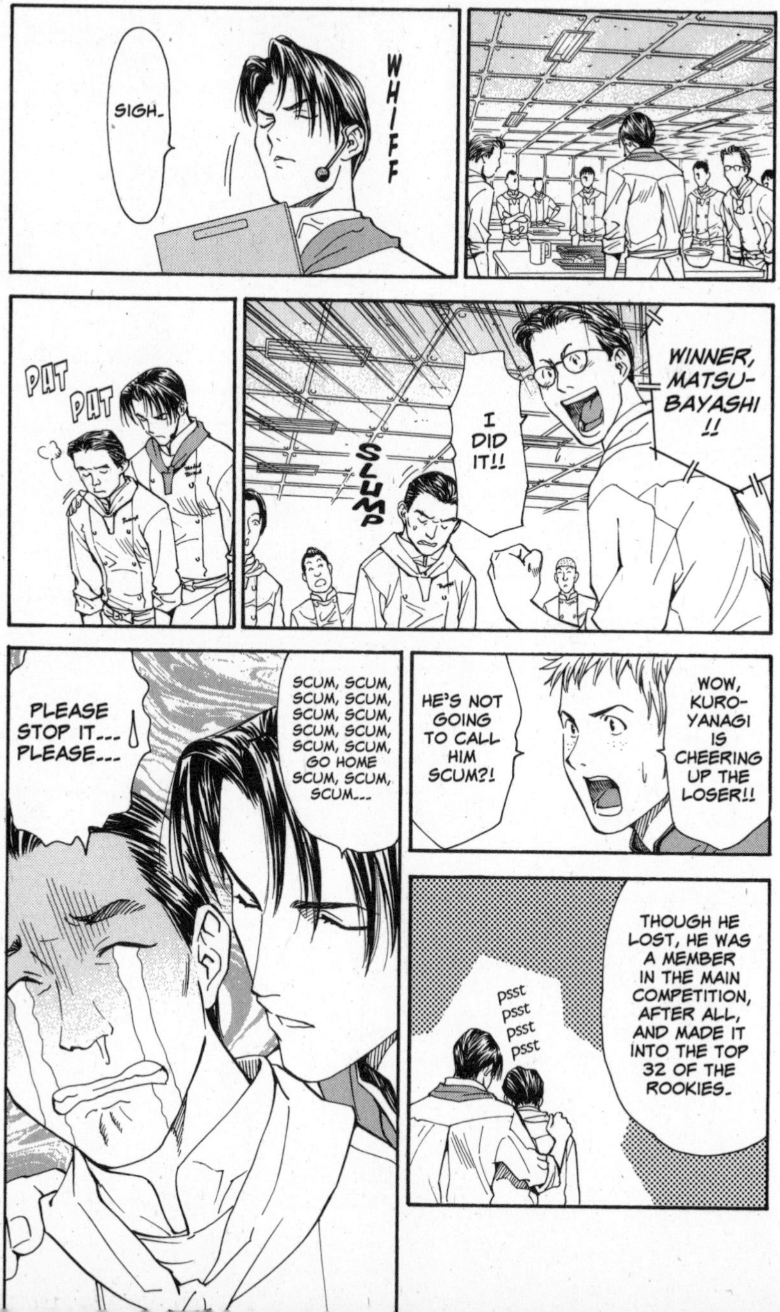
WHIFF
SIGH_
WINNER, MATSU-BAYASHI !!
I DID IT!!
...
SLUMP
PAT PAT
WOW, KURO-YANAGI IS CHEERING UP THE LOSER!!
HE'S NOT GOING TO CALL HIM SCUM?!
THOUGH HE LOST, HE WAS A MEMBER IN THE MAIN COMPETITION, AFTER ALL, AND MADE IT INTO THE TOP 32 OF THE ROOKIES_
psst psst psst psst
SCUM, SCUM, SCUM, SCUM, SCUM, SCUM, SCUM, SCUM, SCUM, SCUM, GO HOME SCUM, SCUM, SCUM...
PLEASE STOP IT... PLEASE...

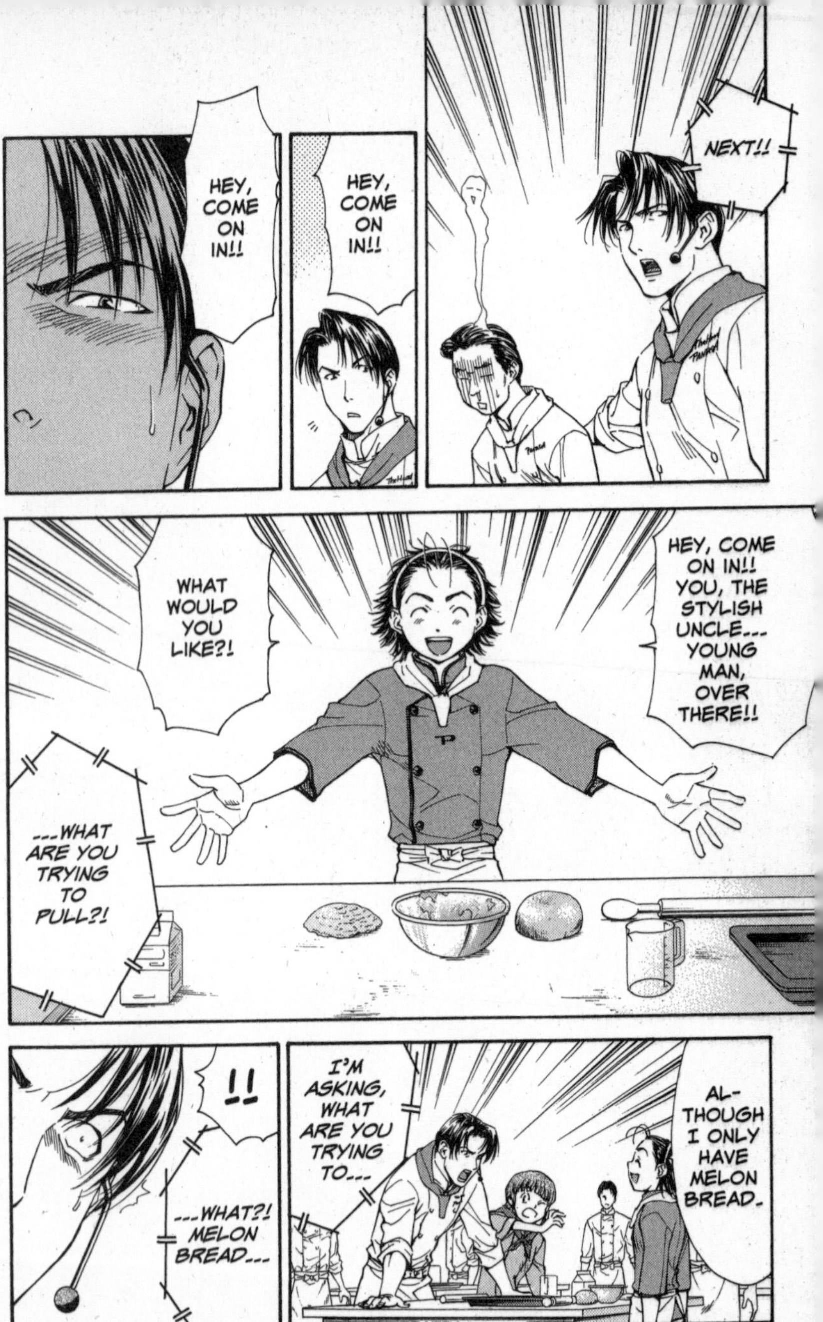
NEXT!!
HEY, COME ON IN!!
HEY, COME ON IN!!
HEY, COME ON IN!! YOU, THE STYLISH UNCLE... YOUNG MAN, OVER THERE!!
WHAT WOULD YOU LIKE?!
...WHAT ARE YOU TRYING TO PULL?!
AL-THOUGH I ONLY HAVE MELON BREAD.
I'M ASKING, WHAT ARE YOU TRYING TO...
!!
...WHAT?! MELON BREAD...

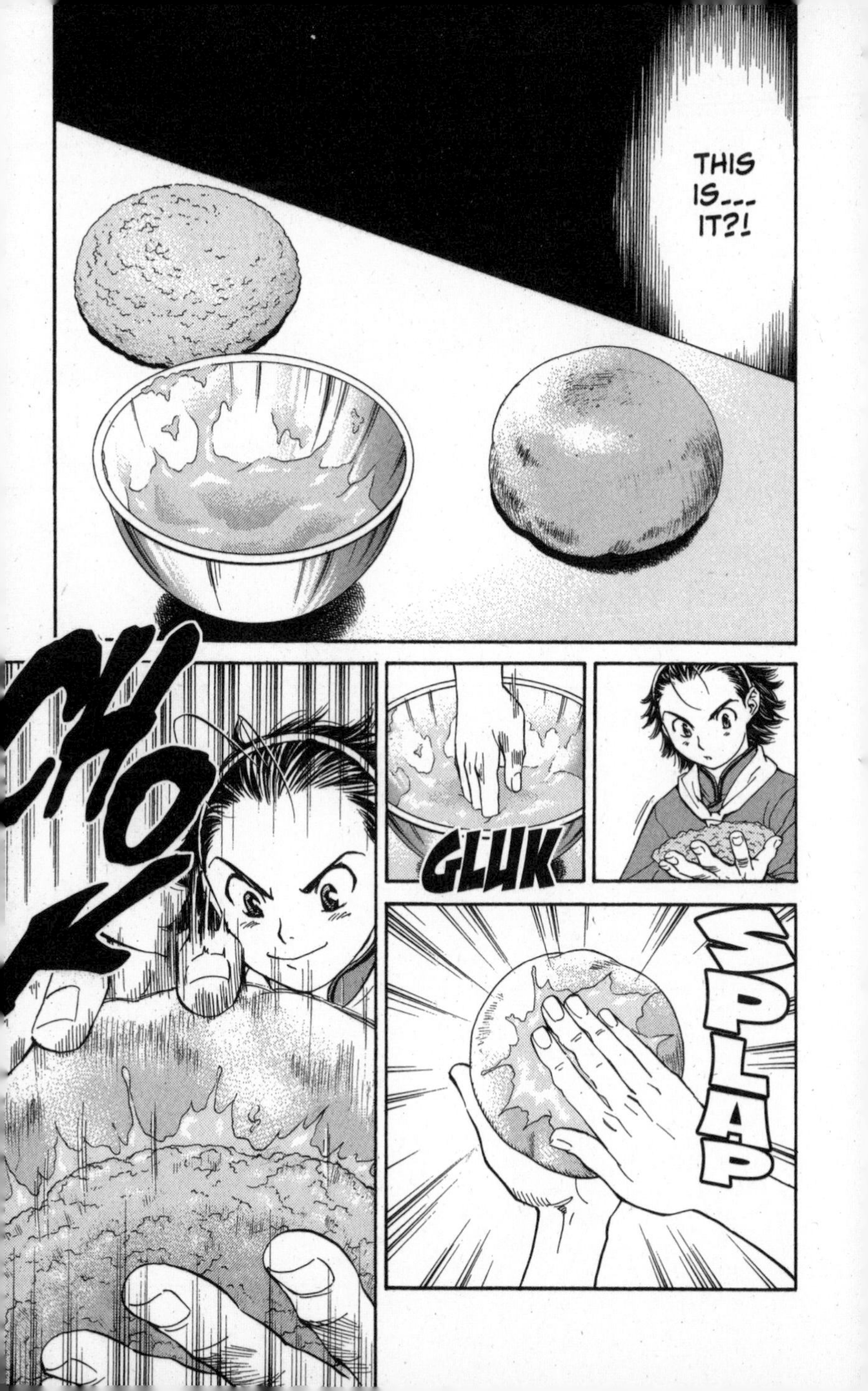
THIS IS... IT?!
GLUK
SPLAP
CHOK

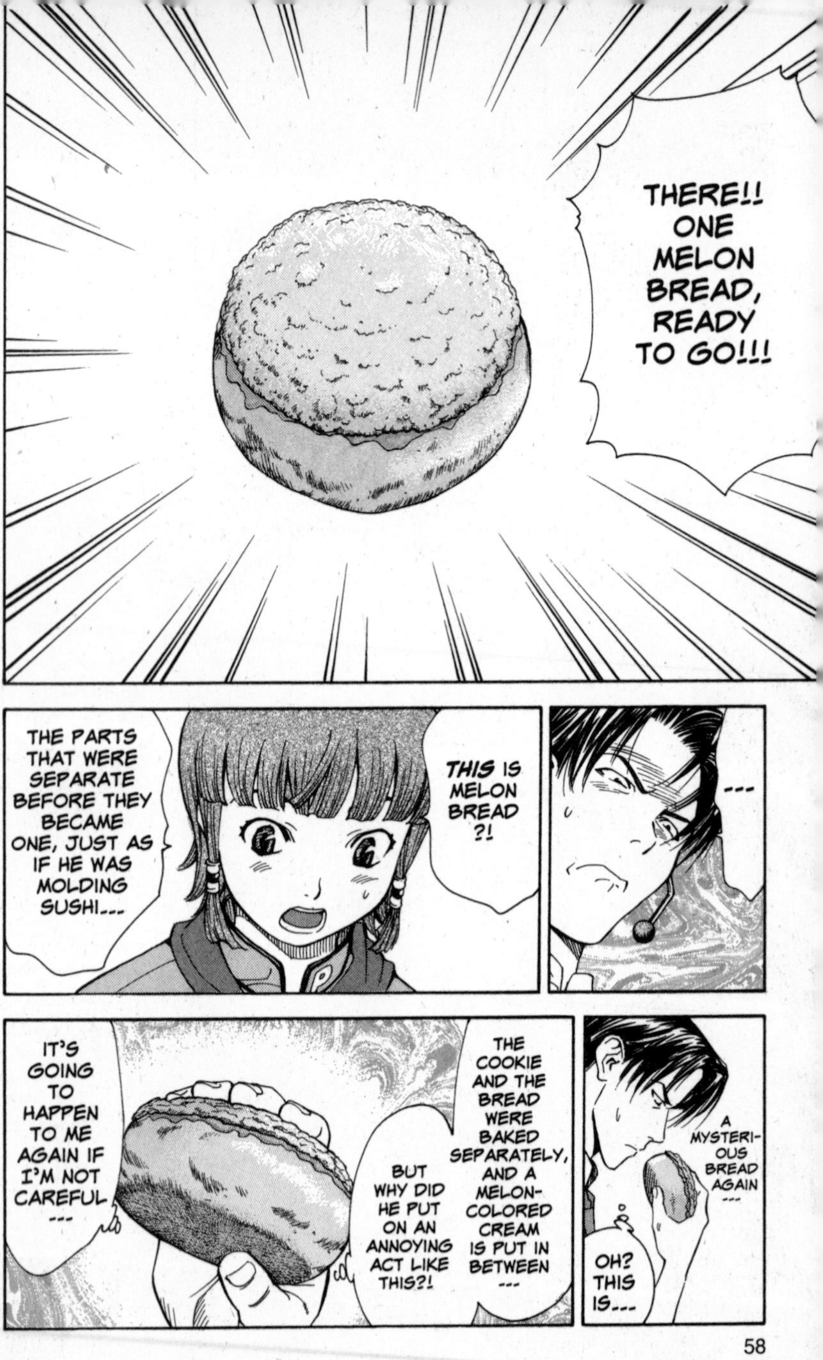
THERE!! ONE MELON BREAD, READY TO GO!!!
...
THIS IS MELON BREAD?!
THE PARTS THAT WERE SEPARATE BEFORE THEY BECAME ONE, JUST AS IF HE WAS MOLDING SUSHI...
A MYSTERIOUS BREAD AGAIN...
OH? THIS IS...
THE COOKIE AND THE BREAD WERE BAKED SEPARATELY, AND A MELON-COLORED CREAM IS PUT IN BETWEEN...
BUT WHY DID HE PUT ON AN ANNOYING ACT LIKE THIS?!
IT'S GOING TO HAPPEN TO ME AGAIN IF I'M NOT CAREFUL...

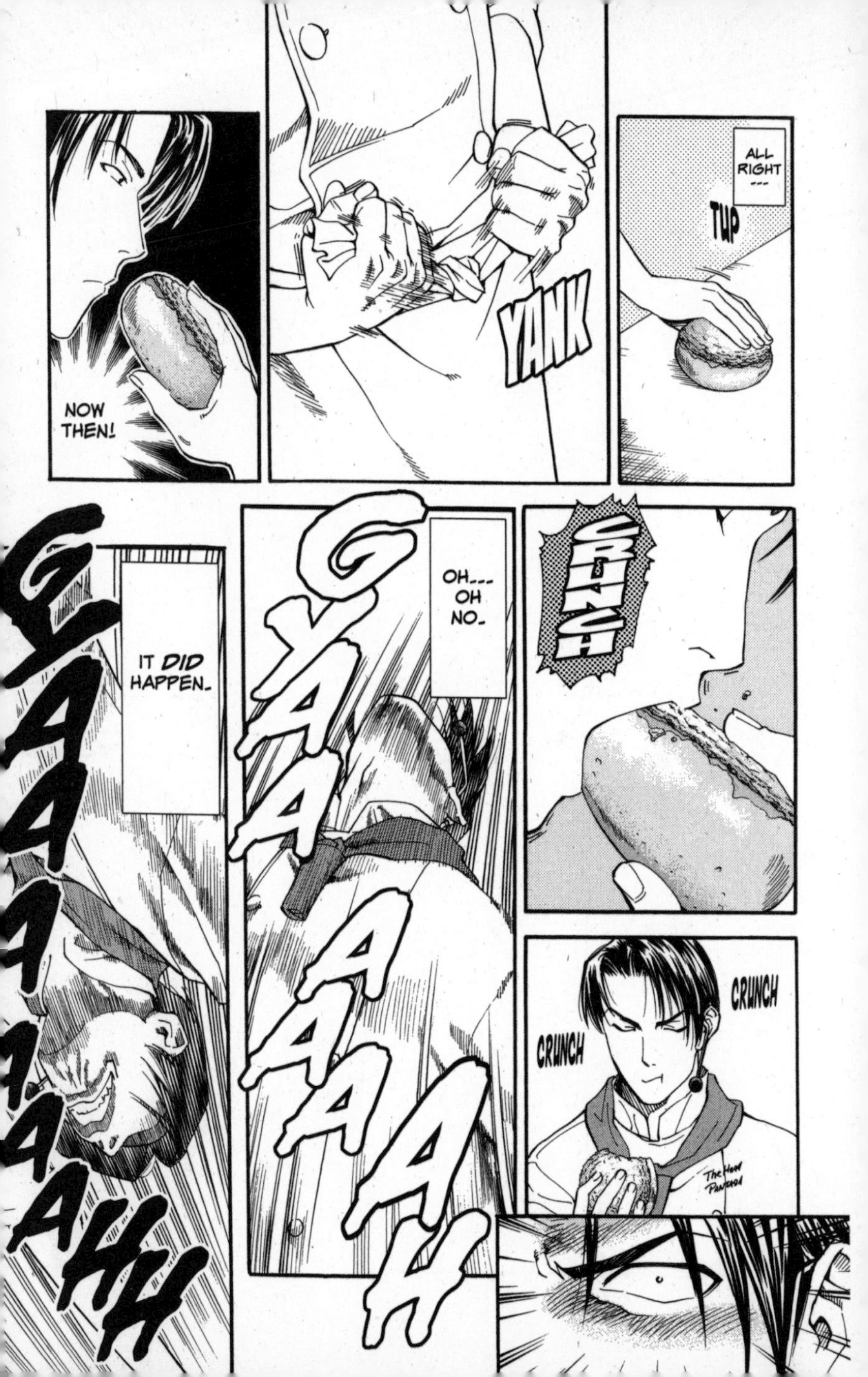
ALL RIGHT---
TUP
YANK
NOW THEN!
CRUNCH
CRUNCH
CRUNCH
OH--- OH NO-
GYAAAAAAH
IT *DID* HAPPEN-
GAAAAAAAHH

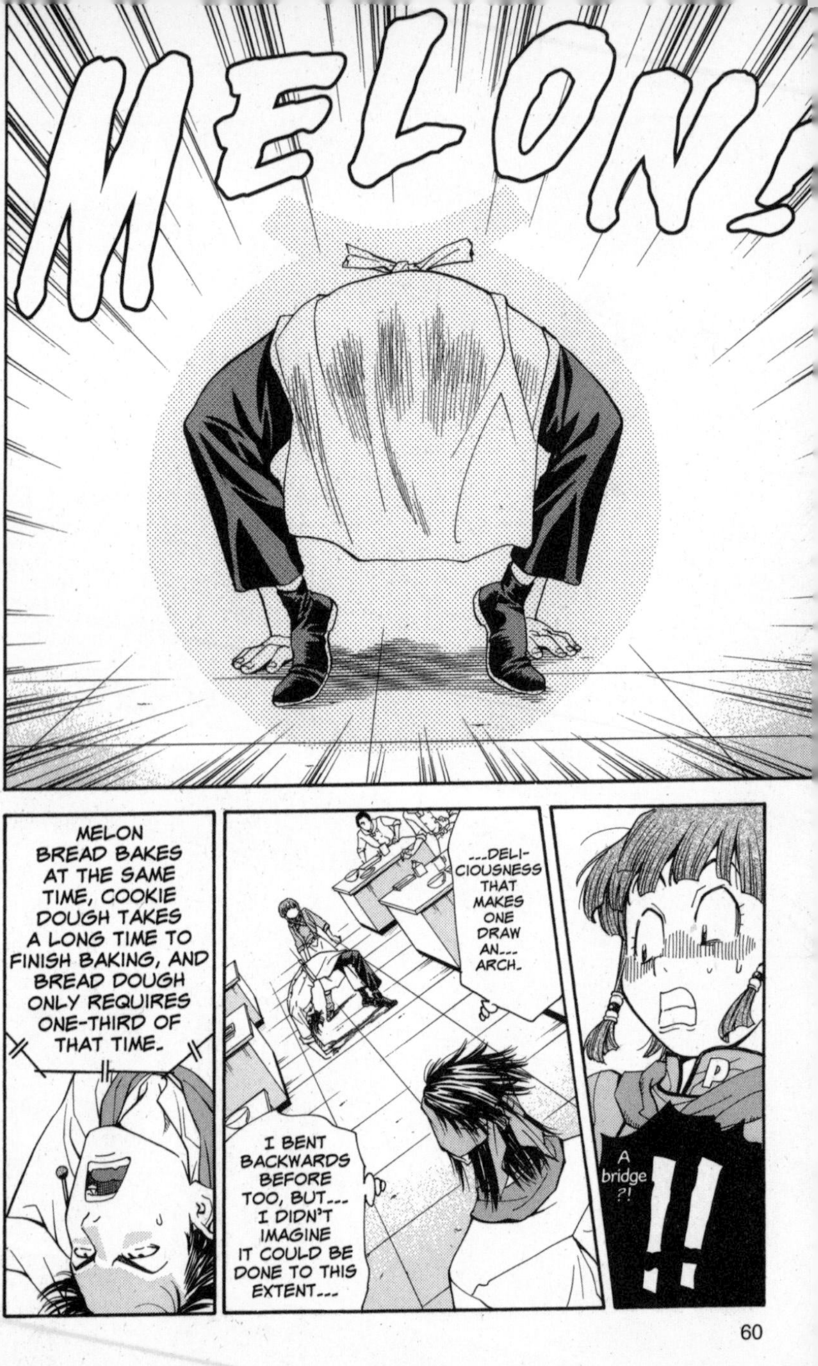
MELON!
A bridge?!
...DELI-CIOUSNESS THAT MAKES ONE DRAW AN... ARCH.
I BENT BACKWARDS BEFORE TOO, BUT... I DIDN'T IMAGINE IT COULD BE DONE TO THIS EXTENT...
MELON BREAD BAKES AT THE SAME TIME, COOKIE DOUGH TAKES A LONG TIME TO FINISH BAKING, AND BREAD DOUGH ONLY REQUIRES ONE-THIRD OF THAT TIME.

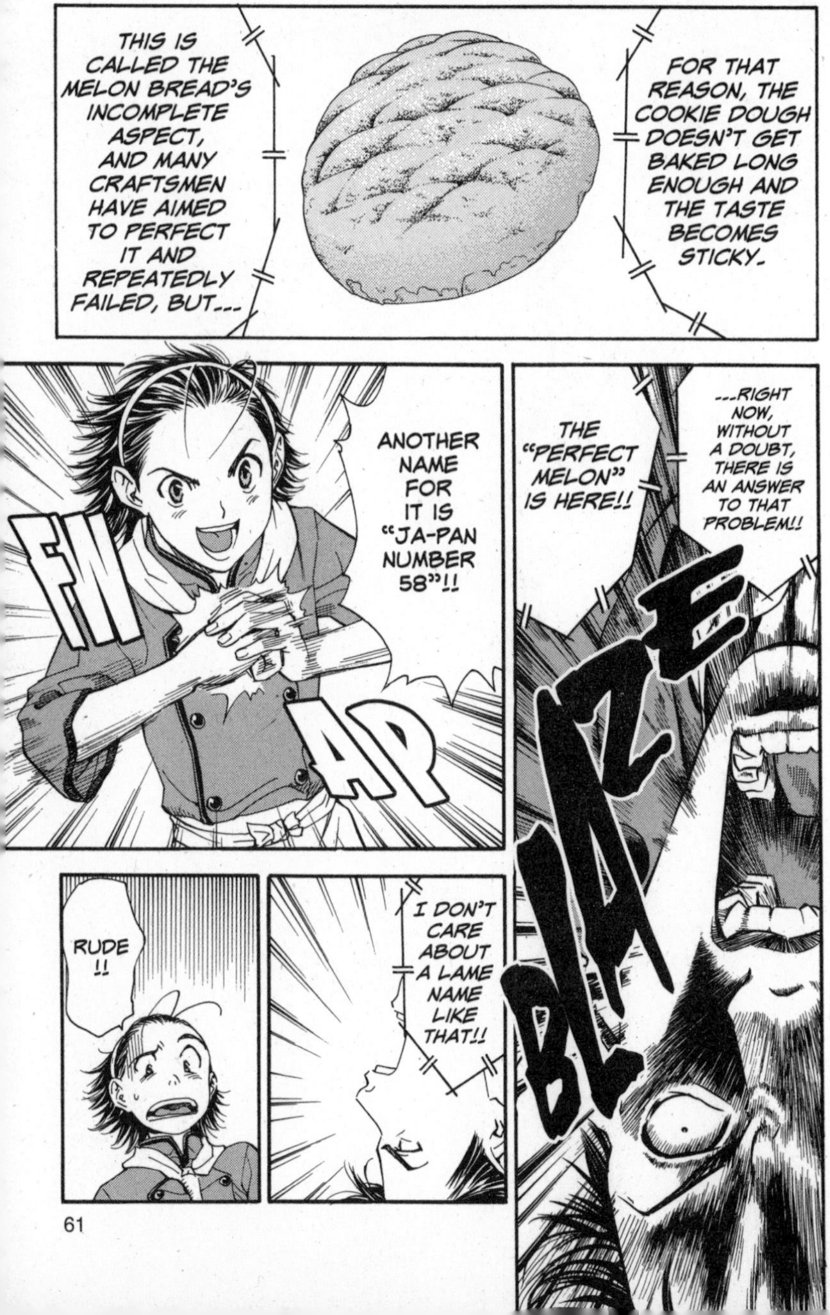
FOR THAT REASON, THE COOKIE DOUGH DOESN'T GET BAKED LONG ENOUGH AND THE TASTE BECOMES STICKY...
THIS IS CALLED THE MELON BREAD'S INCOMPLETE ASPECT, AND MANY CRAFTSMEN HAVE AIMED TO PERFECT IT AND REPEATEDLY FAILED, BUT...
...RIGHT NOW, WITHOUT A DOUBT, THERE IS AN ANSWER TO THAT PROBLEM!!
THE "PERFECT MELON" IS HERE!!
BLAZE
ANOTHER NAME FOR IT IS "JA-PAN NUMBER 58"!!
FWAP
I DON'T CARE ABOUT A LAME NAME LIKE THAT!!
RUDE!!

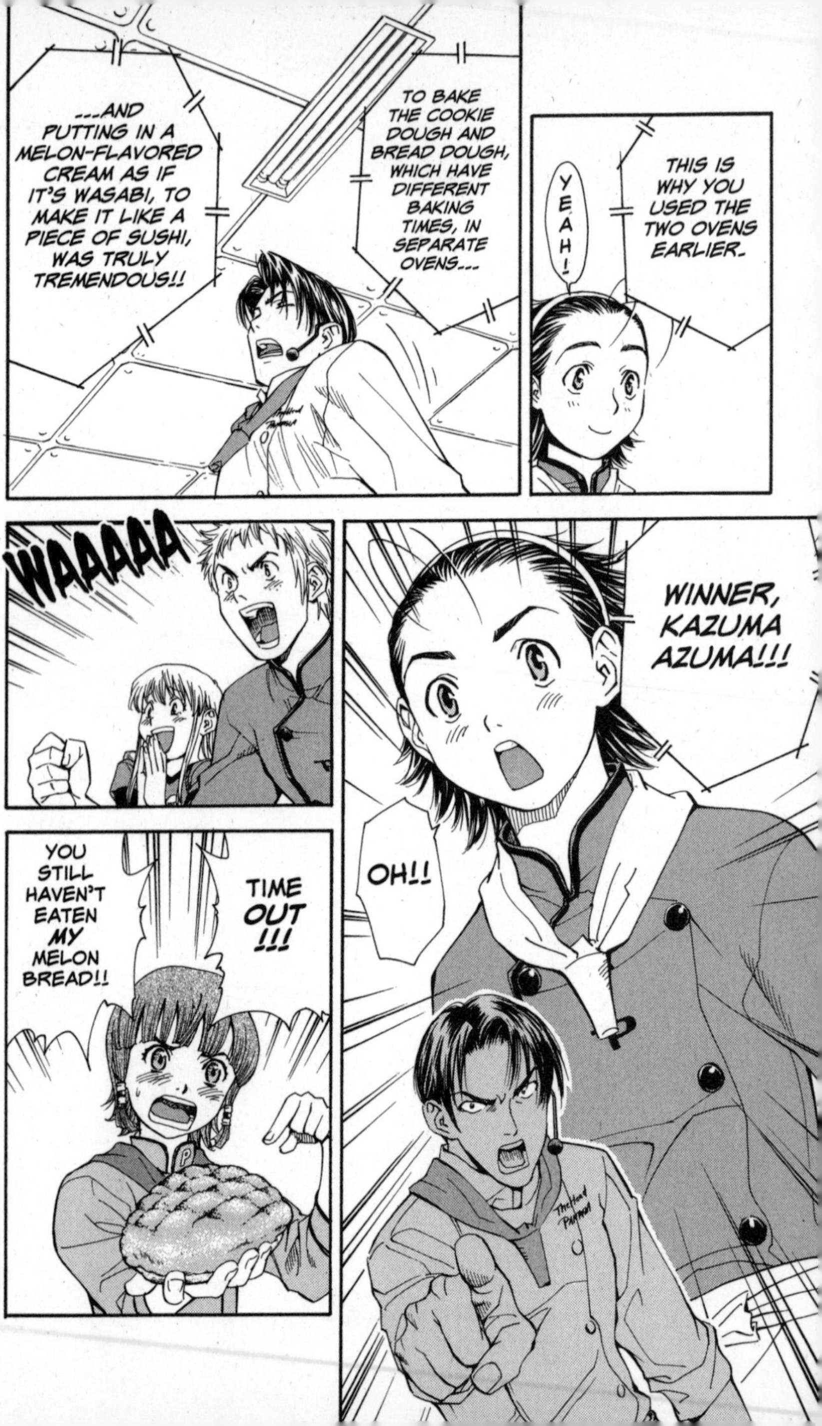
THIS IS WHY YOU USED THE TWO OVENS EARLIER.
YEAH!
TO BAKE THE COOKIE DOUGH AND BREAD DOUGH, WHICH HAVE DIFFERENT BAKING TIMES, IN SEPARATE OVENS...
...AND PUTTING IN A MELON-FLAVORED CREAM AS IF IT'S WASABI, TO MAKE IT LIKE A PIECE OF SUSHI, WAS TRULY TREMENDOUS!!
WINNER, KAZUMA AZUMA!!!
OH!!
WAAAAA
TIME OUT!!!
YOU STILL HAVEN'T EATEN MY MELON BREAD!!

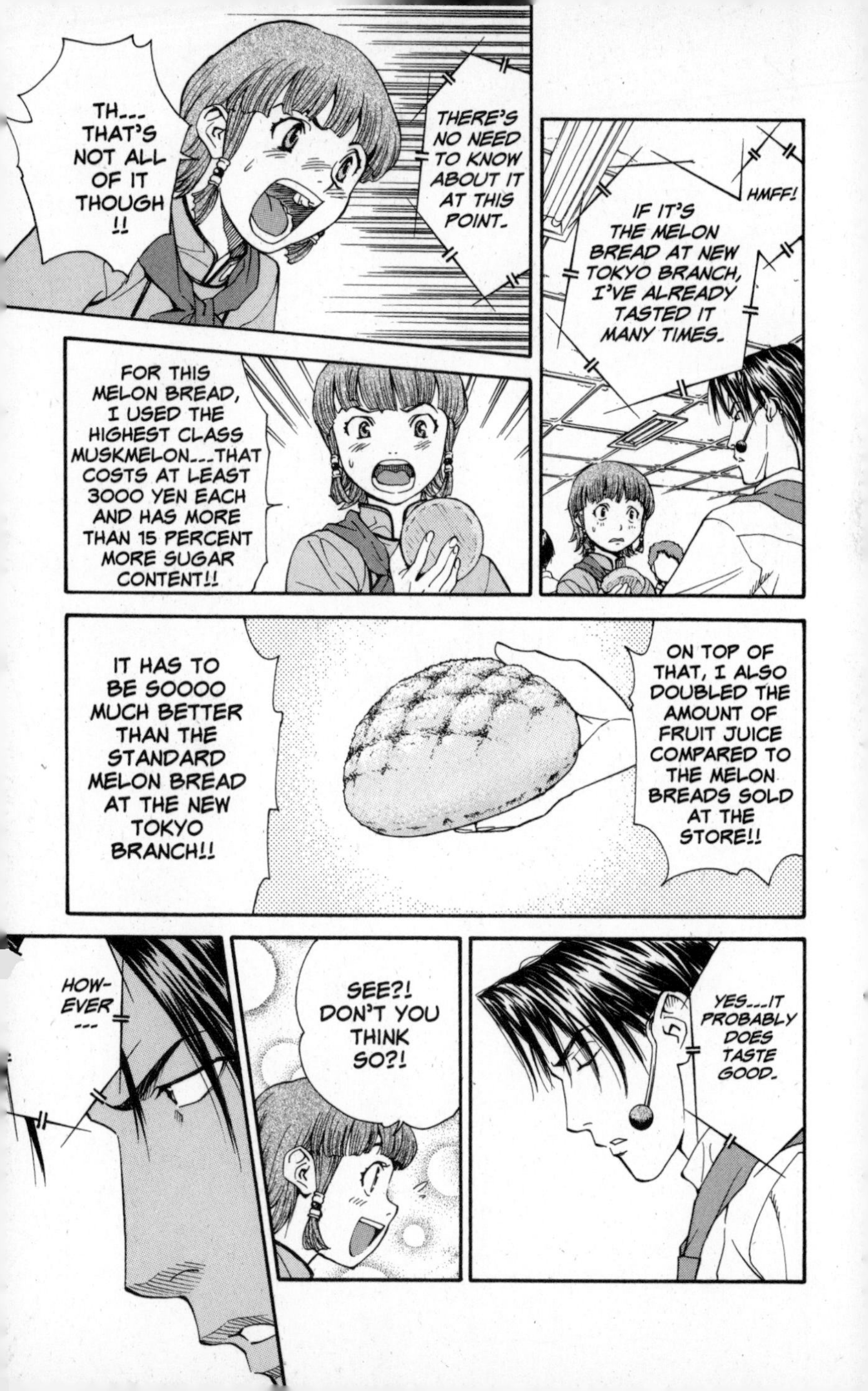
THERE'S NO NEED TO KNOW ABOUT IT AT THIS POINT.
TH... THAT'S NOT ALL OF IT THOUGH!!
HMFF!
IF IT'S THE MELON BREAD AT NEW TOKYO BRANCH, I'VE ALREADY TASTED IT MANY TIMES.
FOR THIS MELON BREAD, I USED THE HIGHEST CLASS MUSKMELON...THAT COSTS AT LEAST 3000 YEN EACH AND HAS MORE THAN 15 PERCENT MORE SUGAR CONTENT!!
ON TOP OF THAT, I ALSO DOUBLED THE AMOUNT OF FRUIT JUICE COMPARED TO THE MELON BREADS SOLD AT THE STORE!!
IT HAS TO BE SOOOO MUCH BETTER THAN THE STANDARD MELON BREAD AT THE NEW TOKYO BRANCH!!
YES...IT PROBABLY DOES TASTE GOOD.
SEE?! DON'T YOU THINK SO?!
HOW-EVER...

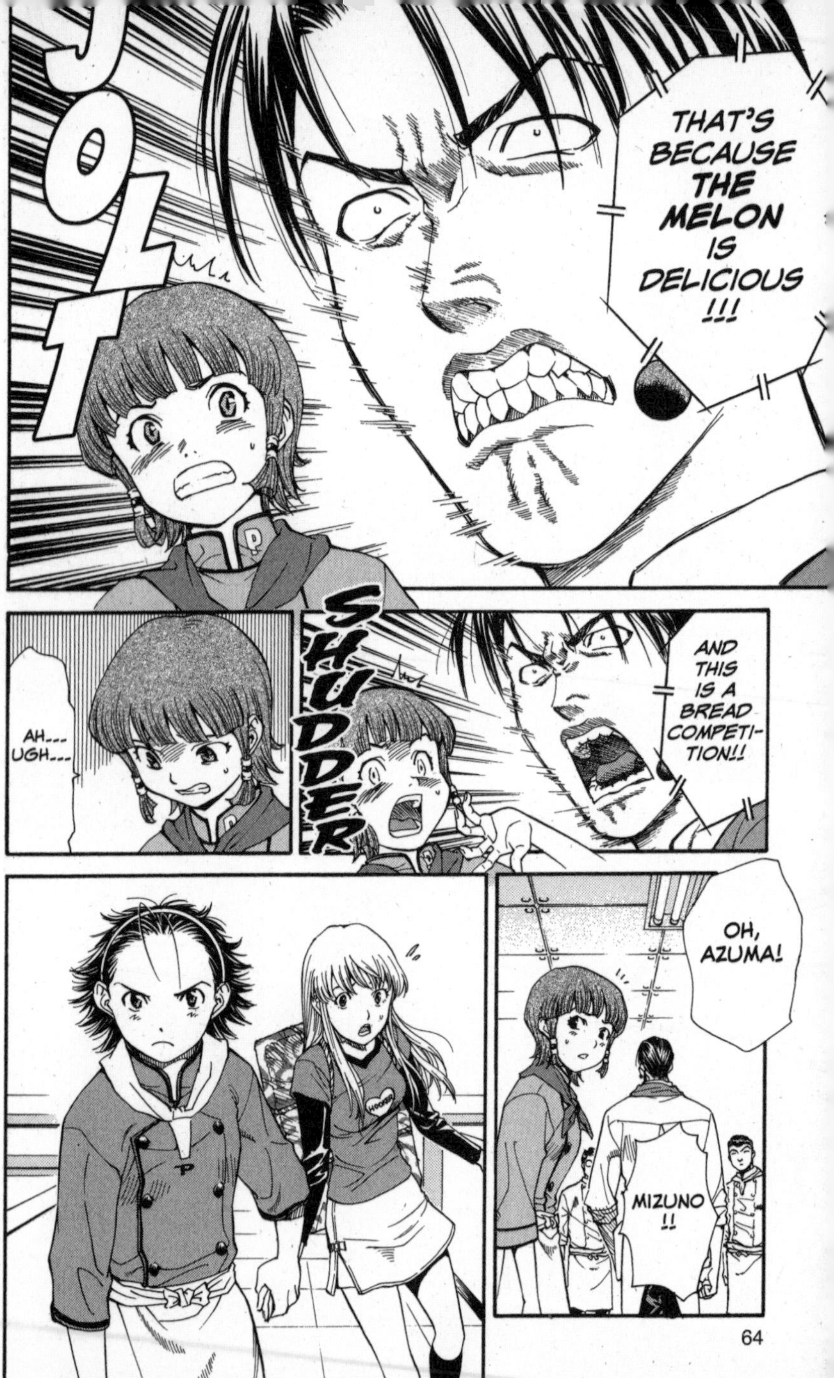
JOLT
THAT'S BECAUSE THE MELON IS DELICIOUS !!!
AND THIS IS A BREAD COMPETITION!!
SHUDDER
AH... UGH...
OH, AZUMA!
MIZUNO !!

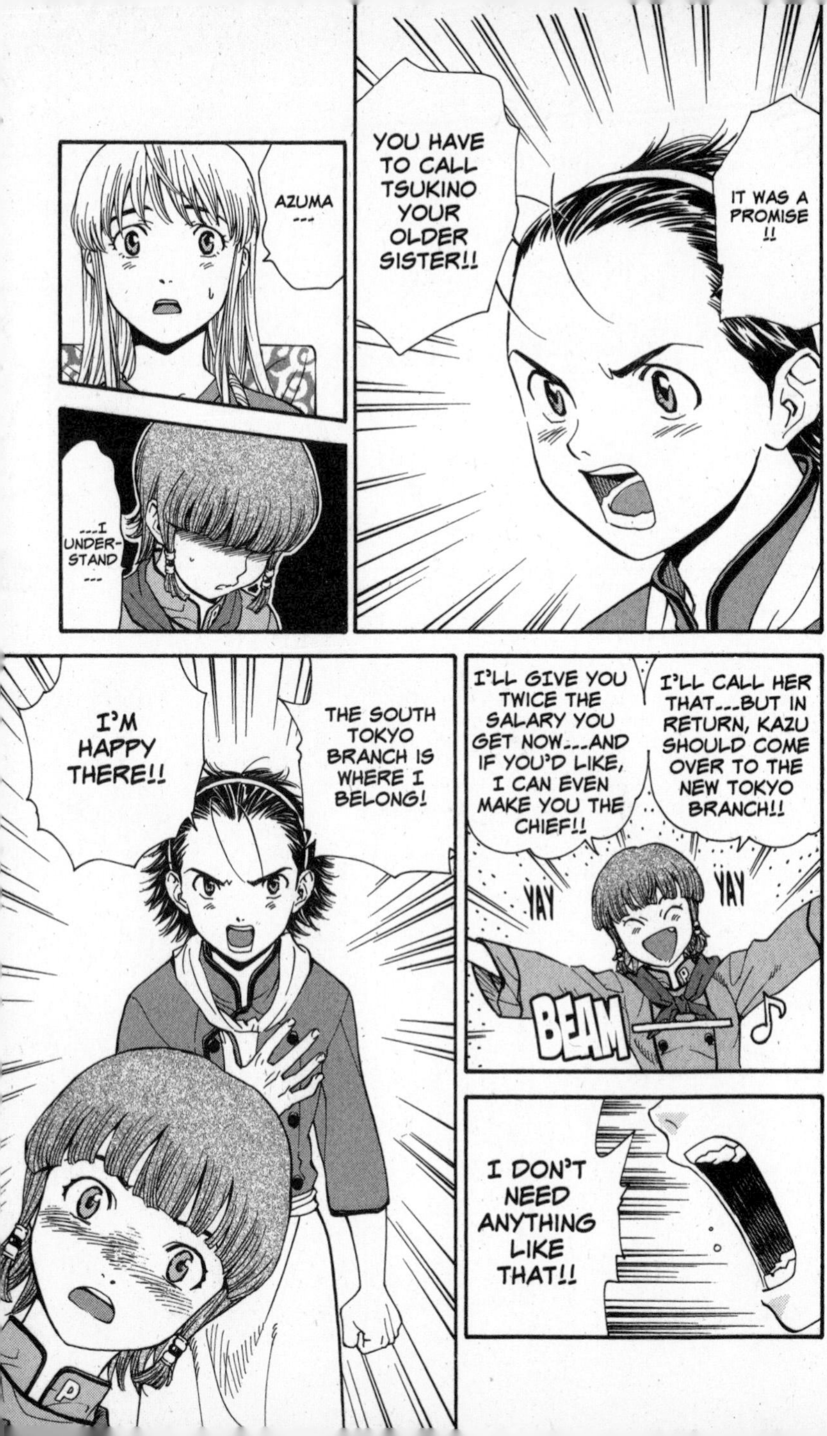
YOU HAVE TO CALL TSUKINO YOUR OLDER SISTER!!
IT WAS A PROMISE!!
AZUMA---
---I UNDERSTAND---
I'LL CALL HER THAT...BUT IN RETURN, KAZU SHOULD COME OVER TO THE NEW TOKYO BRANCH!!
I'LL GIVE YOU TWICE THE SALARY YOU GET NOW...AND IF YOU'D LIKE, I CAN EVEN MAKE YOU THE CHIEF!!
YAY
YAY
BEAM
I DON'T NEED ANYTHING LIKE THAT!!
THE SOUTH TOKYO BRANCH IS WHERE I BELONG!
I'M HAPPY THERE!!

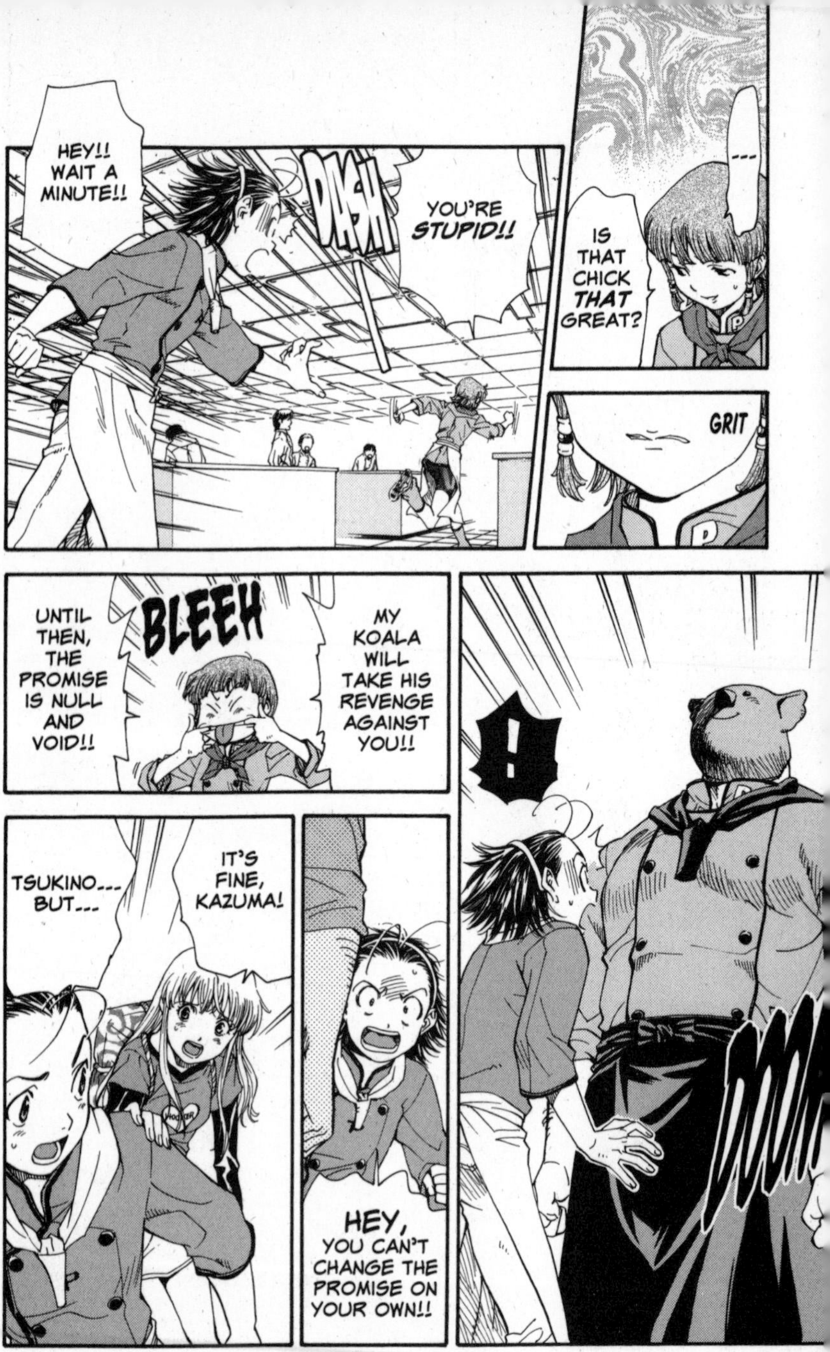
...
IS THAT CHICK THAT GREAT?
GRIT
YOU'RE STUPID!!
DASH
HEY!! WAIT A MINUTE!!
!
MY KOALA WILL TAKE HIS REVENGE AGAINST YOU!!
BLEEH
UNTIL THEN, THE PROMISE IS NULL AND VOID!!
HEY, YOU CAN'T CHANGE THE PROMISE ON YOUR OWN!!
IT'S FINE, KAZUMA!
TSUKINO... BUT...

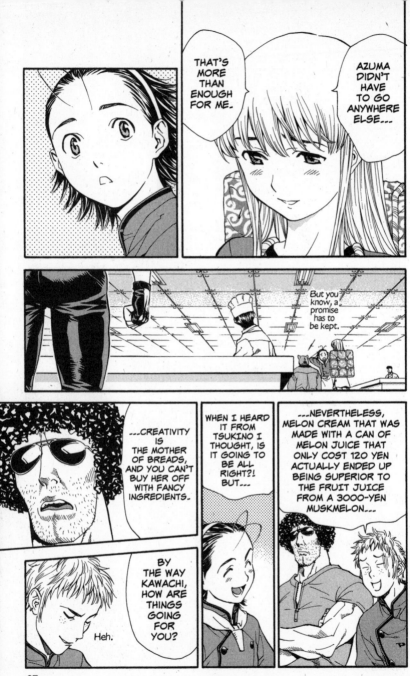

AZUMA DIDN'T HAVE TO GO ANYWHERE ELSE...
THAT'S MORE THAN ENOUGH FOR ME.
But you know, a promise has to be kept.
...NEVERTHELESS, MELON CREAM THAT WAS MADE WITH A CAN OF MELON JUICE THAT ONLY COST 120 YEN ACTUALLY ENDED UP BEING SUPERIOR TO THE FRUIT JUICE FROM A 3000-YEN MUSKMELON...
WHEN I HEARD IT FROM TSUKINO I THOUGHT, IS IT GOING TO BE ALL RIGHT?! BUT...
...CREATIVITY IS THE MOTHER OF BREADS, AND YOU CAN'T BUY HER OFF WITH FANCY INGREDIENTS.
BY THE WAY KAWACHI, HOW ARE THINGS GOING FOR YOU?
Heh.

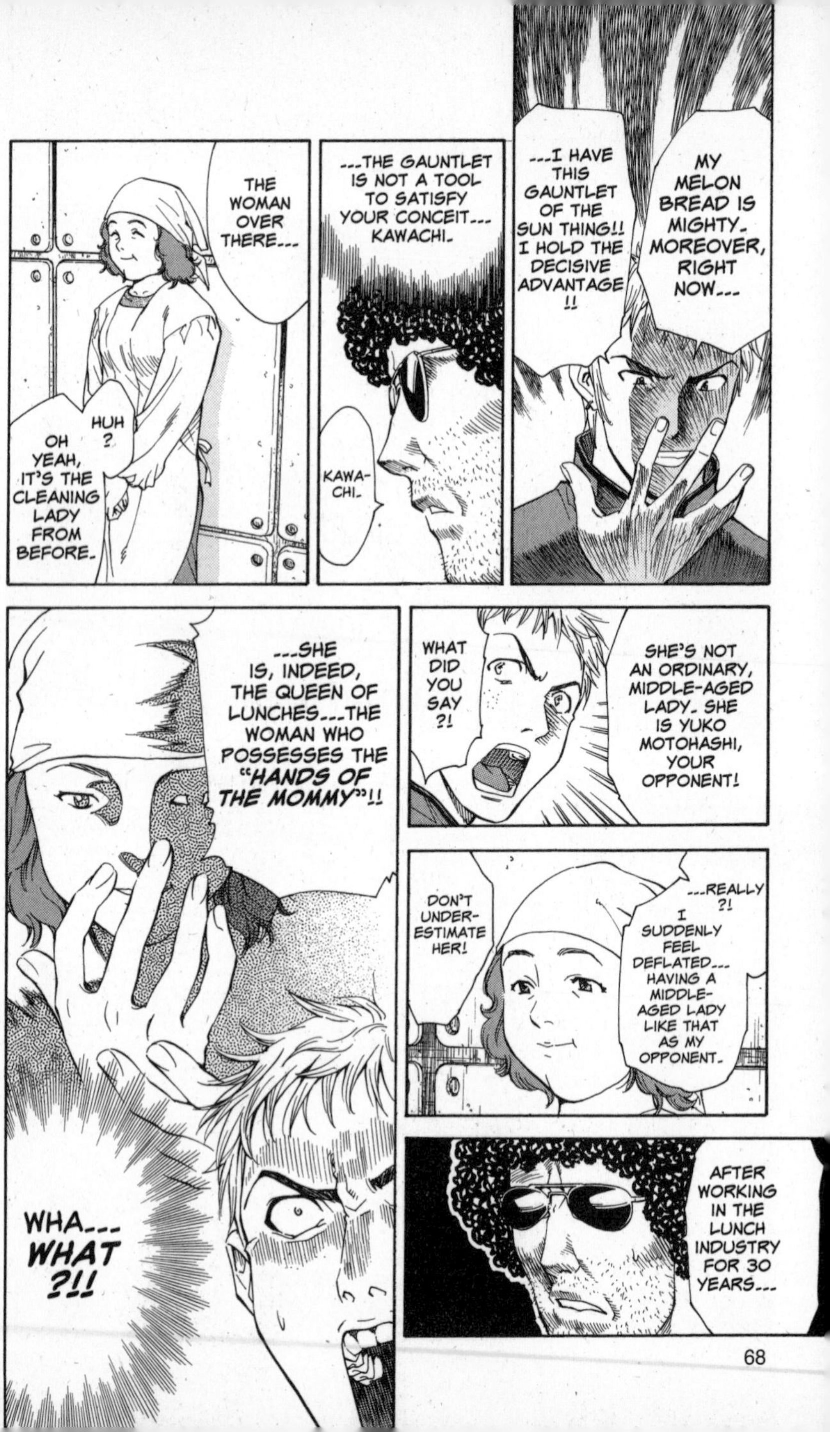
MY MELON BREAD IS MIGHTY. MOREOVER, RIGHT NOW...
...I HAVE THIS GAUNTLET OF THE SUN THING!! I HOLD THE DECISIVE ADVANTAGE!!
...THE GAUNTLET IS NOT A TOOL TO SATISFY YOUR CONCEIT... KAWACHI.
KAWACHI.
THE WOMAN OVER THERE...
HUH?
OH YEAH, IT'S THE CLEANING LADY FROM BEFORE.
SHE'S NOT AN ORDINARY, MIDDLE-AGED LADY. SHE IS YUKO MOTOHASHI, YOUR OPPONENT!
WHAT DID YOU SAY?!
...REALLY?!
I SUDDENLY FEEL DEFLATED... HAVING A MIDDLE-AGED LADY LIKE THAT AS MY OPPONENT.
DON'T UNDER-ESTIMATE HER!
AFTER WORKING IN THE LUNCH INDUSTRY FOR 30 YEARS...
...SHE IS, INDEED, THE QUEEN OF LUNCHES...THE WOMAN WHO POSSESSES THE "*HANDS OF THE MOMMY*"!!
WHA... *WHAT?!!*

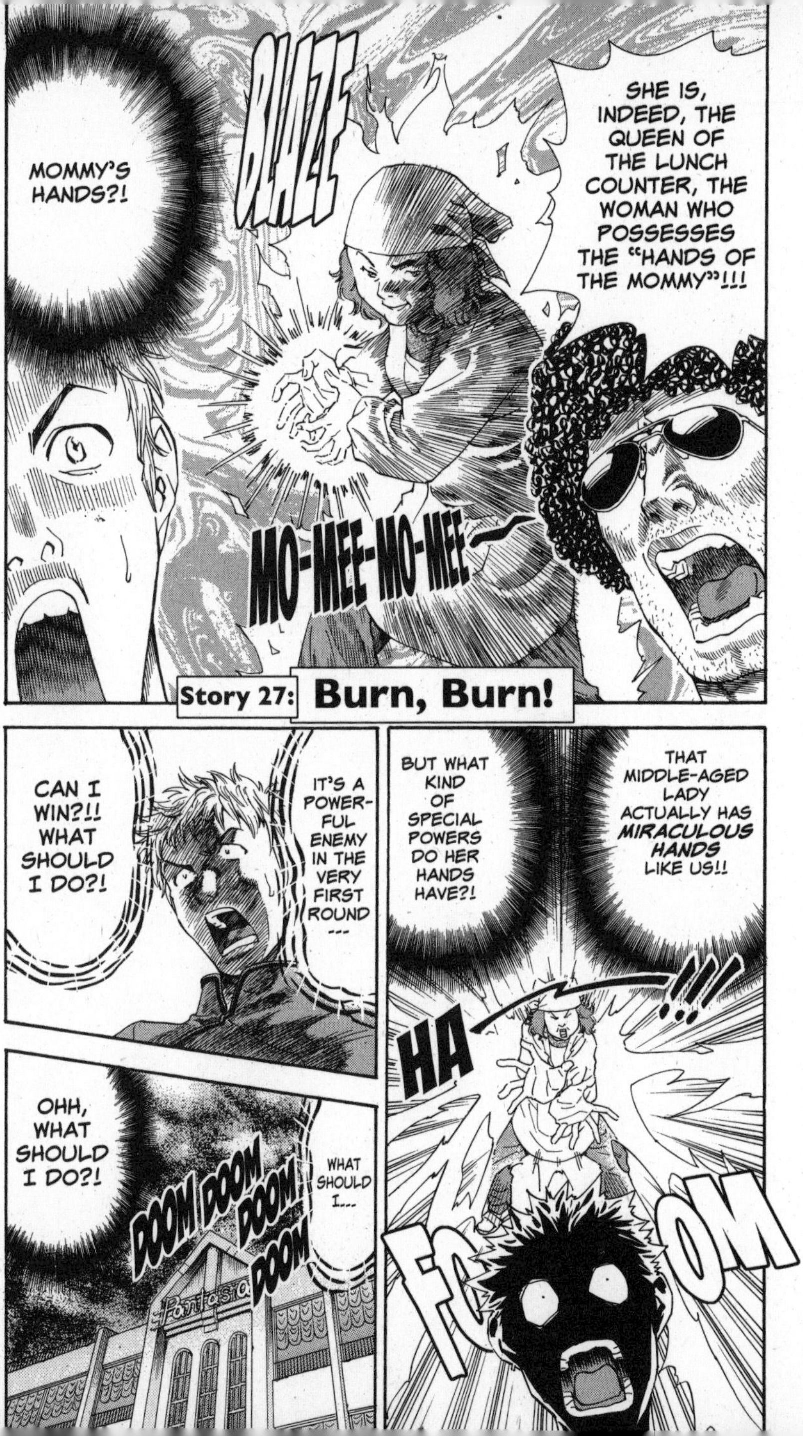
SHE IS, INDEED, THE QUEEN OF THE LUNCH COUNTER, THE WOMAN WHO POSSESSES THE "HANDS OF THE MOMMY"!!!
BLAZE
MOMMY'S HANDS?!
MO-MEE-MO-MEE
Story 27: Burn, Burn!
THAT MIDDLE-AGED LADY ACTUALLY HAS *MIRACULOUS HANDS* LIKE US!!
BUT WHAT KIND OF SPECIAL POWERS DO HER HANDS HAVE?!
HA!!!
FOOM
IT'S A POWERFUL ENEMY IN THE VERY FIRST ROUND---
CAN I WIN?!! WHAT SHOULD I DO?!
WHAT SHOULD I...
OHH, WHAT SHOULD I DO?!
DOOM DOOM DOOM DOOM DOOM
Pantasia

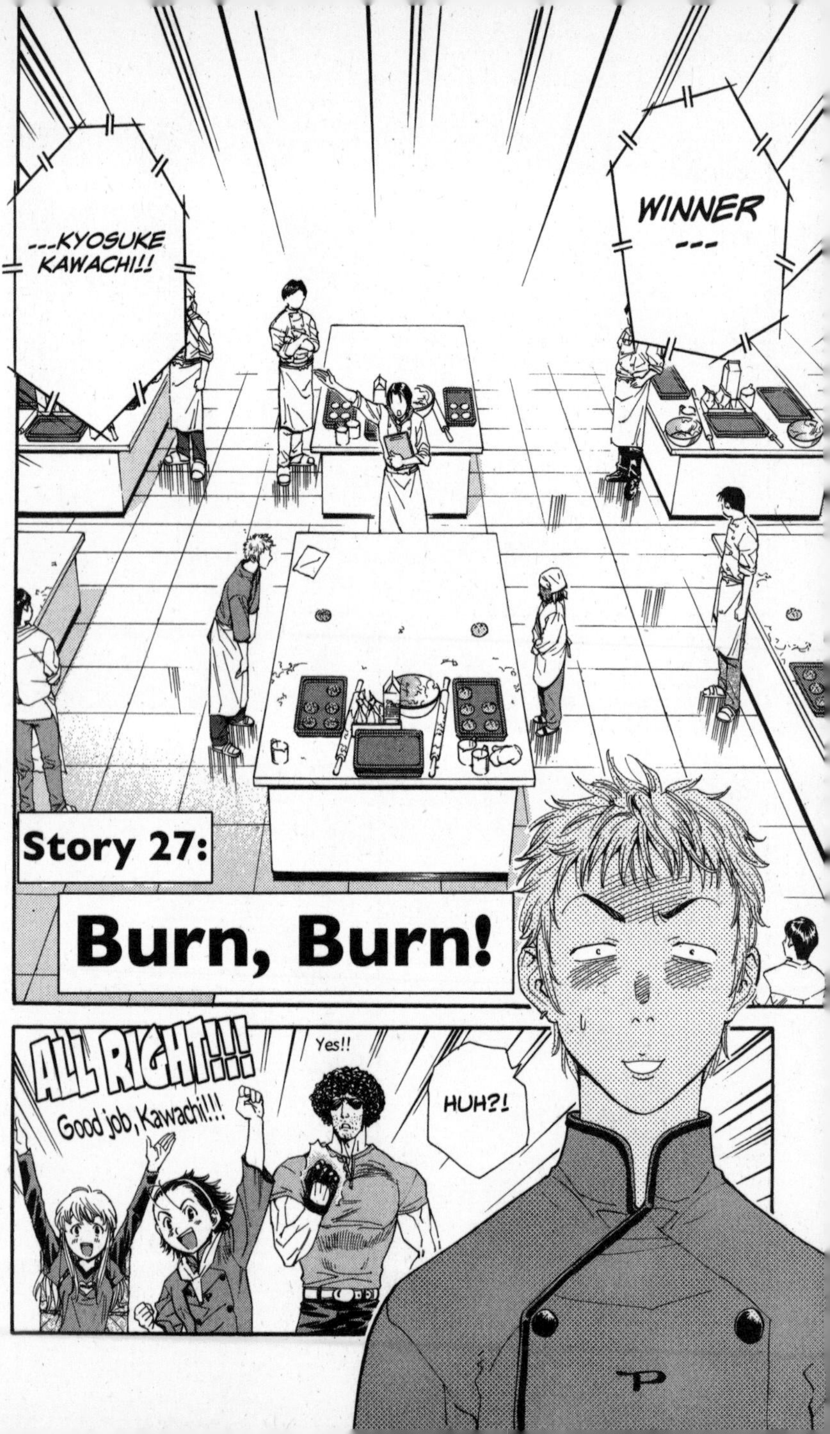
WINNER ---
---KYOSUKE KAWACHI!!
Story 27:
Burn, Burn!
HUH?!
Yes!!
ALL RIGHT!!!
Good job, Kawachi!!!

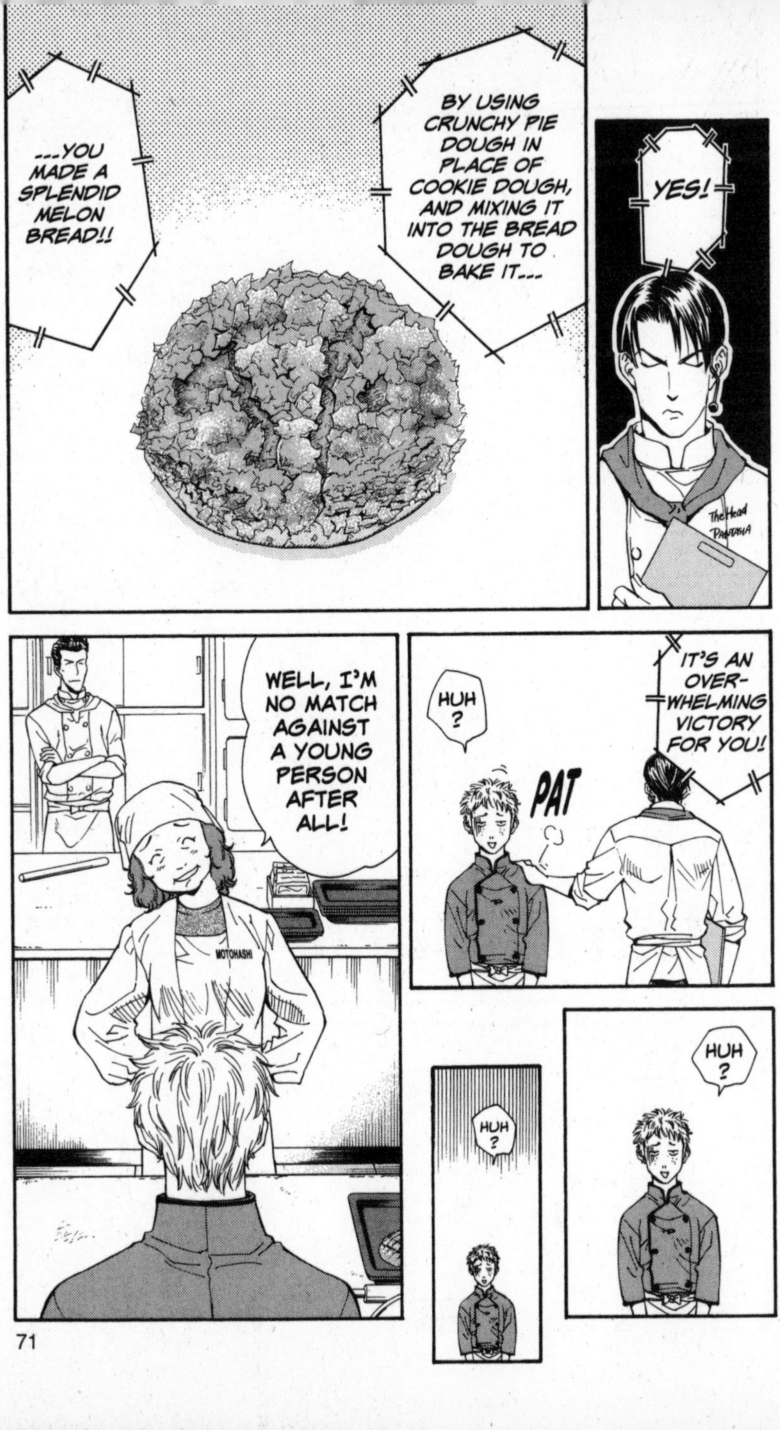
YES!
BY USING CRUNCHY PIE DOUGH IN PLACE OF COOKIE DOUGH, AND MIXING IT INTO THE BREAD DOUGH TO BAKE IT---
---YOU MADE A SPLENDID MELON BREAD!!
The Head PANTASIA
IT'S AN OVER-WHELMING VICTORY FOR YOU!
HUH?
PAT
WELL, I'M NO MATCH AGAINST A YOUNG PERSON AFTER ALL!
MOTOHASHI
HUH?
HUH?

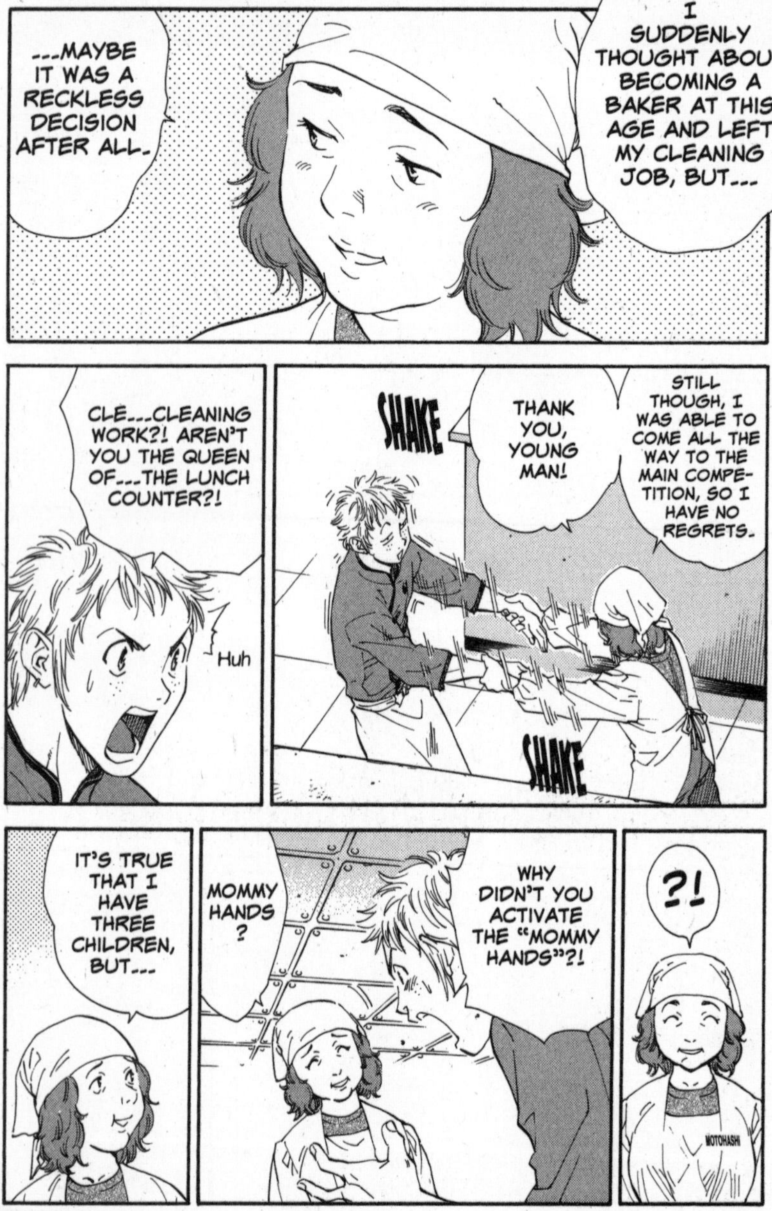
I SUDDENLY THOUGHT ABOUT BECOMING A BAKER AT THIS AGE AND LEFT MY CLEANING JOB, BUT...
...MAYBE IT WAS A RECKLESS DECISION AFTER ALL.
STILL THOUGH, I WAS ABLE TO COME ALL THE WAY TO THE MAIN COMPE-TITION, SO I HAVE NO REGRETS.
THANK YOU, YOUNG MAN!
SHAKE
SHAKE
CLE...CLEANING WORK?! AREN'T YOU THE QUEEN OF...THE LUNCH COUNTER?!
Huh
?!
MOTOHASHI
WHY DIDN'T YOU ACTIVATE THE "MOMMY HANDS"?!
MOMMY HANDS ?
IT'S TRUE THAT I HAVE THREE CHILDREN, BUT...

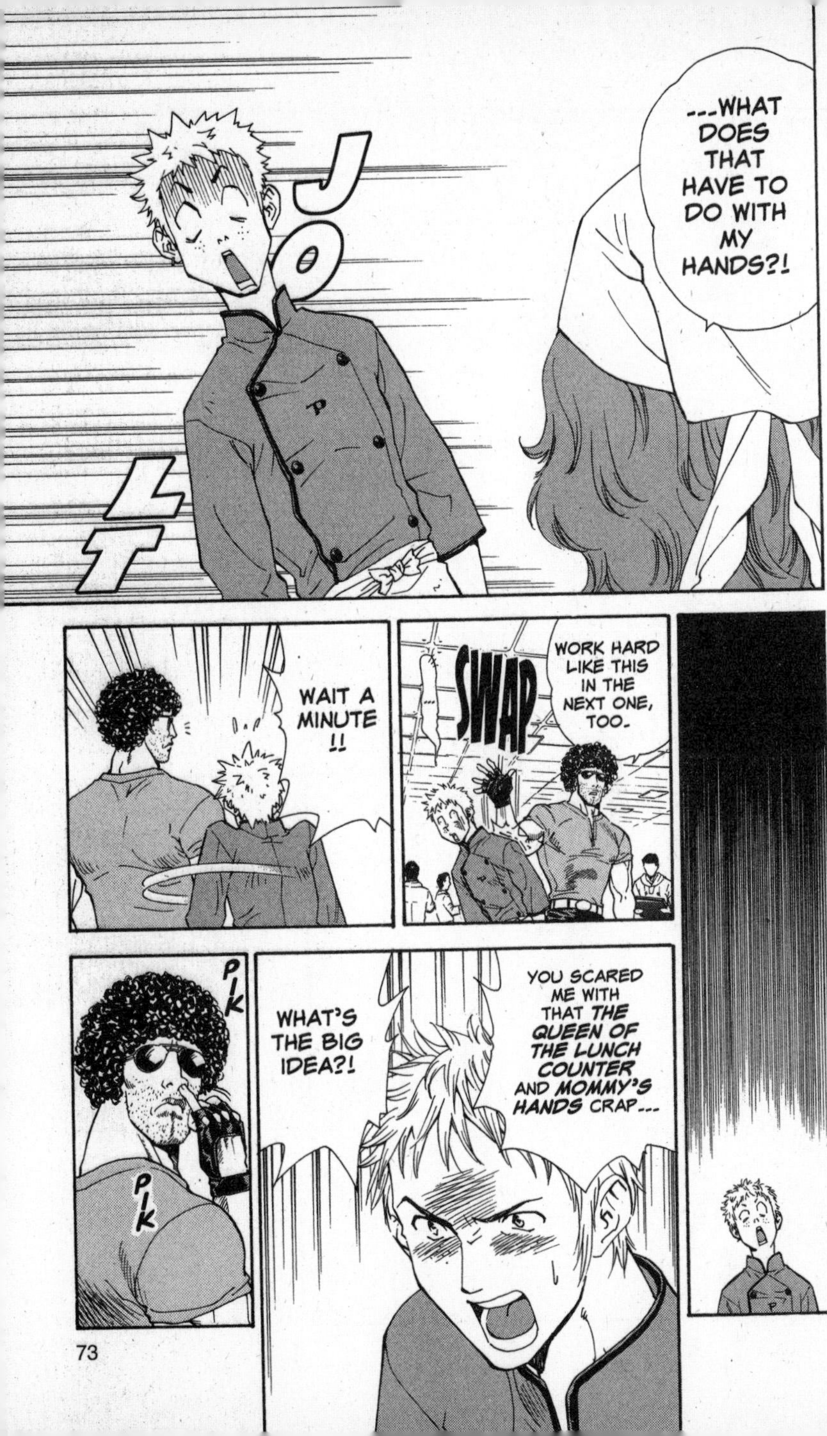
---WHAT DOES THAT HAVE TO DO WITH MY HANDS?!
JOLT
WORK HARD LIKE THIS IN THE NEXT ONE, TOO.
SWAP
WAIT A MINUTE !!
YOU SCARED ME WITH THAT *THE QUEEN OF THE LUNCH COUNTER* AND *MOMMY'S HANDS* CRAP...
WHAT'S THE BIG IDEA?!
PIK
PIK

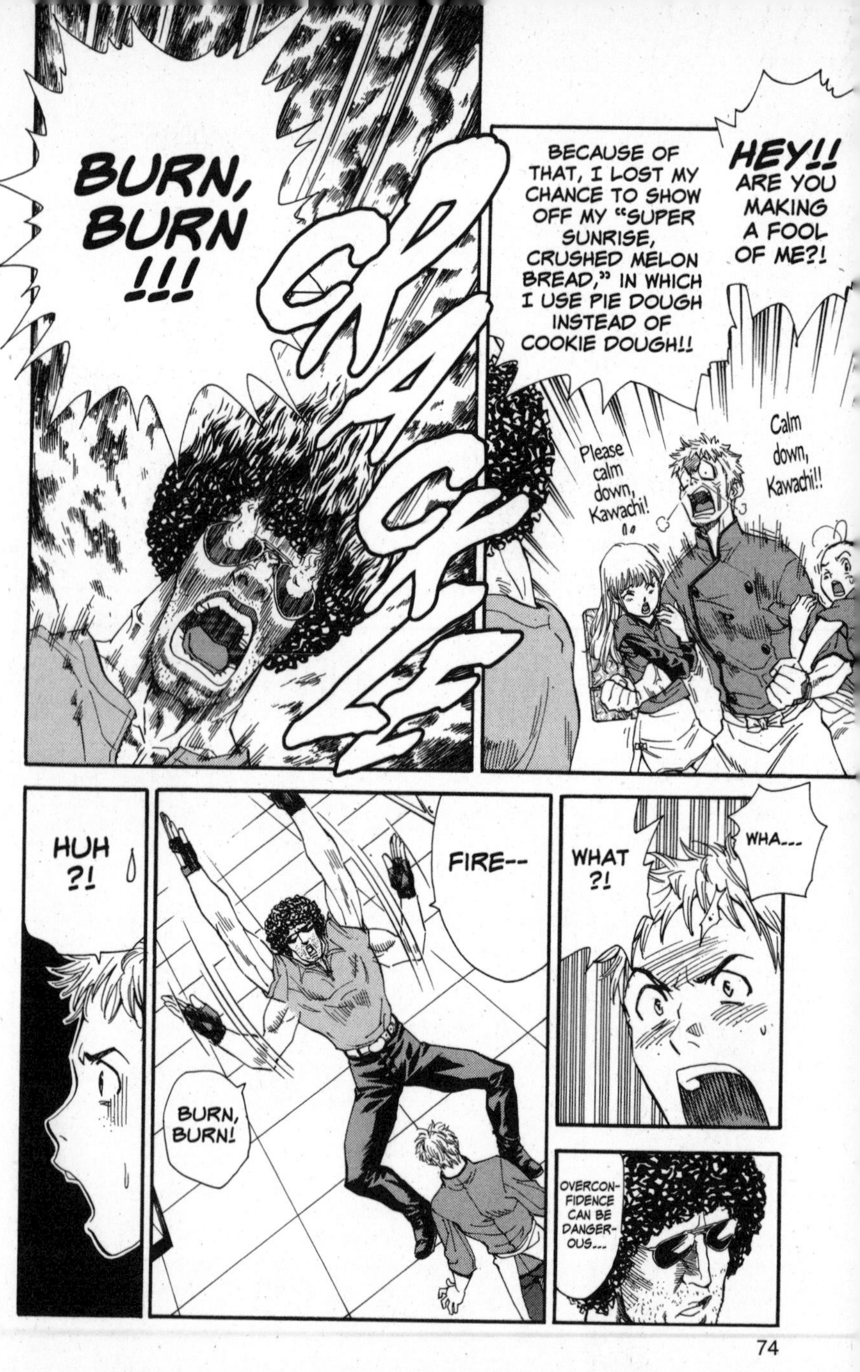
HEY!! ARE YOU MAKING A FOOL OF ME?!
BECAUSE OF THAT, I LOST MY CHANCE TO SHOW OFF MY "SUPER SUNRISE, CRUSHED MELON BREAD," IN WHICH I USE PIE DOUGH INSTEAD OF COOKIE DOUGH!!
Calm down, Kawachi!!
Please calm down, Kawachi!
CRACK
BURN, BURN !!!
WHA...
WHAT ?!
OVERCONFIDENCE CAN BE DANGEROUS...
FIRE--
BURN, BURN!
HUH ?!

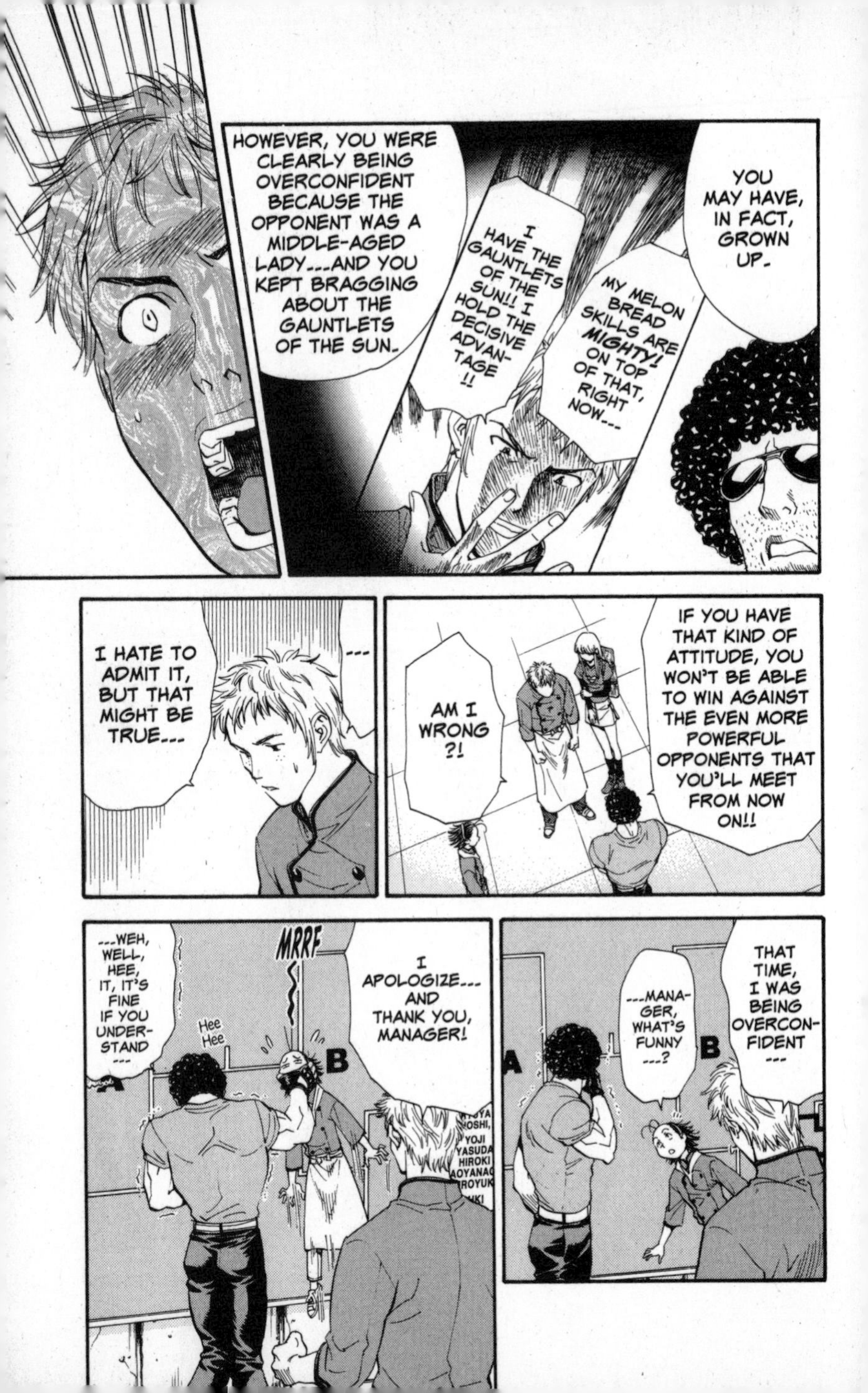
YOU MAY HAVE, IN FACT, GROWN UP.
MY MELON BREAD SKILLS ARE MIGHTY! ON TOP OF THAT, RIGHT NOW...
I HAVE THE GAUNTLETS OF THE SUN!! I HOLD THE DECISIVE ADVAN-TAGE!!
HOWEVER, YOU WERE CLEARLY BEING OVERCONFIDENT BECAUSE THE OPPONENT WAS A MIDDLE-AGED LADY...AND YOU KEPT BRAGGING ABOUT THE GAUNTLETS OF THE SUN.
IF YOU HAVE THAT KIND OF ATTITUDE, YOU WON'T BE ABLE TO WIN AGAINST THE EVEN MORE POWERFUL OPPONENTS THAT YOU'LL MEET FROM NOW ON!!
AM I WRONG?!
...
I HATE TO ADMIT IT, BUT THAT MIGHT BE TRUE...
THAT TIME, I WAS BEING OVERCON-FIDENT...
...MANA-GER, WHAT'S FUNNY...?
B
A
I APOLOGIZE... AND THANK YOU, MANAGER!
MRRF
B
Hee Hee
...WEH, WELL, HEE, IT, IT'S FINE IF YOU UNDER-STAND...
A

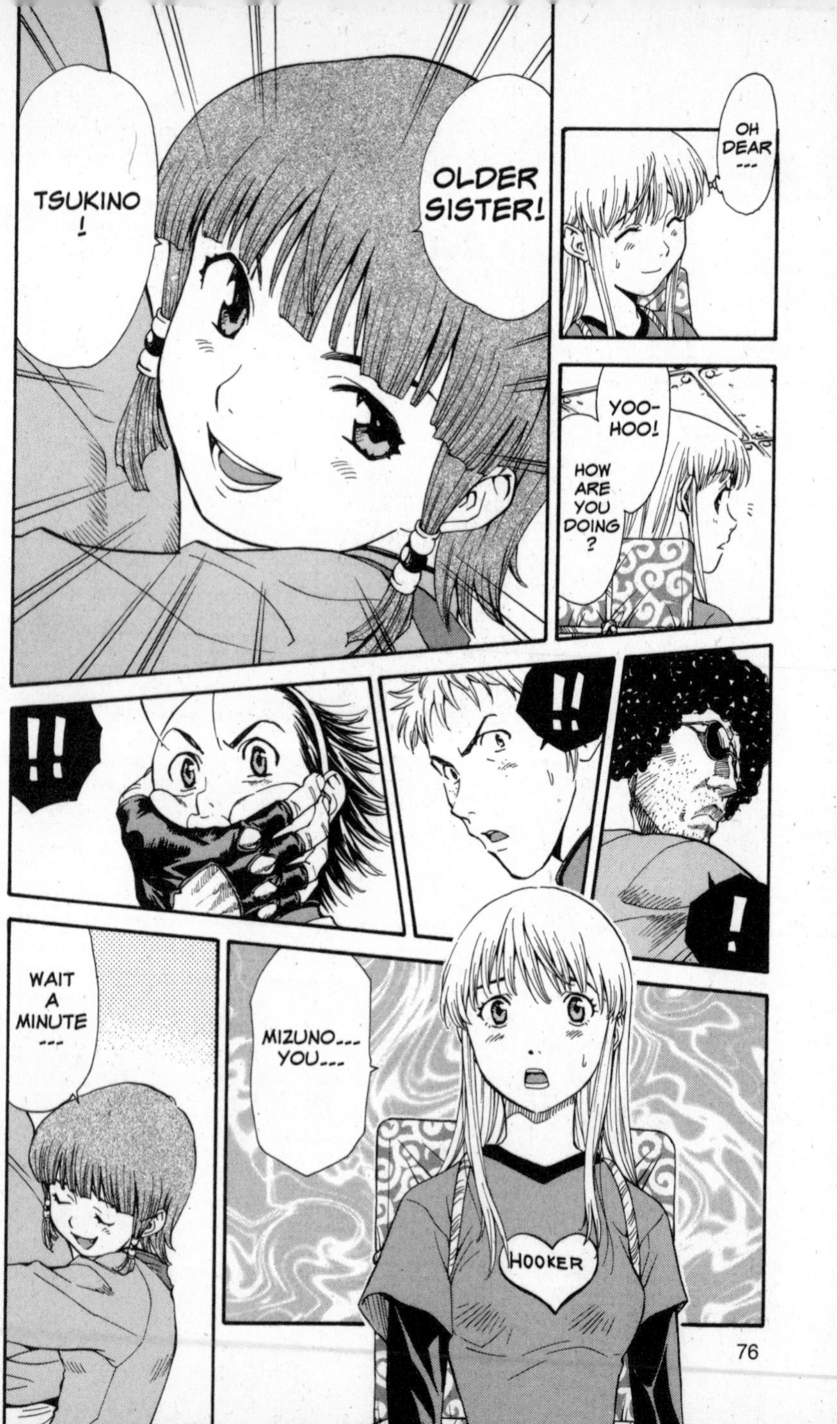

OH DEAR ---
YOO-HOO!
HOW ARE YOU DOING?
OLDER SISTER!
TSUKINO!
!
!!
!!
HOOKER
MIZUNO--- YOU---
WAIT A MINUTE ---

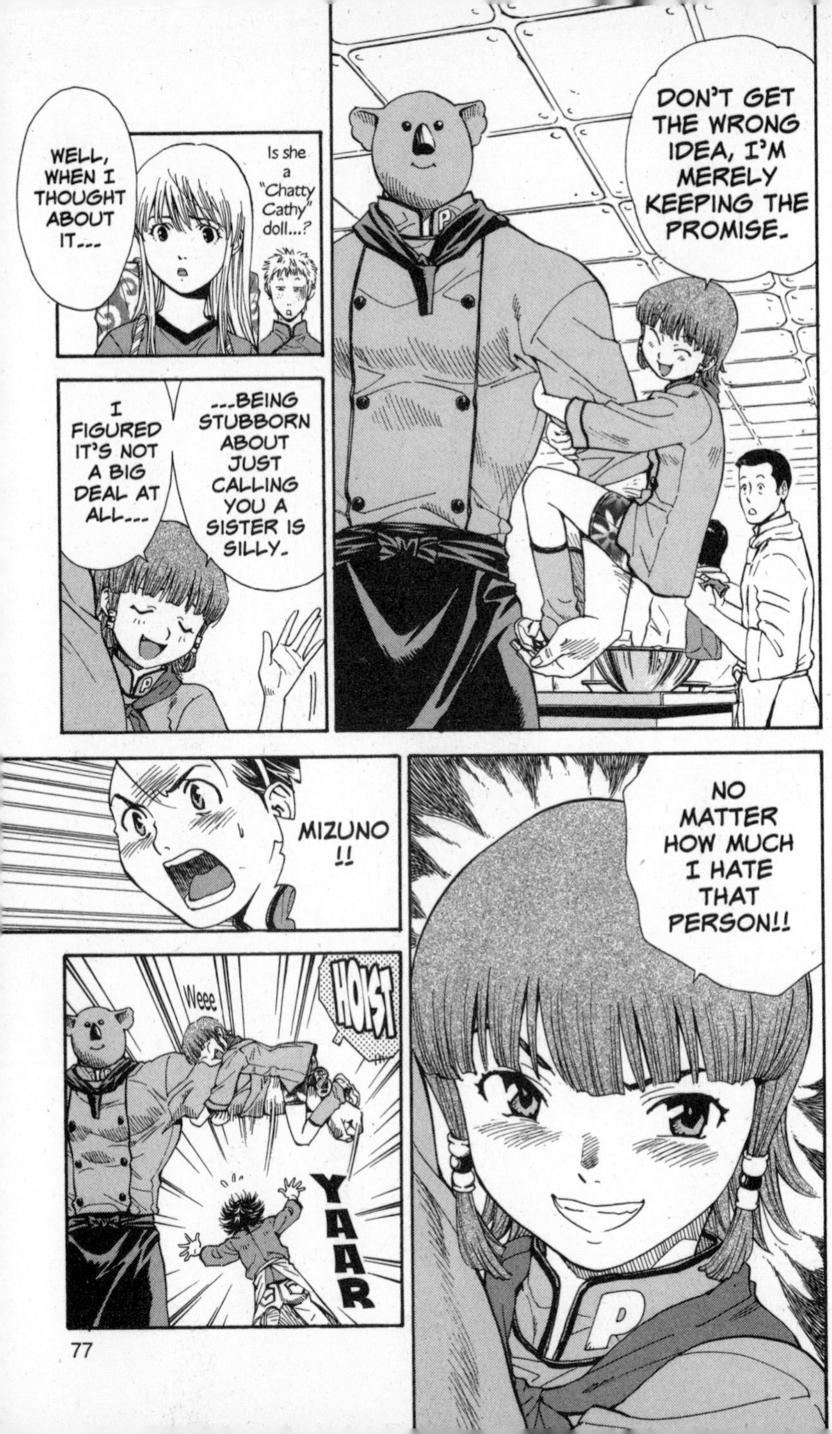
DON'T GET THE WRONG IDEA, I'M MERELY KEEPING THE PROMISE.
WELL, WHEN I THOUGHT ABOUT IT...
Is she a "Chatty Cathy" doll...?
I FIGURED IT'S NOT A BIG DEAL AT ALL...
...BEING STUBBORN ABOUT JUST CALLING YOU A SISTER IS SILLY.
NO MATTER HOW MUCH I HATE THAT PERSON!!
MIZUNO !!
HOIST
Weee
YAAR

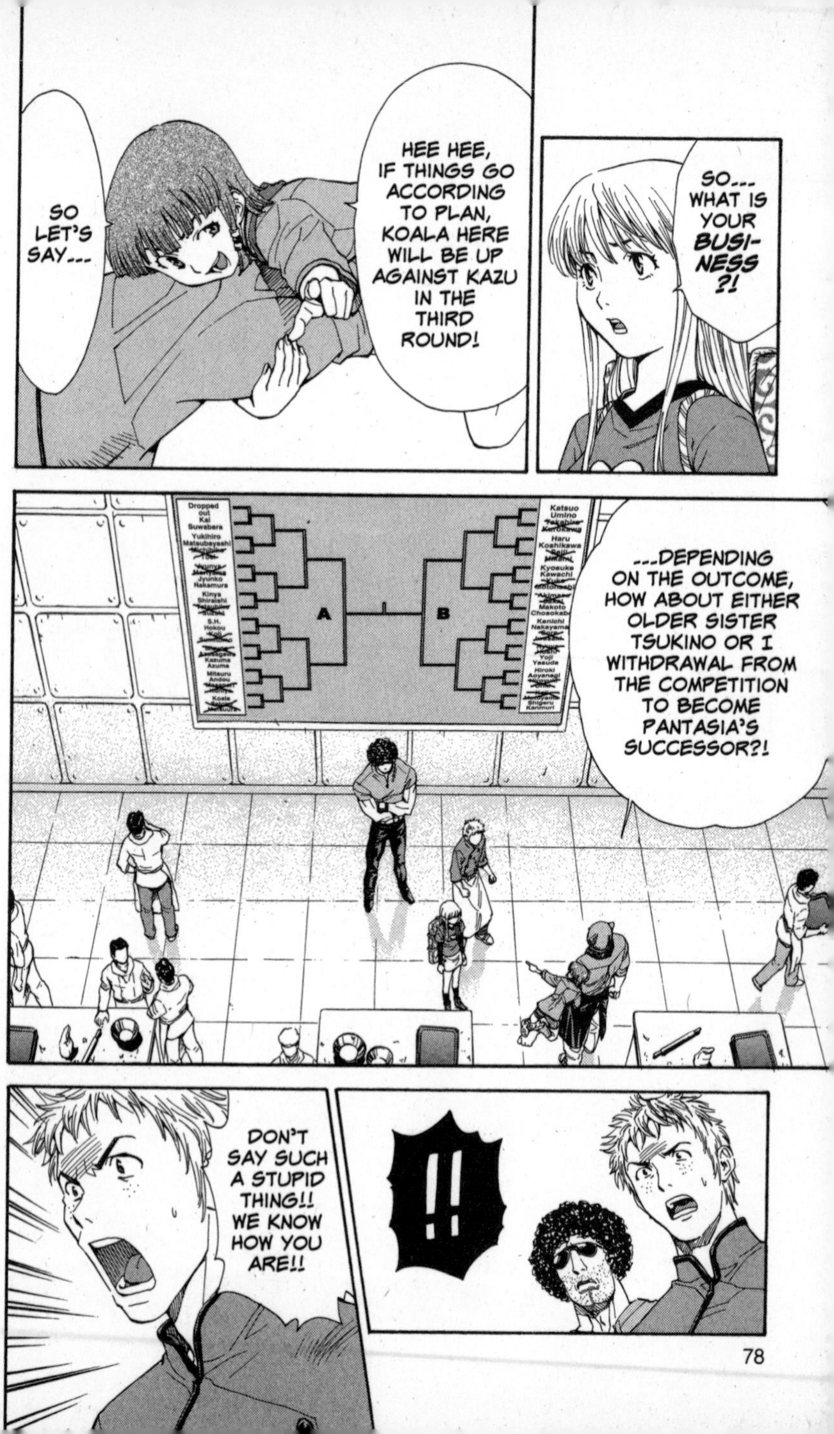
SO... WHAT IS YOUR BUSINESS?!
HEE HEE, IF THINGS GO ACCORDING TO PLAN, KOALA HERE WILL BE UP AGAINST KAZU IN THE THIRD ROUND!
SO LET'S SAY...
A
B
...DEPENDING ON THE OUTCOME, HOW ABOUT EITHER OLDER SISTER TSUKINO OR I WITHDRAWAL FROM THE COMPETITION TO BECOME PANTASIA'S SUCCESSOR?!
!!
DON'T SAY SUCH A STUPID THING!! WE KNOW HOW YOU ARE!!

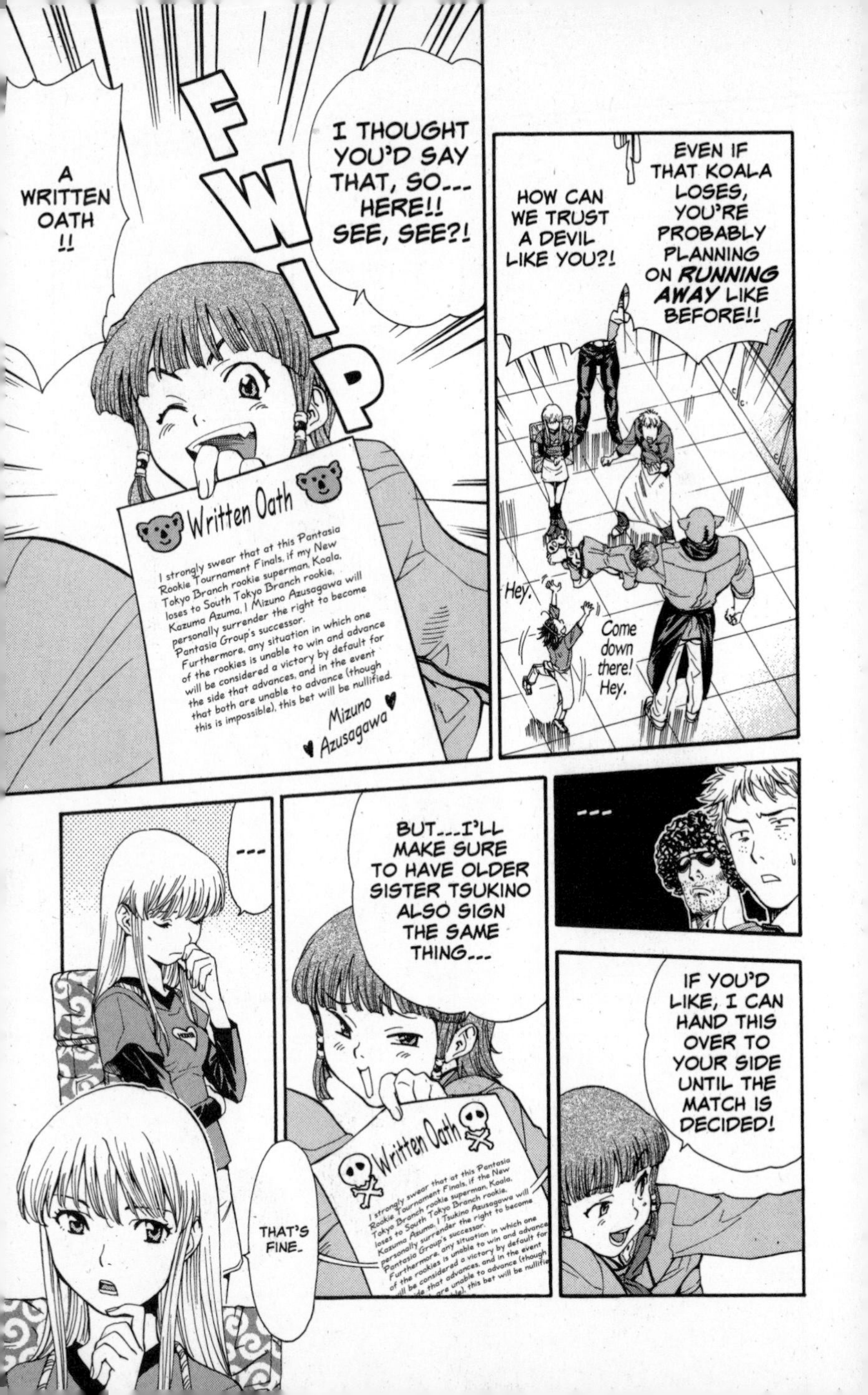
EVEN IF THAT KOALA LOSES, YOU'RE PROBABLY PLANNING ON ***RUNNING AWAY*** LIKE BEFORE!!
HOW CAN WE TRUST A DEVIL LIKE YOU?!
Hey.
Come down there! Hey.
I THOUGHT YOU'D SAY THAT, SO... HERE!! SEE, SEE?!
FWIP
A WRITTEN OATH !!
Written Oath
I strongly swear that at this Pantasia Rookie Tournament Finals, if my New Tokyo Branch rookie superman, Koala, loses to South Tokyo Branch rookie, Kazuma Azuma, I Mizuno Azusagawa will personally surrender the right to become Pantasia Group's successor.
Furthermore, any situation in which one of the rookies is unable to win and advance will be considered a victory by default for the side that advances, and in the event that both are unable to advance (though this is impossible), this bet will be nullified.
Mizuno Azusagawa
...
IF YOU'D LIKE, I CAN HAND THIS OVER TO YOUR SIDE UNTIL THE MATCH IS DECIDED!
BUT...I'LL MAKE SURE TO HAVE OLDER SISTER TSUKINO ALSO SIGN THE SAME THING...
Written Oath
...
THAT'S FINE.

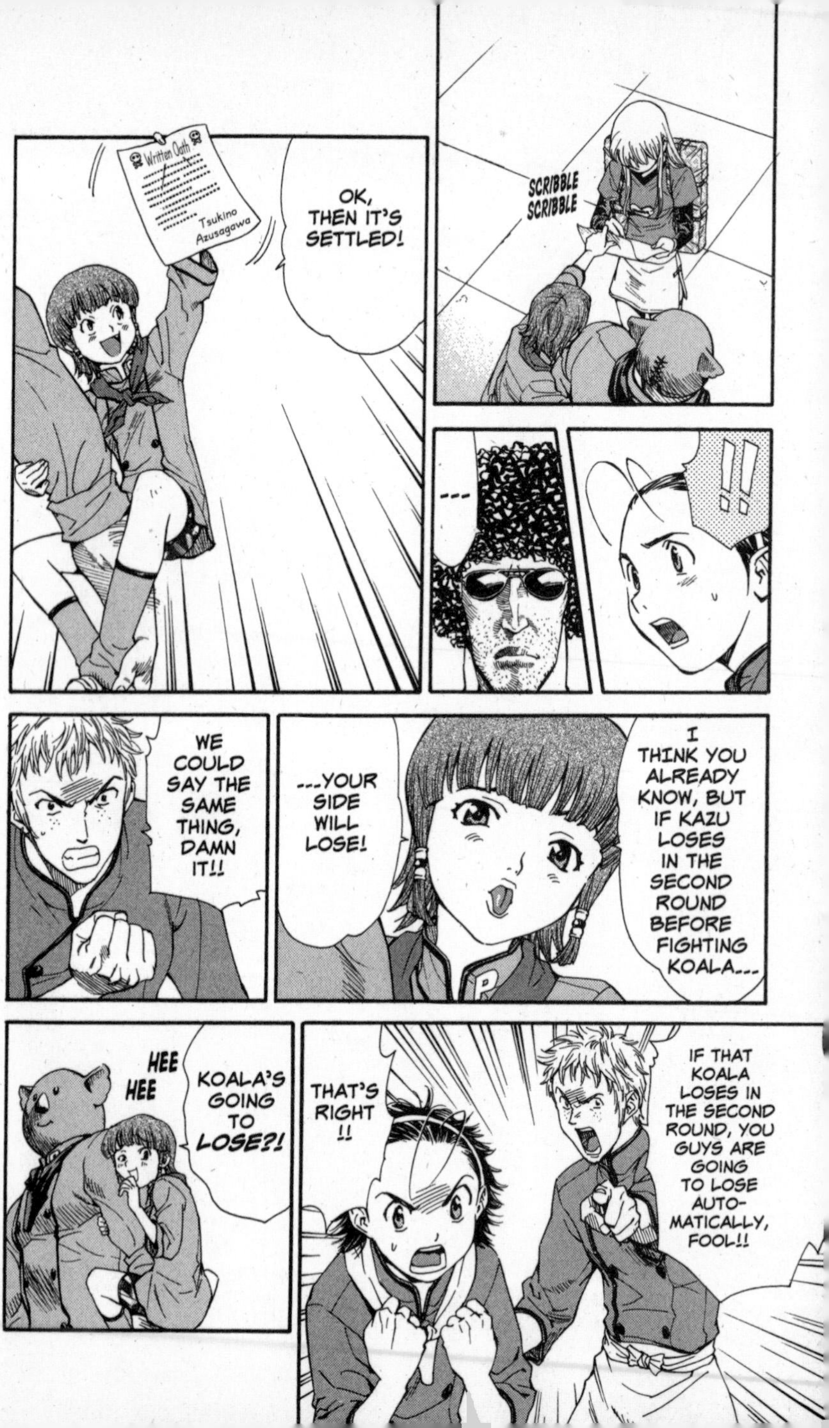
SCRIBBLE SCRIBBLE
!!
...
Written Oath
Tsukino Azusagawa
OK, THEN IT'S SETTLED!
I THINK YOU ALREADY KNOW, BUT IF KAZU LOSES IN THE SECOND ROUND BEFORE FIGHTING KOALA...
...YOUR SIDE WILL LOSE!
WE COULD SAY THE SAME THING, DAMN IT!!
IF THAT KOALA LOSES IN THE SECOND ROUND, YOU GUYS ARE GOING TO LOSE AUTO-MATICALLY, FOOL!!
THAT'S RIGHT !!
HEE HEE
KOALA'S GOING TO LOSE?!

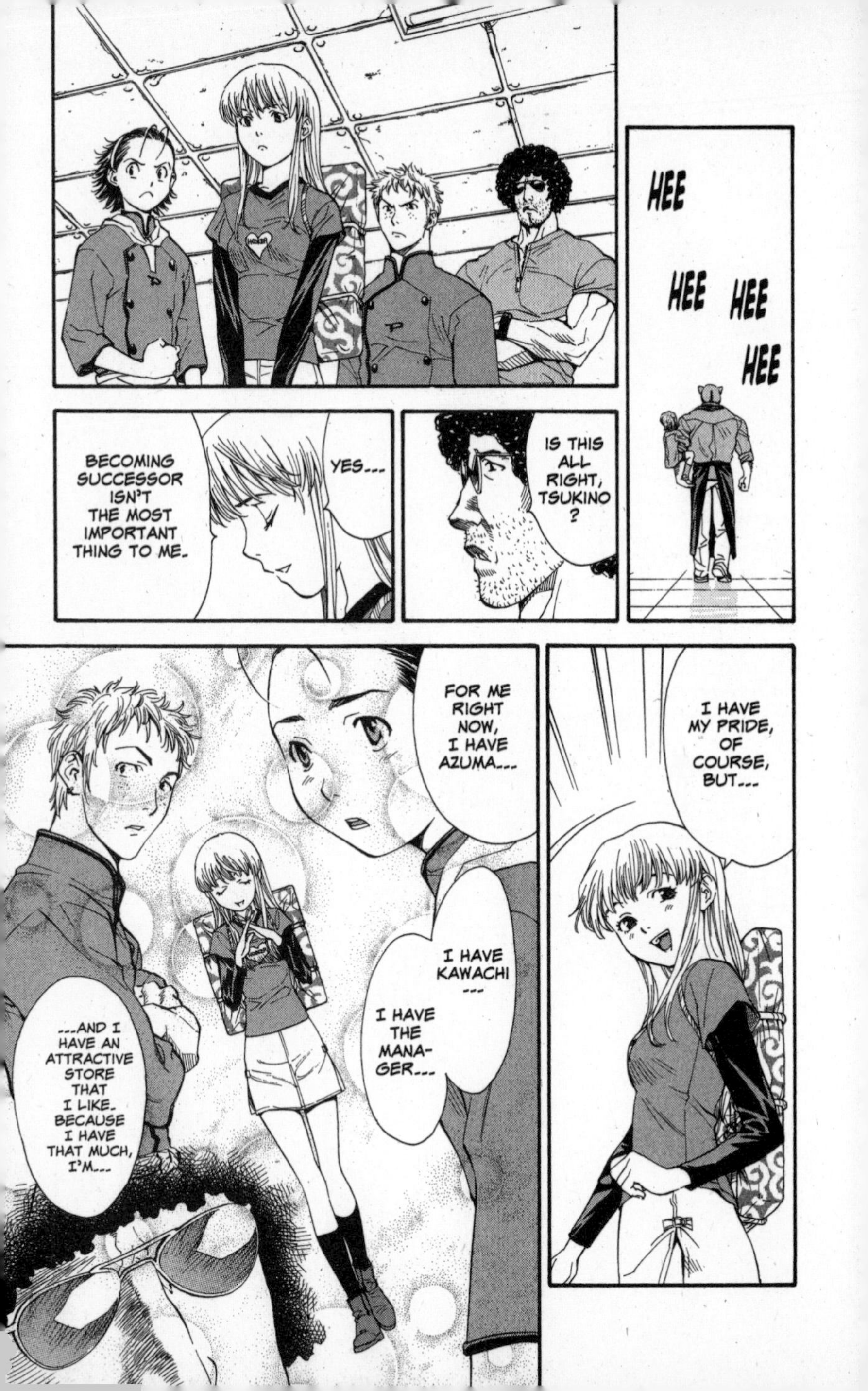
HEE
HEE HEE
HEE
IS THIS ALL RIGHT, TSUKINO?
YES...
BECOMING SUCCESSOR ISN'T THE MOST IMPORTANT THING TO ME.
I HAVE MY PRIDE, OF COURSE, BUT...
FOR ME RIGHT NOW, I HAVE AZUMA...
I HAVE KAWACHI...
I HAVE THE MANAGER...
...AND I HAVE AN ATTRACTIVE STORE THAT I LIKE. BECAUSE I HAVE THAT MUCH, I'M...

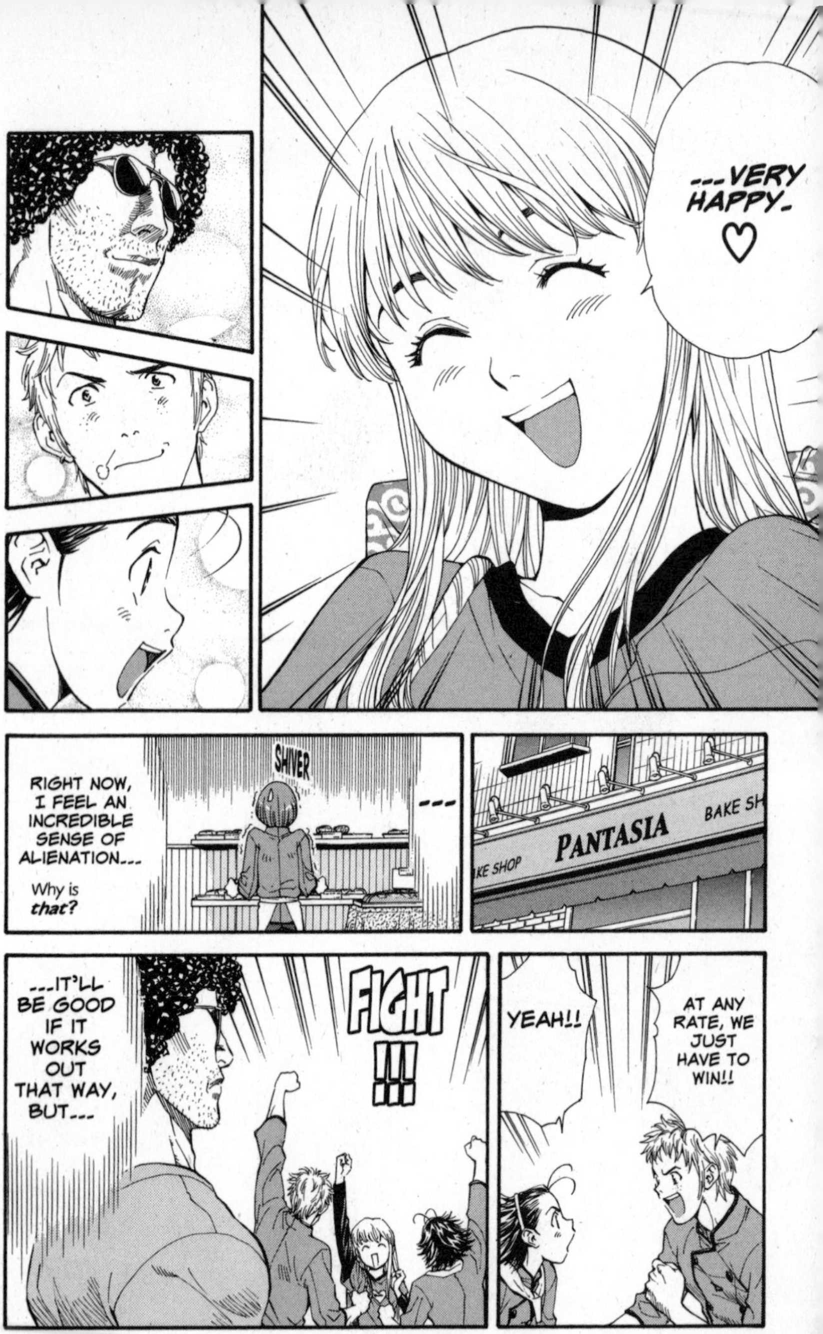
---VERY HAPPY-
♡
PANTASIA

SHIVER
RIGHT NOW, I FEEL AN INCREDIBLE SENSE OF ALIENATION---
Why is *that?*
AT ANY RATE, WE JUST HAVE TO WIN!!
YEAH!!
FIGHT!!!
---IT'LL BE GOOD IF IT WORKS OUT THAT WAY, BUT---

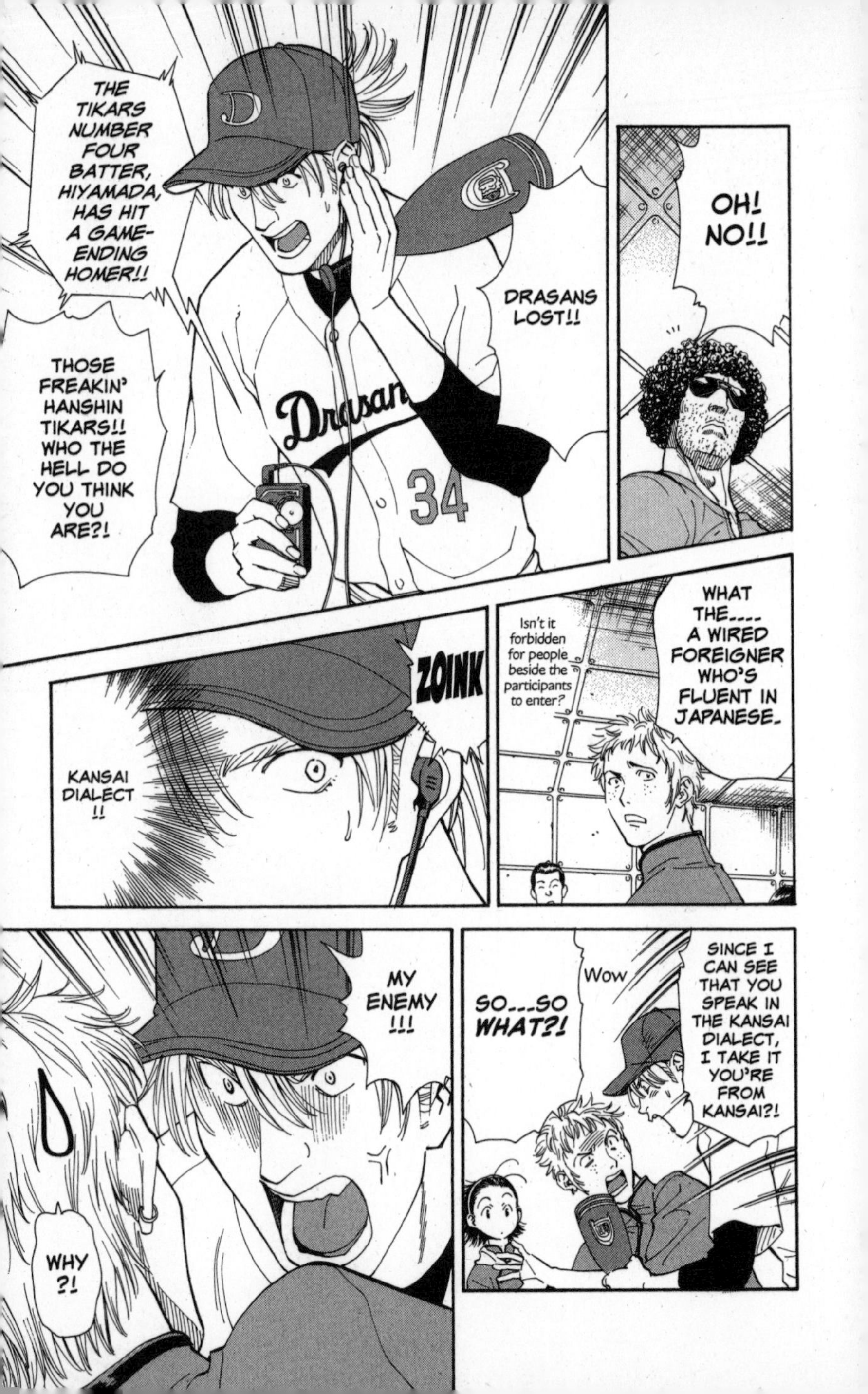

OH! NO!!
DRASANS LOST!!
THE TIKARS NUMBER FOUR BATTER, HIYAMADA, HAS HIT A GAME-ENDING HOMER!!
THOSE FREAKIN' HANSHIN TIKARS!! WHO THE HELL DO YOU THINK YOU ARE?!
34
WHAT THE.... A WIRED FOREIGNER WHO'S FLUENT IN JAPANESE.
Isn't it forbidden for people beside the participants to enter?
ZOINK
KANSAI DIALECT !!
SINCE I CAN SEE THAT YOU SPEAK IN THE KANSAI DIALECT, I TAKE IT YOU'RE FROM KANSAI?!
Wow
SO...SO WHAT?!
MY ENEMY !!!
WHY ?!

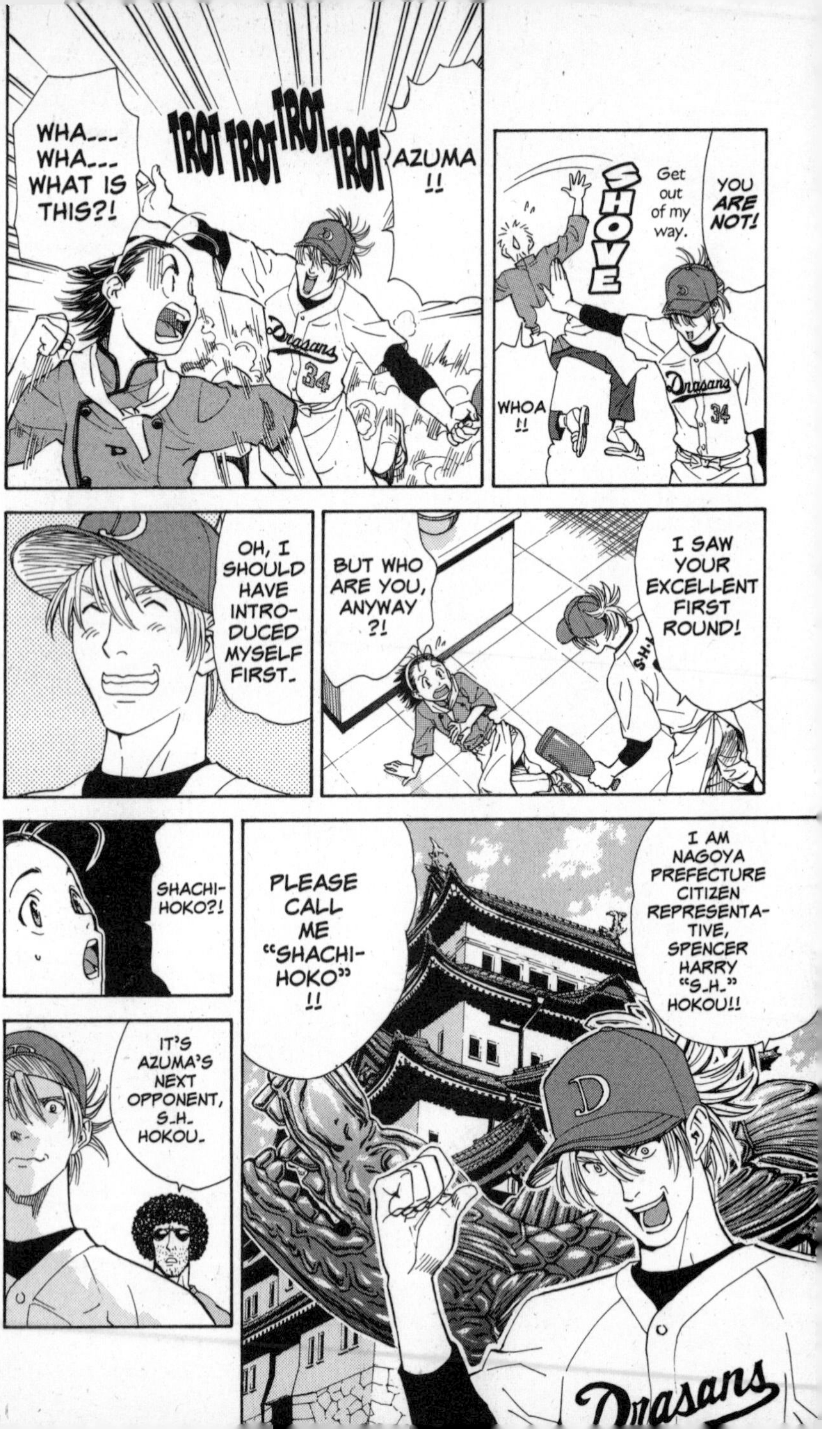
YOU ARE NOT!
Get out of my way.
SHOVE
WHOA !!
AZUMA !!
TROT TROT TROT TROT
WHA... WHA... WHAT IS THIS?!
I SAW YOUR EXCELLENT FIRST ROUND!
BUT WHO ARE YOU, ANYWAY?!
OH, I SHOULD HAVE INTRODUCED MYSELF FIRST.
I AM NAGOYA PREFECTURE CITIZEN REPRESENTATIVE, SPENCER HARRY "S.H." HOKOU!!
PLEASE CALL ME "SHACHI-HOKO" !!
SHACHI-HOKO?!
IT'S AZUMA'S NEXT OPPONENT, S.H. HOKOU.

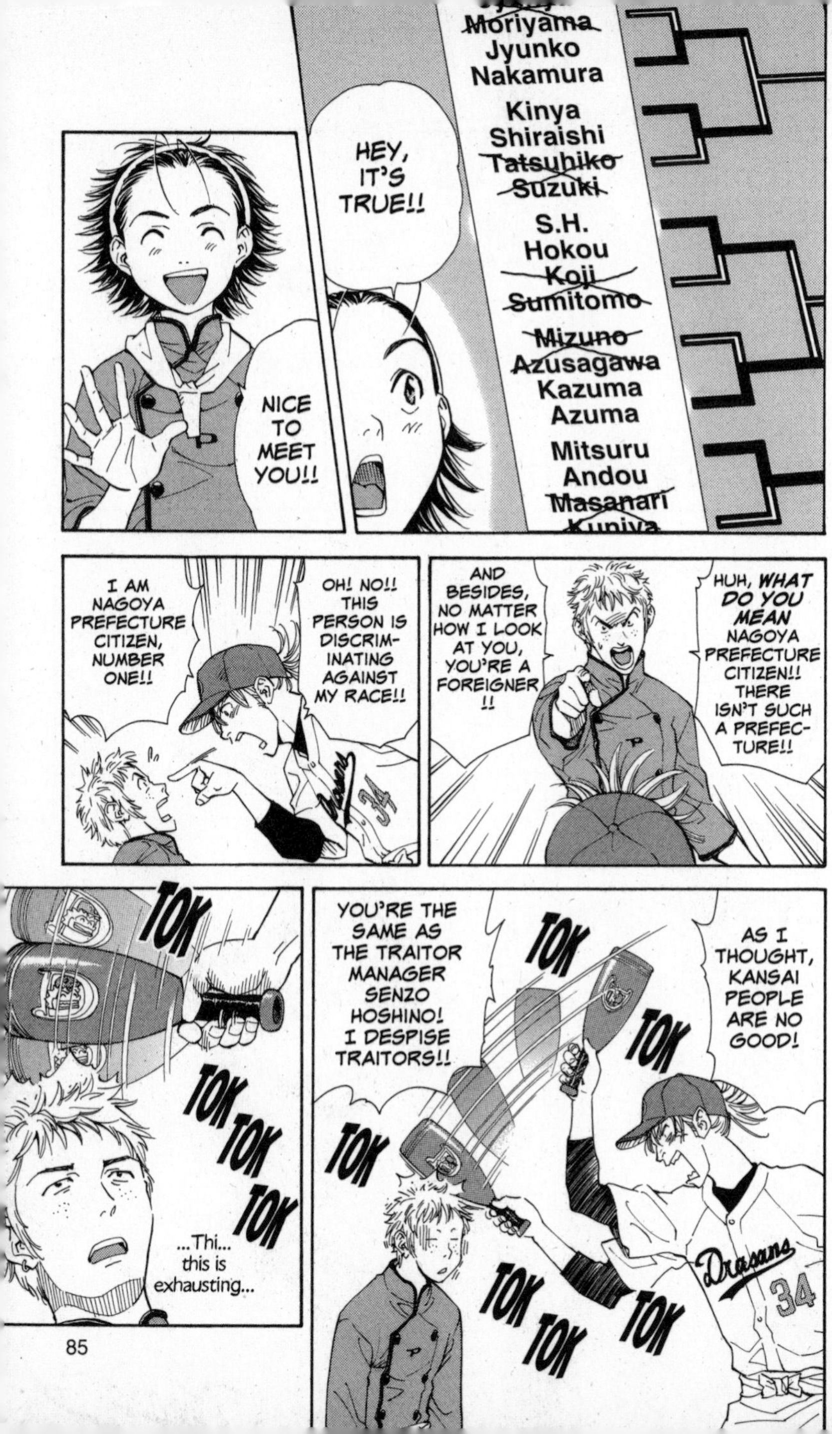
Moriyama
Jyunko Nakamura
Kinya Shiraishi
Tatsuhiko Suzuki
S.H. Hokou
Koji Sumitomo
Mizuno Azusagawa
Kazuma Azuma
Mitsuru Andou
Masanari Kuniya
HEY, IT'S TRUE!!
NICE TO MEET YOU!!
HUH, WHAT DO YOU MEAN NAGOYA PREFECTURE CITIZEN!! THERE ISN'T SUCH A PREFECTURE!!
AND BESIDES, NO MATTER HOW I LOOK AT YOU, YOU'RE A FOREIGNER!!
OH! NO!! THIS PERSON IS DISCRIMINATING AGAINST MY RACE!!
I AM NAGOYA PREFECTURE CITIZEN, NUMBER ONE!!
AS I THOUGHT, KANSAI PEOPLE ARE NO GOOD!
YOU'RE THE SAME AS THE TRAITOR MANAGER SENZO HOSHINO! I DESPISE TRAITORS!!
TOK
TOK
TOK
TOK
TOK
TOK
TOK
TOK
TOK
TOK
TOK
...Thi... this is exhausting...

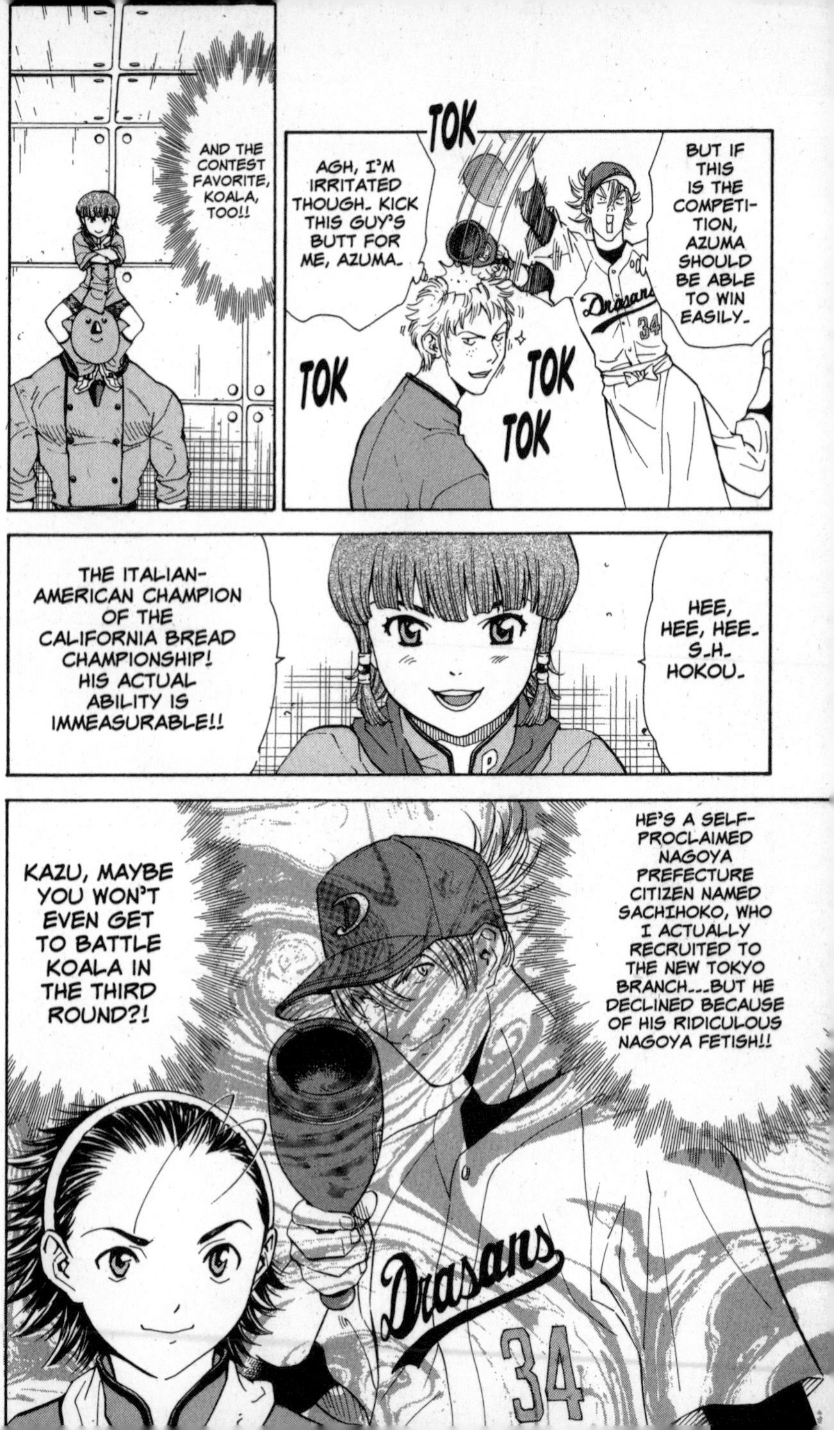
BUT IF THIS IS THE COMPETITION, AZUMA SHOULD BE ABLE TO WIN EASILY.
TOK
AGH, I'M IRRITATED THOUGH. KICK THIS GUY'S BUTT FOR ME, AZUMA.
Drasans
34
TOK
TOK
TOK
AND THE CONTEST FAVORITE, KOALA, TOO!!
HEE, HEE, HEE. S..H.. HOKOU.
THE ITALIAN-AMERICAN CHAMPION OF THE CALIFORNIA BREAD CHAMPIONSHIP! HIS ACTUAL ABILITY IS IMMEASURABLE!!
HE'S A SELF-PROCLAIMED NAGOYA PREFECTURE CITIZEN NAMED SACHIHOKO, WHO I ACTUALLY RECRUITED TO THE NEW TOKYO BRANCH...BUT HE DECLINED BECAUSE OF HIS RIDICULOUS NAGOYA FETISH!!
KAZU, MAYBE YOU WON'T EVEN GET TO BATTLE KOALA IN THE THIRD ROUND?!
Drasans
34

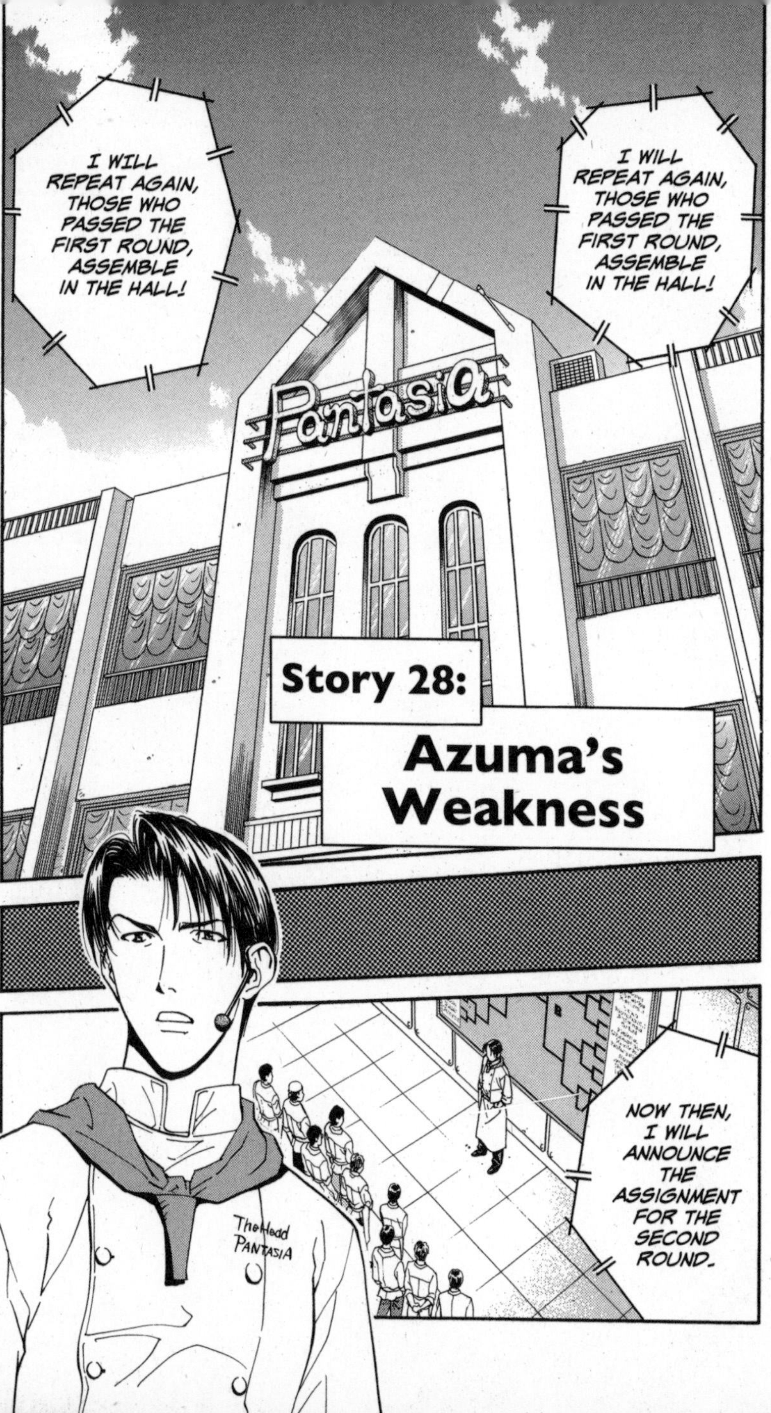
I WILL REPEAT AGAIN, THOSE WHO PASSED THE FIRST ROUND, ASSEMBLE IN THE HALL!
I WILL REPEAT AGAIN, THOSE WHO PASSED THE FIRST ROUND, ASSEMBLE IN THE HALL!
Pantasia
Story 28:
Azuma's Weakness
NOW THEN, I WILL ANNOUNCE THE ASSIGNMENT FOR THE SECOND ROUND...
The Head PANTASIA

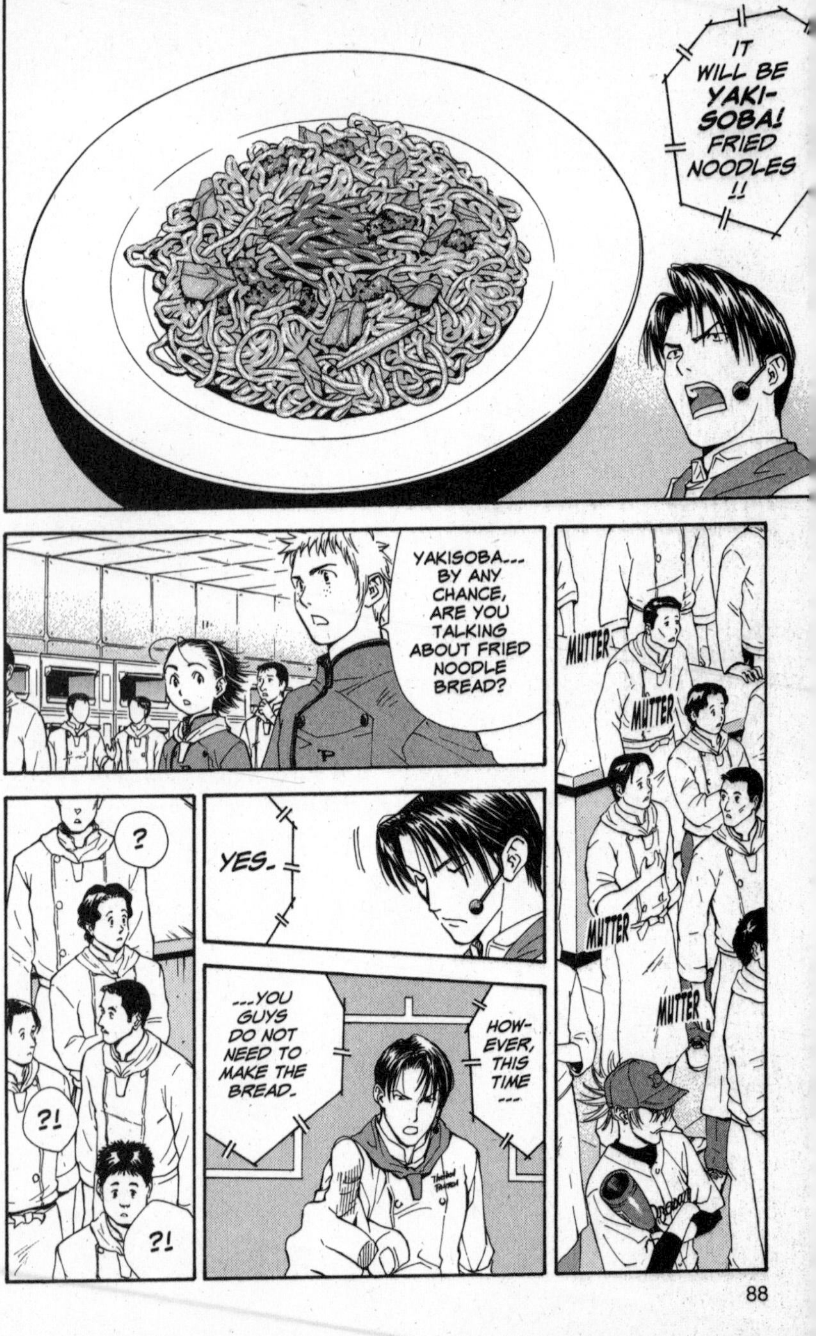
IT WILL BE YAKI-SOBA! FRIED NOODLES !!
MUTTER
MUTTER
MUTTER
MUTTER
YAKISOBA... BY ANY CHANCE, ARE YOU TALKING ABOUT FRIED NOODLE BREAD?
YES.
HOW-EVER, THIS TIME---
---YOU GUYS DO NOT NEED TO MAKE THE BREAD.
?
?!
?!

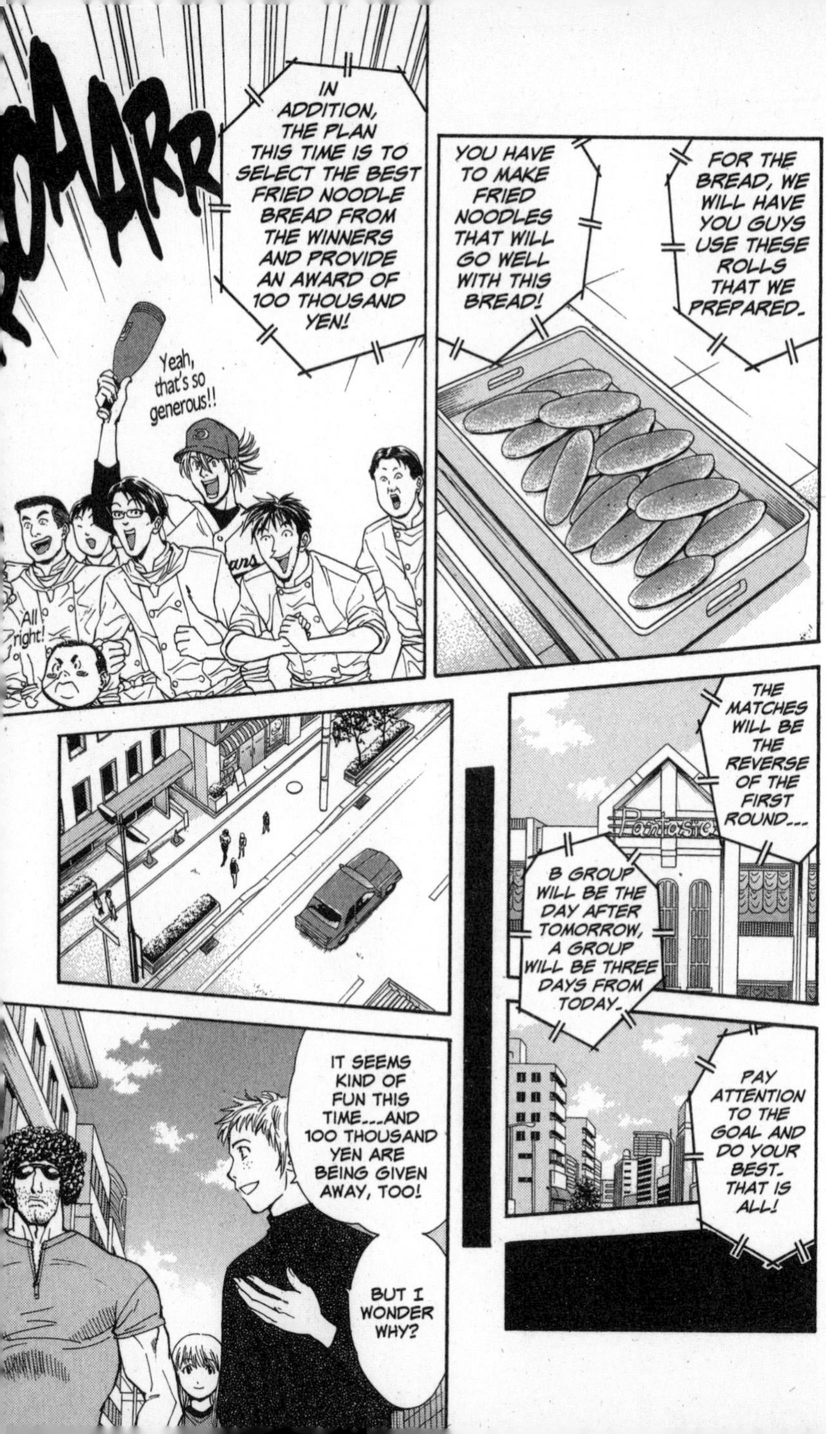

FOR THE BREAD, WE WILL HAVE YOU GUYS USE THESE ROLLS THAT WE PREPARED.
YOU HAVE TO MAKE FRIED NOODLES THAT WILL GO WELL WITH THIS BREAD!
IN ADDITION, THE PLAN THIS TIME IS TO SELECT THE BEST FRIED NOODLE BREAD FROM THE WINNERS AND PROVIDE AN AWARD OF 100 THOUSAND YEN!
Yeah, that's so generous!!
All right!
THE MATCHES WILL BE THE REVERSE OF THE FIRST ROUND...
B GROUP WILL BE THE DAY AFTER TOMORROW, A GROUP WILL BE THREE DAYS FROM TODAY.
PAY ATTENTION TO THE GOAL AND DO YOUR BEST. THAT IS ALL!
IT SEEMS KIND OF FUN THIS TIME...AND 100 THOUSAND YEN ARE BEING GIVEN AWAY, TOO!
BUT I WONDER WHY?

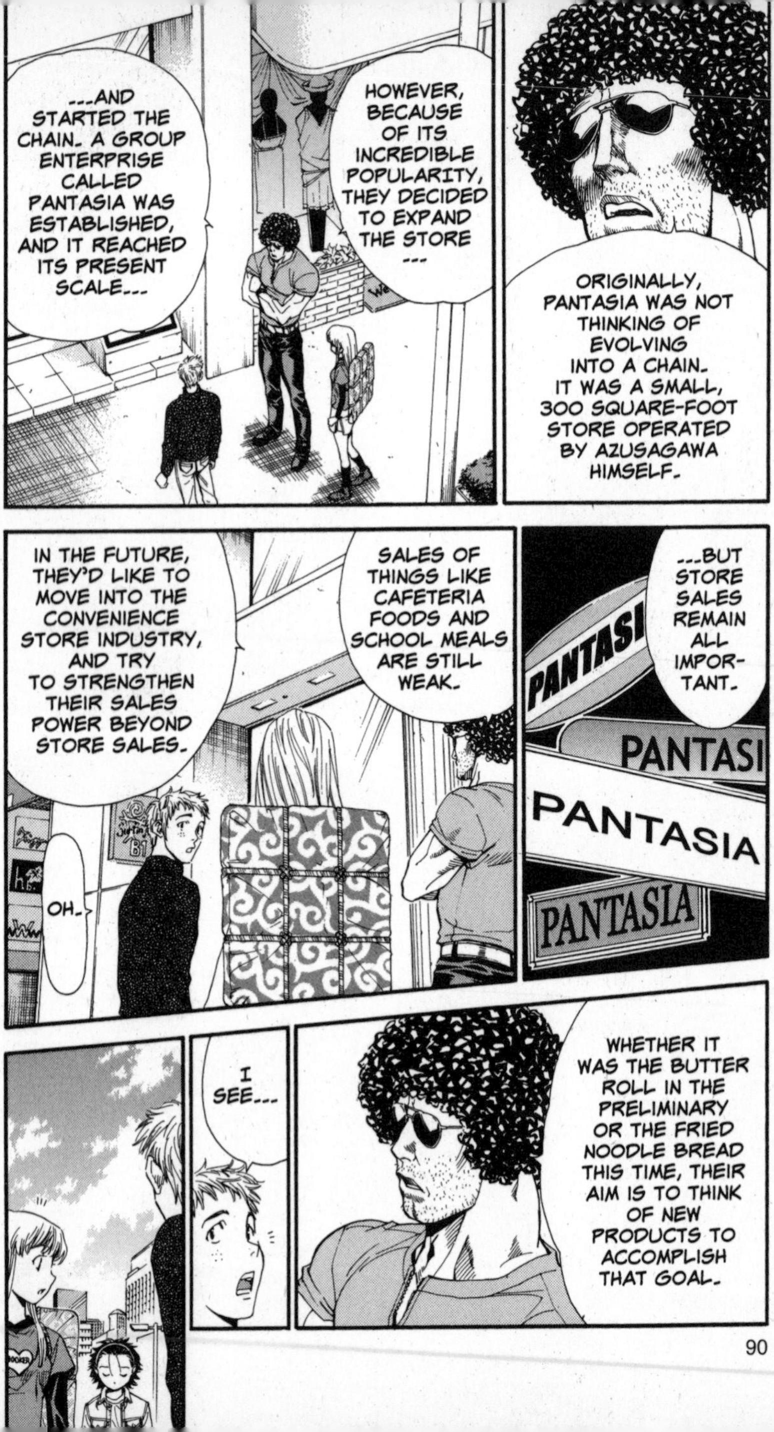
ORIGINALLY, PANTASIA WAS NOT THINKING OF EVOLVING INTO A CHAIN. IT WAS A SMALL, 300 SQUARE-FOOT STORE OPERATED BY AZUSAGAWA HIMSELF.
HOWEVER, BECAUSE OF ITS INCREDIBLE POPULARITY, THEY DECIDED TO EXPAND THE STORE ...
...AND STARTED THE CHAIN. A GROUP ENTERPRISE CALLED PANTASIA WAS ESTABLISHED, AND IT REACHED ITS PRESENT SCALE...
...BUT STORE SALES REMAIN ALL IMPOR-TANT.
PANTASI
PANTASI
PANTASIA
PANTASIA
SALES OF THINGS LIKE CAFETERIA FOODS AND SCHOOL MEALS ARE STILL WEAK.
IN THE FUTURE, THEY'D LIKE TO MOVE INTO THE CONVENIENCE STORE INDUSTRY, AND TRY TO STRENGTHEN THEIR SALES POWER BEYOND STORE SALES.
OH.
WHETHER IT WAS THE BUTTER ROLL IN THE PRELIMINARY OR THE FRIED NOODLE BREAD THIS TIME, THEIR AIM IS TO THINK OF NEW PRODUCTS TO ACCOMPLISH THAT GOAL.
I SEE...

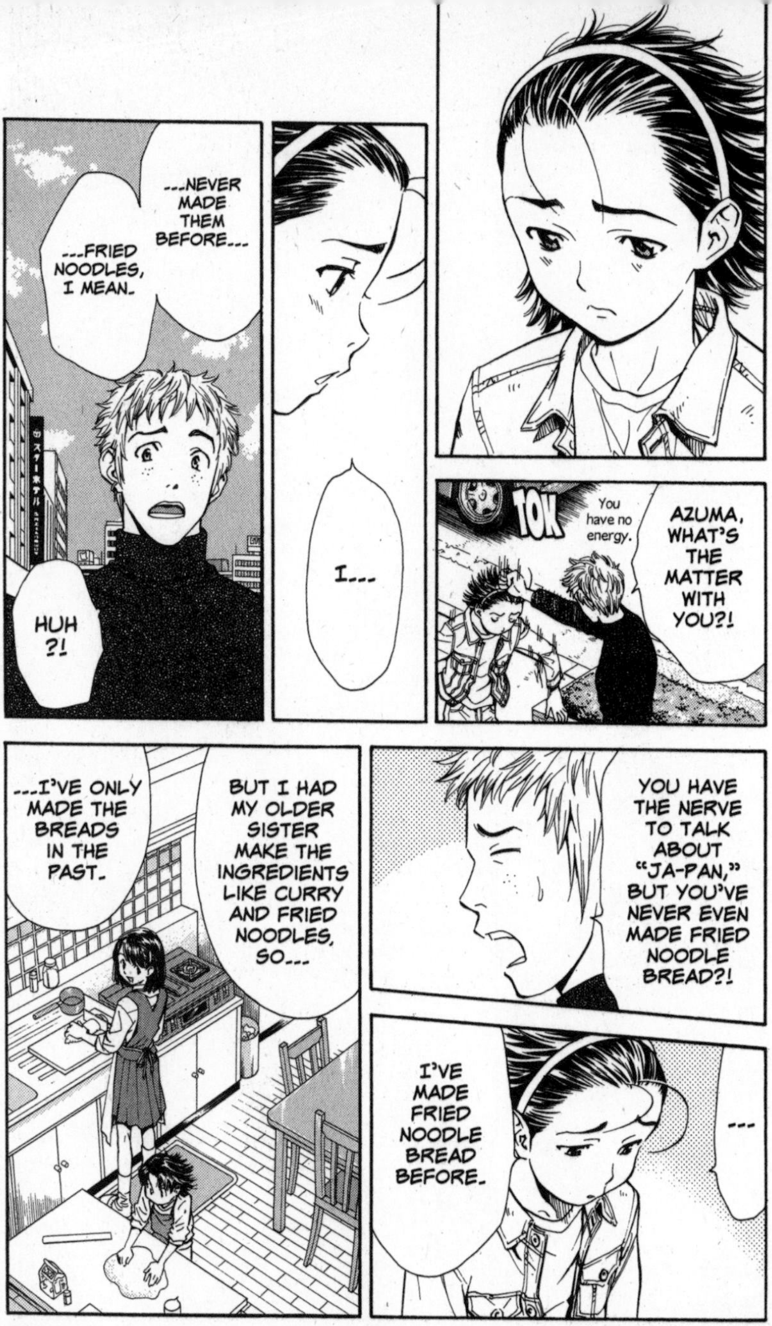
TOK
AZUMA, WHAT'S THE MATTER WITH YOU?!
You have no energy.
I...
...NEVER MADE THEM BEFORE...
...FRIED NOODLES, I MEAN.
HUH ?!
YOU HAVE THE NERVE TO TALK ABOUT "JA-PAN," BUT YOU'VE NEVER EVEN MADE FRIED NOODLE BREAD?!
...
I'VE MADE FRIED NOODLE BREAD BEFORE.
BUT I HAD MY OLDER SISTER MAKE THE INGREDIENTS LIKE CURRY AND FRIED NOODLES, SO...
...I'VE ONLY MADE THE BREADS IN THE PAST.

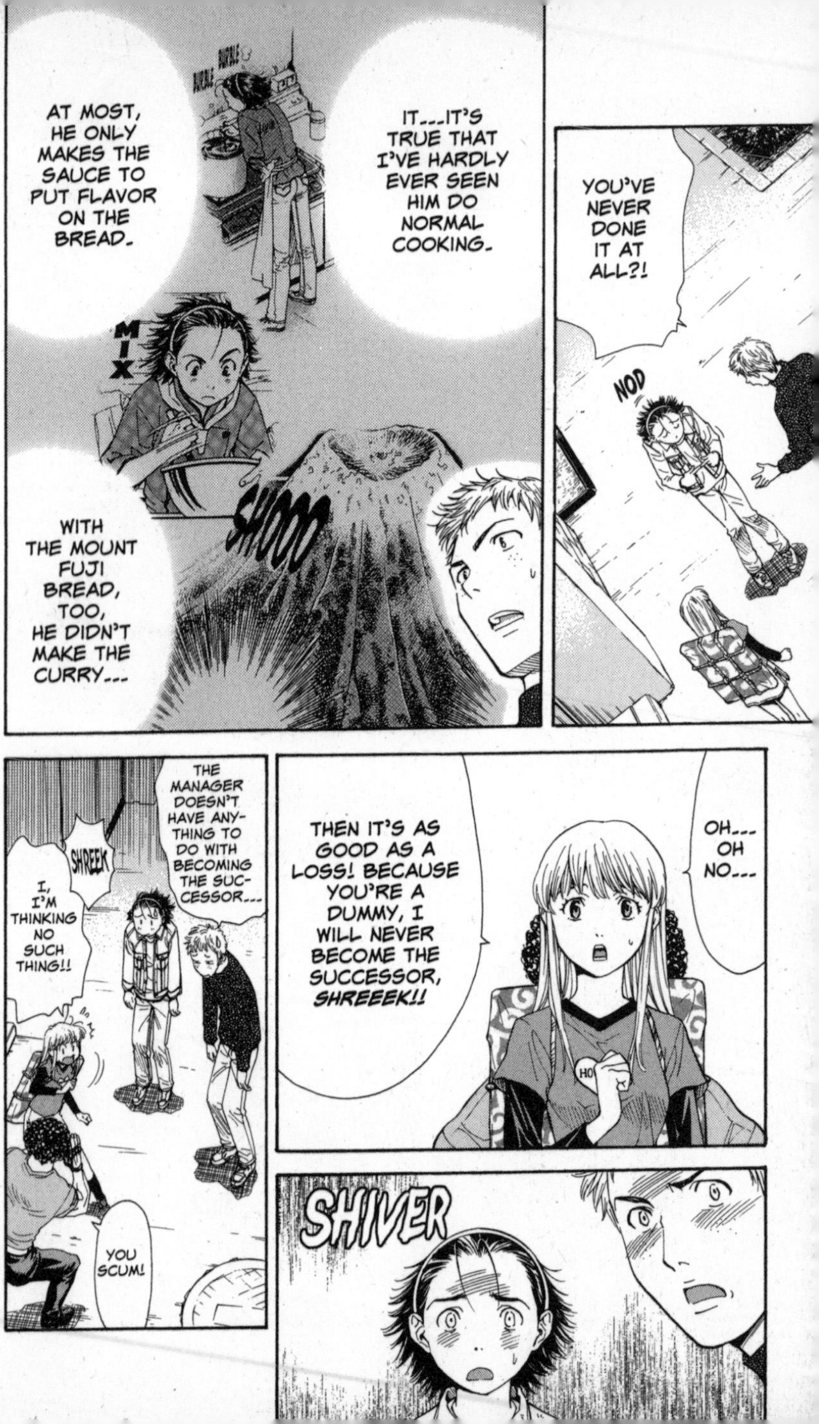
YOU'VE NEVER DONE IT AT ALL?!
NOD
IT...IT'S TRUE THAT I'VE HARDLY EVER SEEN HIM DO NORMAL COOKING.
BUBBLE BUBBLE
AT MOST, HE ONLY MAKES THE SAUCE TO PUT FLAVOR ON THE BREAD.
MIX
SHOOO
WITH THE MOUNT FUJI BREAD, TOO, HE DIDN'T MAKE THE CURRY...
OH... OH NO...
THEN IT'S AS GOOD AS A LOSS! BECAUSE YOU'RE A DUMMY, I WILL NEVER BECOME THE SUCCESSOR, SHREEEK!!
SHIVER
THE MANAGER DOESN'T HAVE ANYTHING TO DO WITH BECOMING THE SUCCESSOR...
SHREEK
I, I'M THINKING NO SUCH THING!!
YOU SCUM!

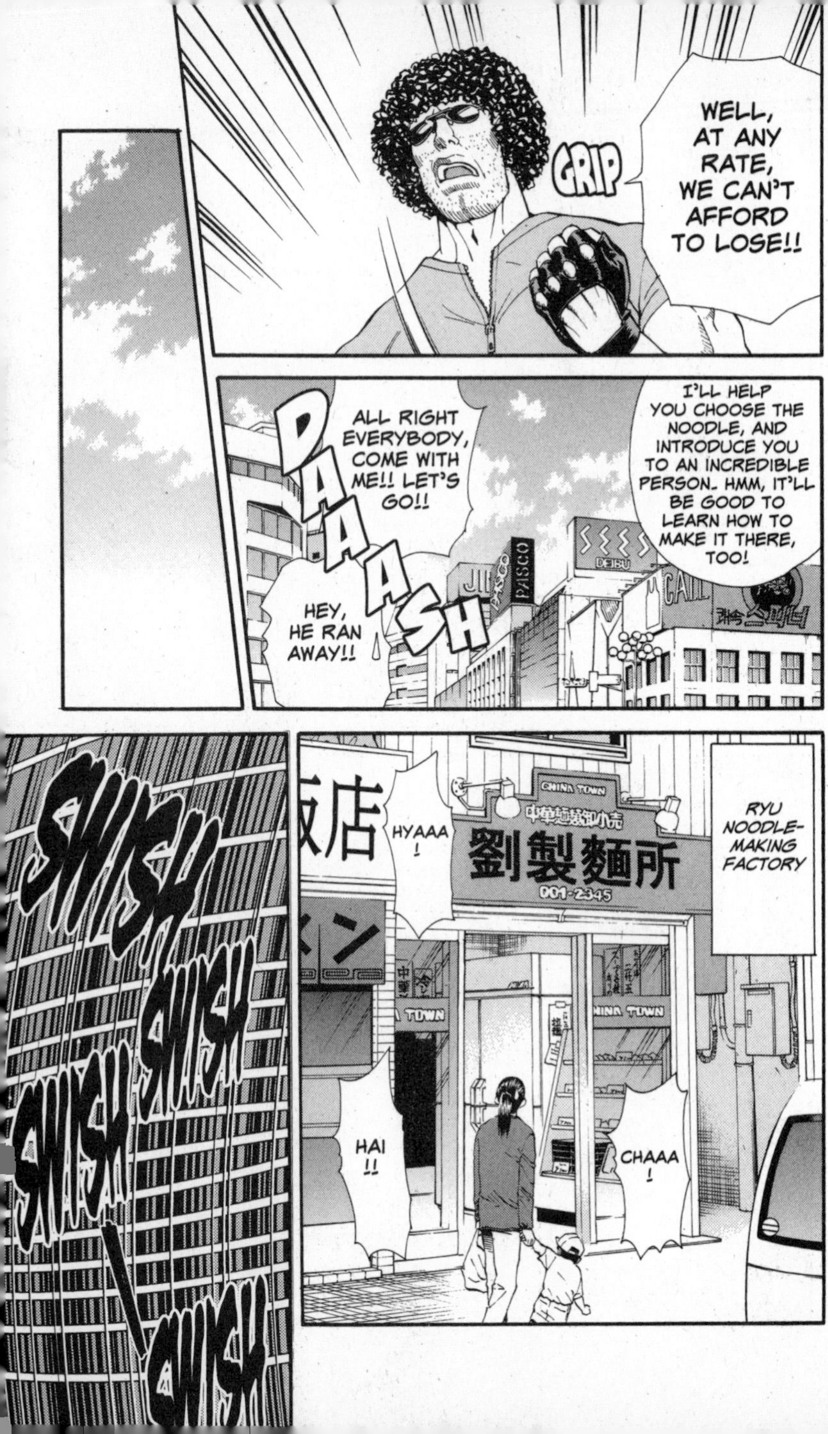
WELL, AT ANY RATE, WE CAN'T AFFORD TO LOSE!!
GRIP
I'LL HELP YOU CHOOSE THE NOODLE, AND INTRODUCE YOU TO AN INCREDIBLE PERSON. HMM, IT'LL BE GOOD TO LEARN HOW TO MAKE IT THERE, TOO!
ALL RIGHT EVERYBODY, COME WITH ME!! LET'S GO!!
DAAAASH
HEY, HE RAN AWAY!!
RYU NOODLE-MAKING FACTORY
CHINA TOWN
劉製麵所
001-2345
CHAAA!
HYAAA!
飯店
HAI!!
SWISH
SWISH
SWISH
SWISH

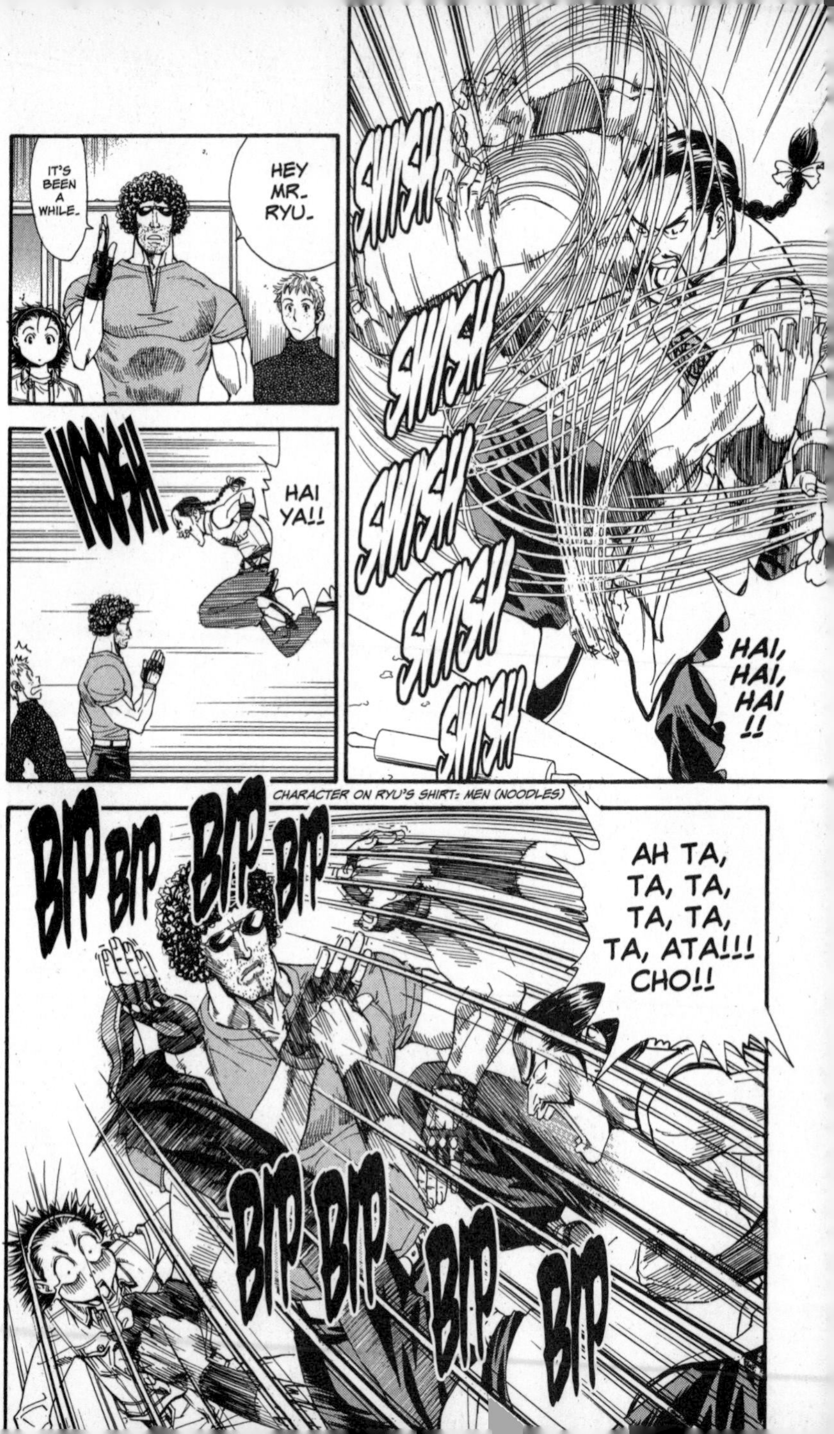
SWISH
SWISH
SWISH
SWISH
SWISH
SWISH
HAI, HAI, HAI!!
HEY MR. RYU.
IT'S BEEN A WHILE.
WOOSH
HAI YA!!
CHARACTER ON RYU'S SHIRT: MEN (NOODLES)
AH TA, TA, TA, TA, TA, TA, ATA!!! CHO!!
BIP BIP BIP BIP
BIP BIP BIP BIP

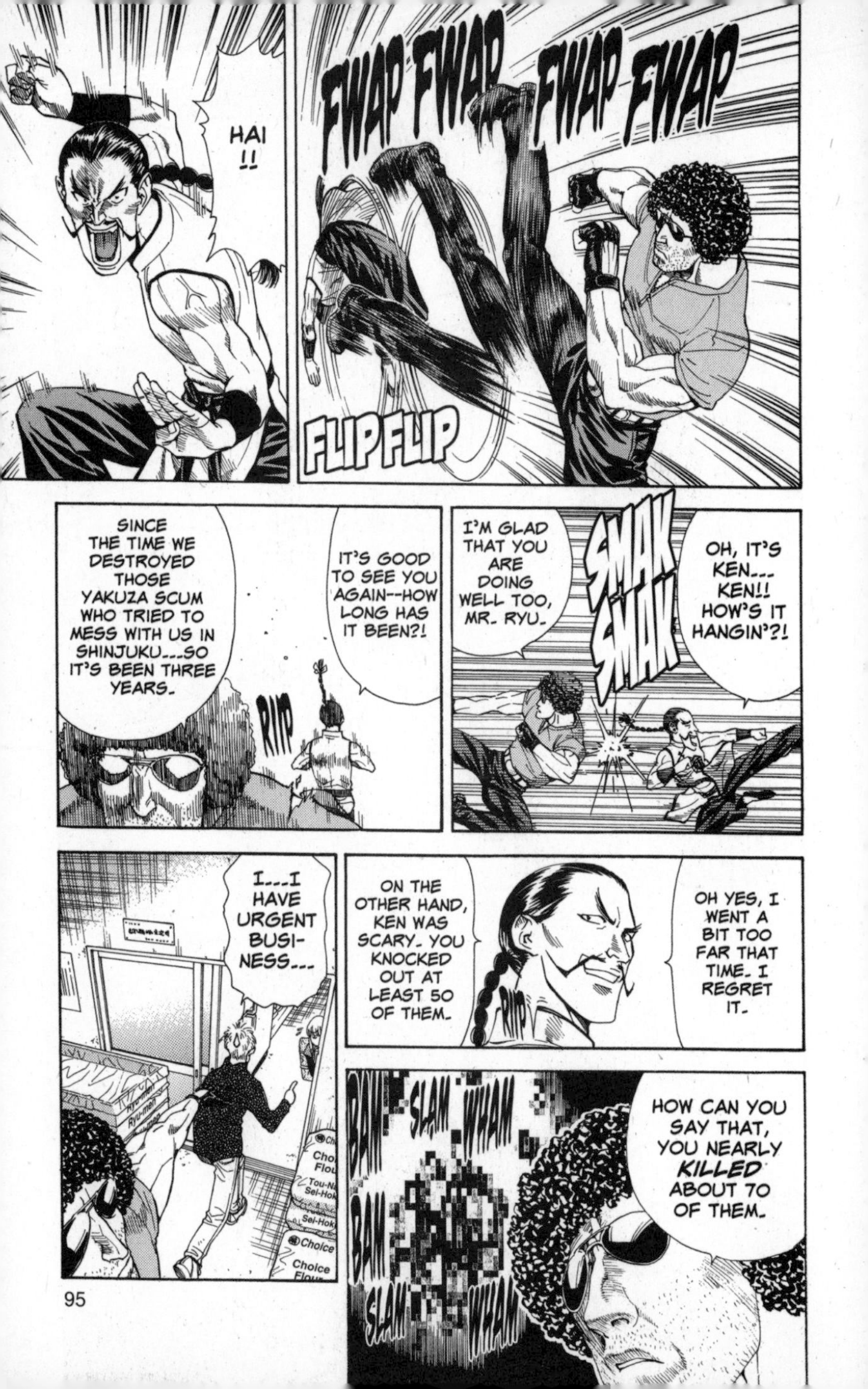
FWAP FWAP FWAP FWAP
FLIP FLIP
HAI !!
OH, IT'S KEN... KEN!! HOW'S IT HANGIN'?!
SMAK SMAK
I'M GLAD THAT YOU ARE DOING WELL TOO, MR. RYU.
IT'S GOOD TO SEE YOU AGAIN--HOW LONG HAS IT BEEN?!
SINCE THE TIME WE DESTROYED THOSE YAKUZA SCUM WHO TRIED TO MESS WITH US IN SHINJUKU...SO IT'S BEEN THREE YEARS.
RIP
OH YES, I WENT A BIT TOO FAR THAT TIME. I REGRET IT.
ON THE OTHER HAND, KEN WAS SCARY. YOU KNOCKED OUT AT LEAST 50 OF THEM.
RIP
HOW CAN YOU SAY THAT, YOU NEARLY ***KILLED*** ABOUT 70 OF THEM.
BAM SLAM WHAM BAM SLAM WHAM
I...I HAVE URGENT BUSI-NESS...
Choice
Choice

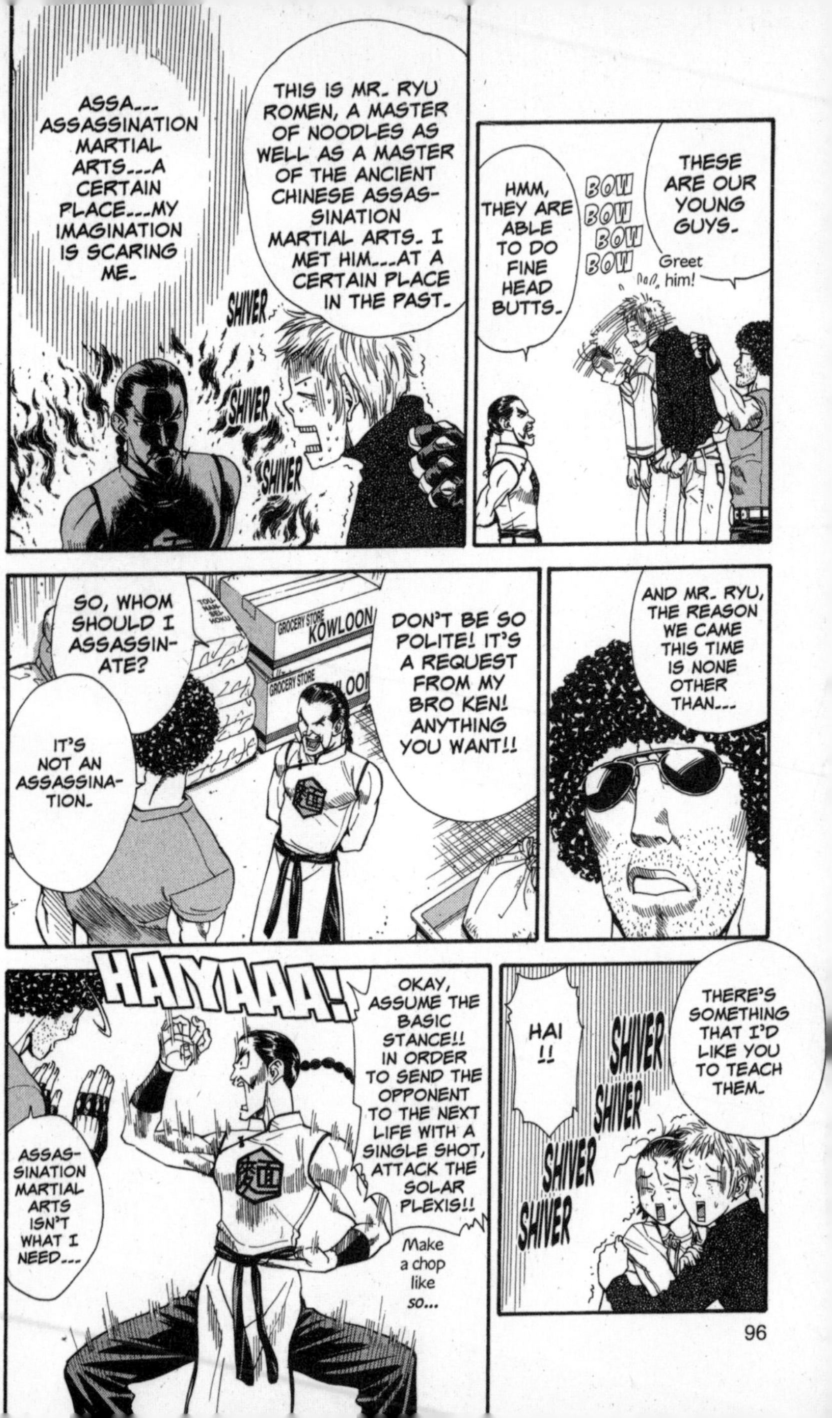
THESE ARE OUR YOUNG GUYS.
Greet him!
BOW BOW BOW BOW
HMM, THEY ARE ABLE TO DO FINE HEAD BUTTS.
THIS IS MR. RYU ROMEN, A MASTER OF NOODLES AS WELL AS A MASTER OF THE ANCIENT CHINESE ASSASSINATION MARTIAL ARTS. I MET HIM...AT A CERTAIN PLACE IN THE PAST.
ASSA... ASSASSINATION MARTIAL ARTS...A CERTAIN PLACE...MY IMAGINATION IS SCARING ME.
SHIVER
SHIVER
SHIVER
AND MR. RYU, THE REASON WE CAME THIS TIME IS NONE OTHER THAN...
SO, WHOM SHOULD I ASSASSINATE?
IT'S NOT AN ASSASSINATION.
DON'T BE SO POLITE! IT'S A REQUEST FROM MY BRO KEN! ANYTHING YOU WANT!!
GROCERY STORE KOWLOON
THERE'S SOMETHING THAT I'D LIKE YOU TO TEACH THEM.
HAI !!
SHIVER SHIVER SHIVER SHIVER
HAIYAAA!
OKAY, ASSUME THE BASIC STANCE!! IN ORDER TO SEND THE OPPONENT TO THE NEXT LIFE WITH A SINGLE SHOT, ATTACK THE SOLAR PLEXIS!!
Make a chop like so...
ASSASSINATION MARTIAL ARTS ISN'T WHAT I NEED...

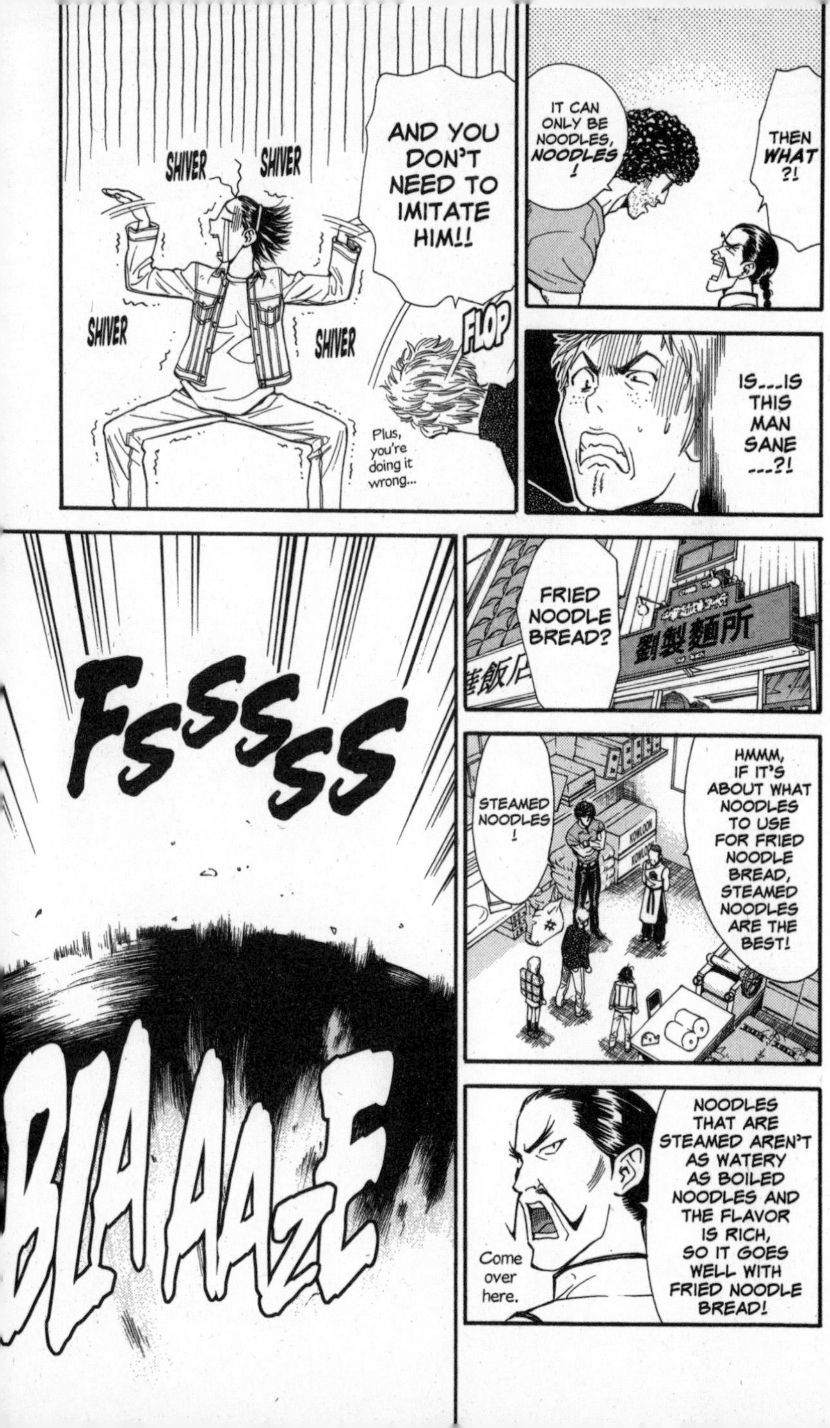
THEN WHAT?!
IT CAN ONLY BE NOODLES, NOODLES!
IS...IS THIS MAN SANE...?!
AND YOU DON'T NEED TO IMITATE HIM!!
FLOP
SHIVER
SHIVER
SHIVER
SHIVER
Plus, you're doing it wrong...
FRIED NOODLE BREAD?
HMMM, IF IT'S ABOUT WHAT NOODLES TO USE FOR FRIED NOODLE BREAD, STEAMED NOODLES ARE THE BEST!
STEAMED NOODLES!
NOODLES THAT ARE STEAMED AREN'T AS WATERY AS BOILED NOODLES AND THE FLAVOR IS RICH, SO IT GOES WELL WITH FRIED NOODLE BREAD!
Come over here.
FSSSSSS
BLAAAZE

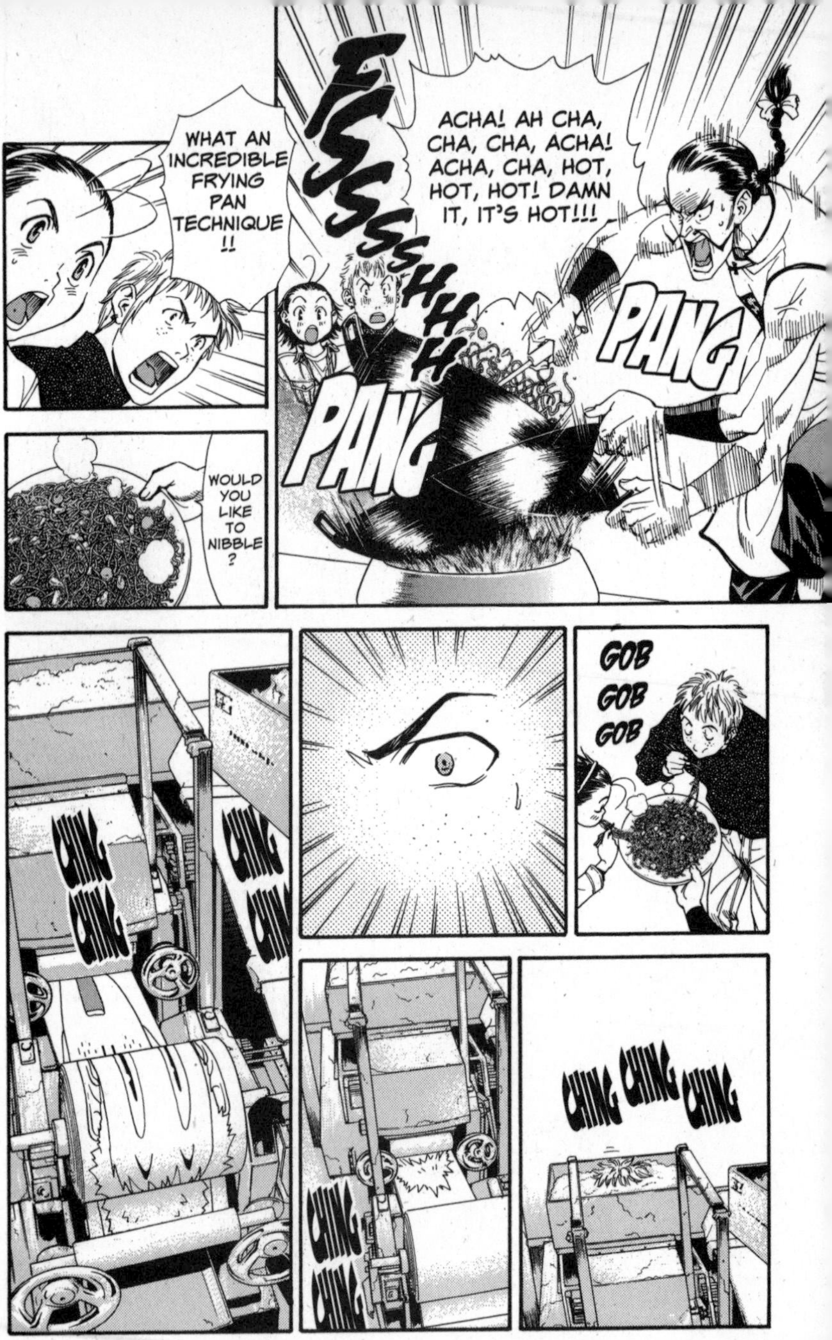
FSSSSHHHH
ACHA! AH CHA, CHA, CHA, ACHA! ACHA, CHA, HOT, HOT, HOT! DAMN IT, IT'S HOT!!!
PANG
PANG
WHAT AN INCREDIBLE FRYING PAN TECHNIQUE!!
WOULD YOU LIKE TO NIBBLE?
GOB GOB GOB
CHING CHING CHING
CHING CHING
CHING CHING
CHING CHING

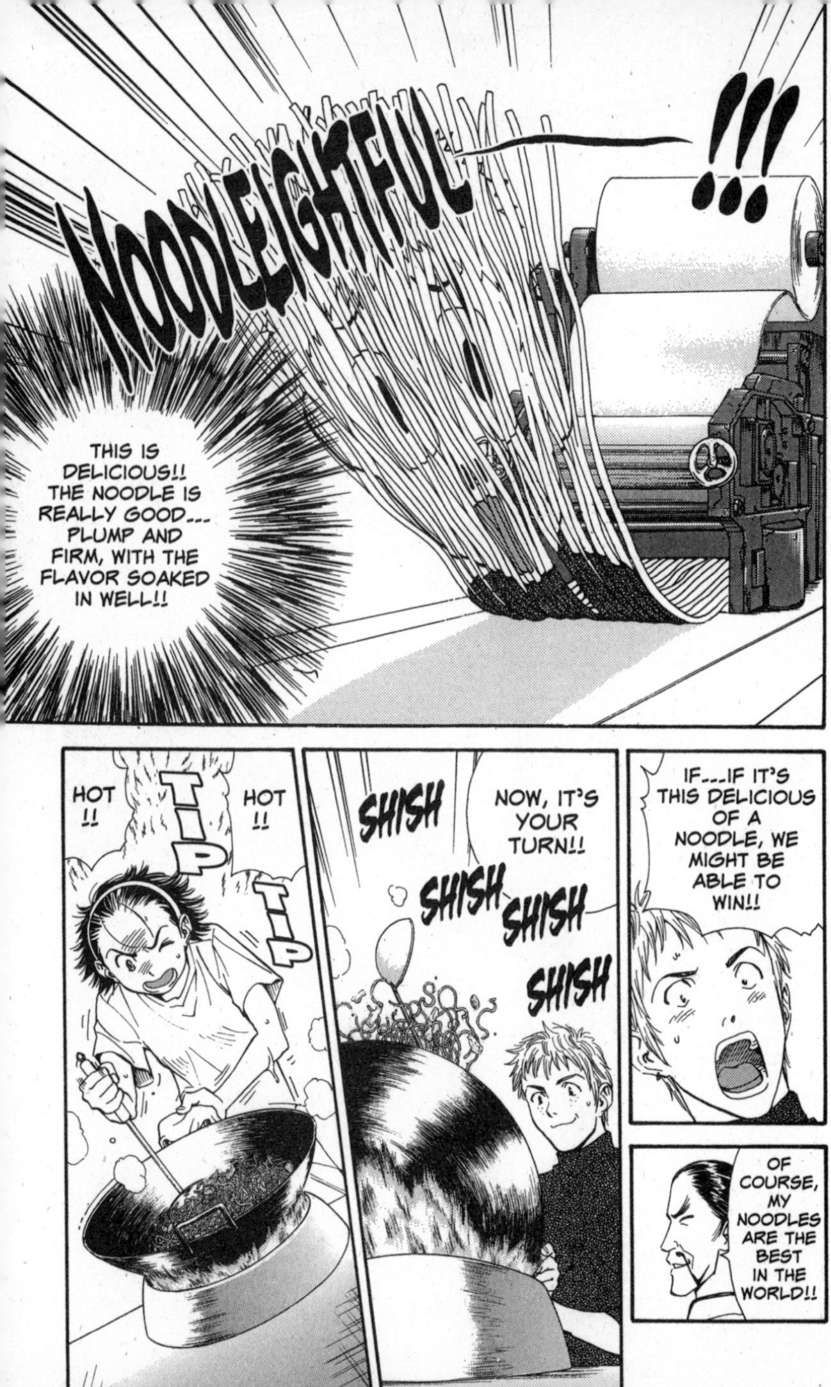
NOODLEIGHTFUL—!!!
THIS IS DELICIOUS!! THE NOODLE IS REALLY GOOD... PLUMP AND FIRM, WITH THE FLAVOR SOAKED IN WELL!!
IF...IF IT'S THIS DELICIOUS OF A NOODLE, WE MIGHT BE ABLE TO WIN!!
OF COURSE, MY NOODLES ARE THE BEST IN THE WORLD!!
NOW, IT'S YOUR TURN!!
SHISH
SHISH
SHISH
SHISH
HOT!!
TIP
TIP
HOT!!

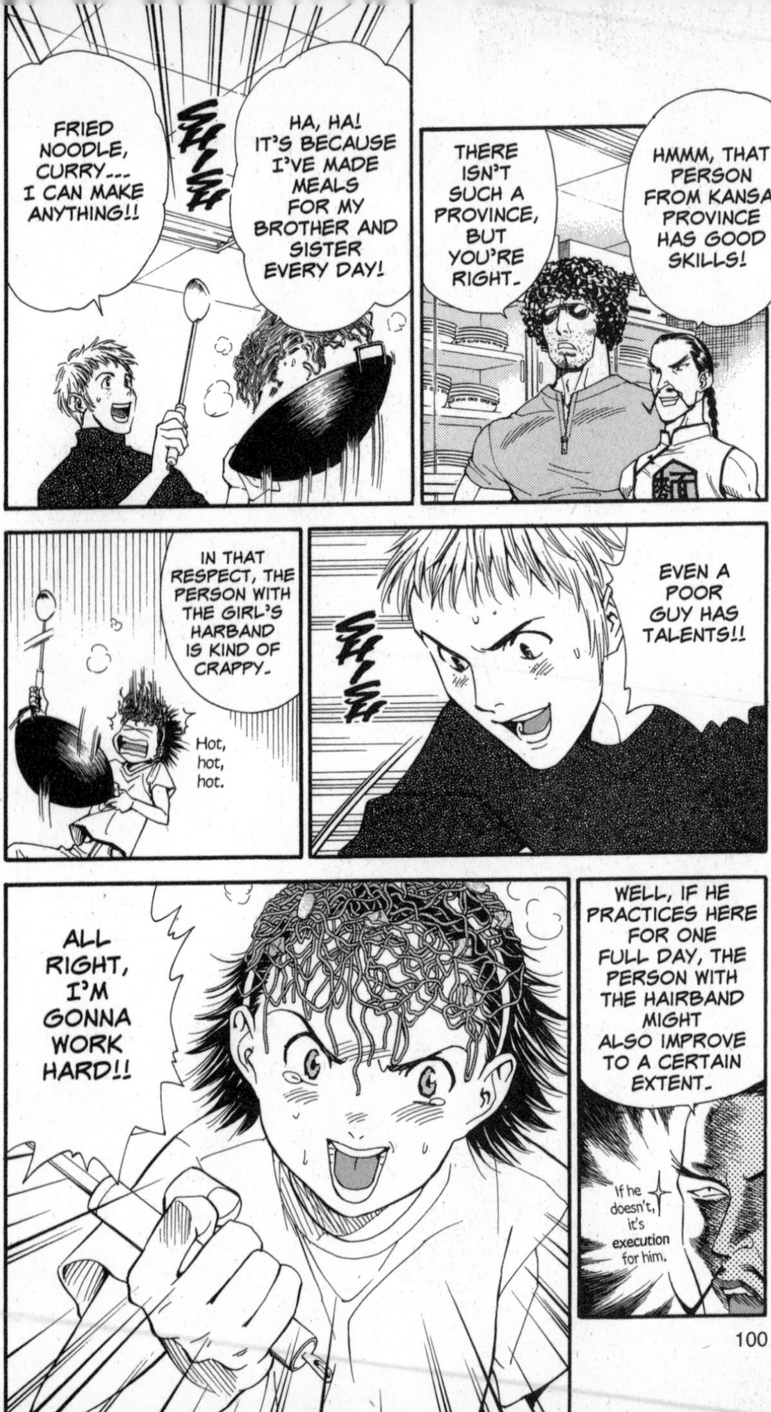
HMMM, THAT PERSON FROM KANSAI PROVINCE HAS GOOD SKILLS!
THERE ISN'T SUCH A PROVINCE, BUT YOU'RE RIGHT.
HA, HA! IT'S BECAUSE I'VE MADE MEALS FOR MY BROTHER AND SISTER EVERY DAY!
SHISH
FRIED NOODLE, CURRY... I CAN MAKE ANYTHING!!
EVEN A POOR GUY HAS TALENTS!!
SHISH
IN THAT RESPECT, THE PERSON WITH THE GIRL'S HARBAND IS KIND OF CRAPPY.
Hot, hot, hot.
WELL, IF HE PRACTICES HERE FOR ONE FULL DAY, THE PERSON WITH THE HAIRBAND MIGHT ALSO IMPROVE TO A CERTAIN EXTENT.
If he doesn't, it's execution for him.
ALL RIGHT, I'M GONNA WORK HARD!!

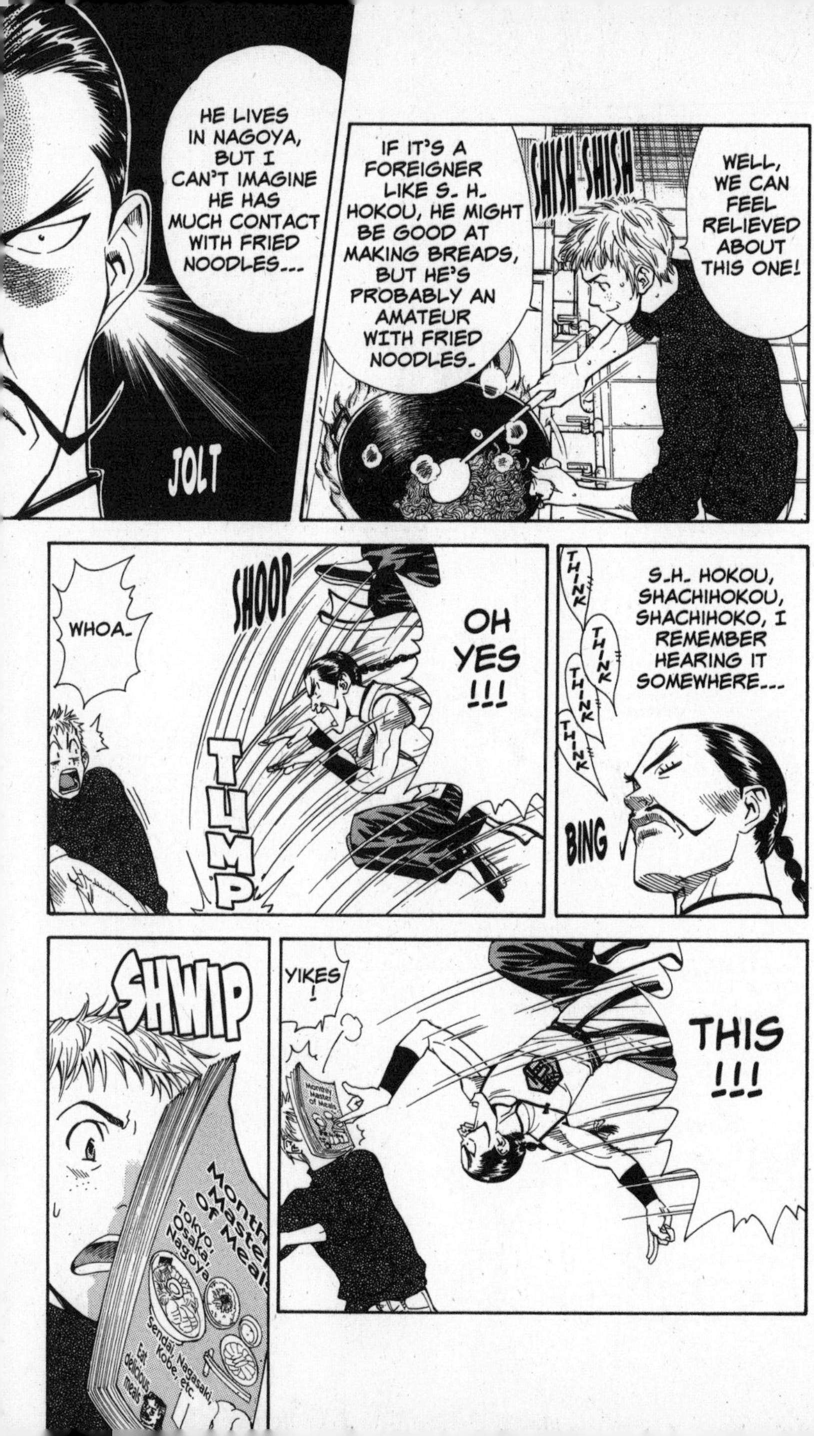
WELL, WE CAN FEEL RELIEVED ABOUT THIS ONE!
SHISH SHISH
IF IT'S A FOREIGNER LIKE S. H. HOKOU, HE MIGHT BE GOOD AT MAKING BREADS, BUT HE'S PROBABLY AN AMATEUR WITH FRIED NOODLES.
HE LIVES IN NAGOYA, BUT I CAN'T IMAGINE HE HAS MUCH CONTACT WITH FRIED NOODLES...
JOLT
THINK
THINK
THINK
THINK
S.H. HOKOU, SHACHIHOKOU, SHACHIHOKO, I REMEMBER HEARING IT SOMEWHERE...
BING
OH YES!!!
SHOOP
TUMP
WHOA.
THIS!!!
YIKES!
Monthly Master of Meals
SHWIP
Monthly Master of Meals
Tokyo, Osaka, Nagoya
Sendai, Nagasaki, Kobe, etc.
Eat delicious meals

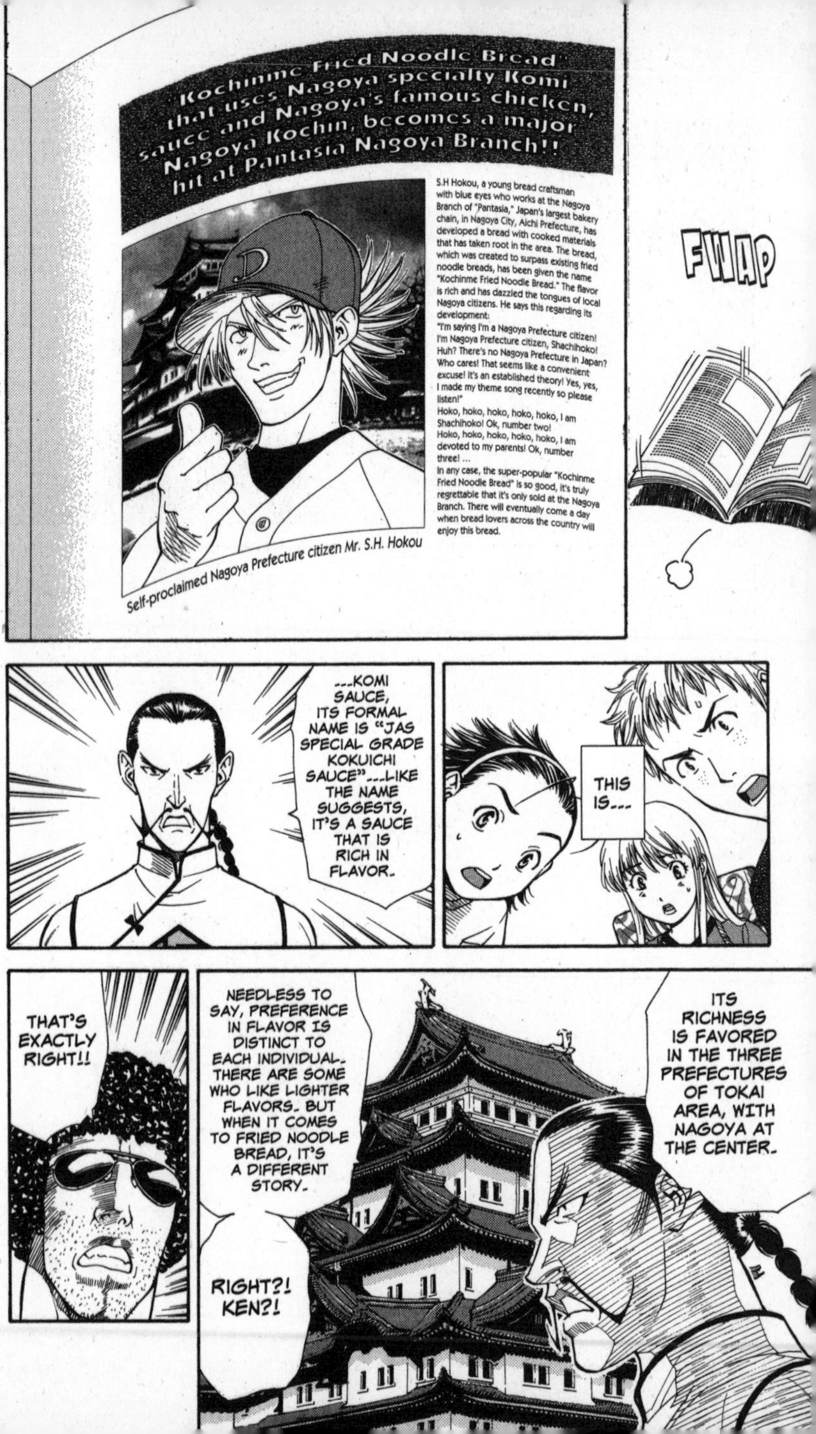
"Kochinme Fried Noodle Bread" that uses Nagoya specialty Komi sauce and Nagoya's famous chicken, Nagoya Kochin, becomes a major hit at Pantasia Nagoya Branch!!
S.H Hokou, a young bread craftsman with blue eyes who works at the Nagoya Branch of "Pantasia," Japan's largest bakery chain, in Nagoya City, Aichi Prefecture, has developed a bread with cooked materials that has taken root in the area. The bread, which was created to surpass existing fried noodle breads, has been given the name "Kochinme Fried Noodle Bread." The flavor is rich and has dazzled the tongues of local Nagoya citizens. He says this regarding its development:
"I'm saying I'm a Nagoya Prefecture citizen! I'm Nagoya Prefecture citizen, Shachihoko! Huh? There's no Nagoya Prefecture in Japan? Who cares! That seems like a convenient excuse! It's an established theory! Yes, yes, I made my theme song recently so please listen!"
Hoko, hoko, hoko, hoko, hoko, I am Shachihoko! Ok, number two!
Hoko, hoko, hoko, hoko, hoko, I am devoted to my parents! Ok, number three! ...
In any case, the super-popular "Kochinme Fried Noodle Bread" is so good, it's truly regrettable that it's only sold at the Nagoya Branch. There will eventually come a day when bread lovers across the country will enjoy this bread.
Self-proclaimed Nagoya Prefecture citizen Mr. S.H. Hokou
FWAP
THIS IS...
...KOMI SAUCE, ITS FORMAL NAME IS "JAS SPECIAL GRADE KOKUICHI SAUCE"...LIKE THE NAME SUGGESTS, IT'S A SAUCE THAT IS RICH IN FLAVOR.
ITS RICHNESS IS FAVORED IN THE THREE PREFECTURES OF TOKAI AREA, WITH NAGOYA AT THE CENTER.
NEEDLESS TO SAY, PREFERENCE IN FLAVOR IS DISTINCT TO EACH INDIVIDUAL. THERE ARE SOME WHO LIKE LIGHTER FLAVORS. BUT WHEN IT COMES TO FRIED NOODLE BREAD, IT'S A DIFFERENT STORY.
RIGHT?! KEN?!
THAT'S EXACTLY RIGHT!!

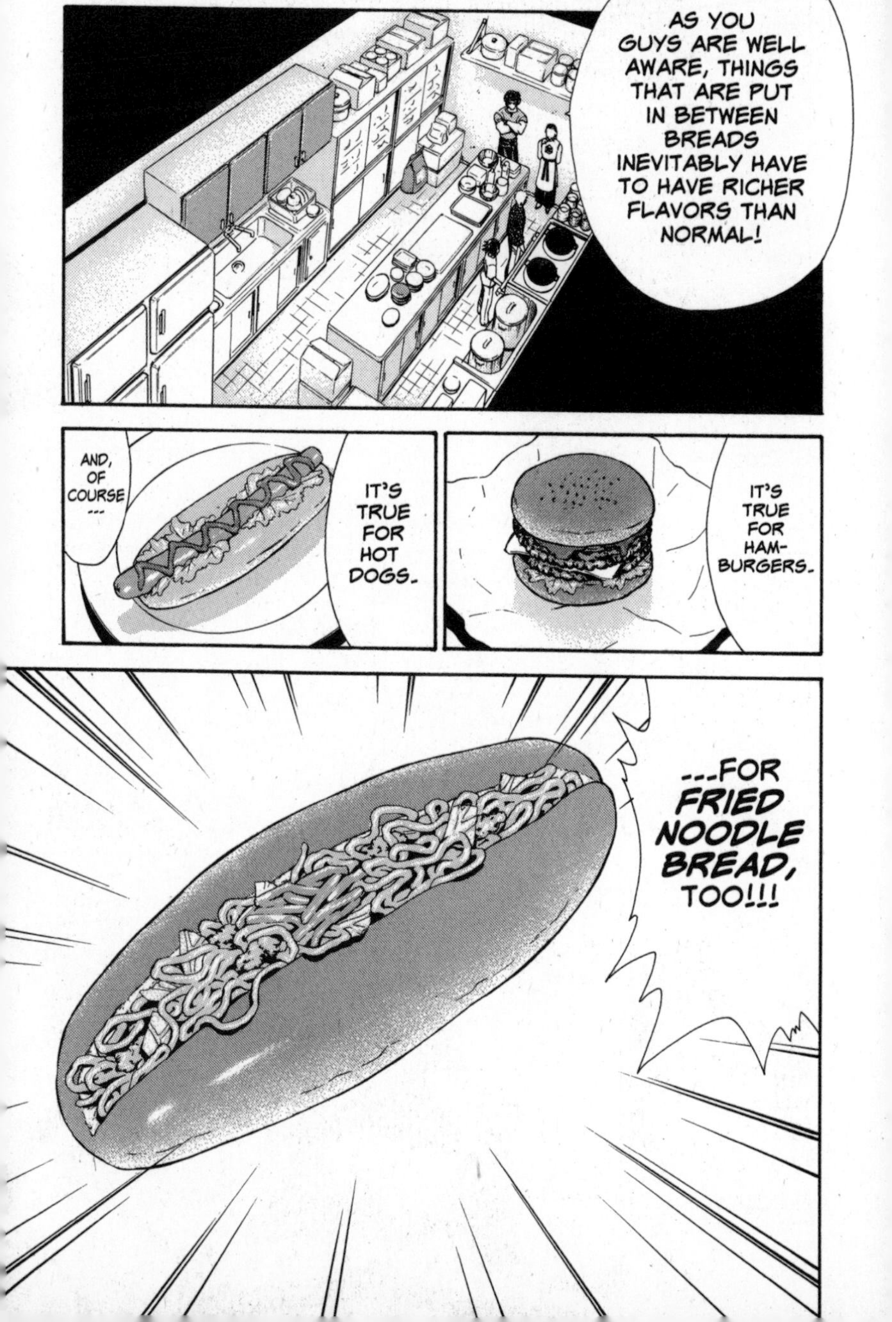
AS YOU GUYS ARE WELL AWARE, THINGS THAT ARE PUT IN BETWEEN BREADS INEVITABLY HAVE TO HAVE RICHER FLAVORS THAN NORMAL!
IT'S TRUE FOR HAM-BURGERS.
IT'S TRUE FOR HOT DOGS.
AND, OF COURSE---
---FOR FRIED NOODLE BREAD, TOO!!!

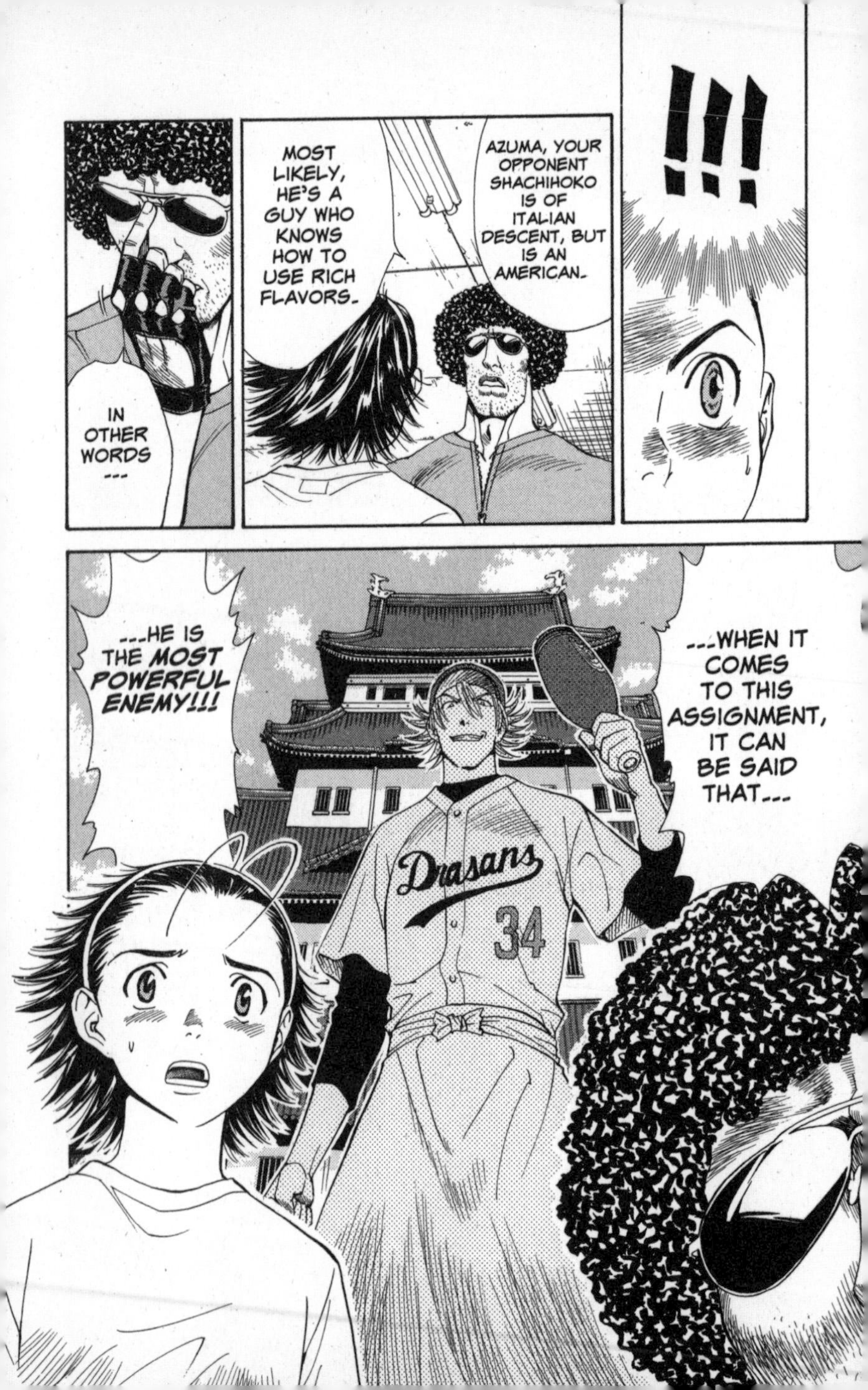
!!!
AZUMA, YOUR OPPONENT SHACHIHOKO IS OF ITALIAN DESCENT, BUT IS AN AMERICAN...
MOST LIKELY, HE'S A GUY WHO KNOWS HOW TO USE RICH FLAVORS...
IN OTHER WORDS ---
---WHEN IT COMES TO THIS ASSIGNMENT, IT CAN BE SAID THAT---
---HE IS THE *MOST POWERFUL* ENEMY!!!
Drasans
34

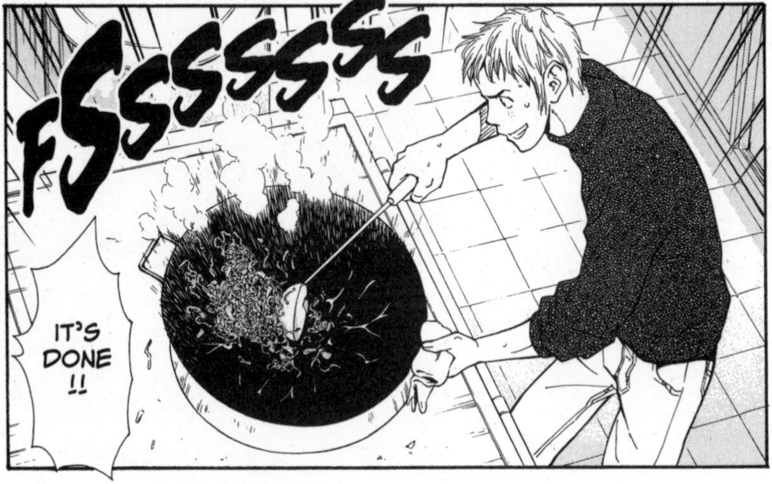
FSSSSSSS
IT'S DONE !!

Story 29:

A Good Team

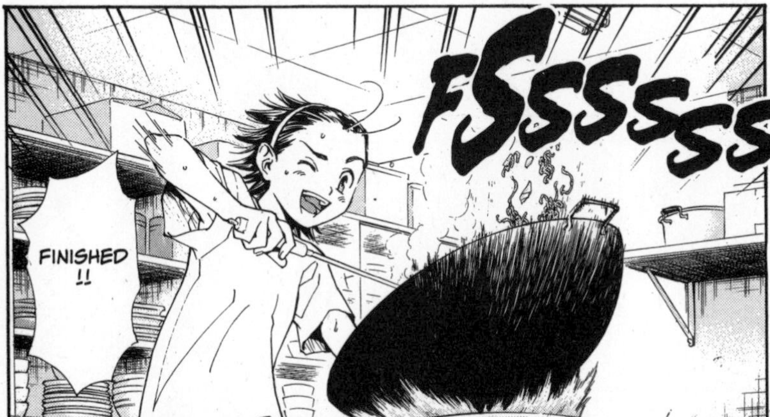
FSSSSSS
FINISHED !!

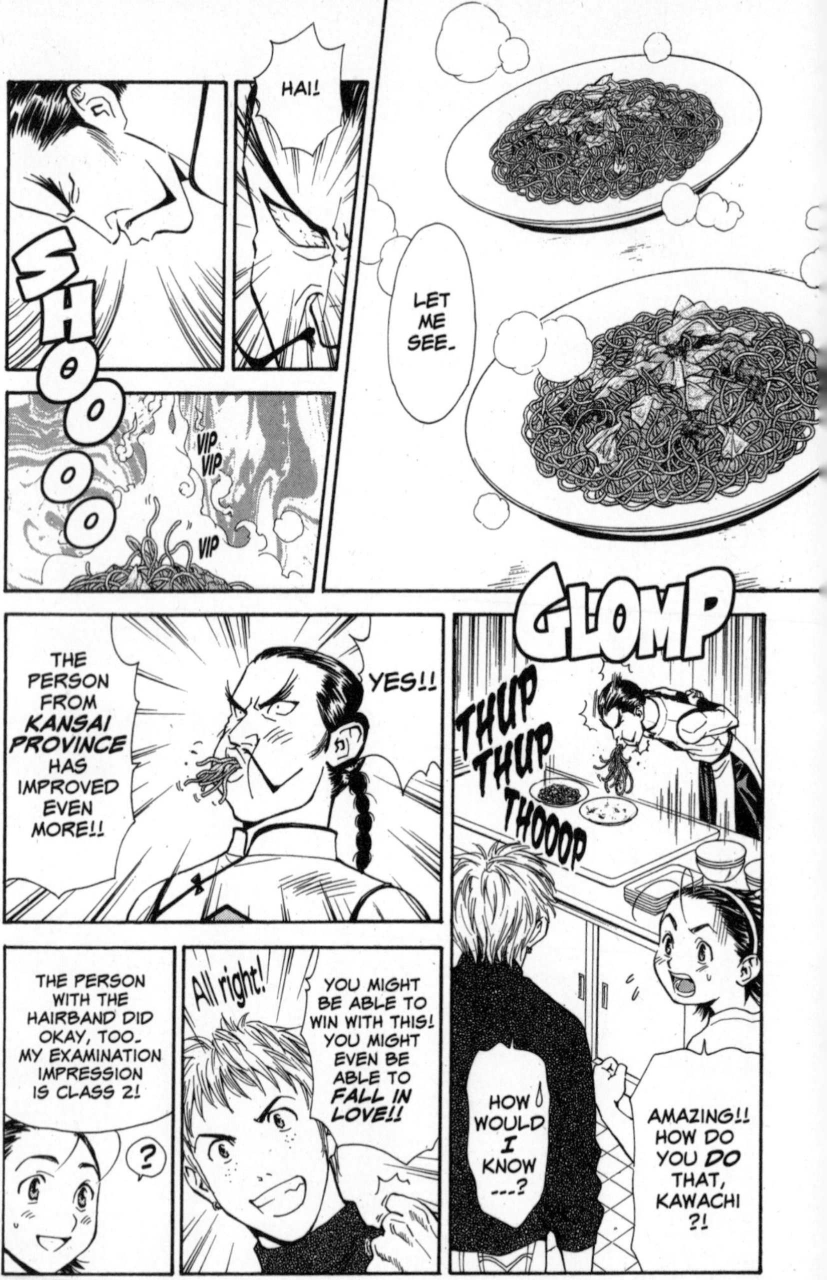
LET ME SEE...
HAI!
SHOOOOOO
VIP VIP
VIP
GLOMP
THUP THUP THOOOP
AMAZING!! HOW DO YOU DO THAT, KAWACHI?!
HOW WOULD I KNOW...?
YES!!
THE PERSON FROM KANSAI PROVINCE HAS IMPROVED EVEN MORE!!
YOU MIGHT BE ABLE TO WIN WITH THIS! YOU MIGHT EVEN BE ABLE TO FALL IN LOVE!!
All right!
THE PERSON WITH THE HAIRBAND DID OKAY, TOO. MY EXAMINATION IMPRESSION IS CLASS 2!
?

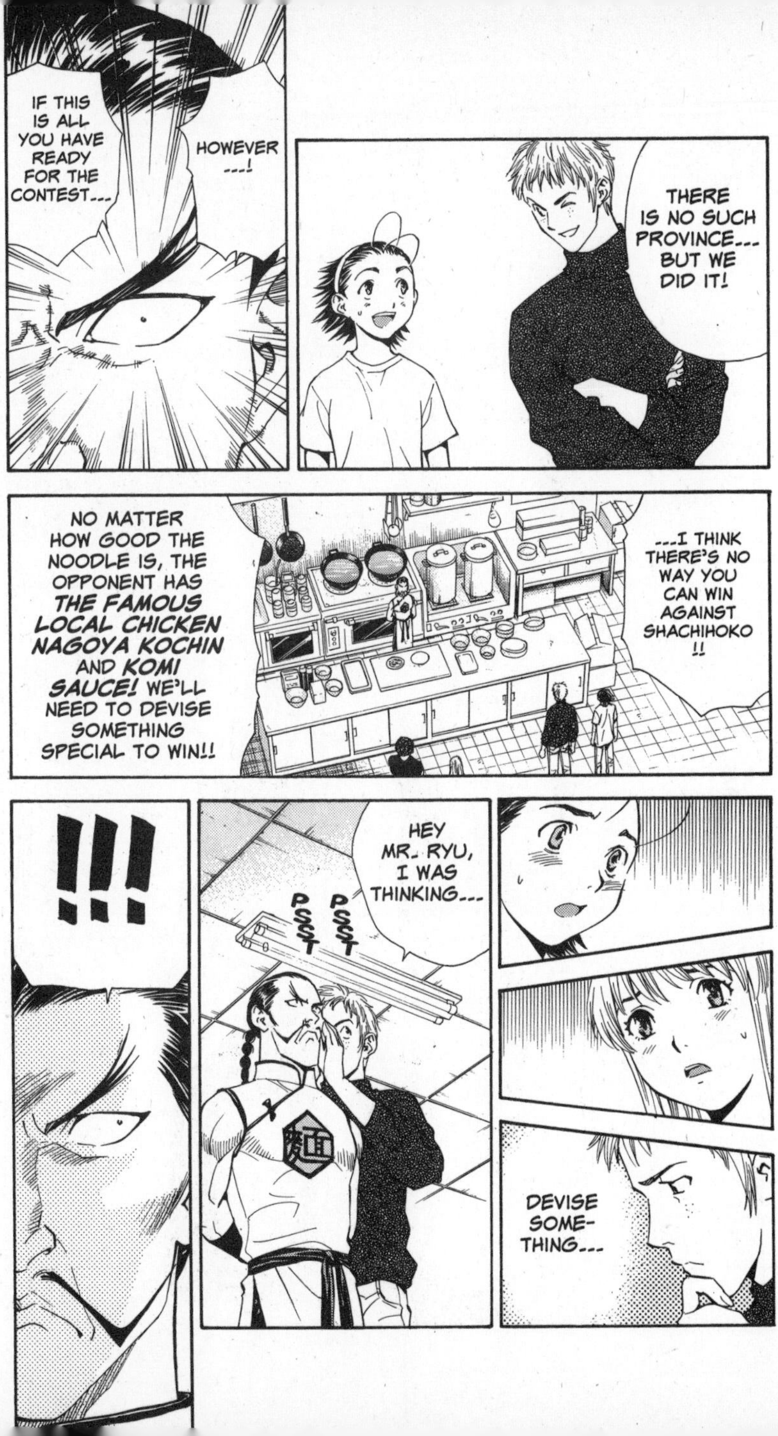
THERE IS NO SUCH PROVINCE... BUT WE DID IT!
HOWEVER...!
IF THIS IS ALL YOU HAVE READY FOR THE CONTEST...
...I THINK THERE'S NO WAY YOU CAN WIN AGAINST SHACHIHOKO!!
NO MATTER HOW GOOD THE NOODLE IS, THE OPPONENT HAS THE FAMOUS LOCAL CHICKEN NAGOYA KOCHIN AND KOMI SAUCE! WE'LL NEED TO DEVISE SOMETHING SPECIAL TO WIN!!
DEVISE SOME-THING...
HEY MR. RYU, I WAS THINKING...
PSST PSST
!!!

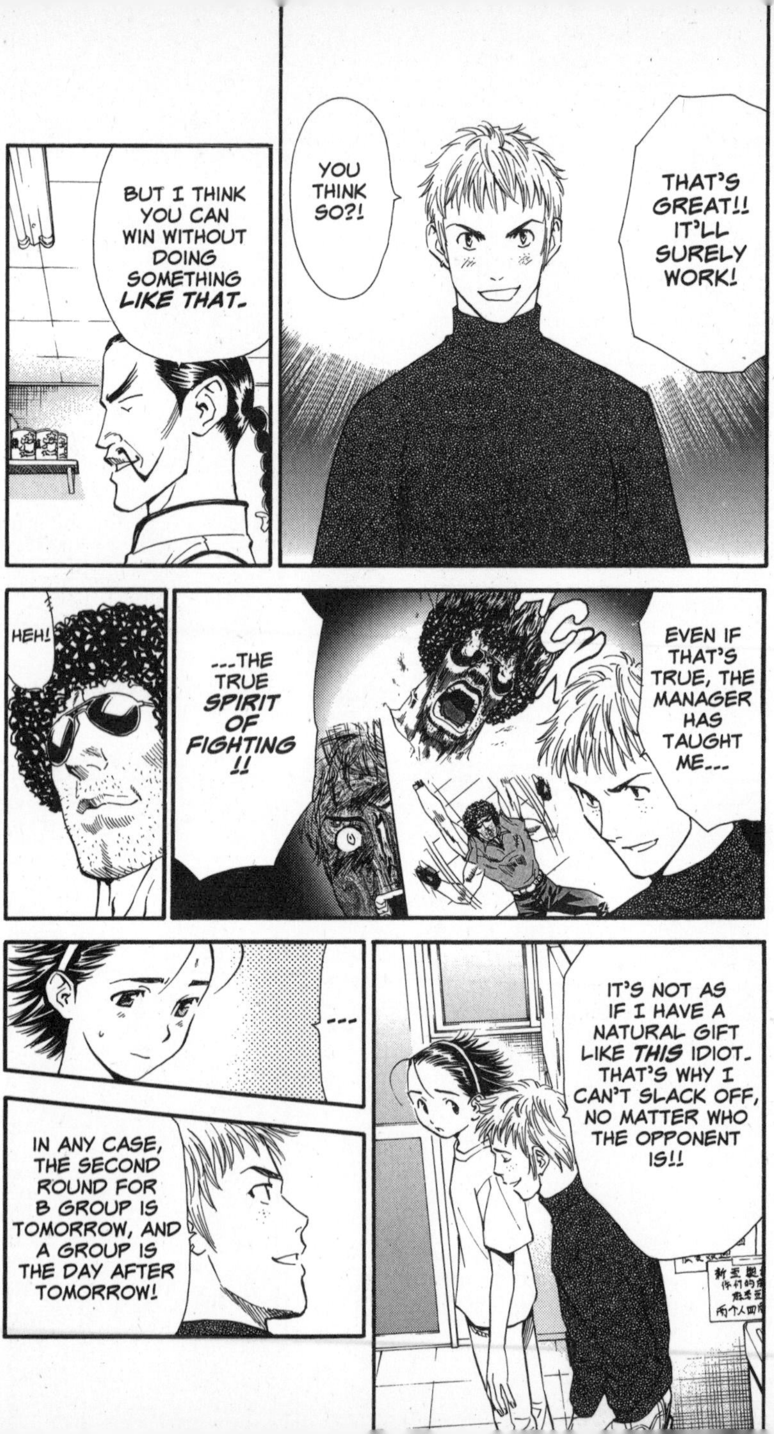
THAT'S GREAT!! IT'LL SURELY WORK!
YOU THINK SO?!
BUT I THINK YOU CAN WIN WITHOUT DOING SOMETHING LIKE THAT.
EVEN IF THAT'S TRUE, THE MANAGER HAS TAUGHT ME...
...THE TRUE SPIRIT OF FIGHTING!!
HEH!
IT'S NOT AS IF I HAVE A NATURAL GIFT LIKE THIS IDIOT. THAT'S WHY I CAN'T SLACK OFF, NO MATTER WHO THE OPPONENT IS!!
...
IN ANY CASE, THE SECOND ROUND FOR B GROUP IS TOMORROW, AND A GROUP IS THE DAY AFTER TOMORROW!

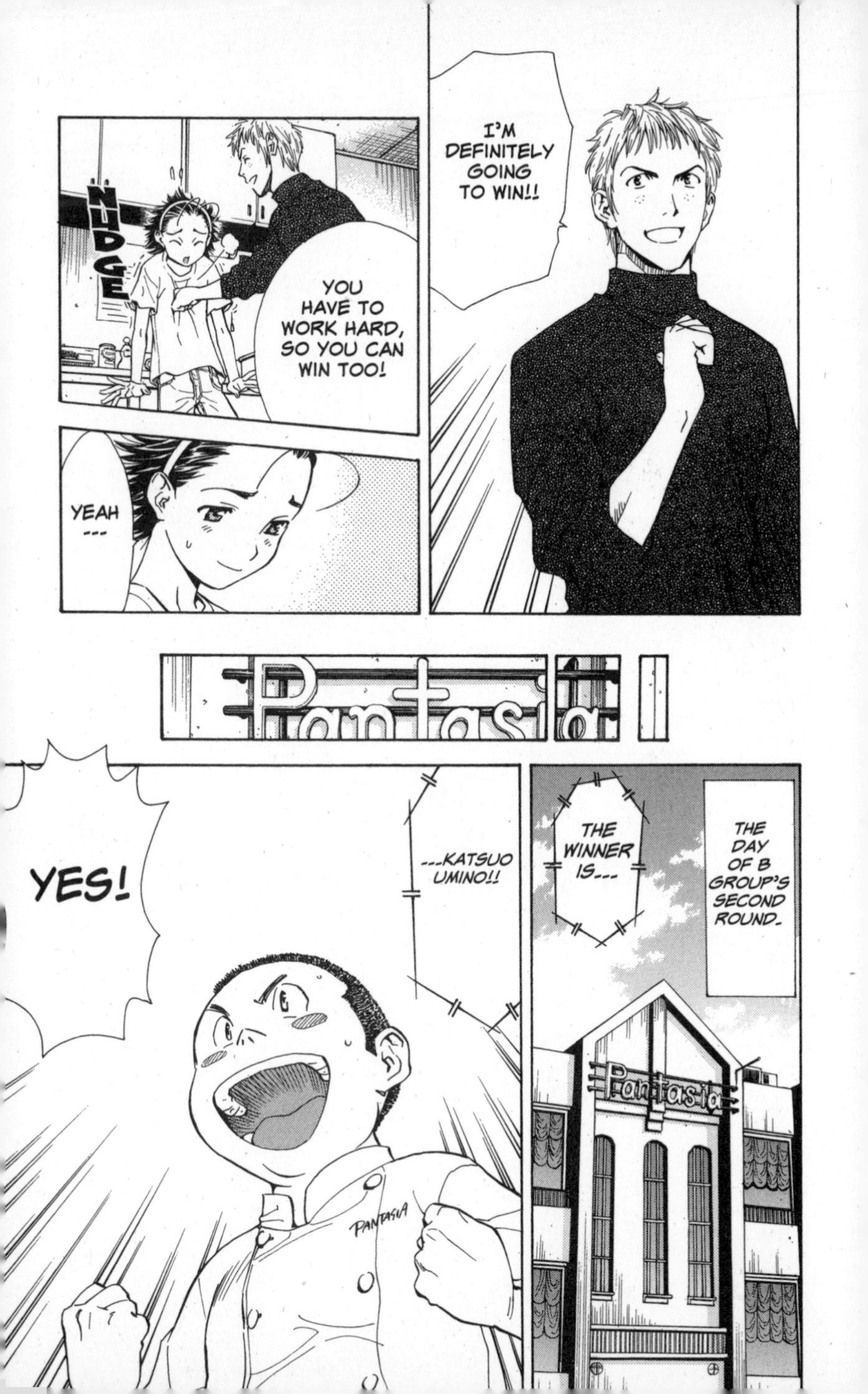
I'M DEFINITELY GOING TO WIN!!
NUDGE
YOU HAVE TO WORK HARD, SO YOU CAN WIN TOO!
YEAH ---
Pantasia
THE DAY OF B GROUP'S SECOND ROUND.
THE WINNER IS---
Pantasia
---KATSUO UMINO!!
YES!
PANTASIA

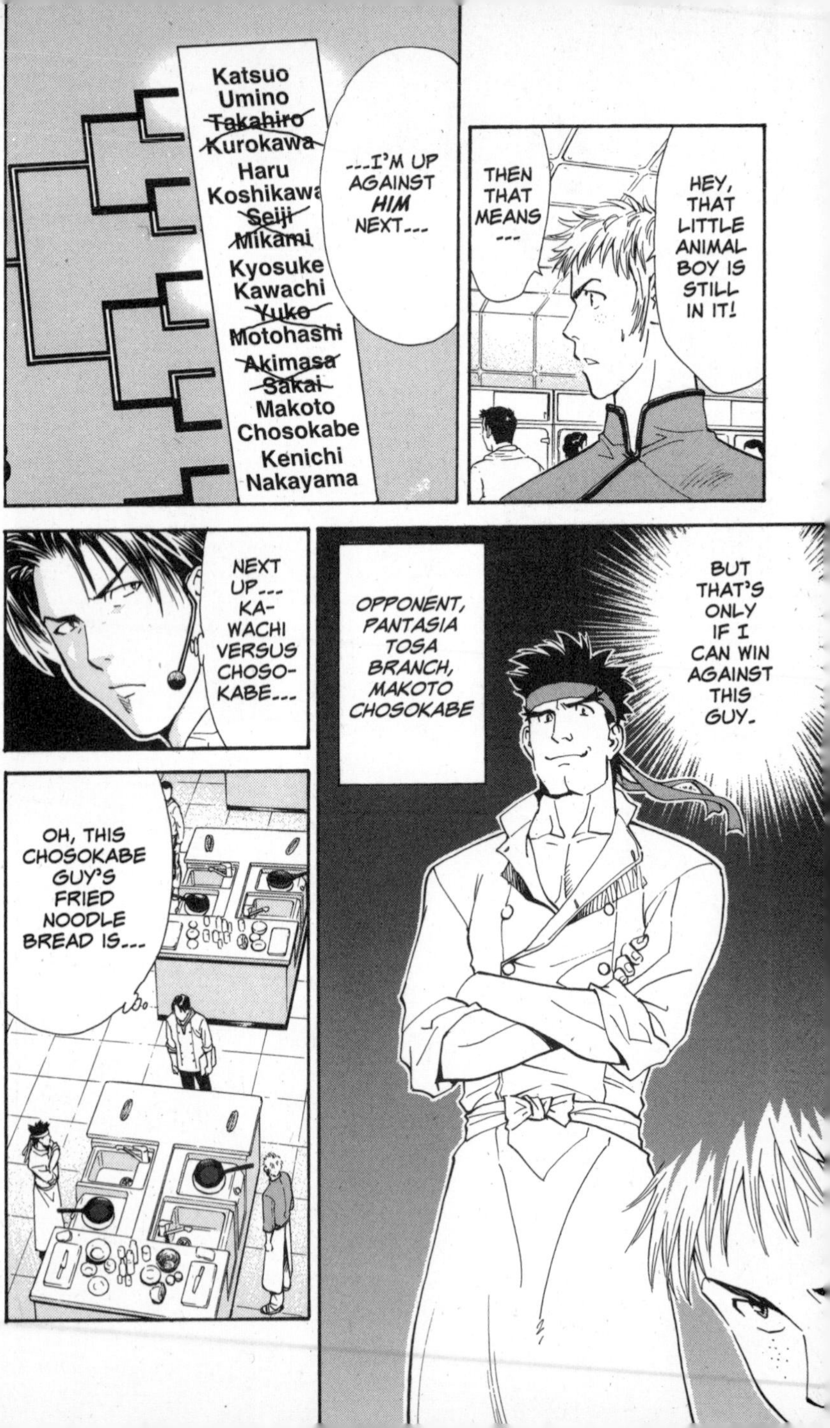
HEY, THAT LITTLE ANIMAL BOY IS STILL IN IT!
THEN THAT MEANS ---
Katsuo Umino
Takahiro Kurokawa
Haru Koshikawa
Seiji Mikami
Kyosuke Kawachi
Yuko Motohashi
Akimasa Sakai
Makoto Chosokabe
Kenichi Nakayama
---I'M UP AGAINST *HIM* NEXT---
BUT THAT'S ONLY IF I CAN WIN AGAINST THIS GUY.
OPPONENT, PANTASIA TOSA BRANCH, MAKOTO CHOSOKABE
NEXT UP--- KAWACHI VERSUS CHOSOKABE---
OH, THIS CHOSOKABE GUY'S FRIED NOODLE BREAD IS---

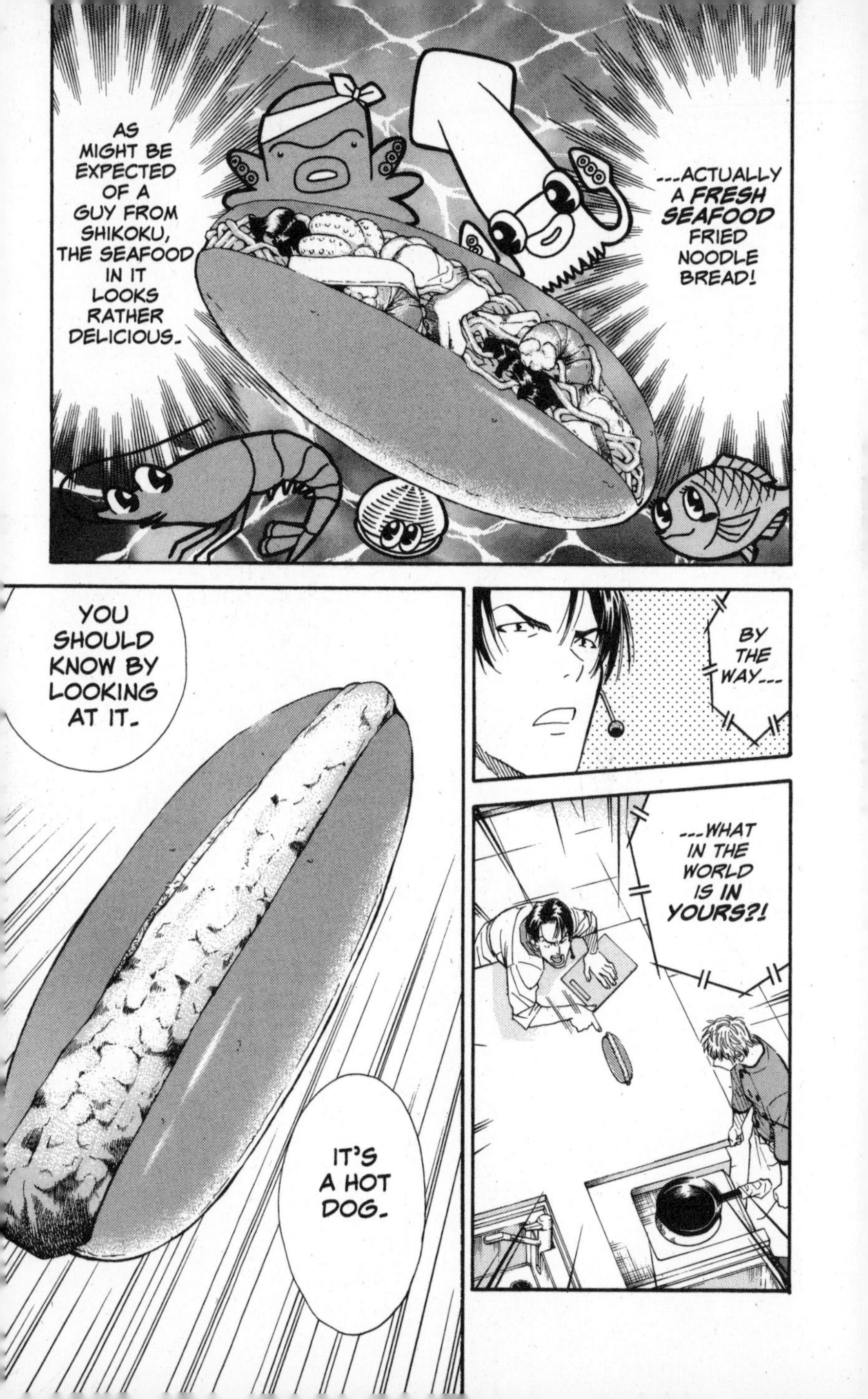

...ACTUALLY A FRESH SEAFOOD FRIED NOODLE BREAD!
AS MIGHT BE EXPECTED OF A GUY FROM SHIKOKU, THE SEAFOOD IN IT LOOKS RATHER DELICIOUS.
BY THE WAY...
...WHAT IN THE WORLD IS IN YOURS?!
YOU SHOULD KNOW BY LOOKING AT IT.
IT'S A HOT DOG.

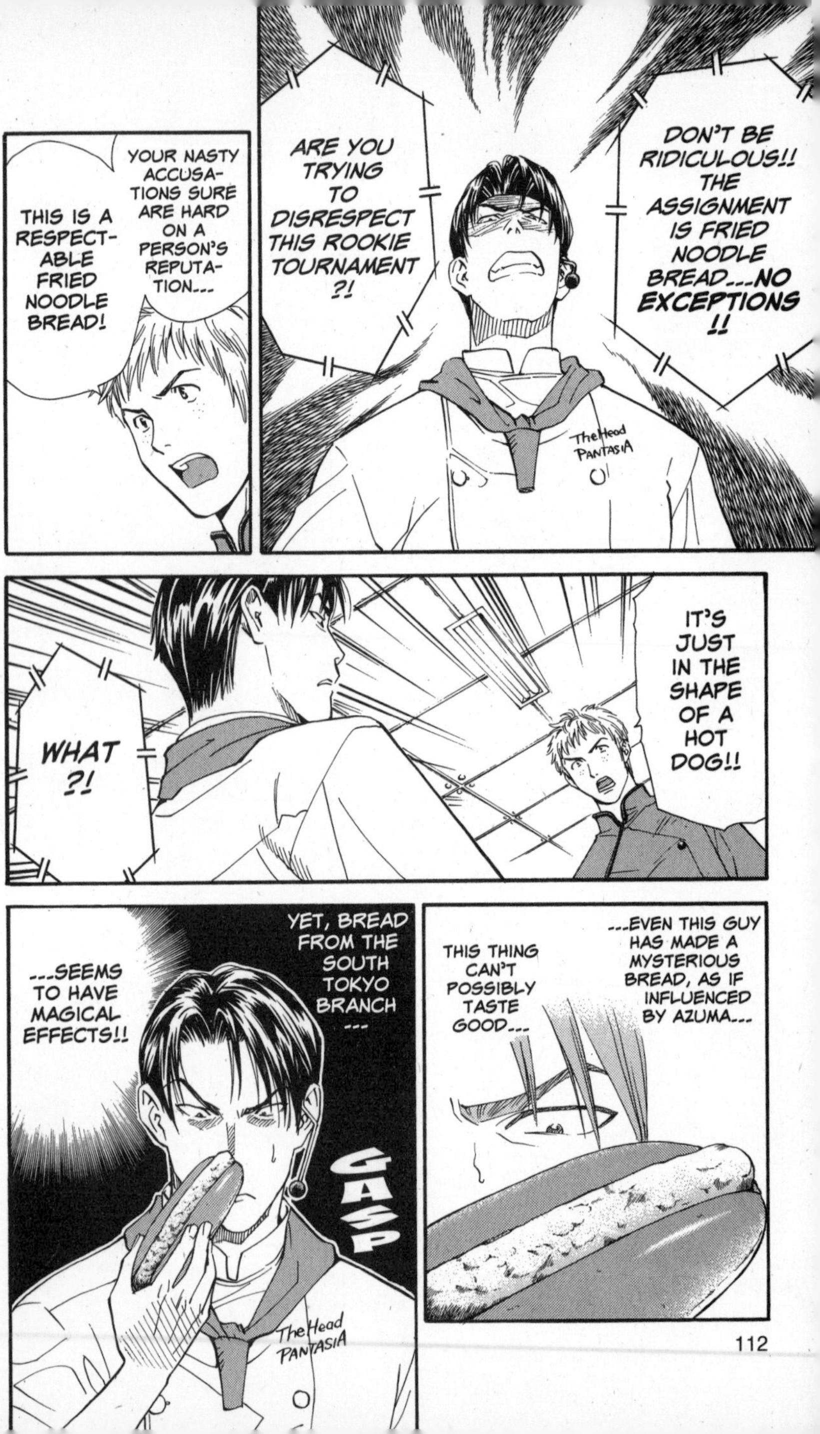

ARE YOU TRYING TO DISRESPECT THIS ROOKIE TOURNAMENT?!
DON'T BE RIDICULOUS!! THE ASSIGNMENT IS FRIED NOODLE BREAD...NO EXCEPTIONS!!
The Head PANTASIA
YOUR NASTY ACCUSATIONS SURE ARE HARD ON A PERSON'S REPUTATION...
THIS IS A RESPECTABLE FRIED NOODLE BREAD!
IT'S JUST IN THE SHAPE OF A HOT DOG!!
WHAT?!
...EVEN THIS GUY HAS MADE A MYSTERIOUS BREAD, AS IF INFLUENCED BY AZUMA...
THIS THING CAN'T POSSIBLY TASTE GOOD...
YET, BREAD FROM THE SOUTH TOKYO BRANCH...
GASP
...SEEMS TO HAVE MAGICAL EFFECTS!!
The Head PANTASIA

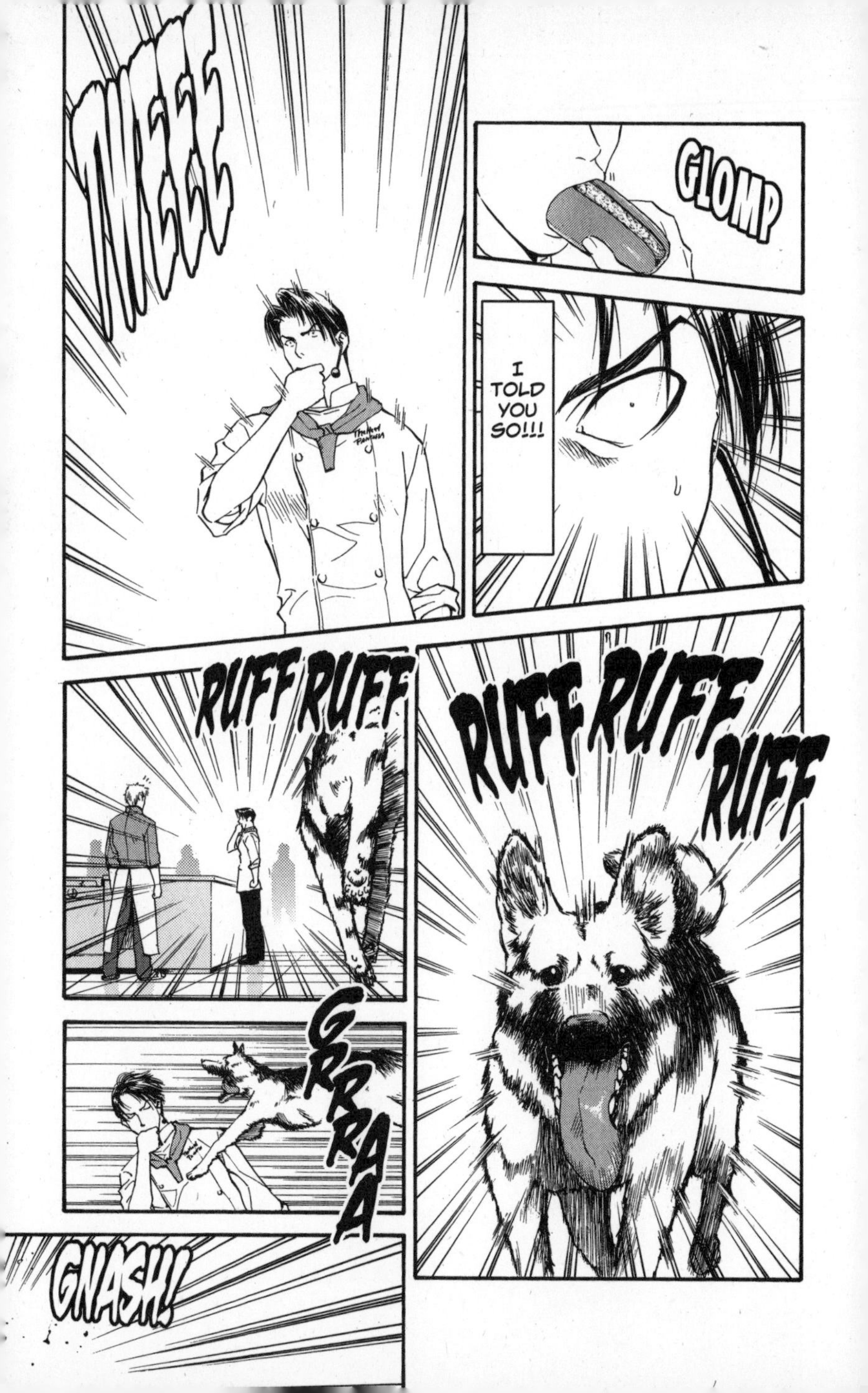

GLOMP
I TOLD YOU SO!!!
TWEEE
RUFF RUFF RUFF RUFF
RUFF RUFF
GRRAA
GNASH!

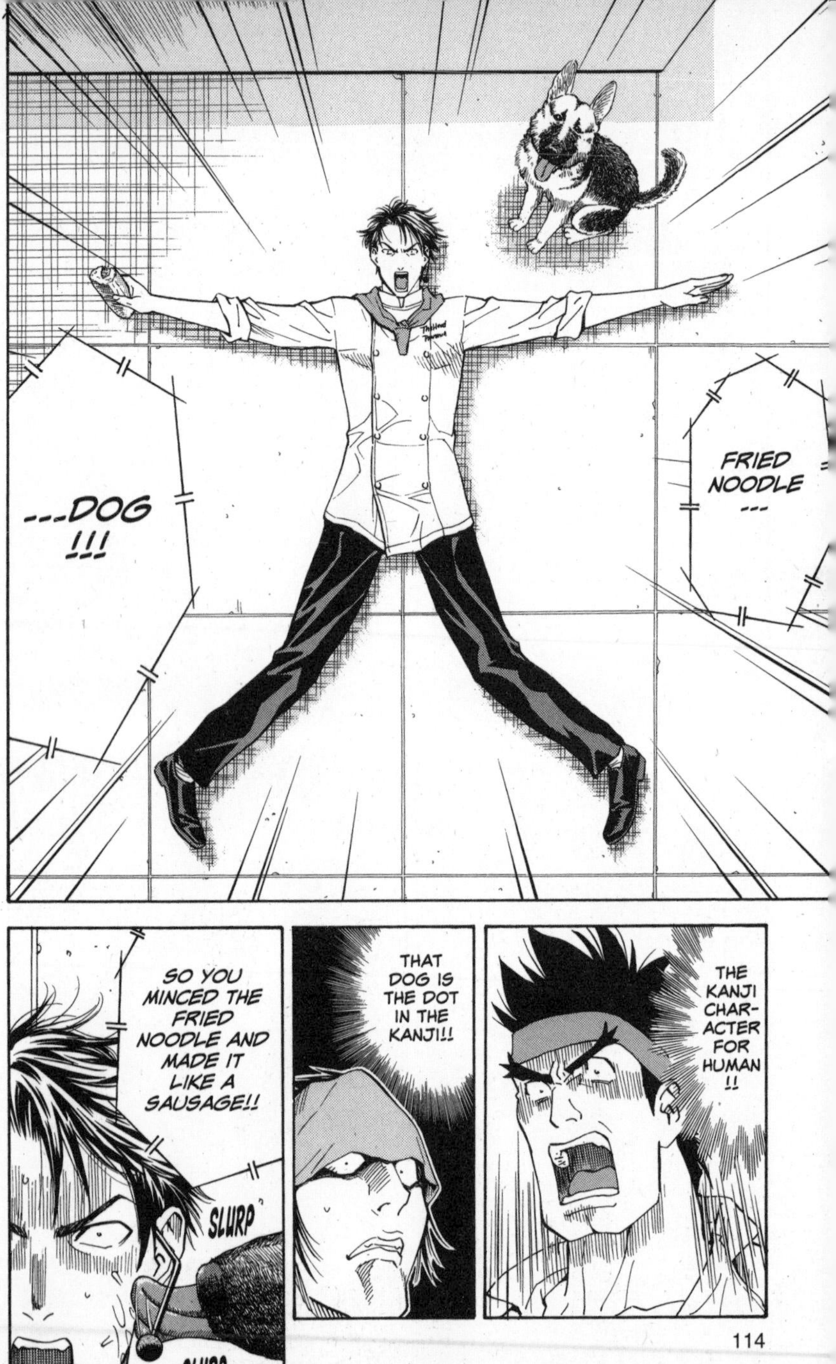
FRIED NOODLE ---
---DOG !!!
THE KANJI CHAR-ACTER FOR HUMAN !!
THAT DOG IS THE DOT IN THE KANJI!!
SO YOU MINCED THE FRIED NOODLE AND MADE IT LIKE A SAUSAGE!!
SLURP
SLURP

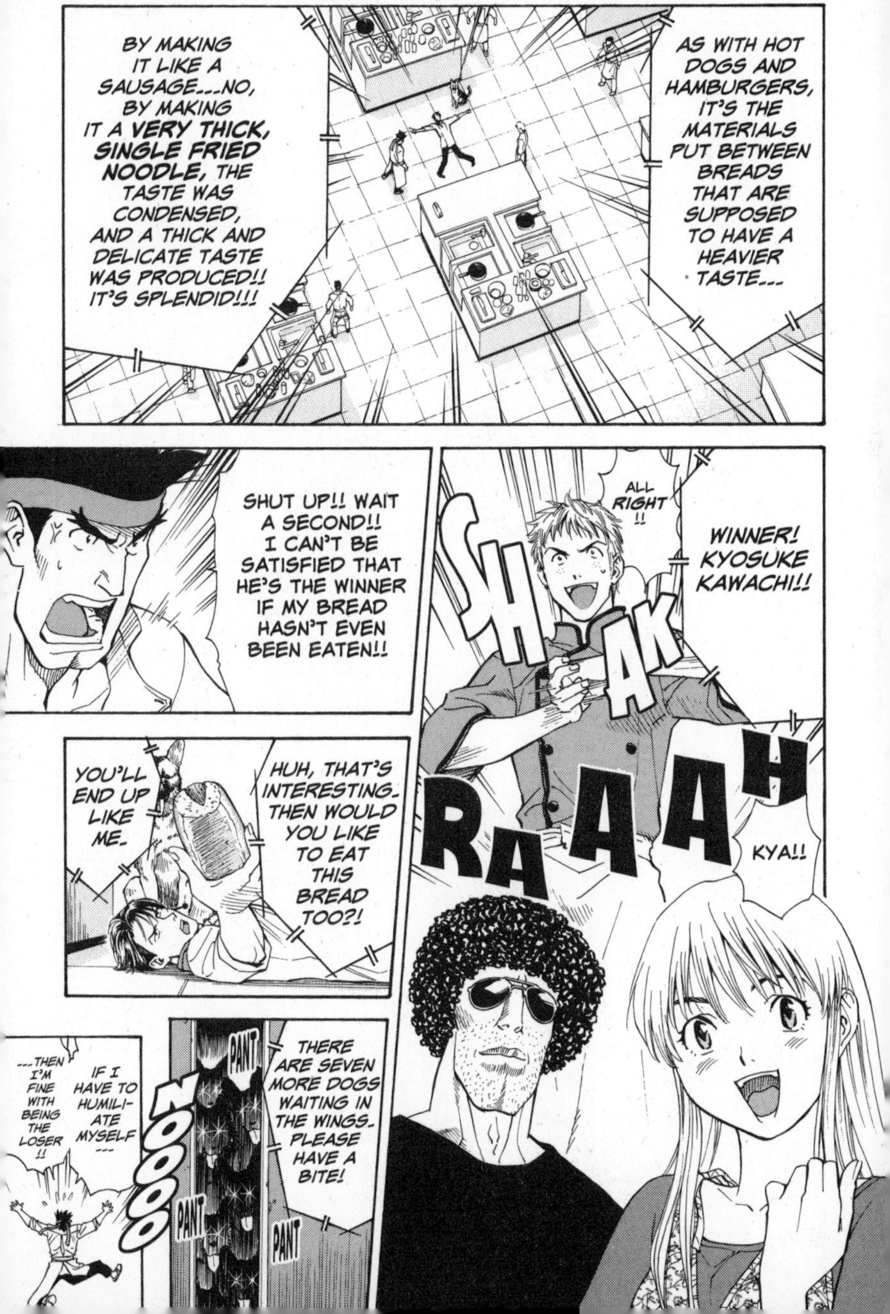
AS WITH HOT DOGS AND HAMBURGERS, IT'S THE MATERIALS PUT BETWEEN BREADS THAT ARE SUPPOSED TO HAVE A HEAVIER TASTE...
BY MAKING IT LIKE A SAUSAGE...NO, BY MAKING IT A **VERY THICK, SINGLE FRIED NOODLE,** THE TASTE WAS CONDENSED, AND A THICK AND DELICATE TASTE WAS PRODUCED!! IT'S SPLENDID!!!
WINNER! KYOSUKE KAWACHI!!
ALL RIGHT!!
SHAAK
RAAAH
KYA!!
SHUT UP!! WAIT A SECOND!! I CAN'T BE SATISFIED THAT HE'S THE WINNER IF MY BREAD HASN'T EVEN BEEN EATEN!!
HUH, THAT'S INTERESTING. THEN WOULD YOU LIKE TO EAT THIS BREAD TOO?!
YOU'LL END UP LIKE ME.
THERE ARE SEVEN MORE DOGS WAITING IN THE WINGS. PLEASE HAVE A BITE!
PANT
PANT
PANT
NOOOOO
IF I HAVE TO HUMILI-ATE MYSELF...
...THEN I'M FINE WITH BEING THE LOSER!!

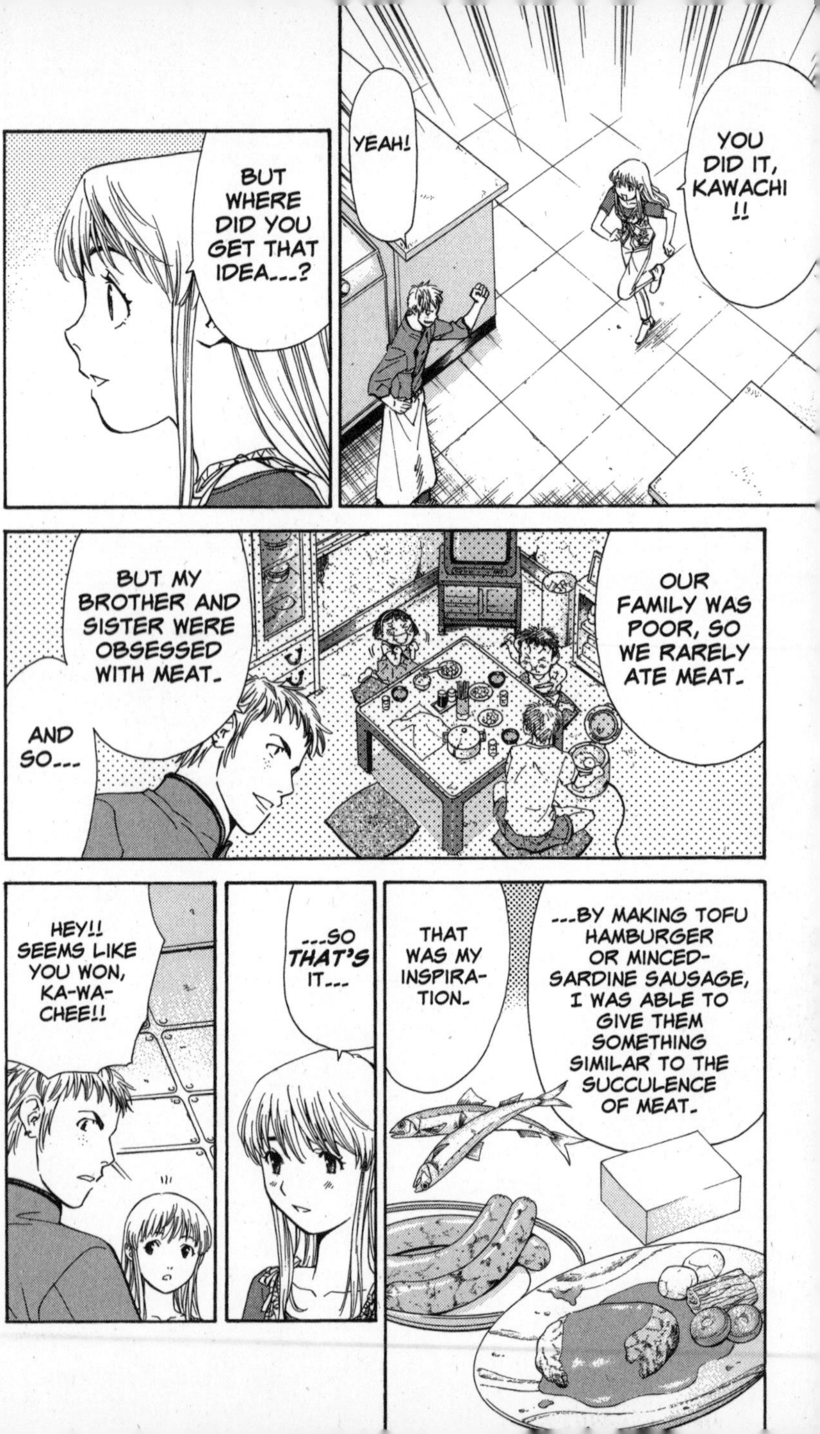
YOU DID IT, KAWACHI!!
YEAH!
BUT WHERE DID YOU GET THAT IDEA...?
OUR FAMILY WAS POOR, SO WE RARELY ATE MEAT.
BUT MY BROTHER AND SISTER WERE OBSESSED WITH MEAT.
AND SO...
...BY MAKING TOFU HAMBURGER OR MINCED-SARDINE SAUSAGE, I WAS ABLE TO GIVE THEM SOMETHING SIMILAR TO THE SUCCULENCE OF MEAT.
THAT WAS MY INSPIRA-TION.
...SO *THAT'S* IT...
HEY!! SEEMS LIKE YOU WON, KA-WA-CHEE!!

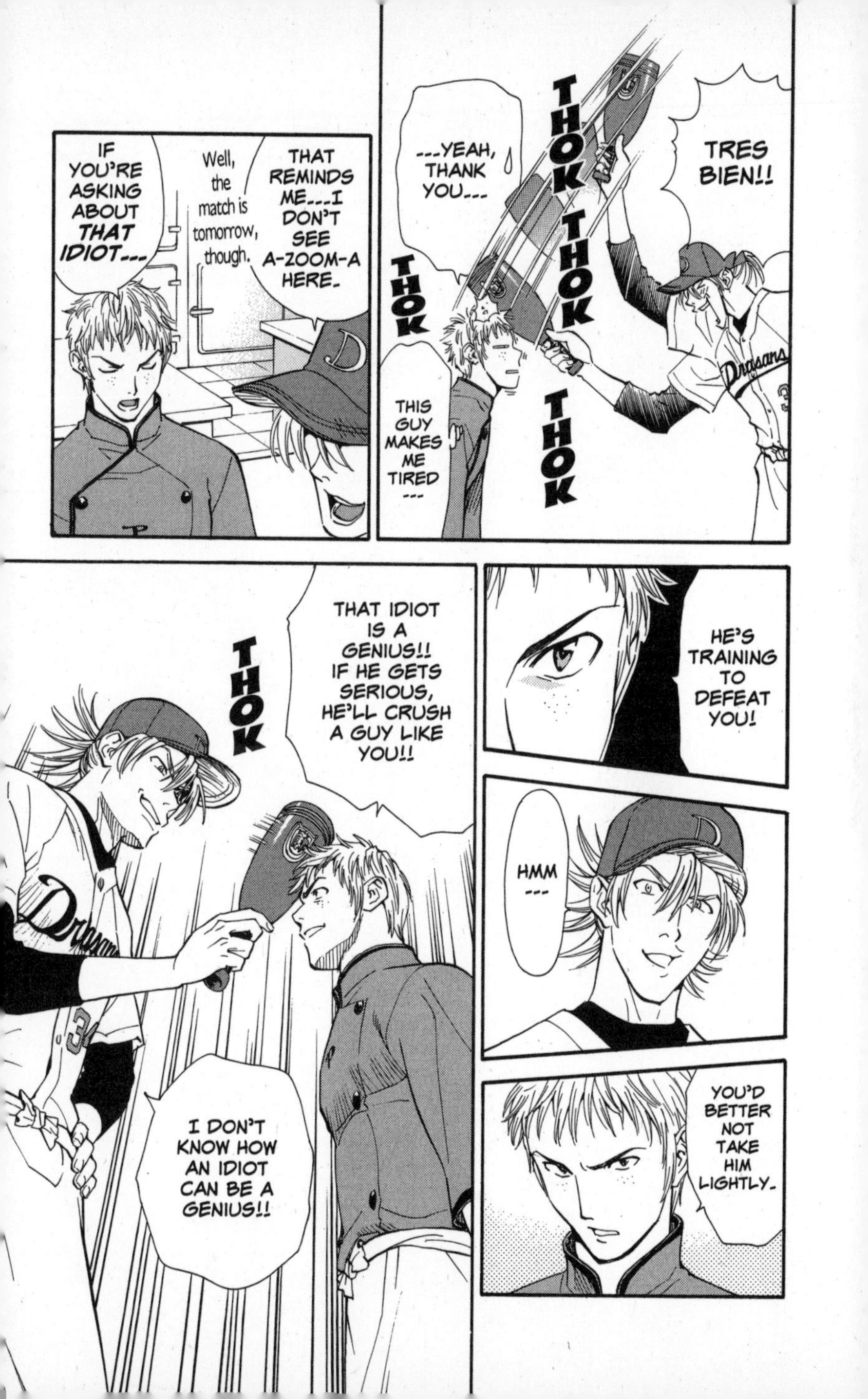
TRES BIEN!!
THOK THOK THOK
...YEAH, THANK YOU...
THOK
THIS GUY MAKES ME TIRED ...
THOK
THAT REMINDS ME...I DON'T SEE A-ZOOM-A HERE.
Well, the match is tomorrow, though.
IF YOU'RE ASKING ABOUT *THAT IDIOT*...
HE'S TRAINING TO DEFEAT YOU!
HMM ...
YOU'D BETTER NOT TAKE HIM LIGHTLY.
THOK
THAT IDIOT IS A GENIUS!! IF HE GETS SERIOUS, HE'LL CRUSH A GUY LIKE YOU!!
I DON'T KNOW HOW AN IDIOT CAN BE A GENIUS!!

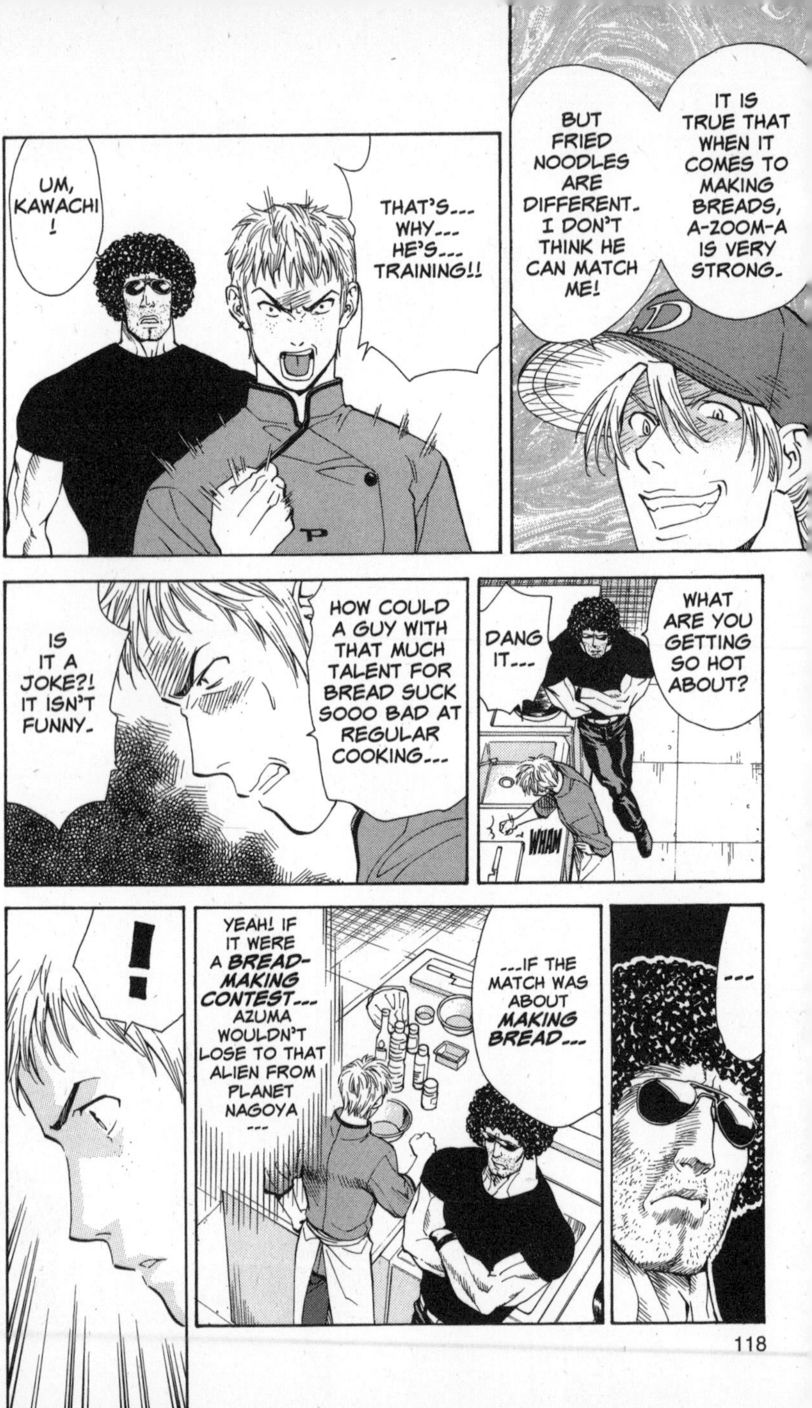
IT IS TRUE THAT WHEN IT COMES TO MAKING BREADS, A-ZOOM-A IS VERY STRONG.
BUT FRIED NOODLES ARE DIFFERENT. I DON'T THINK HE CAN MATCH ME!
THAT'S... WHY... HE'S... TRAINING!!
UM, KAWACHI!
WHAT ARE YOU GETTING SO HOT ABOUT?
DANG IT...
WHAM
HOW COULD A GUY WITH THAT MUCH TALENT FOR BREAD SUCK SOOO BAD AT REGULAR COOKING...
IS IT A JOKE?! IT ISN'T FUNNY.
...
...IF THE MATCH WAS ABOUT *MAKING BREAD*...
YEAH! IF IT WERE A ***BREAD-MAKING CONTEST***... AZUMA WOULDN'T LOSE TO THAT ALIEN FROM PLANET NAGOYA ...
!

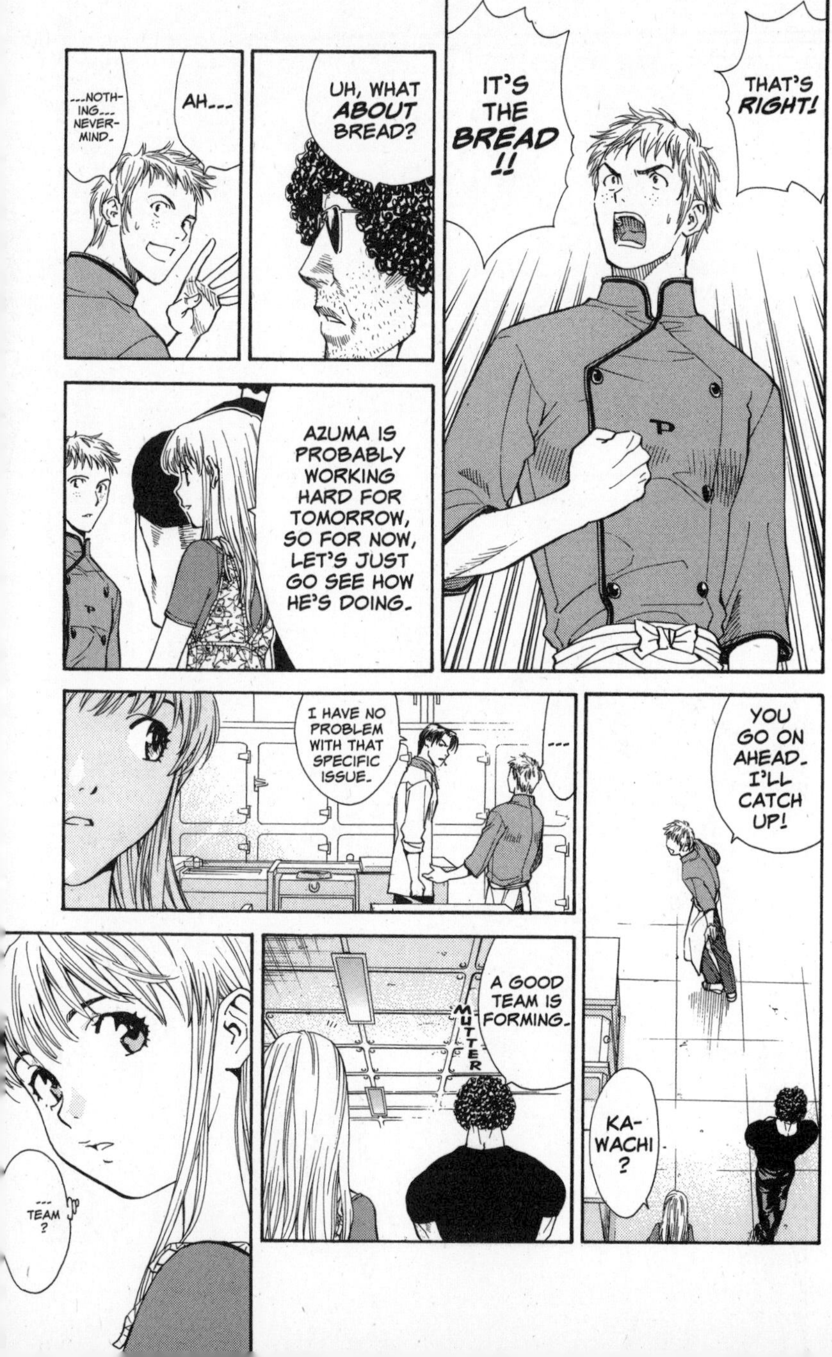
THAT'S RIGHT!
IT'S THE BREAD!!
UH, WHAT ABOUT BREAD?
AH...
...NOTHING... NEVERMIND.
AZUMA IS PROBABLY WORKING HARD FOR TOMORROW, SO FOR NOW, LET'S JUST GO SEE HOW HE'S DOING.
YOU GO ON AHEAD. I'LL CATCH UP!
KA-WACHI?
...
I HAVE NO PROBLEM WITH THAT SPECIFIC ISSUE.
A GOOD TEAM IS FORMING.
MUTTER
...TEAM?

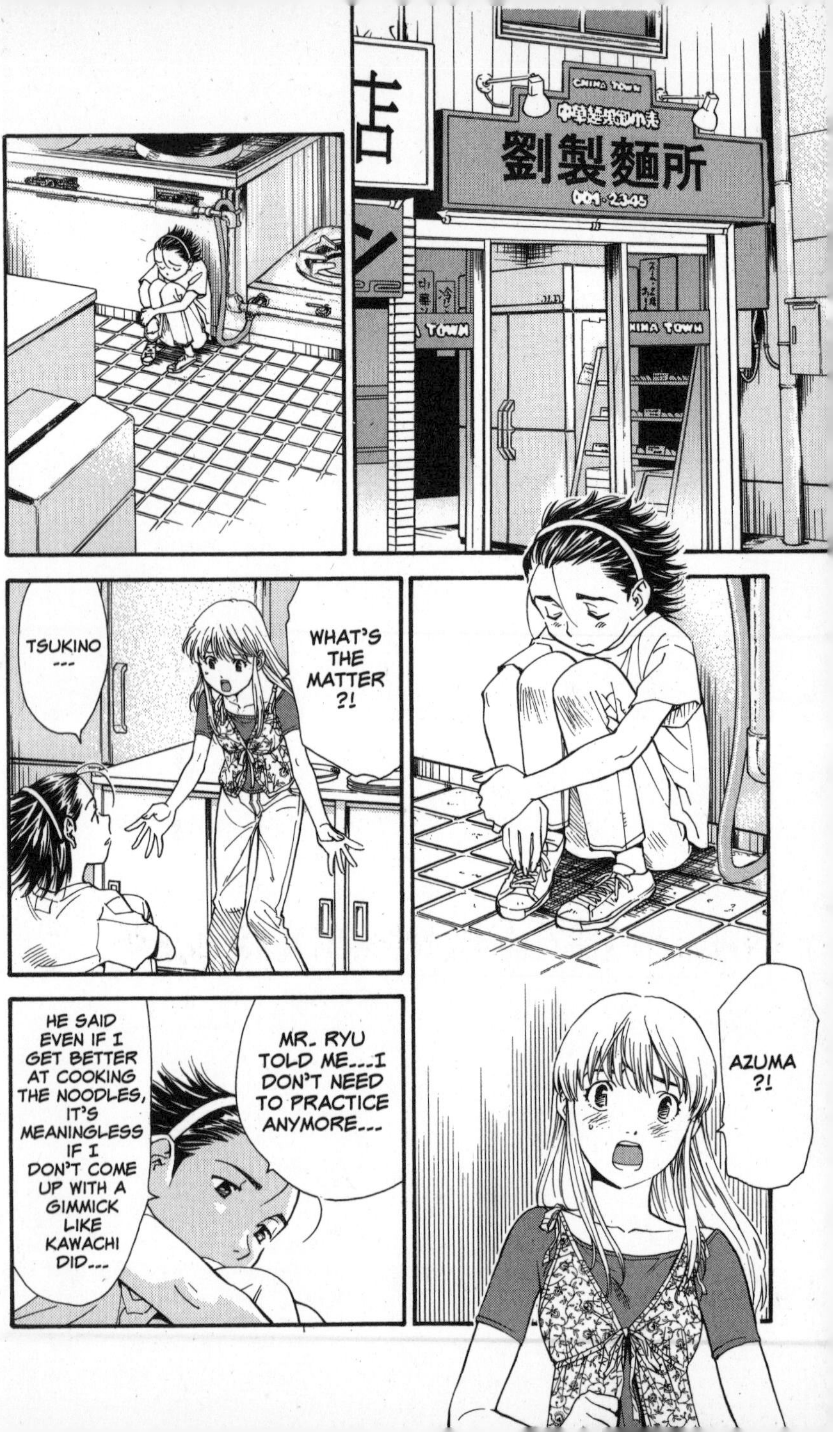
CHINA TOWN
劉製麺所
001-2345
WHAT'S THE MATTER ?!
TSUKINO ---
AZUMA ?!
MR. RYU TOLD ME...I DON'T NEED TO PRACTICE ANYMORE...
HE SAID EVEN IF I GET BETTER AT COOKING THE NOODLES, IT'S MEANINGLESS IF I DON'T COME UP WITH A GIMMICK LIKE KAWACHI DID...

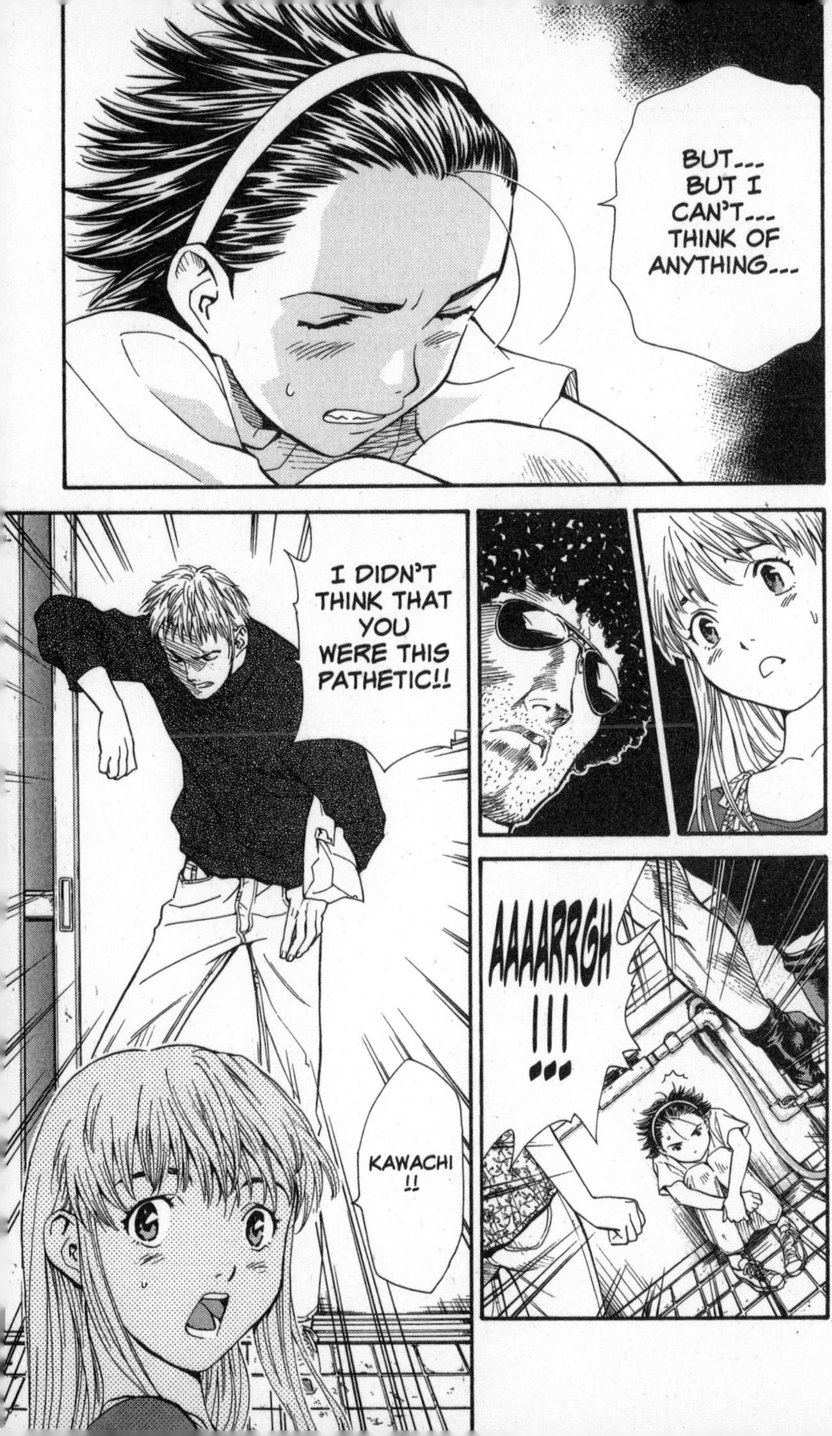
BUT... BUT I CAN'T... THINK OF ANYTHING...
AAAARRGH!!!...
I DIDN'T THINK THAT YOU WERE THIS PATHETIC!!
KAWACHI!!

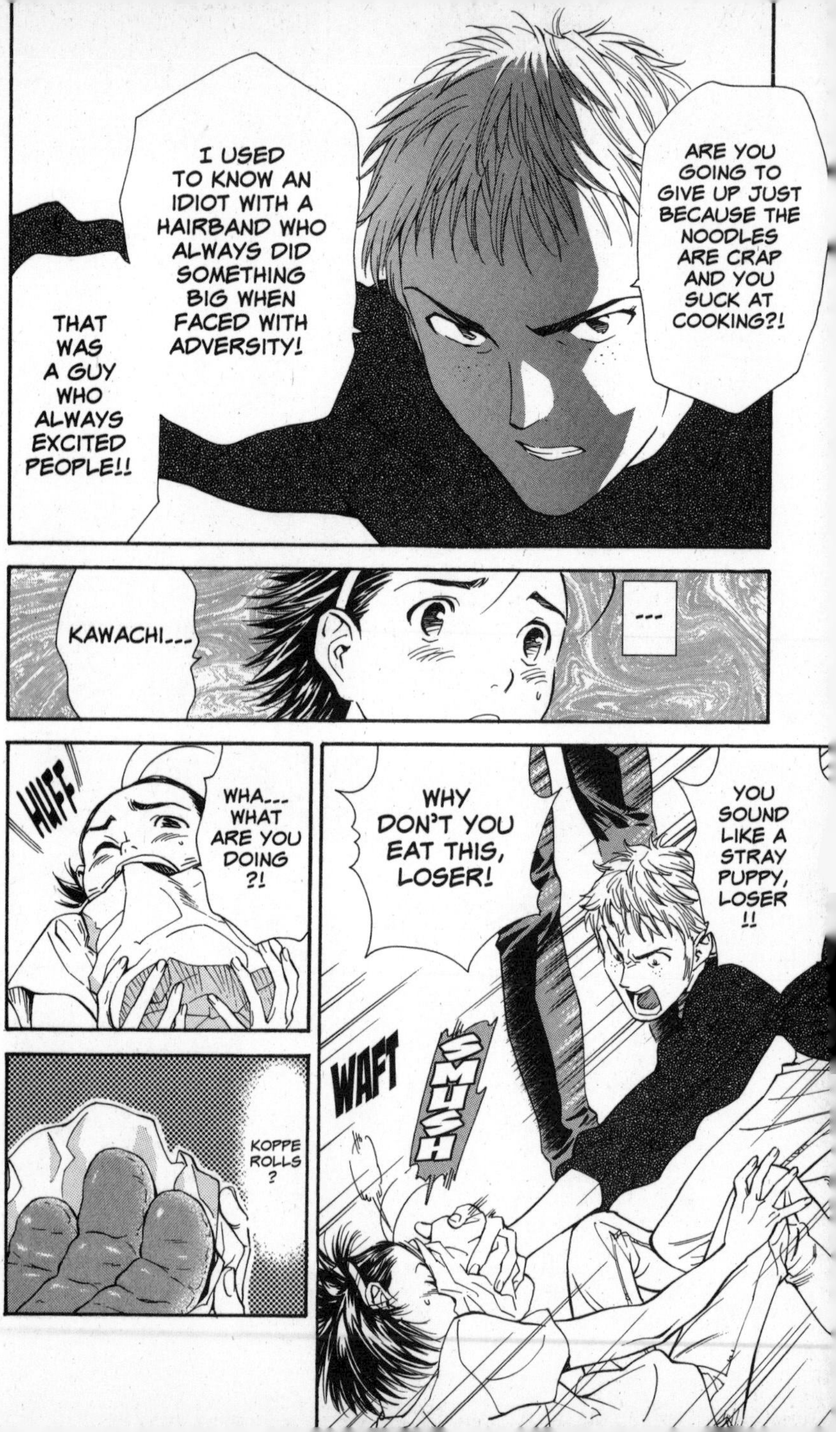
ARE YOU GOING TO GIVE UP JUST BECAUSE THE NOODLES ARE CRAP AND YOU SUCK AT COOKING?!
I USED TO KNOW AN IDIOT WITH A HAIRBAND WHO ALWAYS DID SOMETHING BIG WHEN FACED WITH ADVERSITY!
THAT WAS A GUY WHO ALWAYS EXCITED PEOPLE!!
...
KAWACHI...
YOU SOUND LIKE A STRAY PUPPY, LOSER !!
WHY DON'T YOU EAT THIS, LOSER!
SMUSH
WAFT
HUFF
WHA... WHAT ARE YOU DOING ?!
KOPPE ROLLS ?

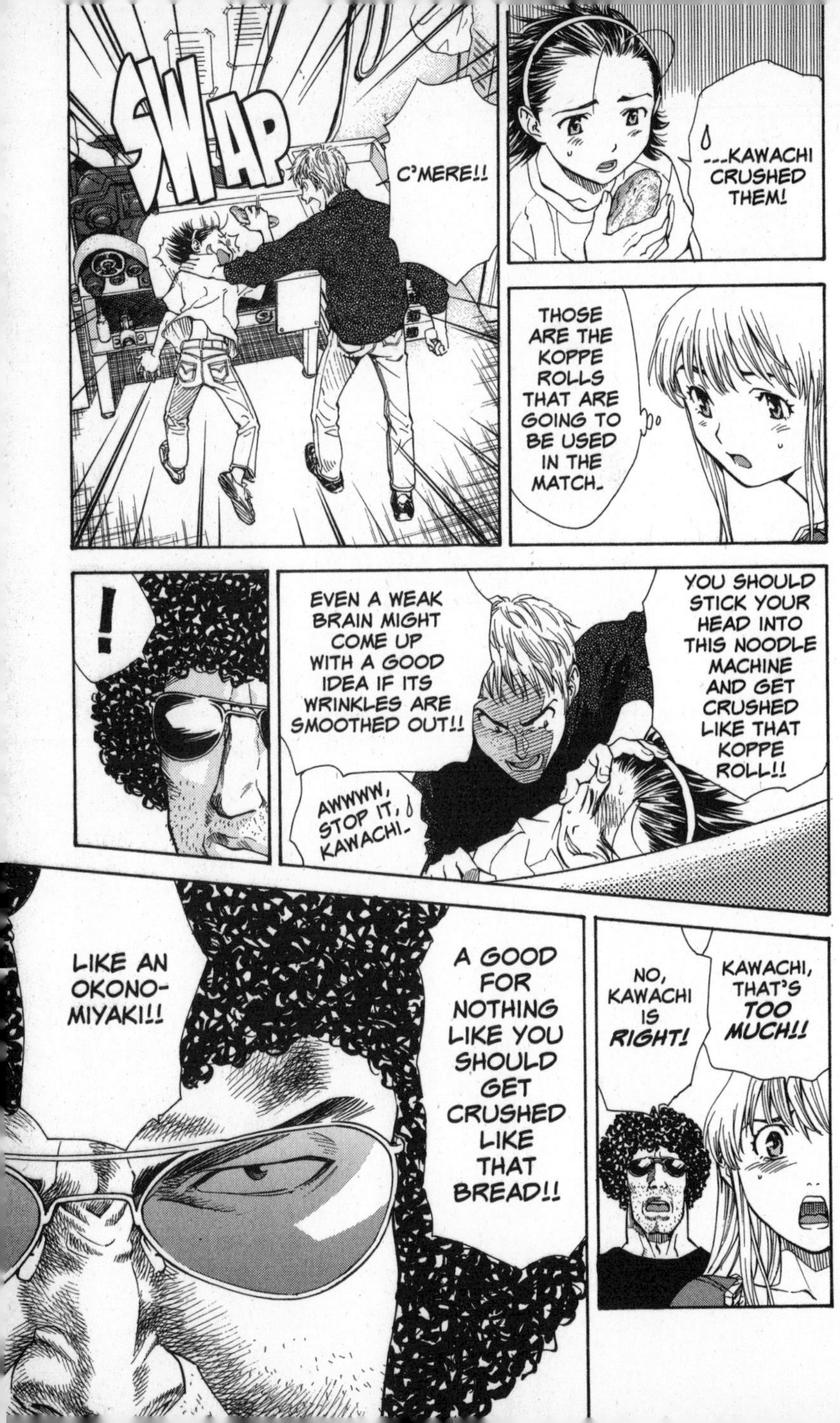
...KAWACHI CRUSHED THEM!
THOSE ARE THE KOPPE ROLLS THAT ARE GOING TO BE USED IN THE MATCH.
SWAP
C'MERE!!
YOU SHOULD STICK YOUR HEAD INTO THIS NOODLE MACHINE AND GET CRUSHED LIKE THAT KOPPE ROLL!!
EVEN A WEAK BRAIN MIGHT COME UP WITH A GOOD IDEA IF ITS WRINKLES ARE SMOOTHED OUT!!
AWWWW, STOP IT, KAWACHI.
!
KAWACHI, THAT'S *TOO MUCH!!*
NO, KAWACHI IS *RIGHT!*
A GOOD FOR NOTHING LIKE YOU SHOULD GET CRUSHED LIKE THAT BREAD!!
LIKE AN OKONO-MIYAKI!!

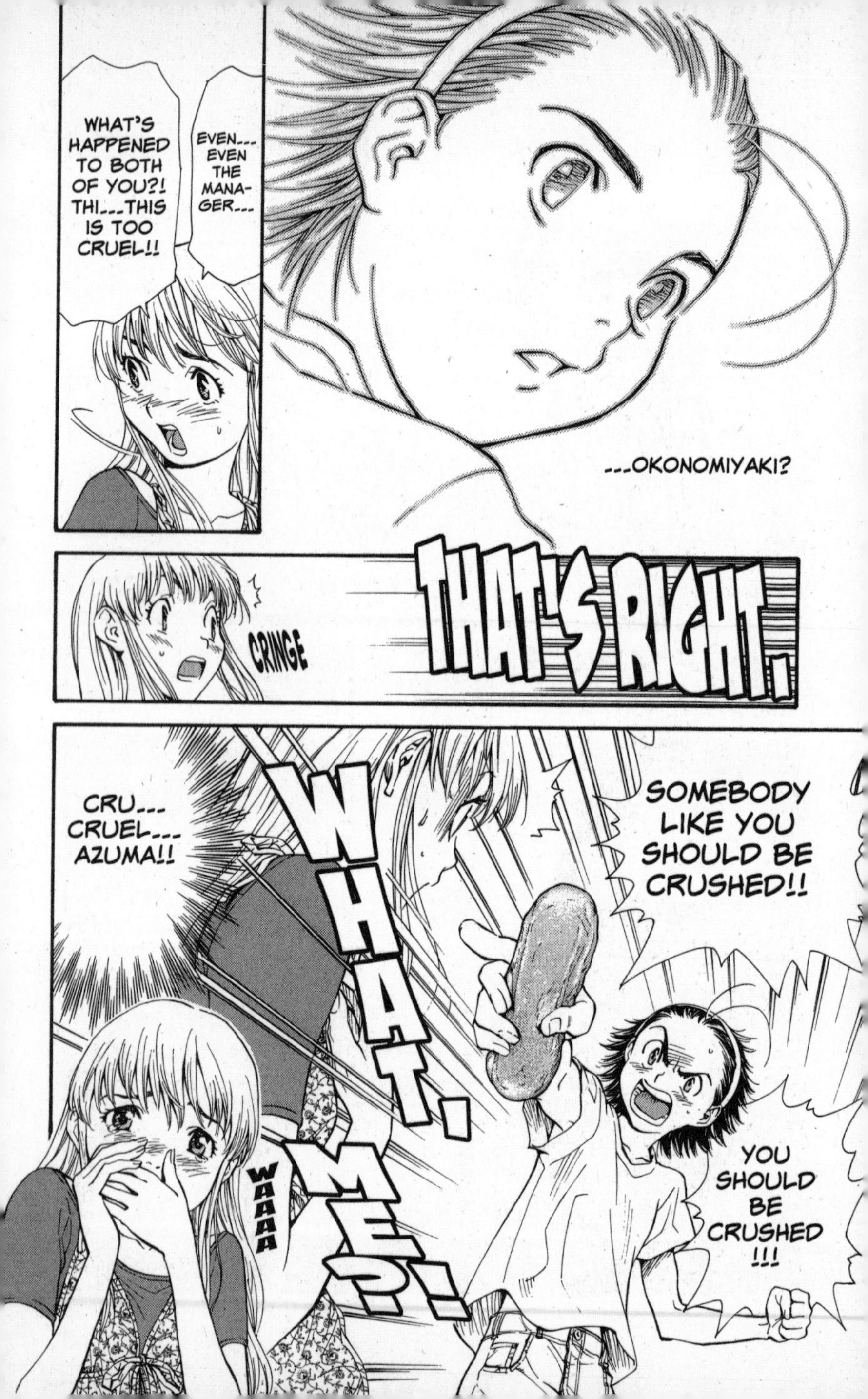
...OKONOMIYAKI?
EVEN... EVEN THE MANAGER...
WHAT'S HAPPENED TO BOTH OF YOU?! THI...THIS IS TOO CRUEL!!
THAT'S RIGHT.
CRINGE
SOMEBODY LIKE YOU SHOULD BE CRUSHED!!
YOU SHOULD BE CRUSHED!!!
WHAT, ME?!
CRU... CRUEL... AZUMA!!
WAAAA

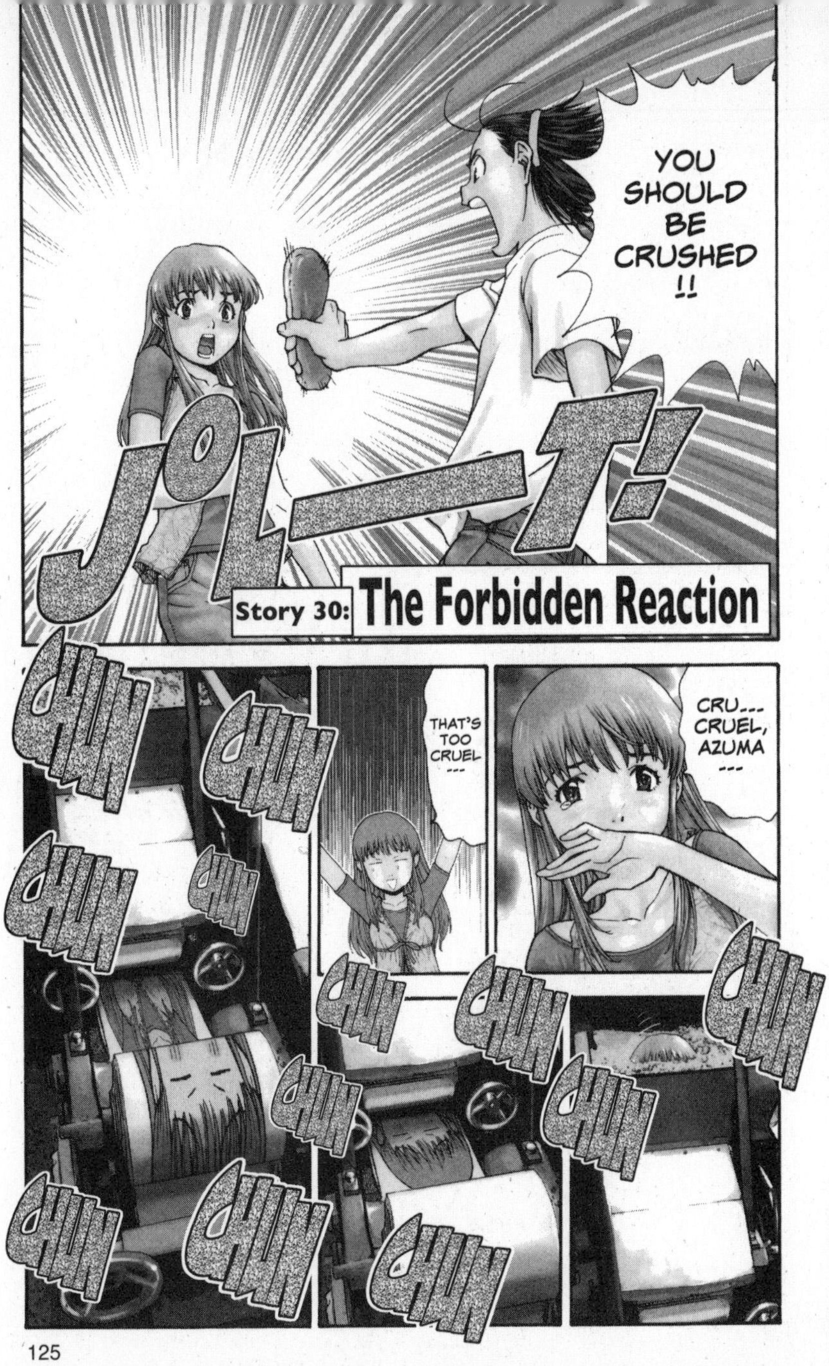
YOU SHOULD BE CRUSHED!!
プレーート!
Story 30: The Forbidden Reaction
CRU... CRUEL, AZUMA...
THAT'S TOO CRUEL...
CHUN
CHUN
CHUN
CHUN
CHUN
CHUN
CHUN
CHUN
CHUN
CHUN
CHUN
CHUN

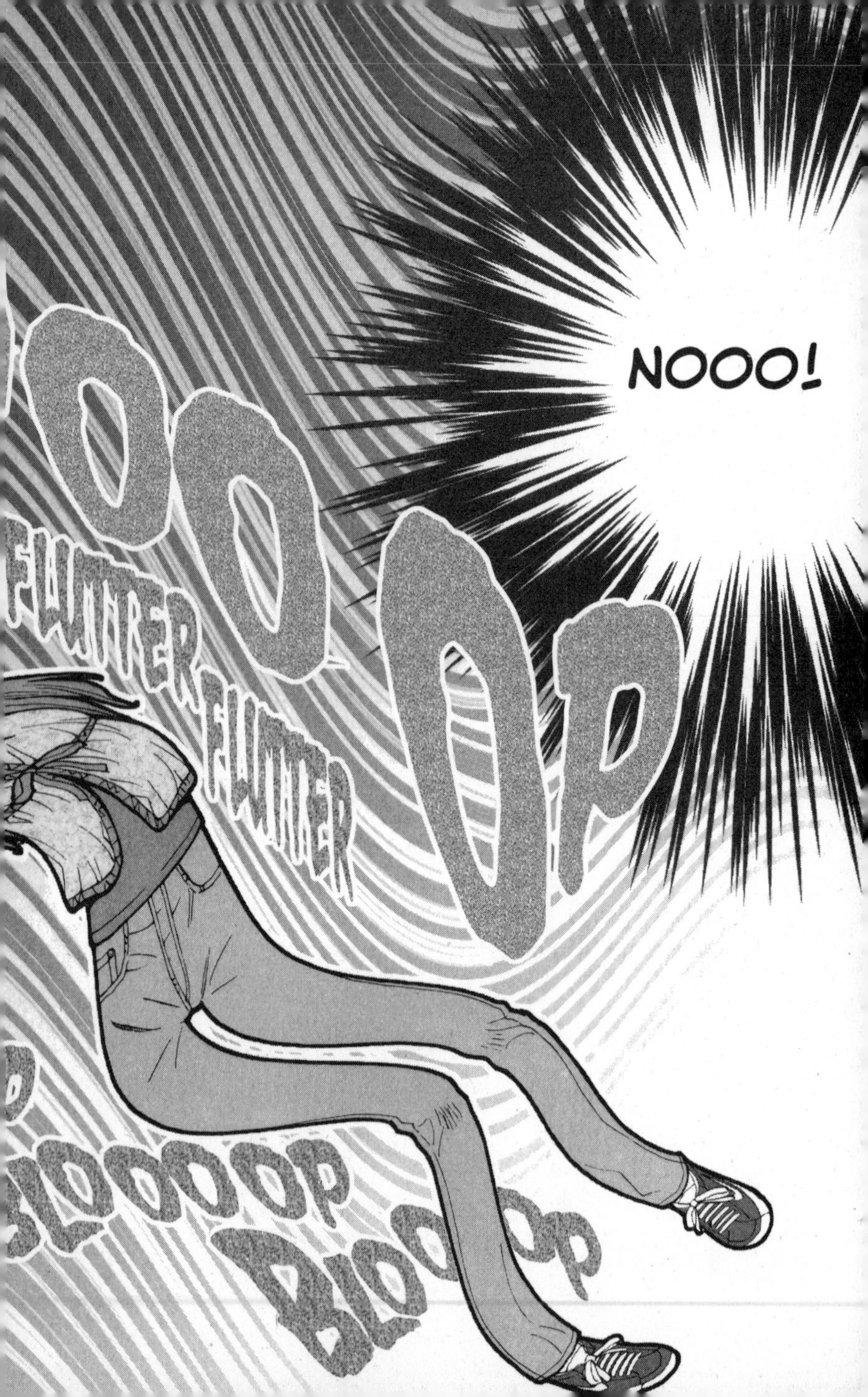
NOOO!
FLUTTER FLUTTER

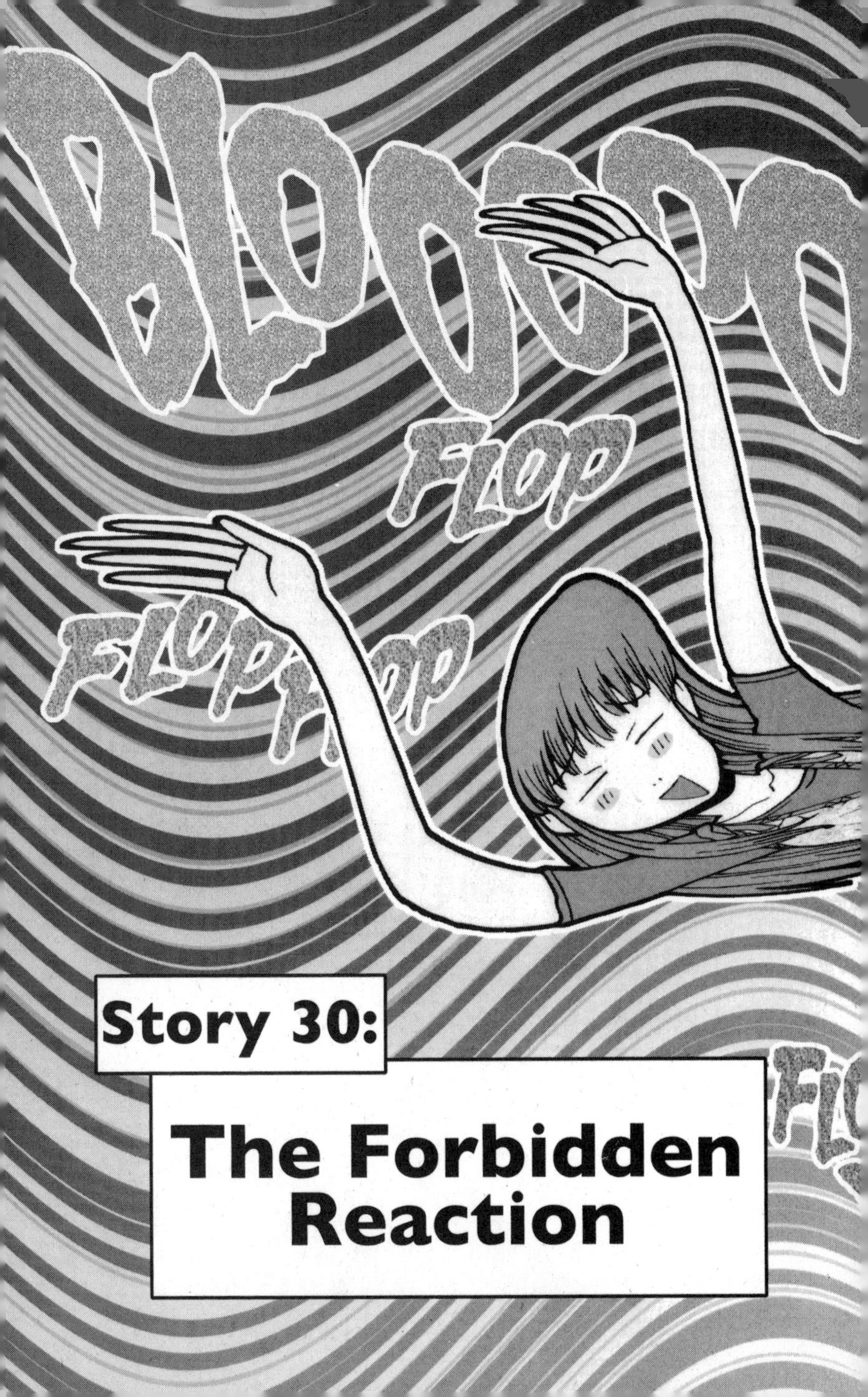
FLOP
FLOP FLOP

Story 30: The Forbidden Reaction

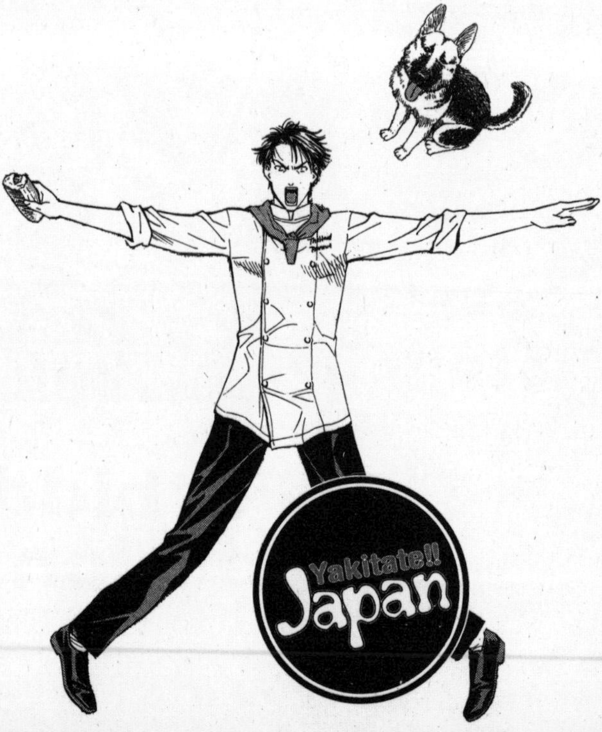
Yakitate!!
Japan

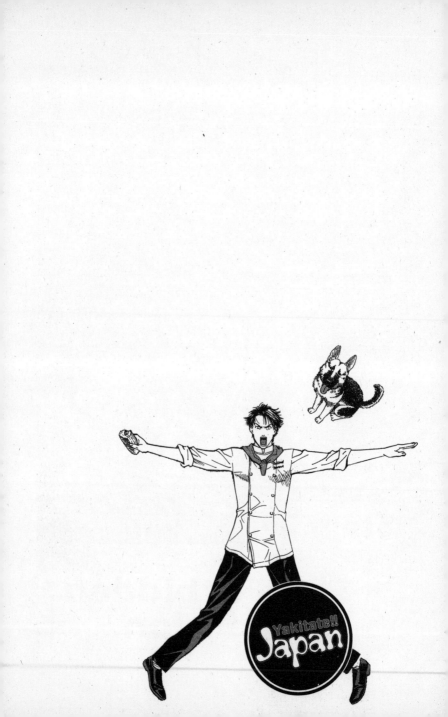

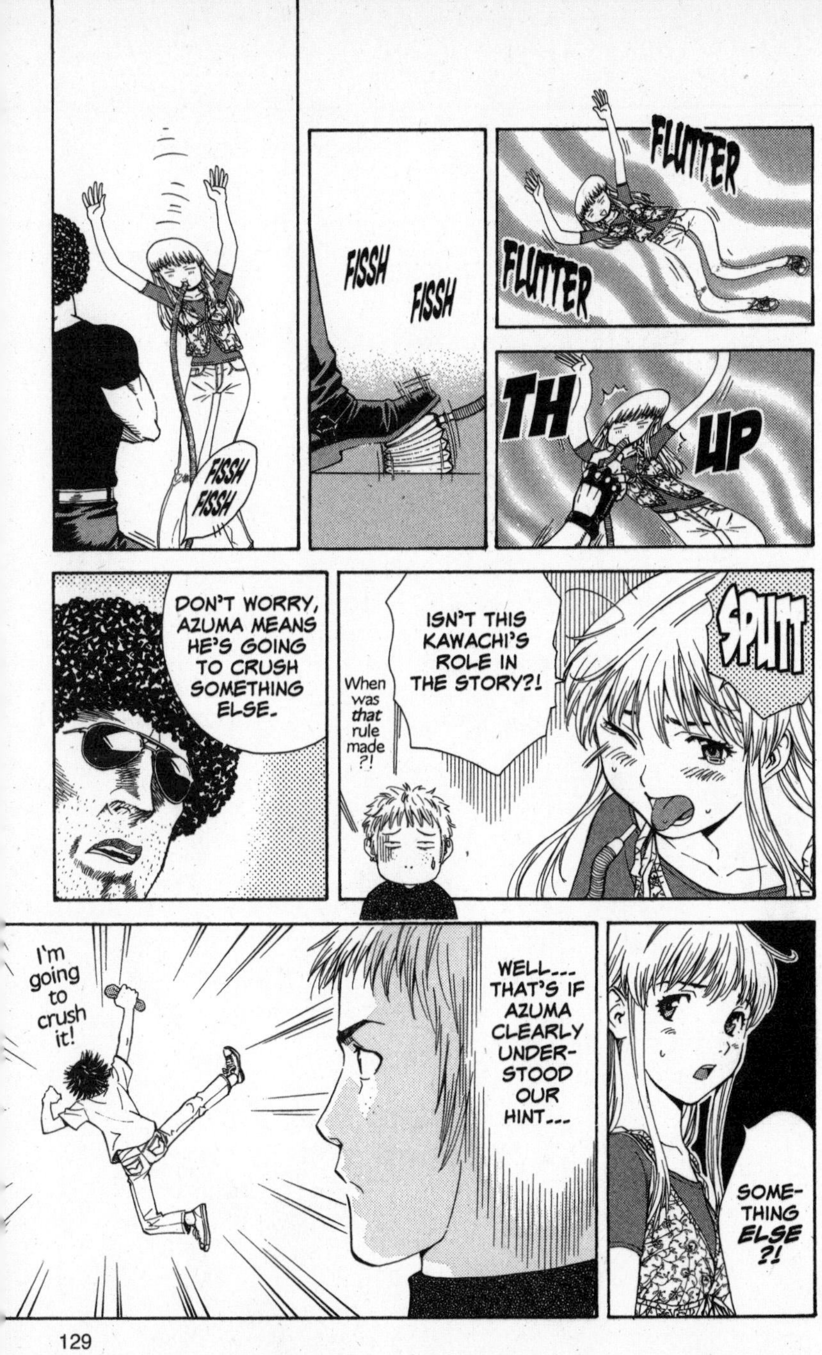
FLUTTER
FLUTTER
TH
UP
FISSH
FISSH
FISSH FISSH
SPUTT
ISN'T THIS KAWACHI'S ROLE IN THE STORY?!
When was *that* rule made?!
DON'T WORRY, AZUMA MEANS HE'S GOING TO CRUSH SOMETHING ELSE.
SOME-THING *ELSE* ?!
WELL... THAT'S IF AZUMA CLEARLY UNDER-STOOD OUR HINT...
I'm going to crush it!

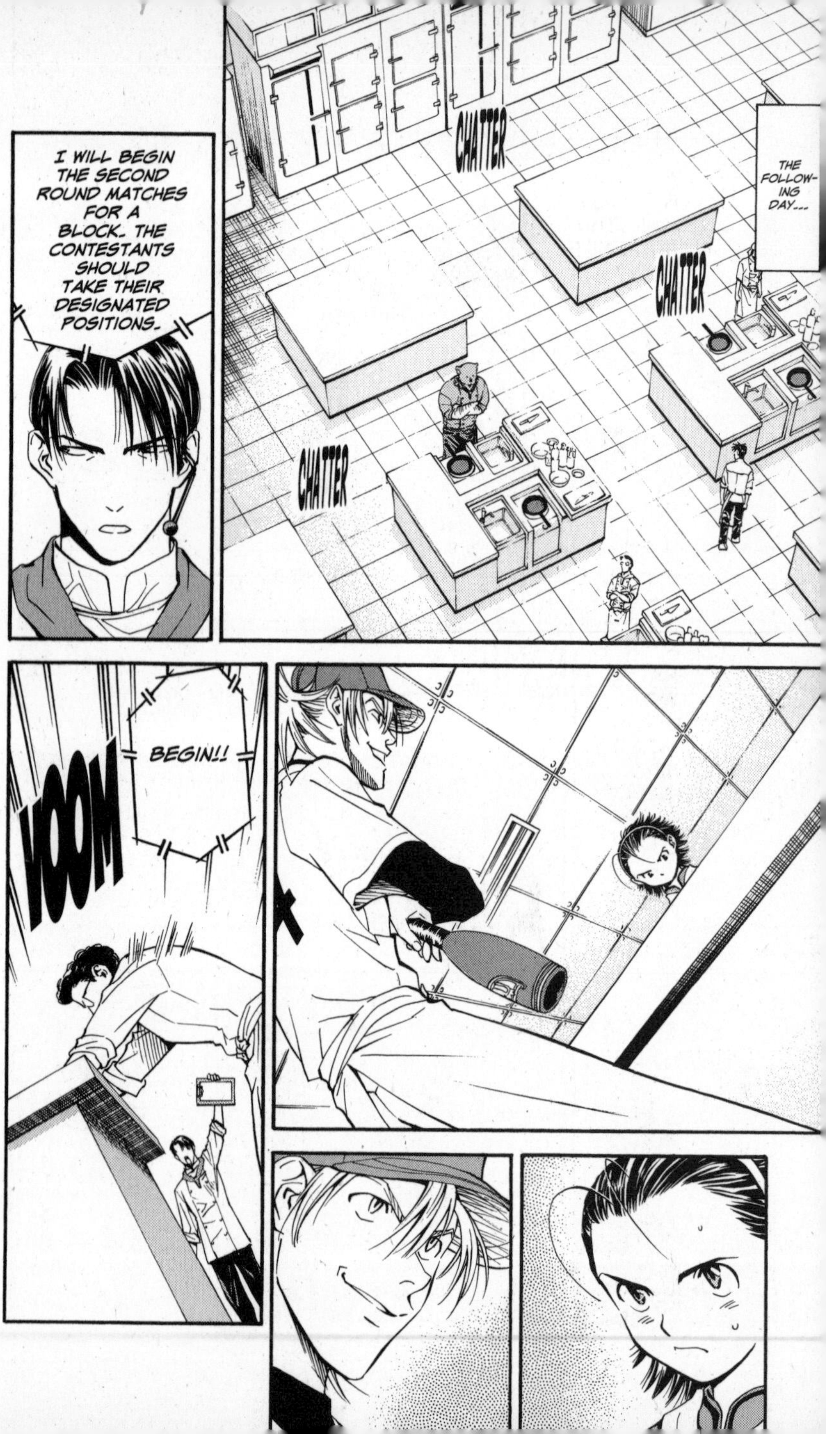
THE FOLLOWING DAY...
CHATTER
CHATTER
CHATTER
I WILL BEGIN THE SECOND ROUND MATCHES FOR A BLOCK. THE CONTESTANTS SHOULD TAKE THEIR DESIGNATED POSITIONS.
BEGIN!!
VOOM

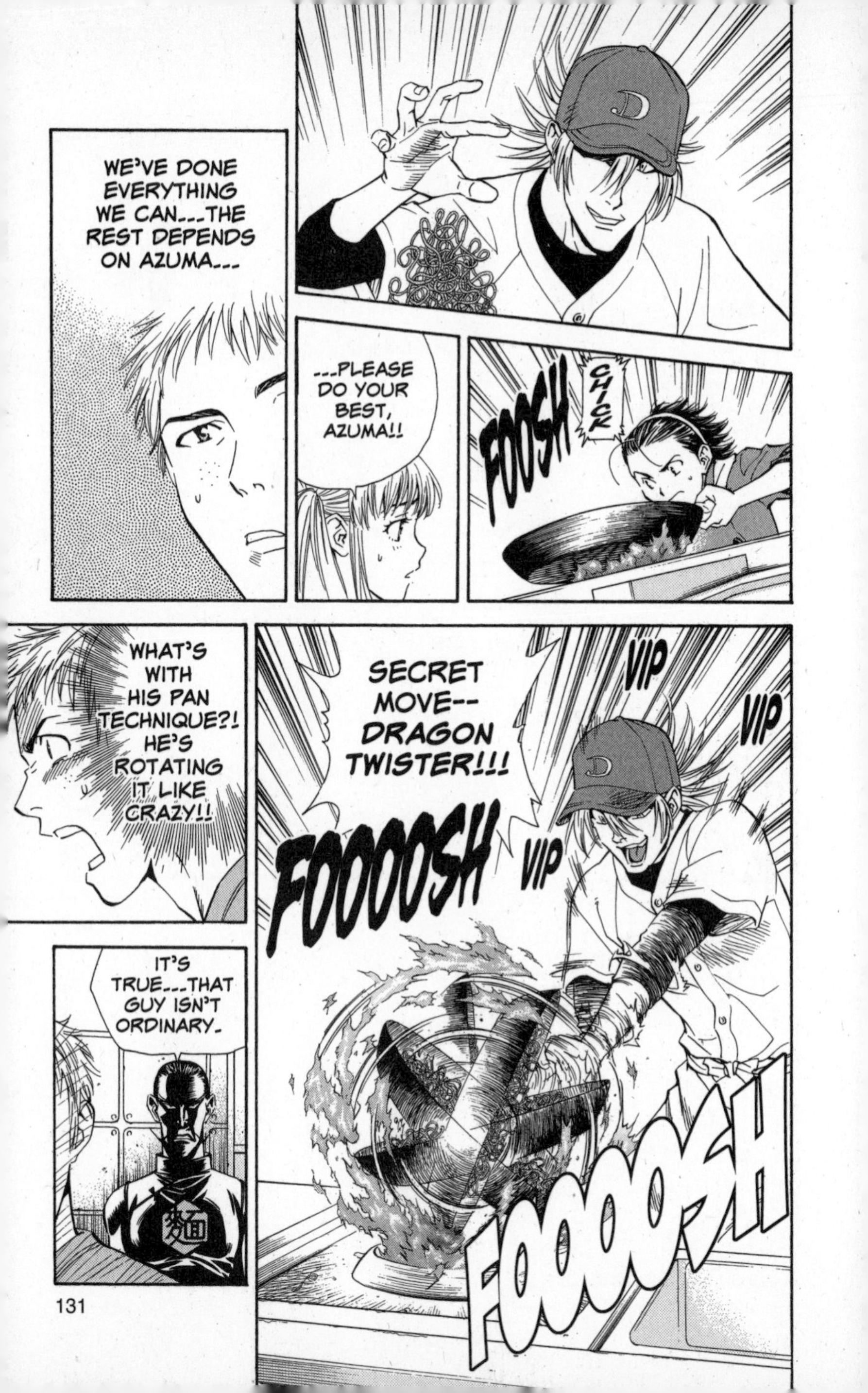
FOOSH
CHICK
...PLEASE DO YOUR BEST, AZUMA!!
WE'VE DONE EVERYTHING WE CAN...THE REST DEPENDS ON AZUMA...
VIP
VIP
SECRET MOVE--DRAGON TWISTER!!!
FOOOOSH
VIP
FOOOOSH
WHAT'S WITH HIS PAN TECHNIQUE?! HE'S ROTATING IT LIKE CRAZY!!
IT'S TRUE...THAT GUY ISN'T ORDINARY.

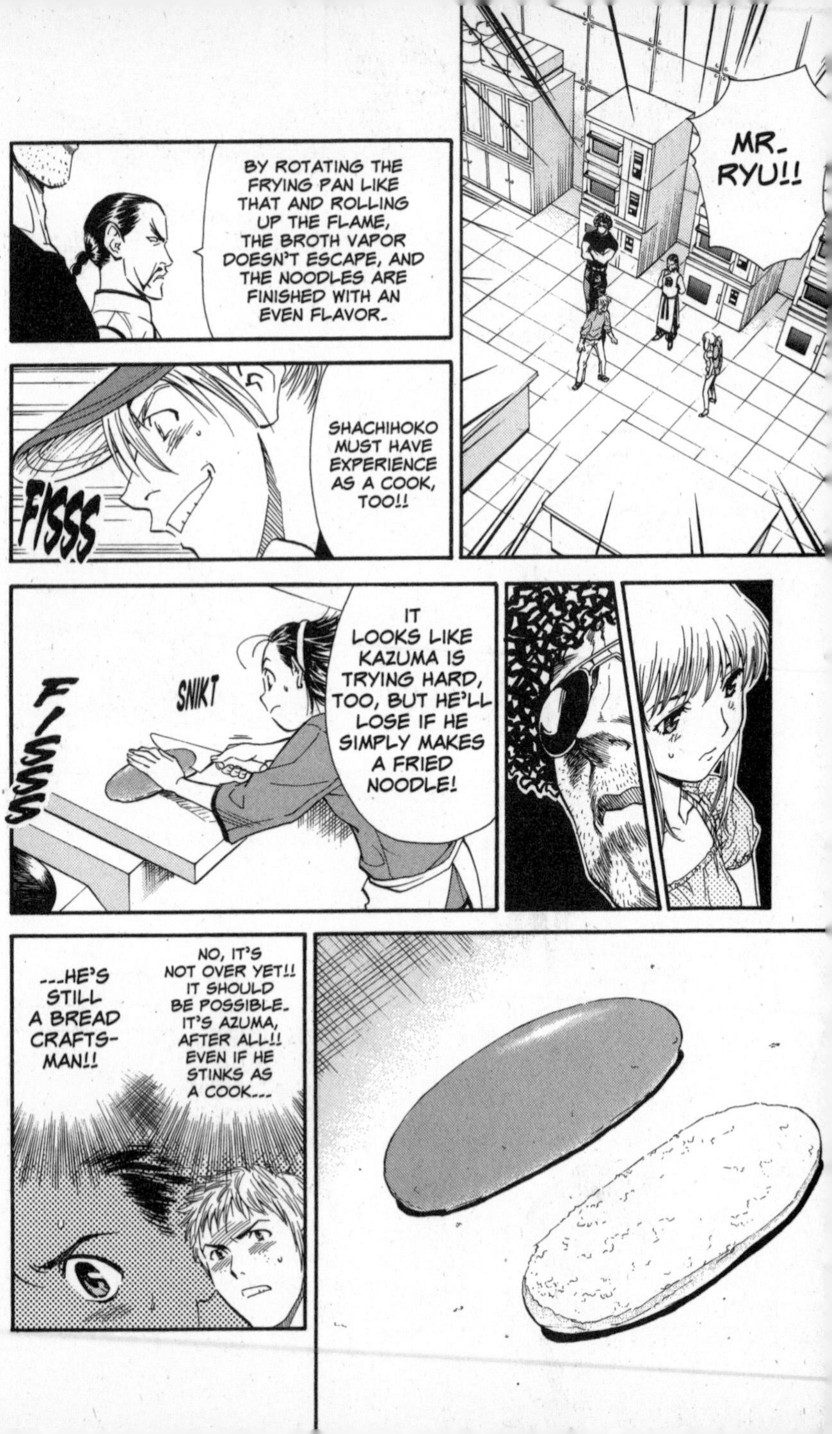
MR. RYU!!
BY ROTATING THE FRYING PAN LIKE THAT AND ROLLING UP THE FLAME, THE BROTH VAPOR DOESN'T ESCAPE, AND THE NOODLES ARE FINISHED WITH AN EVEN FLAVOR.
SHACHIHOKO MUST HAVE EXPERIENCE AS A COOK, TOO!!
FISSS
IT LOOKS LIKE KAZUMA IS TRYING HARD, TOO, BUT HE'LL LOSE IF HE SIMPLY MAKES A FRIED NOODLE!
SNIKT
FISSSS
NO, IT'S NOT OVER YET!! IT SHOULD BE POSSIBLE. IT'S AZUMA, AFTER ALL!! EVEN IF HE STINKS AS A COOK...
...HE'S STILL A BREAD CRAFTS-MAN!!

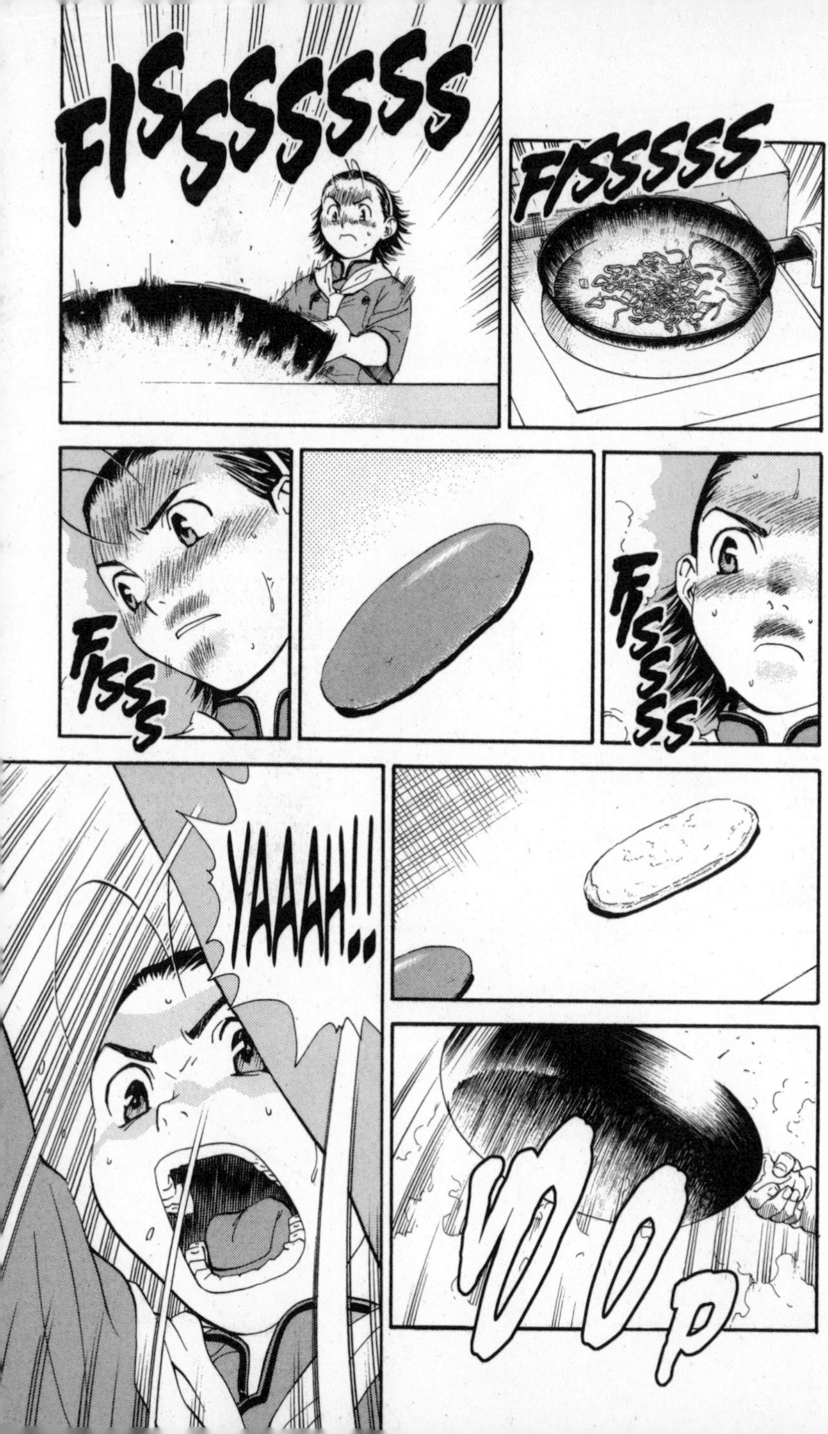
FISSSSS
FISSSSSSS
FISSSSS
FISSS
WOOP
YAAAH!!

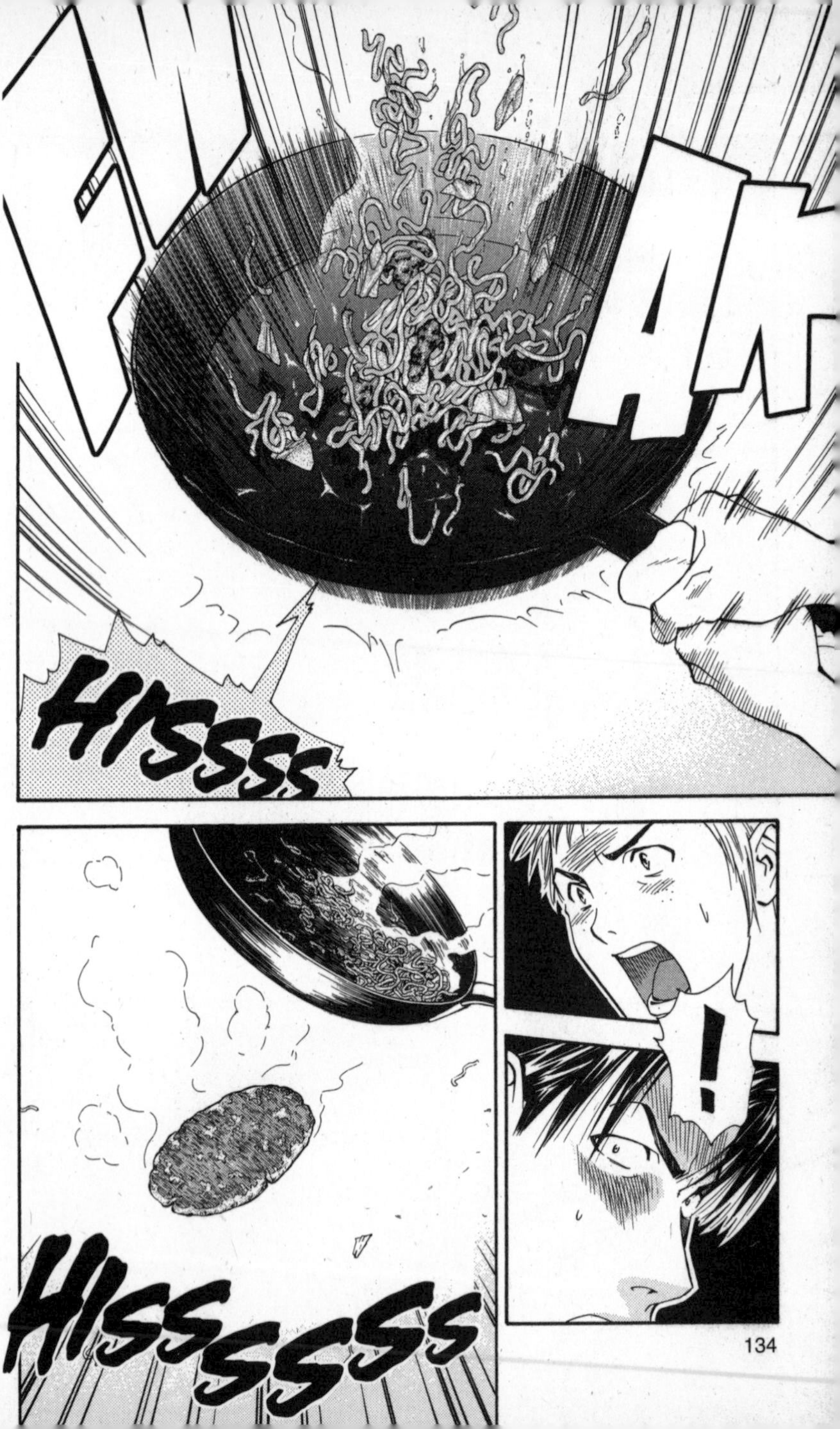
HISSSS
!
HISSSSSS

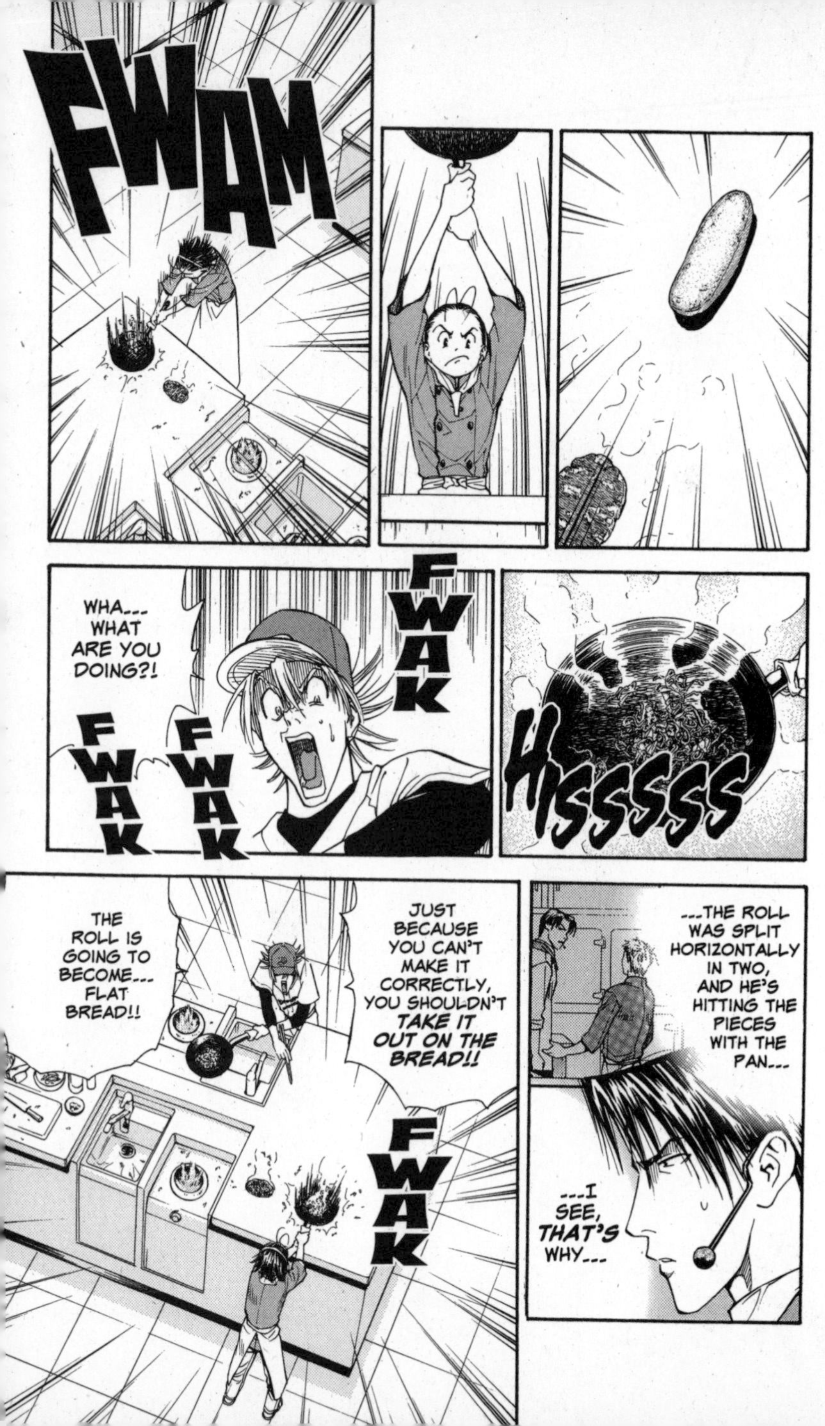
FWAM
HISSSSS
FWAK
WHA... WHAT ARE YOU DOING?!
FWAK
FWAK
...THE ROLL WAS SPLIT HORIZONTALLY IN TWO, AND HE'S HITTING THE PIECES WITH THE PAN...
...I SEE, THAT'S WHY...
JUST BECAUSE YOU CAN'T MAKE IT CORRECTLY, YOU SHOULDN'T *TAKE IT OUT ON THE BREAD!!*
THE ROLL IS GOING TO BECOME... FLAT BREAD!!
FWAK

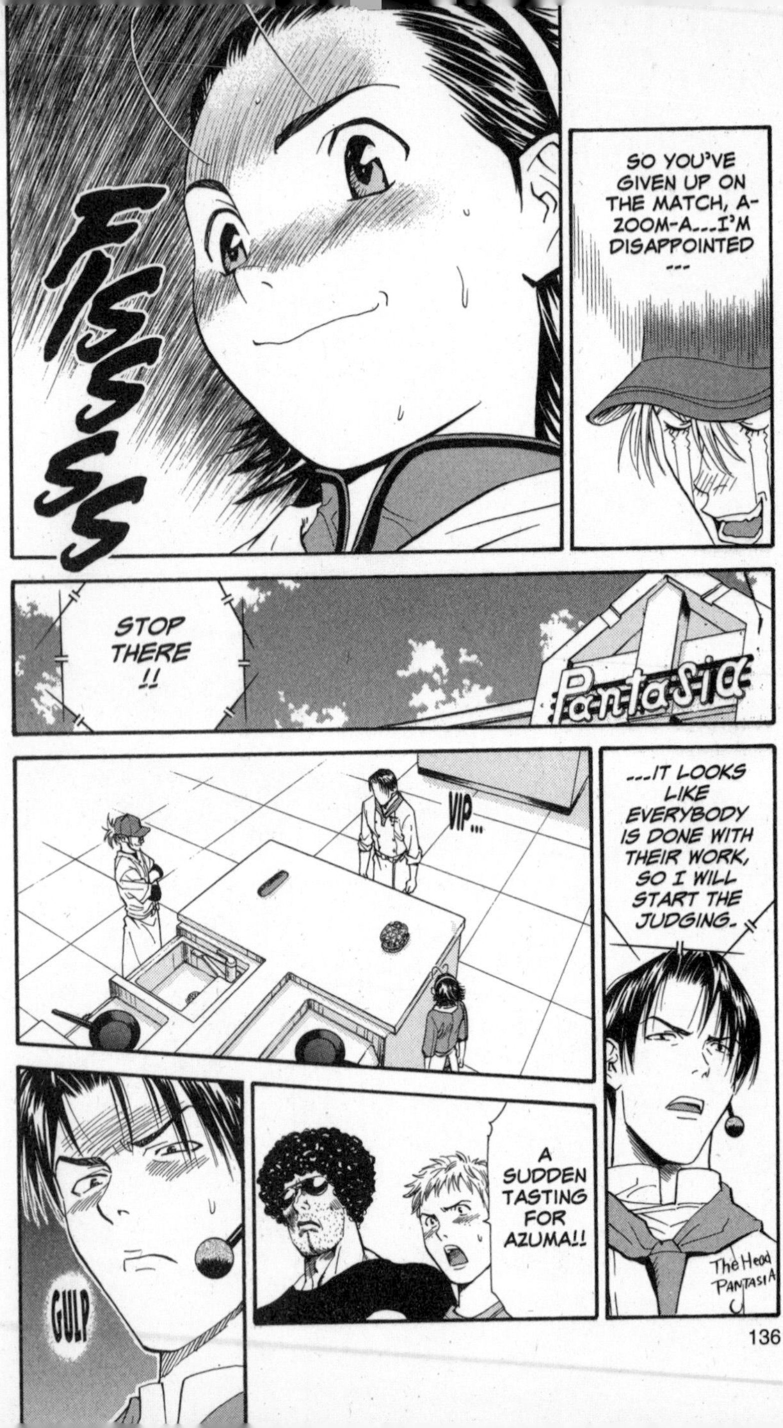
SO YOU'VE GIVEN UP ON THE MATCH, A-ZOOM-A---I'M DISAPPOINTED ---
FISSSSS
STOP THERE !!
Pantasia
---IT LOOKS LIKE EVERYBODY IS DONE WITH THEIR WORK, SO I WILL START THE JUDGING.
The Head PANTASIA
VIP...
A SUDDEN TASTING FOR AZUMA!!
GULP

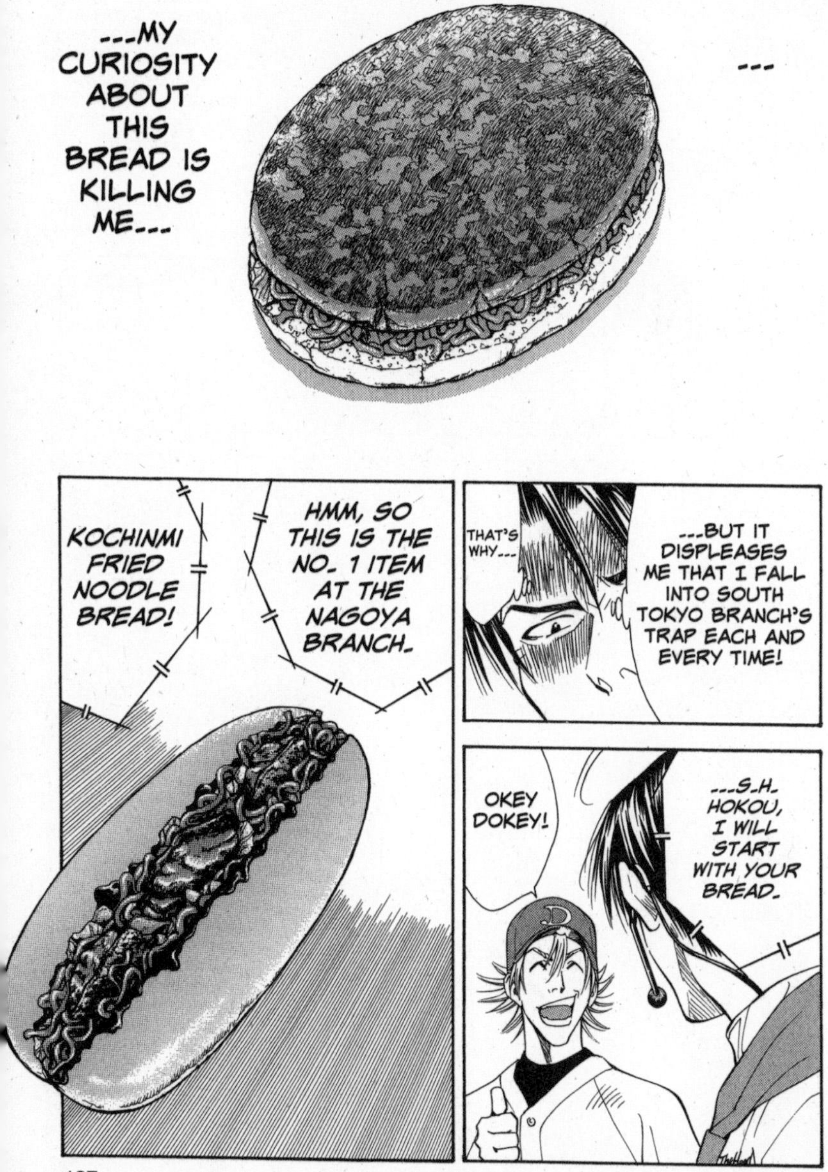

---MY CURIOSITY ABOUT THIS BREAD IS KILLING ME---
THAT'S WHY---
---BUT IT DISPLEASES ME THAT I FALL INTO SOUTH TOKYO BRANCH'S TRAP EACH AND EVERY TIME!
---S.H. HOKOU, I WILL START WITH YOUR BREAD.
OKEY DOKEY!
HMM, SO THIS IS THE NO. 1 ITEM AT THE NAGOYA BRANCH.
KOCHINMI FRIED NOODLE BREAD!

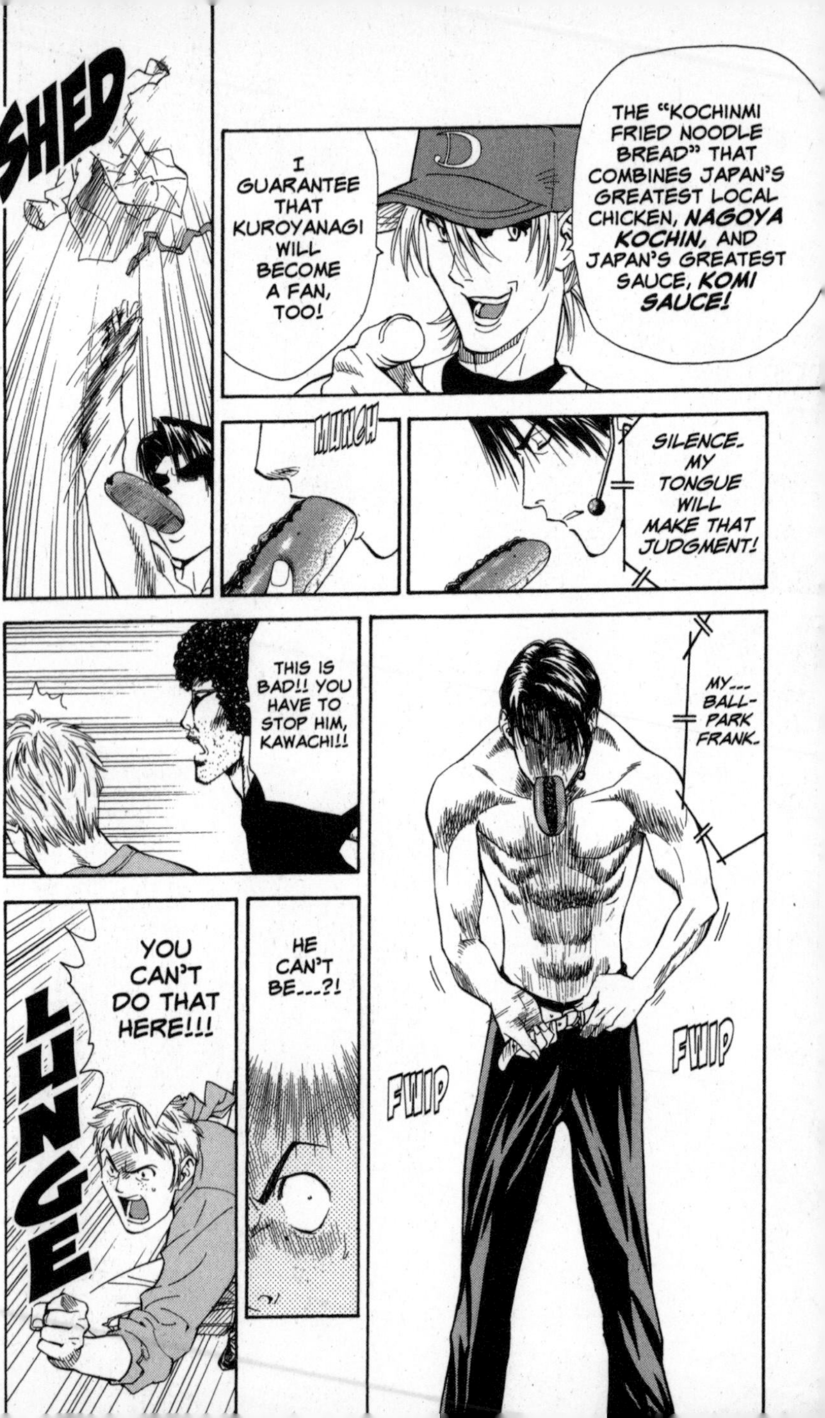
THE "KOCHINMI FRIED NOODLE BREAD" THAT COMBINES JAPAN'S GREATEST LOCAL CHICKEN, **NAGOYA KOCHIN,** AND JAPAN'S GREATEST SAUCE, **KOMI SAUCE!**
I GUARANTEE THAT KUROYANAGI WILL BECOME A FAN, TOO!
SILENCE. MY TONGUE WILL MAKE THAT JUDGMENT!
MUNCH
SHED
MY... BALL-PARK FRANK.
FWIP
FWIP
THIS IS BAD!! YOU HAVE TO STOP HIM, KAWACHI!!
HE CAN'T BE...?!
YOU CAN'T DO THAT HERE!!!
LUNGE

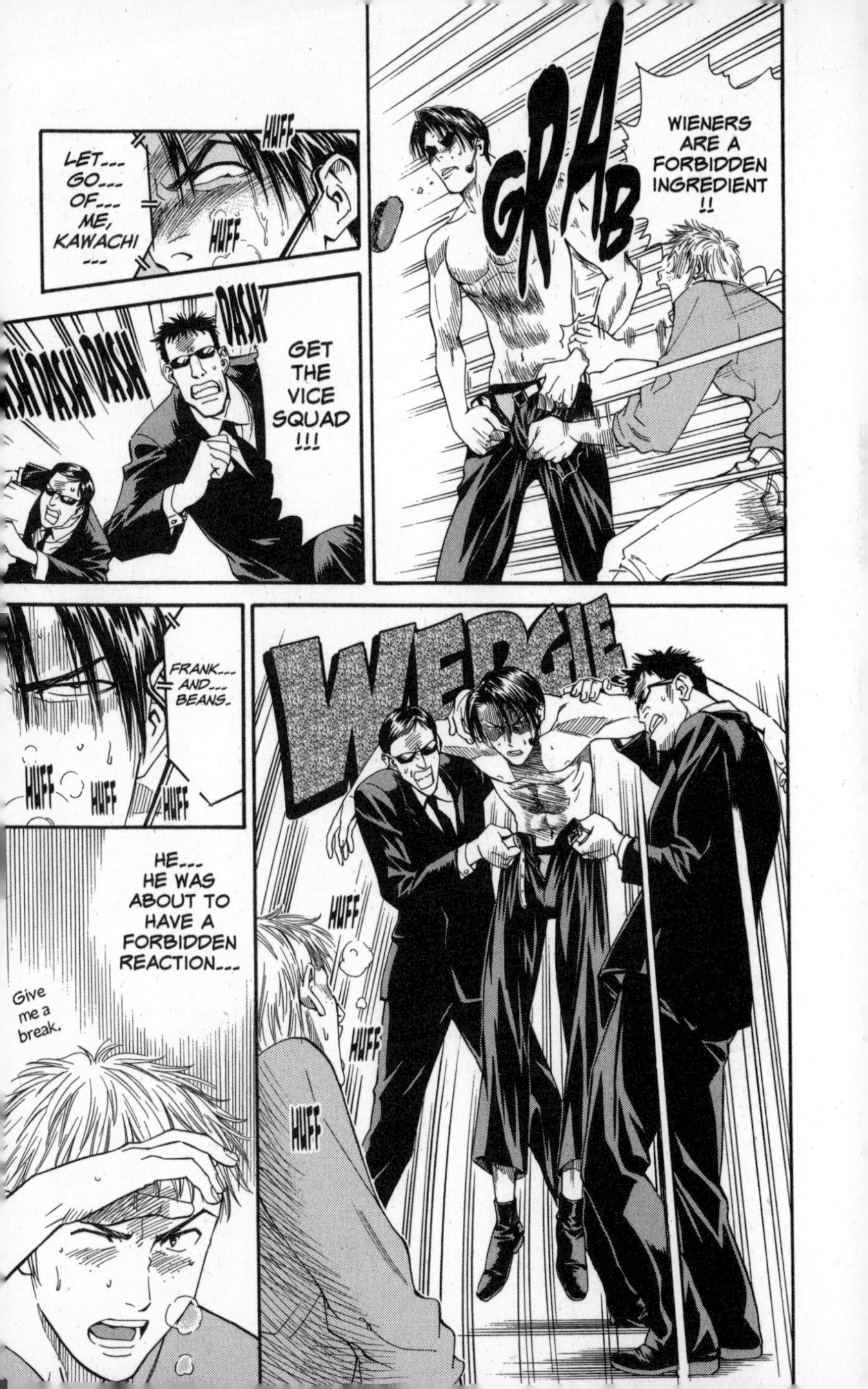
GRAB
WIENERS ARE A FORBIDDEN INGREDIENT !!
HUFF
LET... GO... OF... ME, KAWACHI ...
HUFF
DASH
DASH DASH DASH
GET THE VICE SQUAD !!!
WEDGIE
HUFF
HUFF
HUFF
FRANK... AND... BEANS.
HUFF HUFF HUFF
HE... HE WAS ABOUT TO HAVE A FORBIDDEN REACTION...
Give me a break.

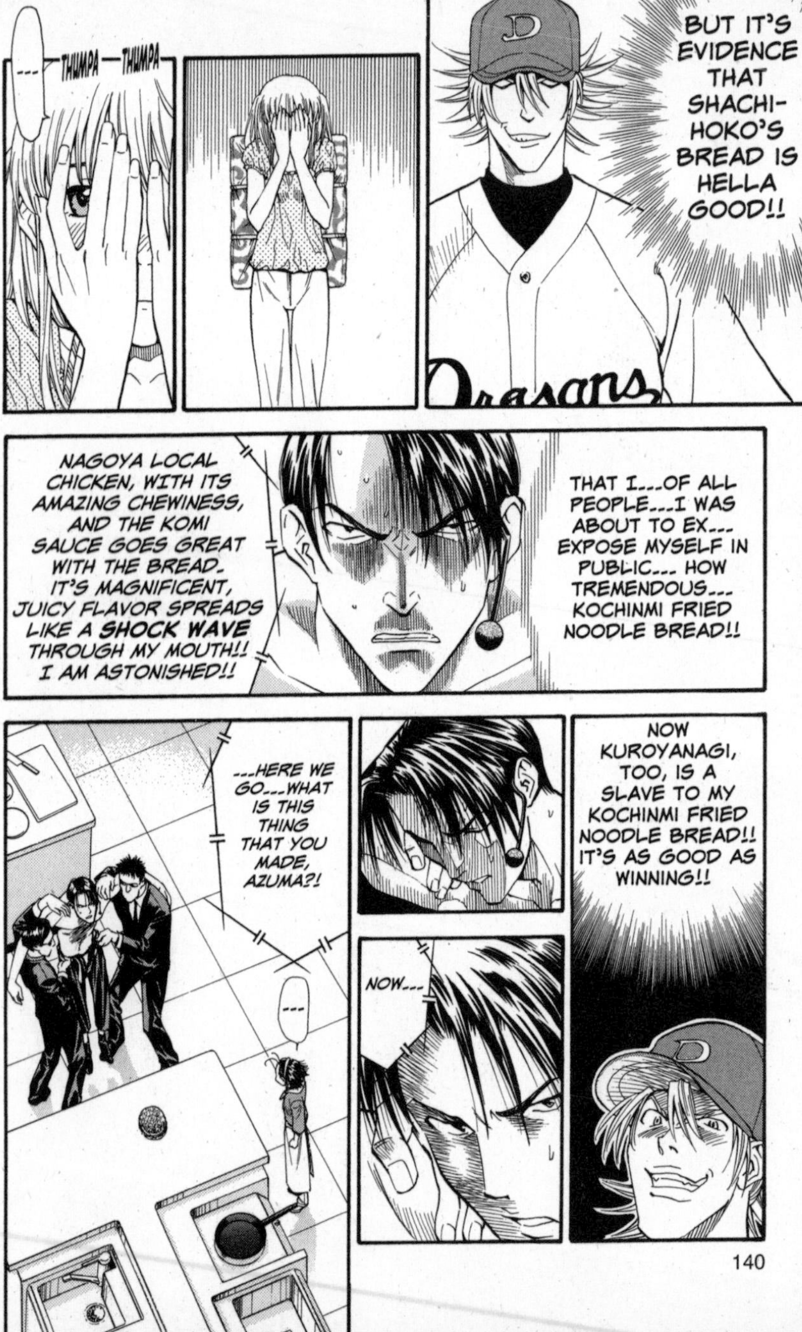
BUT IT'S EVIDENCE THAT SHACHI-HOKO'S BREAD IS HELLA GOOD!!
Dragons
...
THUMPA THUMPA
THAT I...OF ALL PEOPLE...I WAS ABOUT TO EX... EXPOSE MYSELF IN PUBLIC... HOW TREMENDOUS... KOCHINMI FRIED NOODLE BREAD!!
NAGOYA LOCAL CHICKEN, WITH ITS AMAZING CHEWINESS, AND THE KOMI SAUCE GOES GREAT WITH THE BREAD. IT'S MAGNIFICENT, JUICY FLAVOR SPREADS LIKE A **SHOCK WAVE** THROUGH MY MOUTH!! I AM ASTONISHED!!
NOW KUROYANAGI, TOO, IS A SLAVE TO MY KOCHINMI FRIED NOODLE BREAD!! IT'S AS GOOD AS WINNING!!
NOW...
...HERE WE GO...WHAT IS THIS THING THAT YOU MADE, AZUMA?!
...

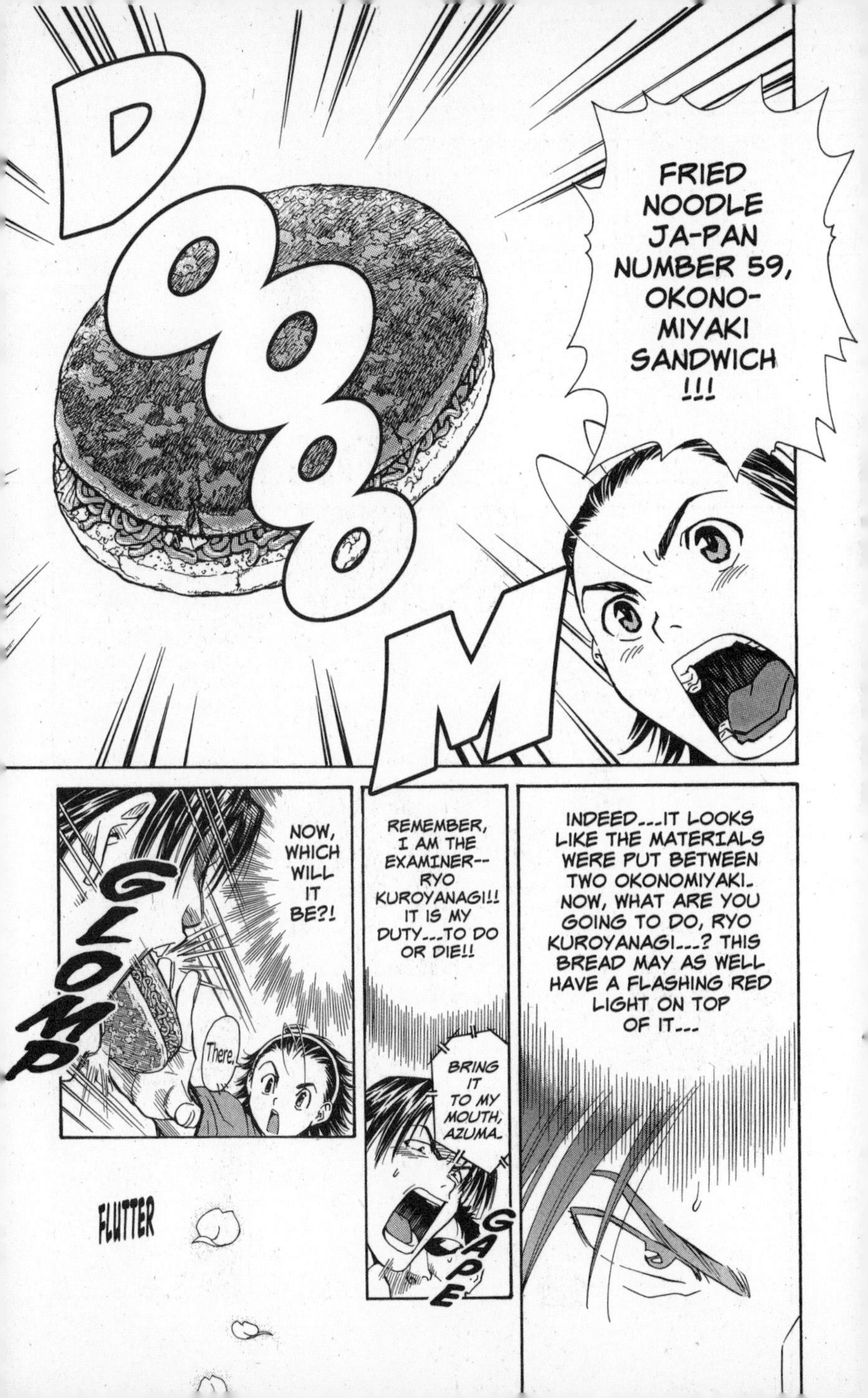
FRIED NOODLE JA-PAN NUMBER 59, OKONOMIYAKI SANDWICH!!!
DOOOOM
INDEED...IT LOOKS LIKE THE MATERIALS WERE PUT BETWEEN TWO OKONOMIYAKI. NOW, WHAT ARE YOU GOING TO DO, RYO KUROYANAGI...? THIS BREAD MAY AS WELL HAVE A FLASHING RED LIGHT ON TOP OF IT...
REMEMBER, I AM THE EXAMINER-- RYO KUROYANAGI!! IT IS MY DUTY...TO DO OR DIE!!
BRING IT TO MY MOUTH, AZUMA.
GAPE
NOW, WHICH WILL IT BE?!
GLOMP
There.
FLUTTER

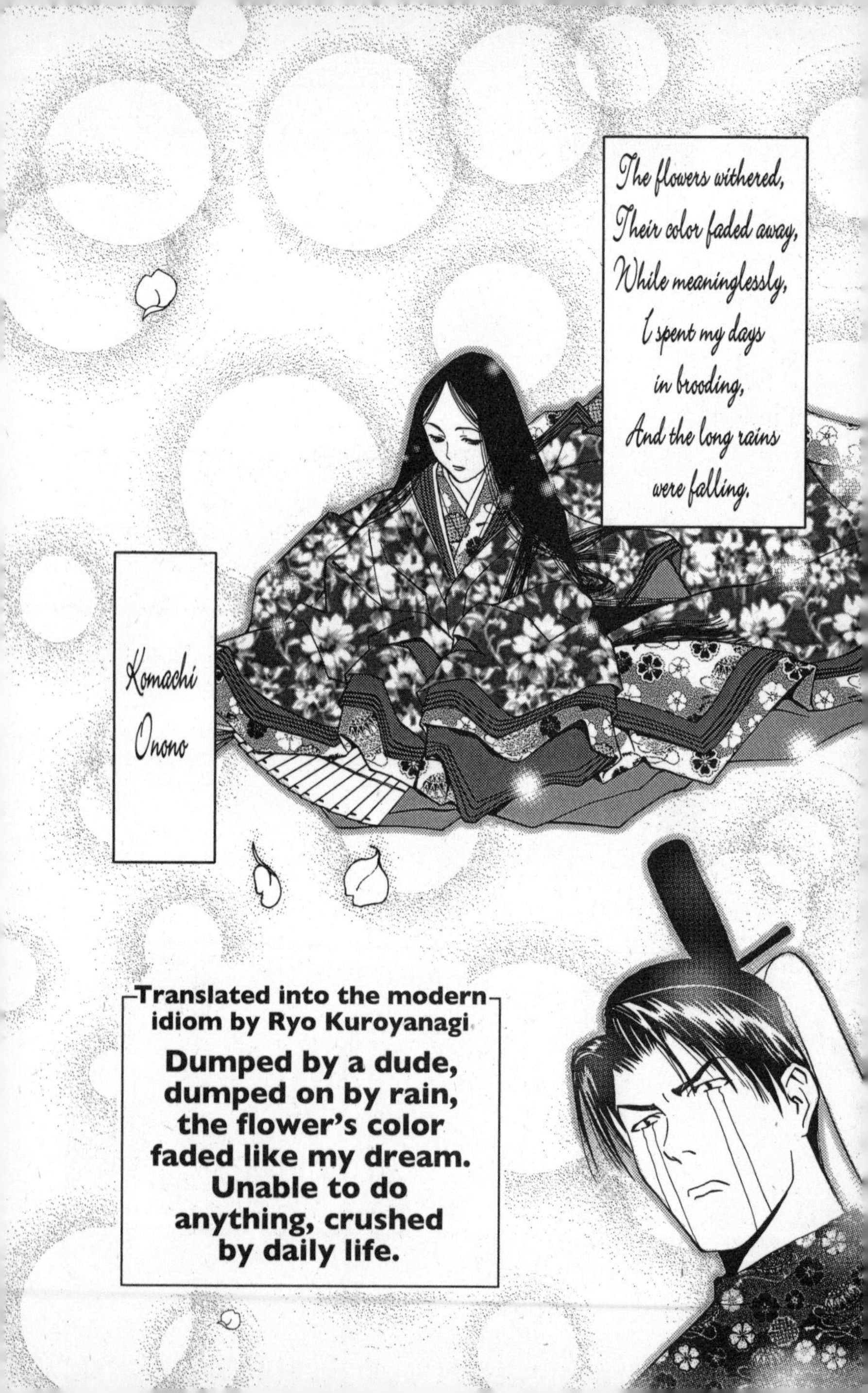
The flowers withered, Their color faded away, While meaninglessly, I spent my days in brooding, And the long rains were falling.
Komachi Onono
-Translated into the modern idiom by Ryo Kuroyanagi
Dumped by a dude, dumped on by rain, the flower's color faded like my dream. Unable to do anything, crushed by daily life.

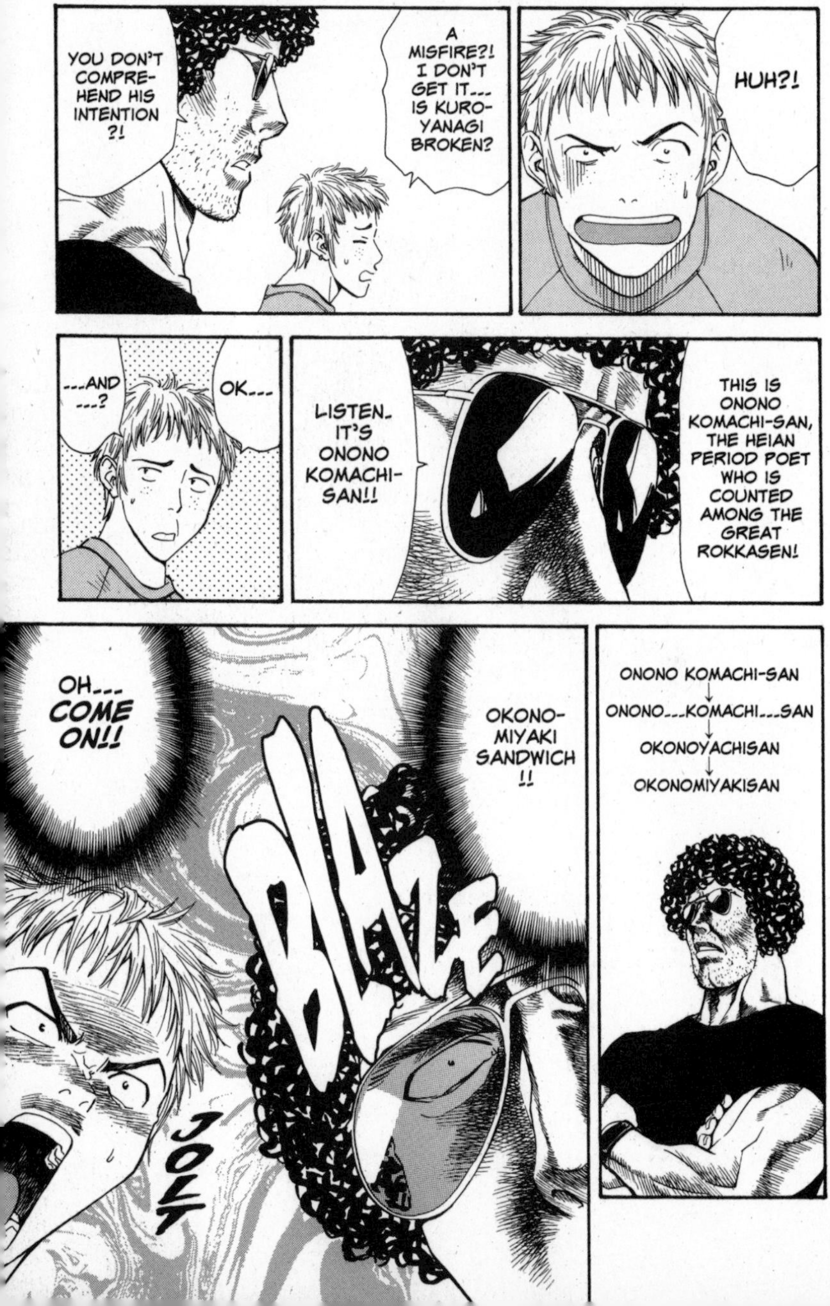
HUH?!
A MISFIRE?! I DON'T GET IT... IS KURO-YANAGI BROKEN?
YOU DON'T COMPRE-HEND HIS INTENTION?!
THIS IS ONONO KOMACHI-SAN, THE HEIAN PERIOD POET WHO IS COUNTED AMONG THE GREAT ROKKASEN!
LISTEN. IT'S ONONO KOMACHI-SAN!!
OK...
...AND ...?
ONONO KOMACHI-SAN
ONONO...KOMACHI...SAN
OKONOYACHISAN
OKONOMIYAKISAN
OKONO-MIYAKI SANDWICH!!
BLAZE
OH... COME ON!!
JOLT

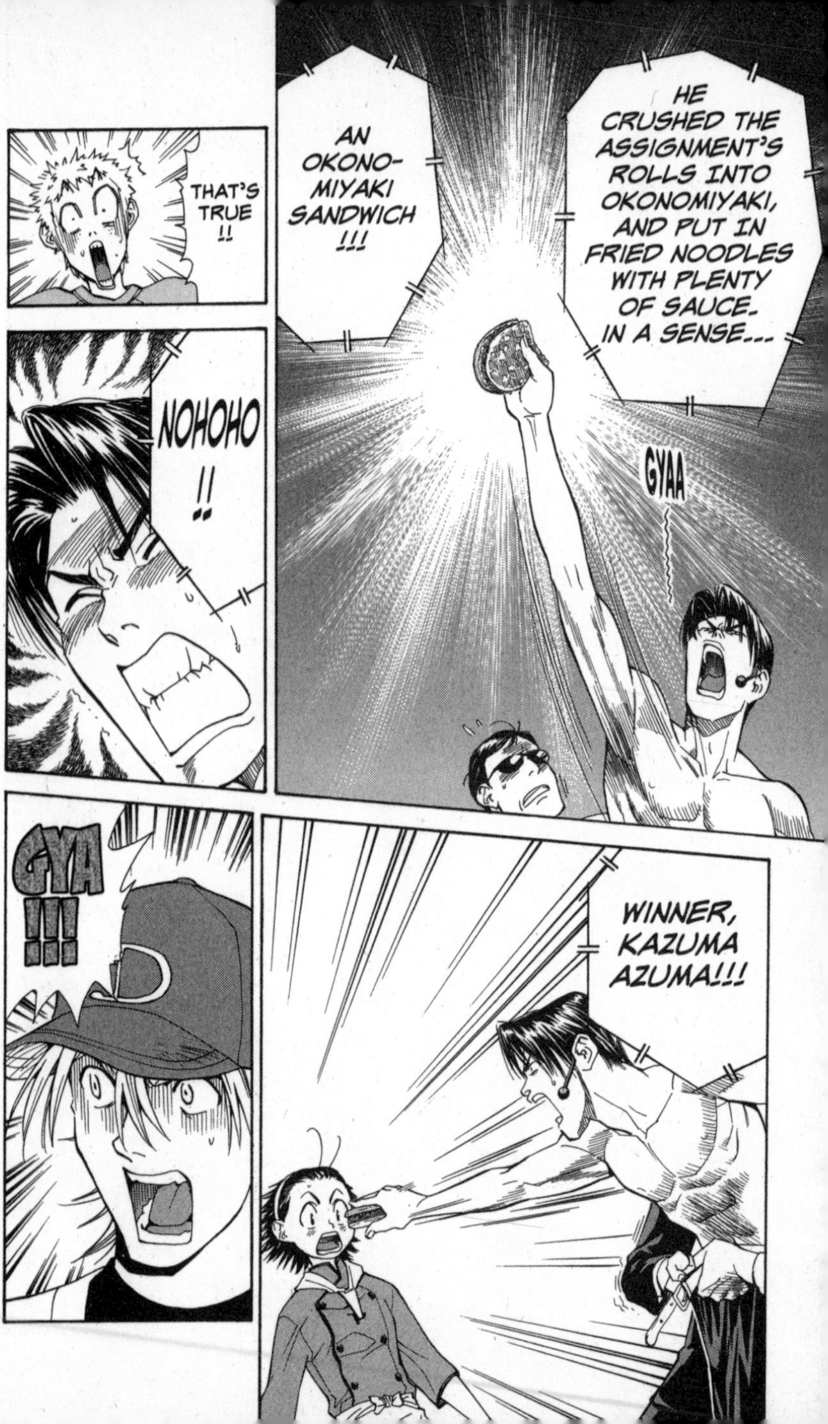
HE CRUSHED THE ASSIGNMENT'S ROLLS INTO OKONOMIYAKI, AND PUT IN FRIED NOODLES WITH PLENTY OF SAUCE. IN A SENSE...
AN OKONOMIYAKI SANDWICH !!!
GYAA
THAT'S TRUE !!
NOHOHO !!
WINNER, KAZUMA AZUMA!!!
GYA !!!

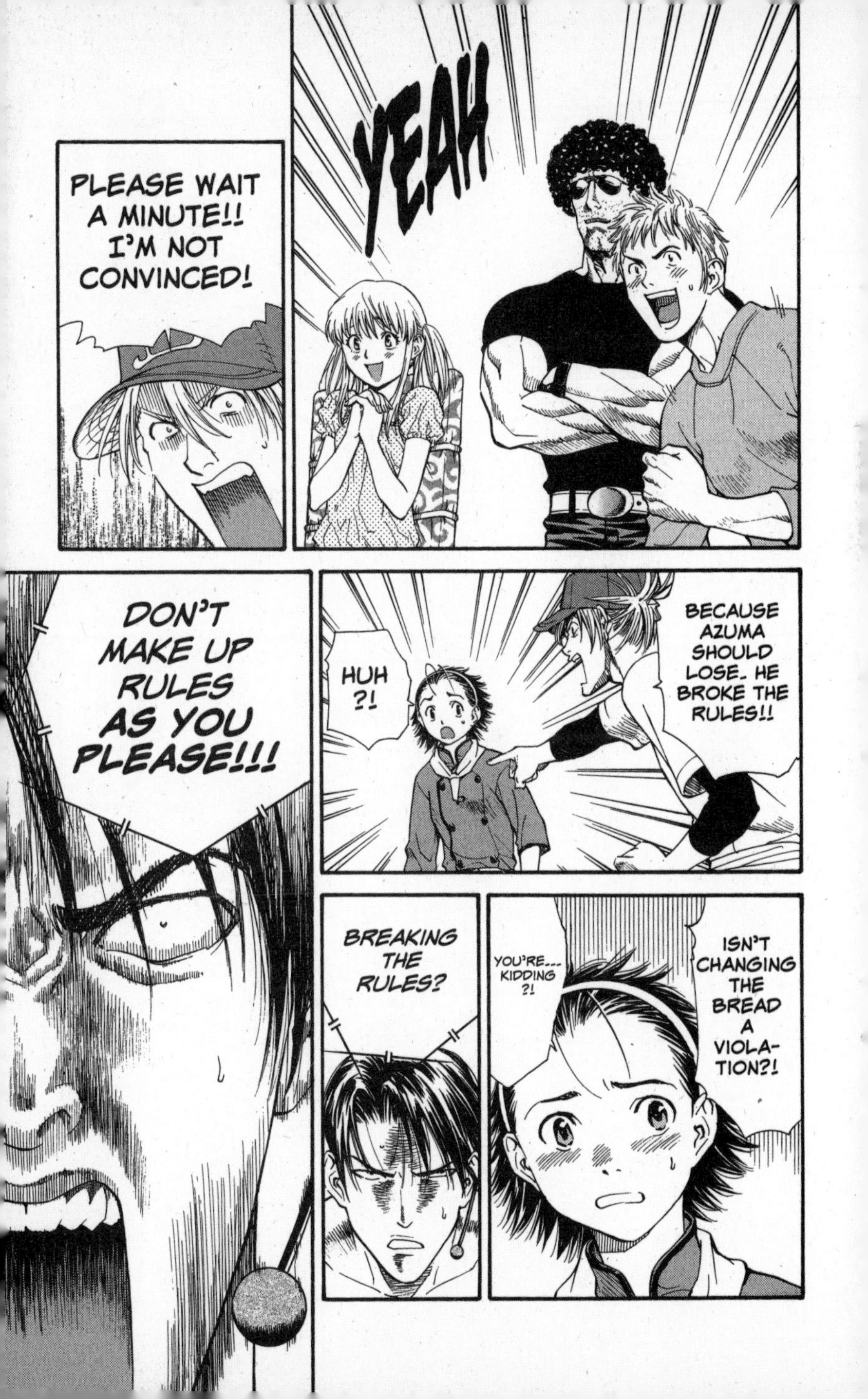
YEAH
PLEASE WAIT A MINUTE!! I'M NOT CONVINCED!
BECAUSE AZUMA SHOULD LOSE. HE BROKE THE RULES!!
HUH ?!
ISN'T CHANGING THE BREAD A VIOLA-TION?!
YOU'RE... KIDDING ?!
BREAKING THE RULES?
DON'T MAKE UP RULES AS YOU PLEASE!!!

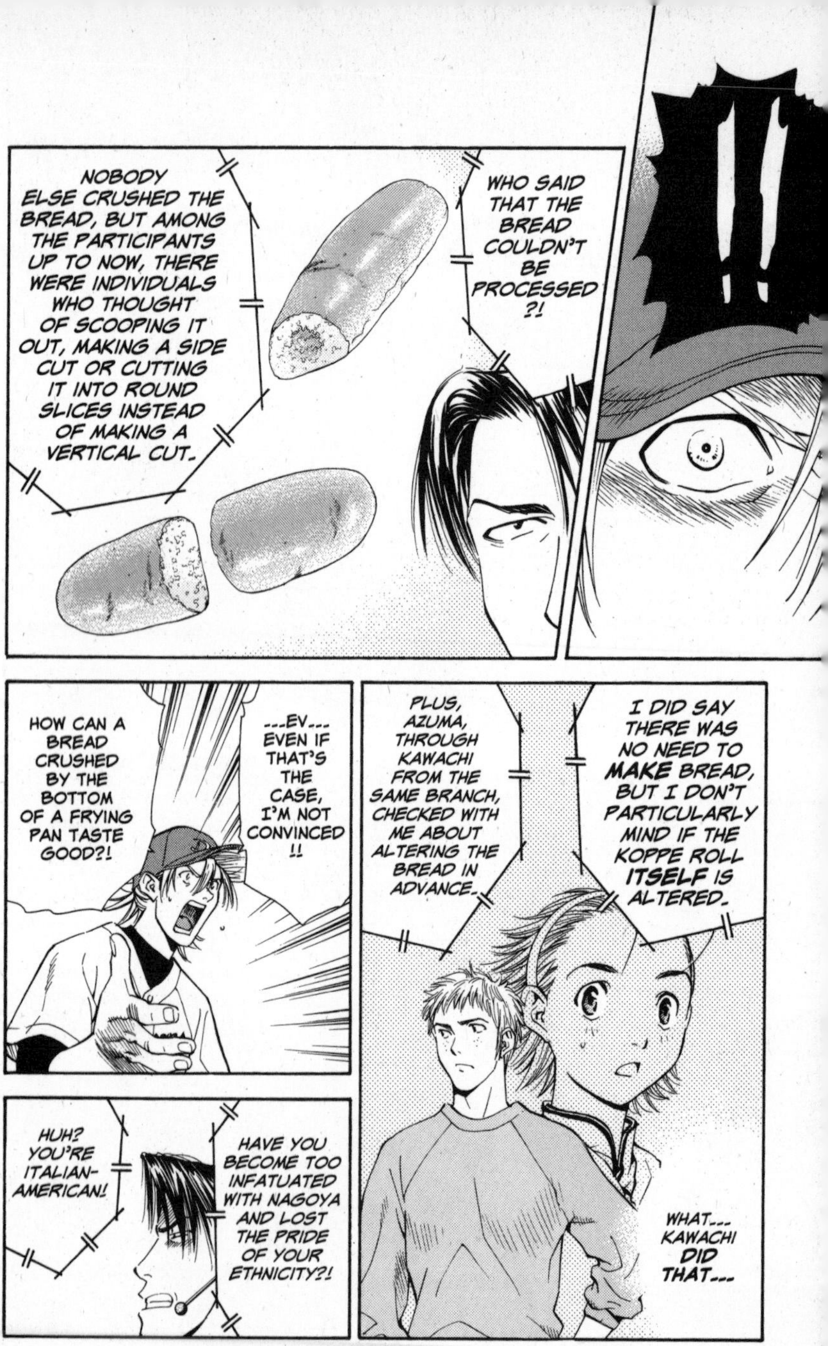
!!
WHO SAID THAT THE BREAD COULDN'T BE PROCESSED?!
NOBODY ELSE CRUSHED THE BREAD, BUT AMONG THE PARTICIPANTS UP TO NOW, THERE WERE INDIVIDUALS WHO THOUGHT OF SCOOPING IT OUT, MAKING A SIDE CUT OR CUTTING IT INTO ROUND SLICES INSTEAD OF MAKING A VERTICAL CUT.
I DID SAY THERE WAS NO NEED TO MAKE BREAD, BUT I DON'T PARTICULARLY MIND IF THE KOPPE ROLL ITSELF IS ALTERED.
PLUS, AZUMA, THROUGH KAWACHI FROM THE SAME BRANCH, CHECKED WITH ME ABOUT ALTERING THE BREAD IN ADVANCE.
...EV... EVEN IF THAT'S THE CASE, I'M NOT CONVINCED!!
HOW CAN A BREAD CRUSHED BY THE BOTTOM OF A FRYING PAN TASTE GOOD?!
WHAT... KAWACHI DID THAT...
HAVE YOU BECOME TOO INFATUATED WITH NAGOYA AND LOST THE PRIDE OF YOUR ETHNICITY?!
HUH? YOU'RE ITALIAN-AMERICAN!

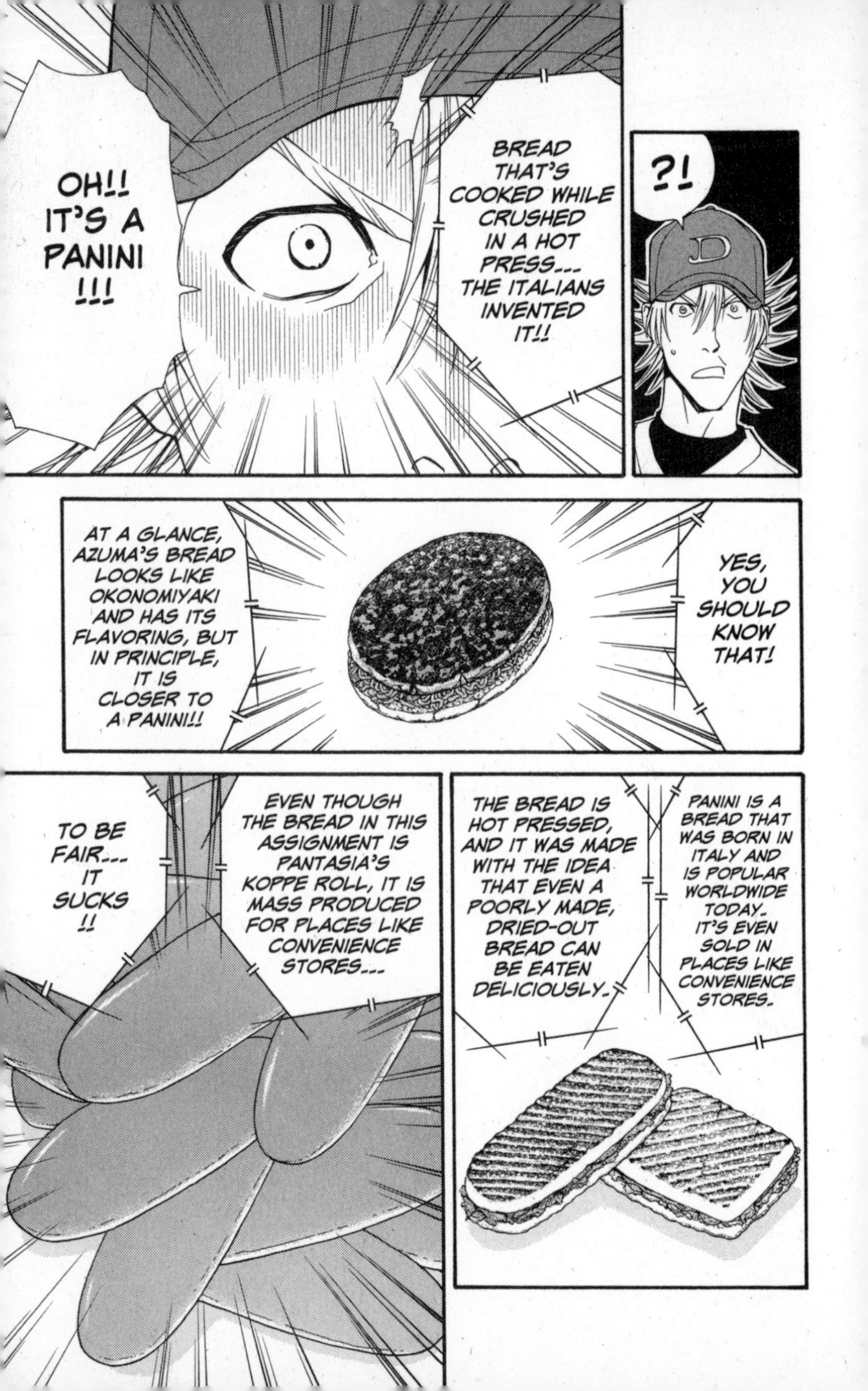
?!
BREAD THAT'S COOKED WHILE CRUSHED IN A HOT PRESS... THE ITALIANS INVENTED IT!!
OH!! IT'S A PANINI !!!
YES, YOU SHOULD KNOW THAT!
AT A GLANCE, AZUMA'S BREAD LOOKS LIKE OKONOMIYAKI AND HAS ITS FLAVORING, BUT IN PRINCIPLE, IT IS CLOSER TO A PANINI!!
PANINI IS A BREAD THAT WAS BORN IN ITALY AND IS POPULAR WORLDWIDE TODAY. IT'S EVEN SOLD IN PLACES LIKE CONVENIENCE STORES.
THE BREAD IS HOT PRESSED, AND IT WAS MADE WITH THE IDEA THAT EVEN A POORLY MADE, DRIED-OUT BREAD CAN BE EATEN DELICIOUSLY.
EVEN THOUGH THE BREAD IN THIS ASSIGNMENT IS PANTASIA'S KOPPE ROLL, IT IS MASS PRODUCED FOR PLACES LIKE CONVENIENCE STORES...
TO BE FAIR... IT SUCKS !!

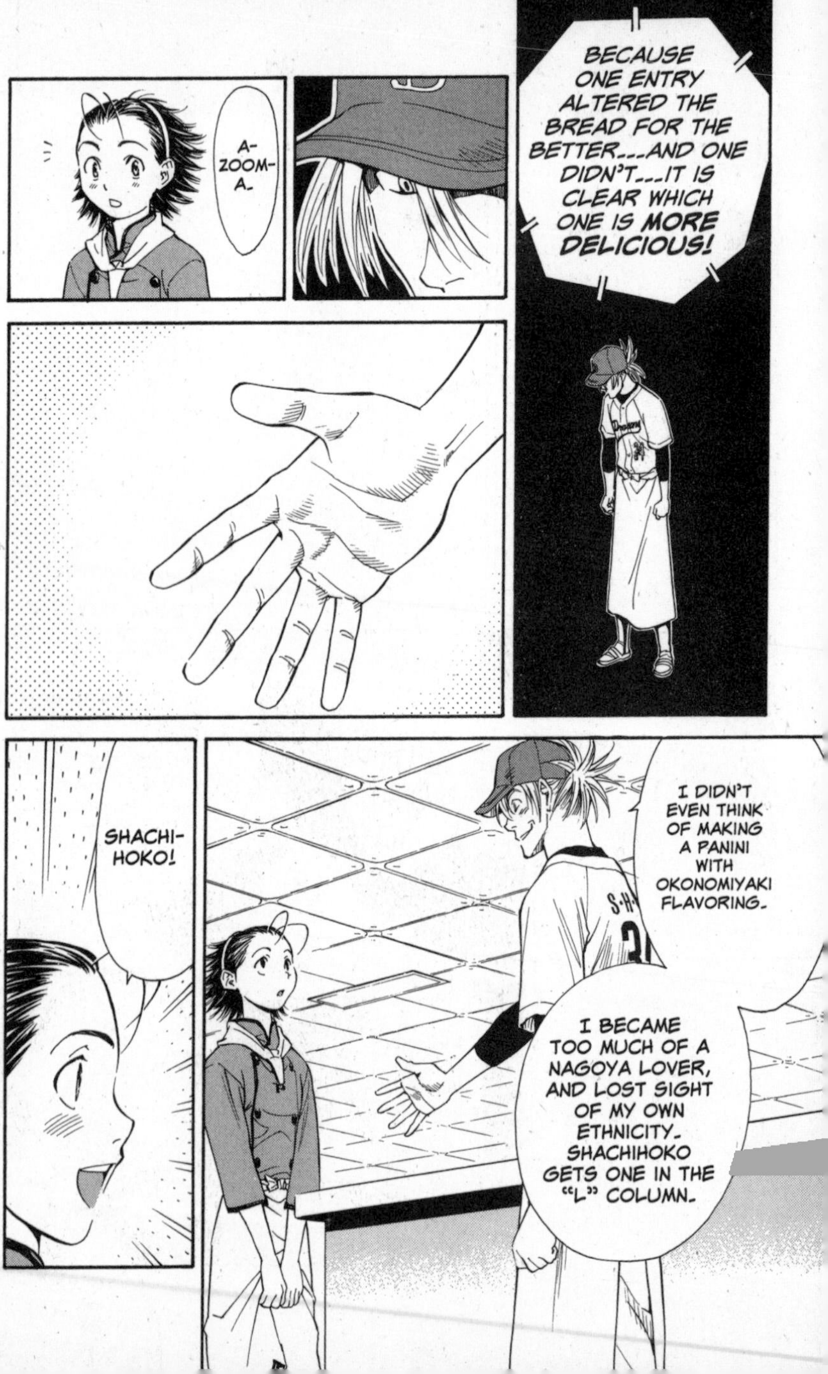
BECAUSE ONE ENTRY ALTERED THE BREAD FOR THE BETTER...AND ONE DIDN'T...IT IS CLEAR WHICH ONE IS **MORE DELICIOUS!**
A-ZOOM-A.
I DIDN'T EVEN THINK OF MAKING A PANINI WITH OKONOMIYAKI FLAVORING.
I BECAME TOO MUCH OF A NAGOYA LOVER, AND LOST SIGHT OF MY OWN ETHNICITY. SHACHIHOKO GETS ONE IN THE "L" COLUMN.
SHACHI-HOKO!

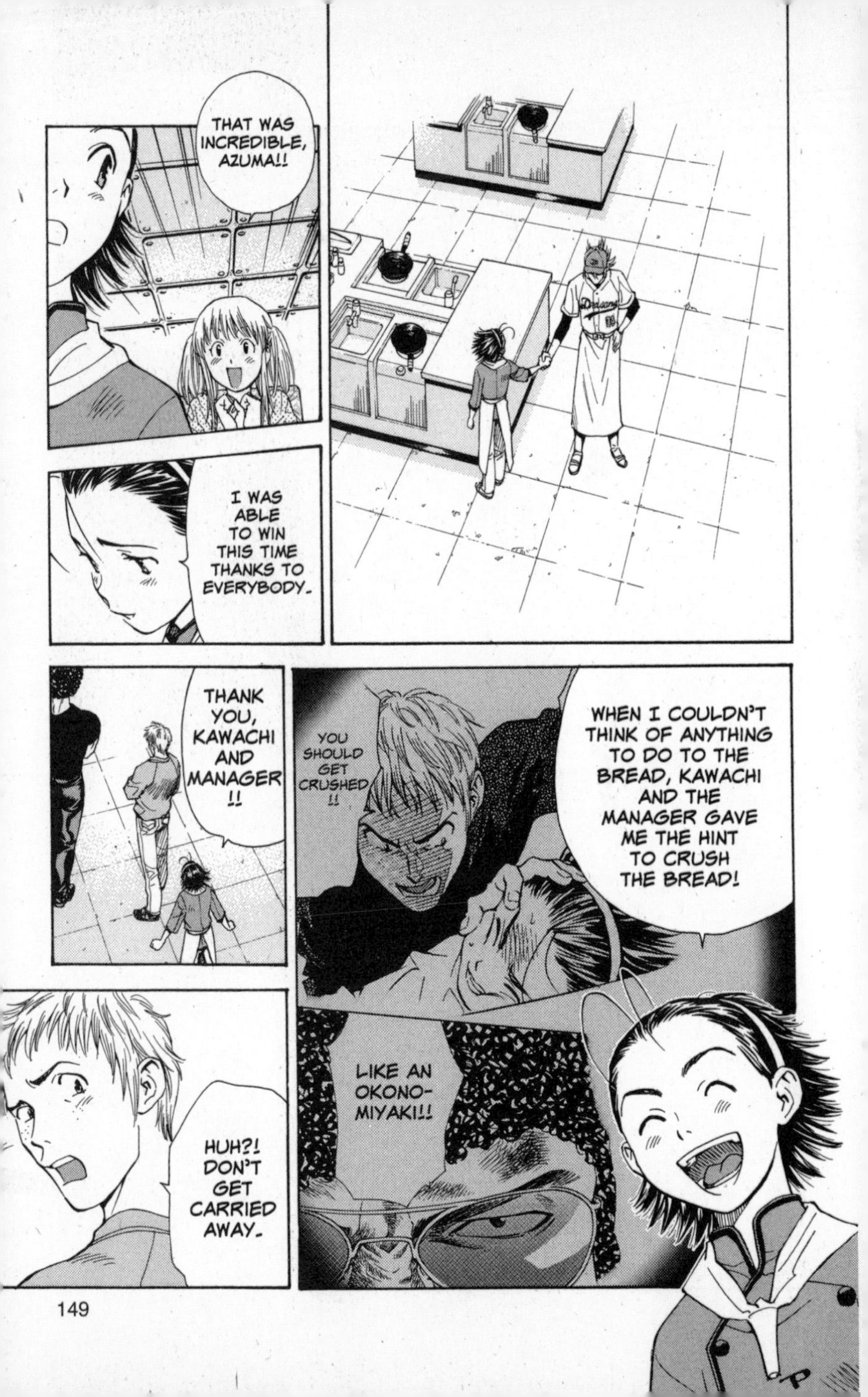
THAT WAS INCREDIBLE, AZUMA!!
I WAS ABLE TO WIN THIS TIME THANKS TO EVERYBODY.
WHEN I COULDN'T THINK OF ANYTHING TO DO TO THE BREAD, KAWACHI AND THE MANAGER GAVE ME THE HINT TO CRUSH THE BREAD!
YOU SHOULD GET CRUSHED!!
THANK YOU, KAWACHI AND MANAGER!!
LIKE AN OKONOMIYAKI!!
HUH?! DON'T GET CARRIED AWAY.

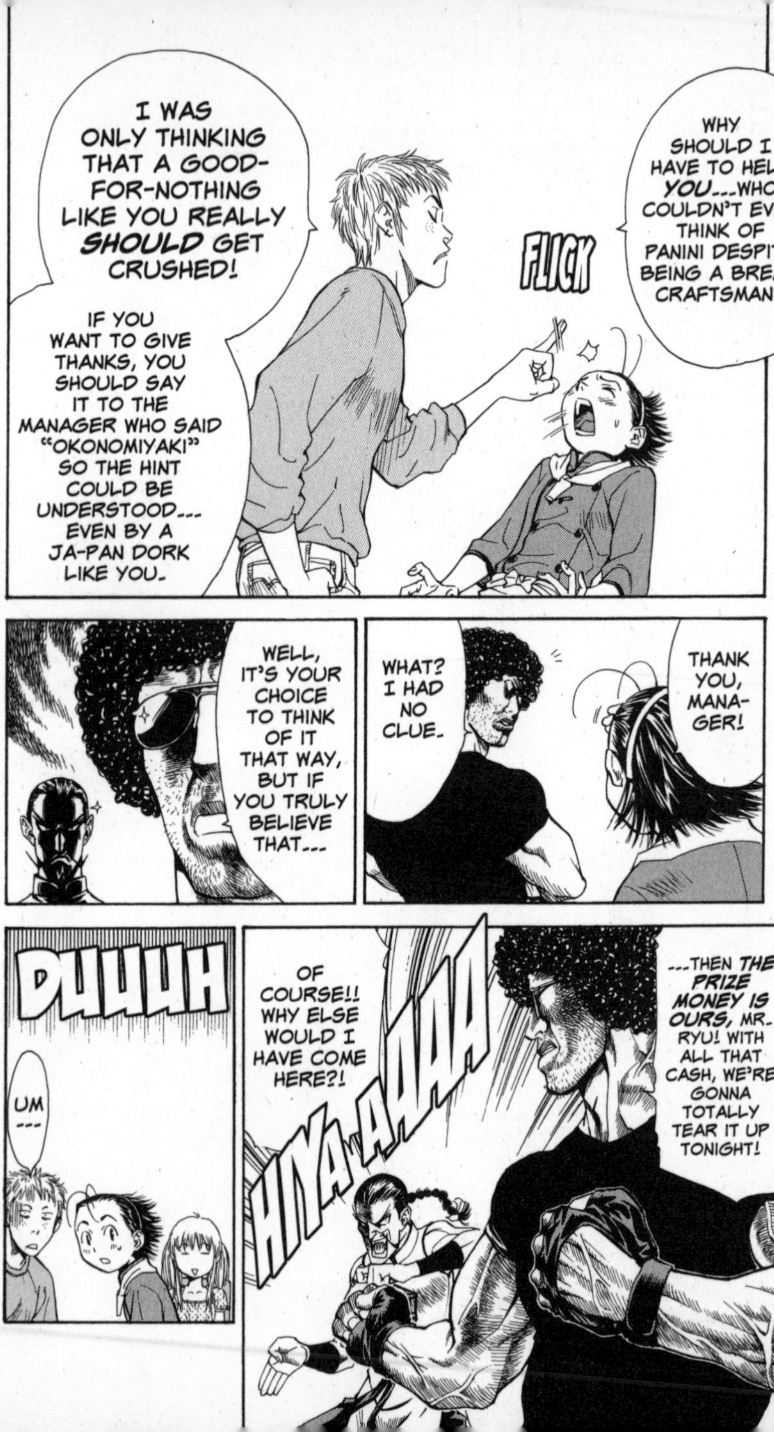
WHY SHOULD I HAVE TO HELP *YOU*...WHO COULDN'T EVEN THINK OF PANINI DESPITE BEING A BREAD CRAFTSMAN?
FLICK
I WAS ONLY THINKING THAT A GOOD-FOR-NOTHING LIKE YOU REALLY ***SHOULD*** GET CRUSHED!
IF YOU WANT TO GIVE THANKS, YOU SHOULD SAY IT TO THE MANAGER WHO SAID "OKONOMIYAKI" SO THE HINT COULD BE UNDERSTOOD... EVEN BY A JA-PAN DORK LIKE YOU.
THANK YOU, MANA-GER!
WHAT? I HAD NO CLUE.
WELL, IT'S YOUR CHOICE TO THINK OF IT THAT WAY, BUT IF YOU TRULY BELIEVE THAT...
...THEN *THE PRIZE MONEY IS OURS,* MR. RYU! WITH ALL THAT CASH, WE'RE GONNA TOTALLY TEAR IT UP TONIGHT!
HIYA-AAAA
OF COURSE!! WHY ELSE WOULD I HAVE COME HERE?!
DUUUH
UM...

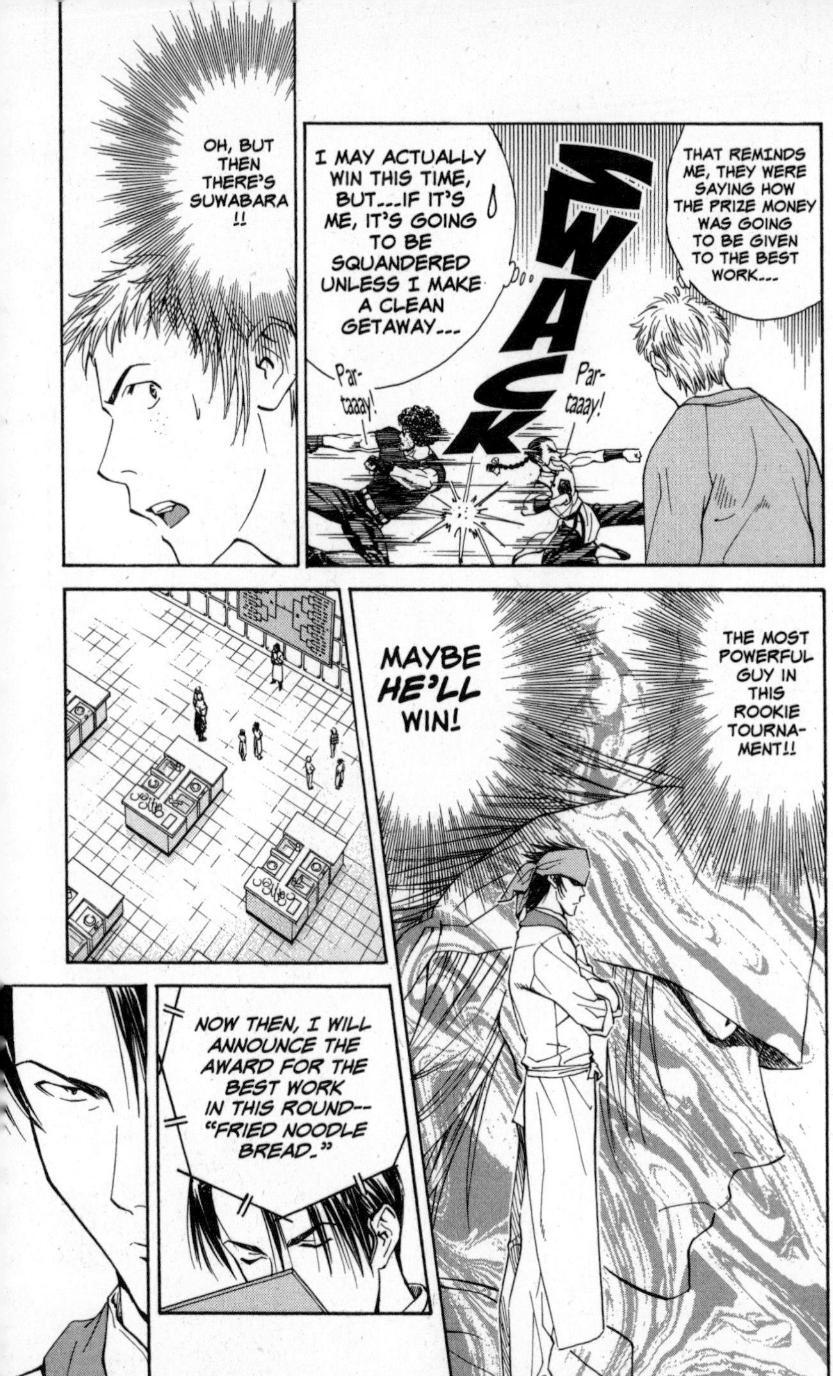
THAT REMINDS ME, THEY WERE SAYING HOW THE PRIZE MONEY WAS GOING TO BE GIVEN TO THE BEST WORK...
I MAY ACTUALLY WIN THIS TIME, BUT...IF IT'S ME, IT'S GOING TO BE SQUANDERED UNLESS I MAKE A CLEAN GETAWAY...
SWACK
Par-taaay!
Par-taaay!
OH, BUT THEN THERE'S SUWABARA !!
THE MOST POWERFUL GUY IN THIS ROOKIE TOURNAMENT!!
MAYBE HE'LL WIN!
NOW THEN, I WILL ANNOUNCE THE AWARD FOR THE BEST WORK IN THIS ROUND-- "FRIED NOODLE BREAD."

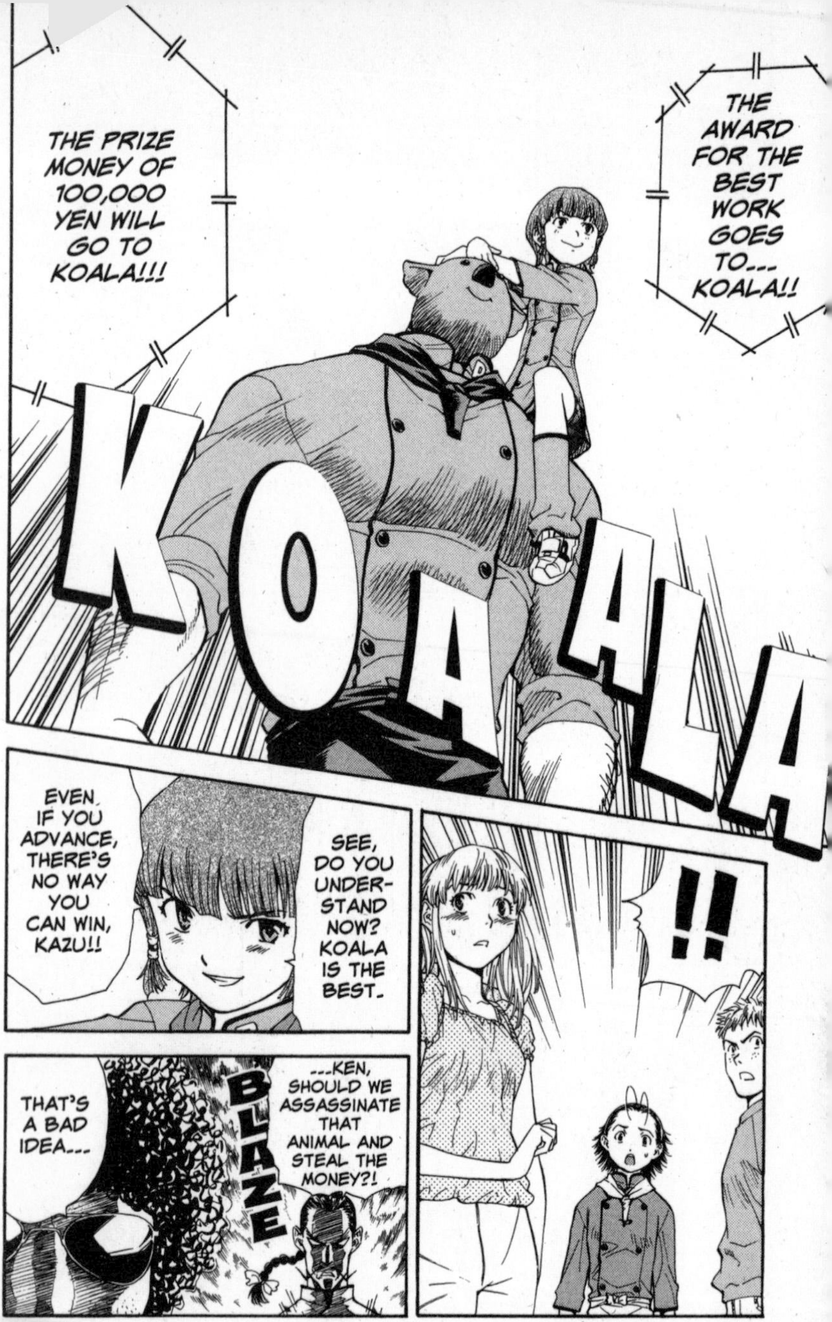
THE AWARD FOR THE BEST WORK GOES TO... KOALA!!
THE PRIZE MONEY OF 100,000 YEN WILL GO TO KOALA!!!
KOALA
!!
SEE, DO YOU UNDERSTAND NOW? KOALA IS THE BEST.
EVEN IF YOU ADVANCE, THERE'S NO WAY YOU CAN WIN, KAZU!!
...KEN, SHOULD WE ASSASSINATE THAT ANIMAL AND STEAL THE MONEY?!
BLAZE
THAT'S A BAD IDEA...

Story 31: Koala's Identity

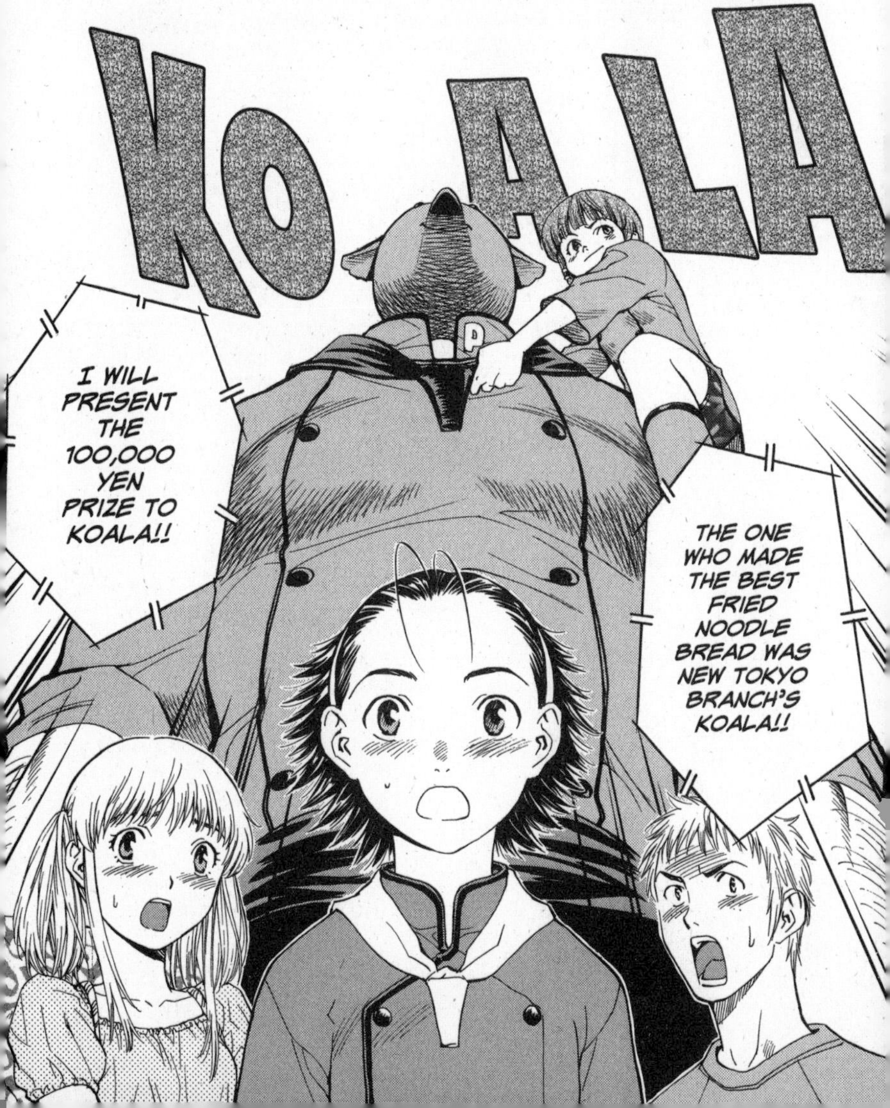
KOALA
THE ONE WHO MADE THE BEST FRIED NOODLE BREAD WAS NEW TOKYO BRANCH'S KOALA!!
I WILL PRESENT THE 100,000 YEN PRIZE TO KOALA!!

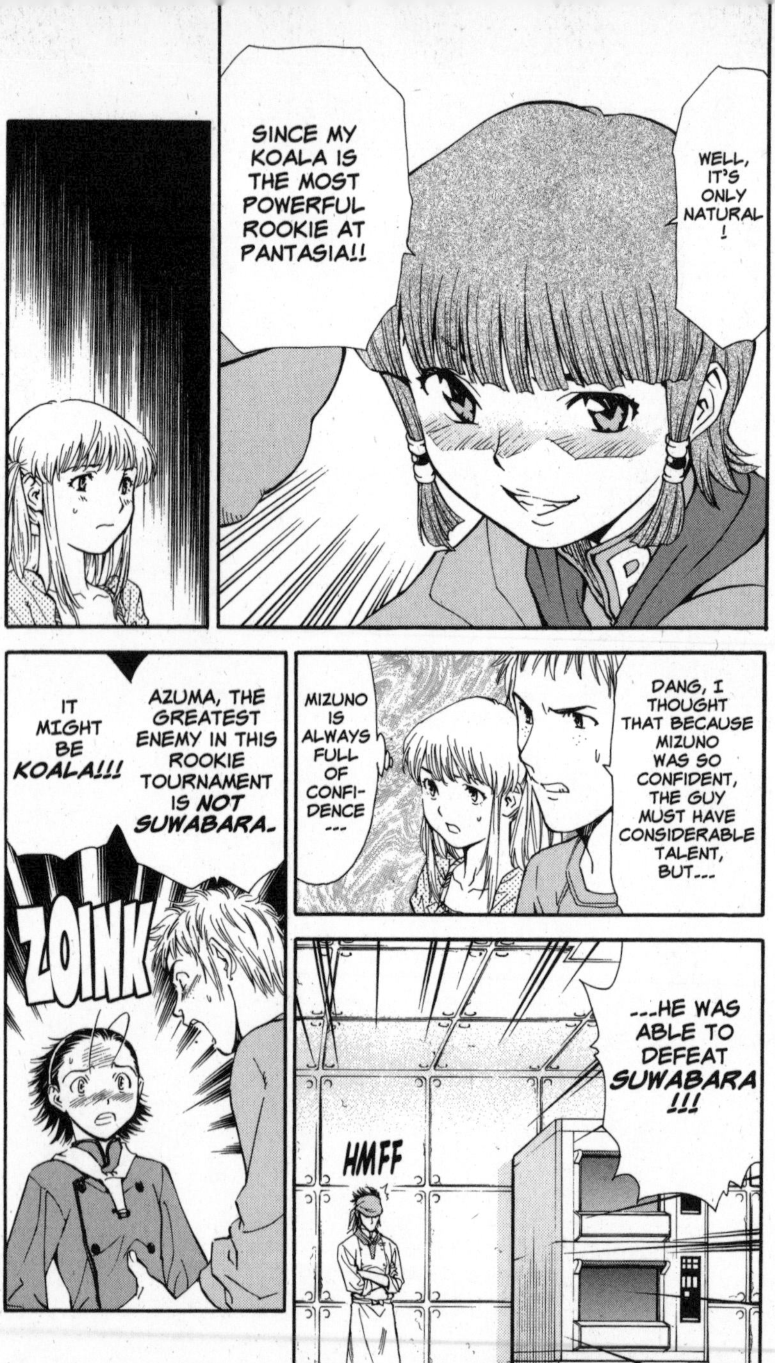
WELL, IT'S ONLY NATURAL!
SINCE MY KOALA IS THE MOST POWERFUL ROOKIE AT PANTASIA!!
DANG, I THOUGHT THAT BECAUSE MIZUNO WAS SO CONFIDENT, THE GUY MUST HAVE CONSIDERABLE TALENT, BUT...
MIZUNO IS ALWAYS FULL OF CONFIDENCE...
...HE WAS ABLE TO DEFEAT SUWABARA!!!
HMFF
AZUMA, THE GREATEST ENEMY IN THIS ROOKIE TOURNAMENT IS NOT SUWABARA.
IT MIGHT BE KOALA!!!
ZOINK

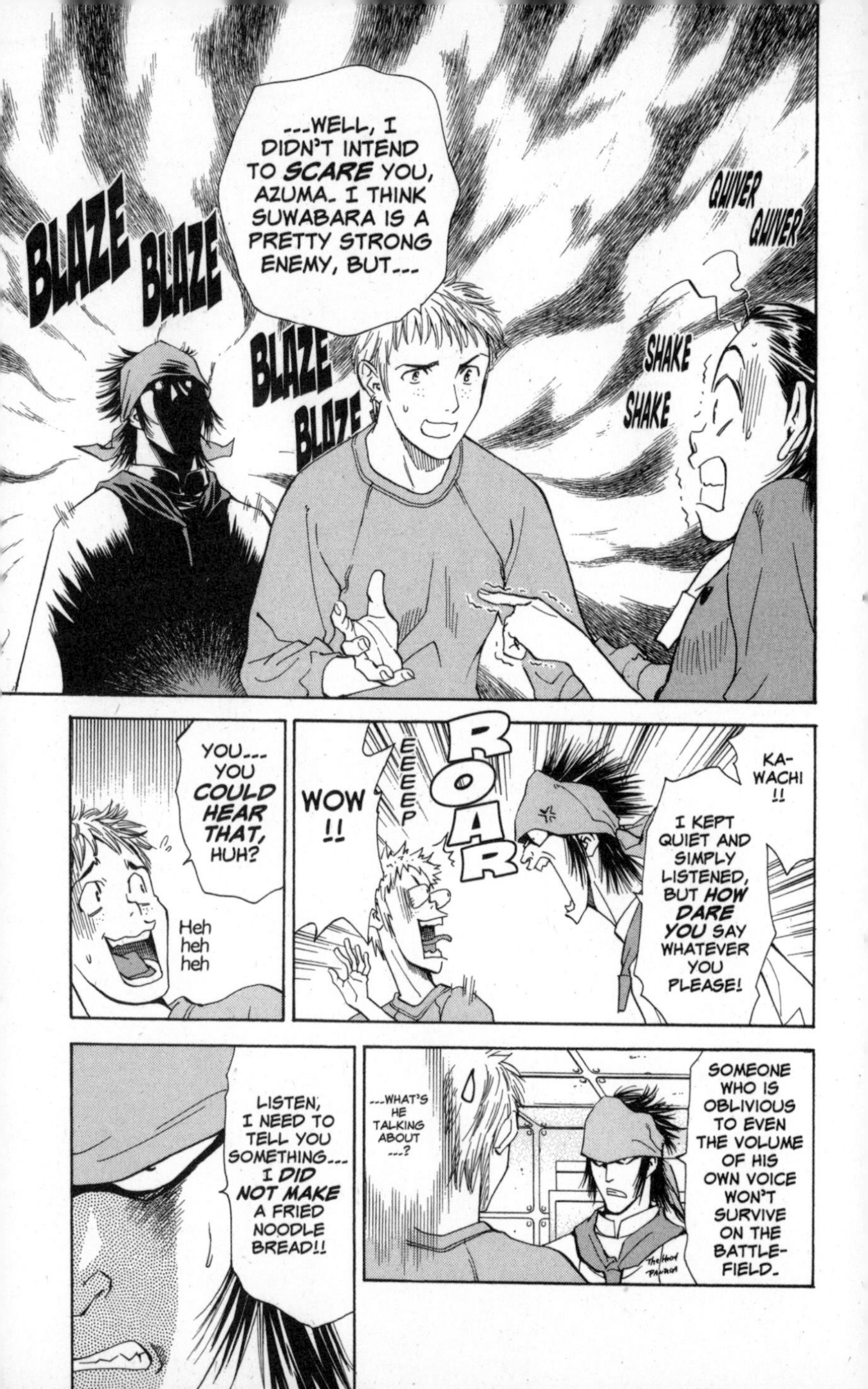
QUIVER
QUIVER
SHAKE
SHAKE
---WELL, I DIDN'T INTEND TO **SCARE** YOU, AZUMA. I THINK SUWABARA IS A PRETTY STRONG ENEMY, BUT---
BLAZE
BLAZE
BLAZE
BLAZE
KA-WACHI!!
I KEPT QUIET AND SIMPLY LISTENED, BUT **HOW DARE YOU** SAY WHATEVER YOU PLEASE!
ROAR
EEEEP
WOW!!
YOU--- YOU **COULD HEAR THAT,** HUH?
Heh heh heh
SOMEONE WHO IS OBLIVIOUS TO EVEN THE VOLUME OF HIS OWN VOICE WON'T SURVIVE ON THE BATTLE-FIELD.
---WHAT'S HE TALKING ABOUT---?
LISTEN, I NEED TO TELL YOU SOMETHING--- I ***DID NOT MAKE*** A FRIED NOODLE BREAD!!

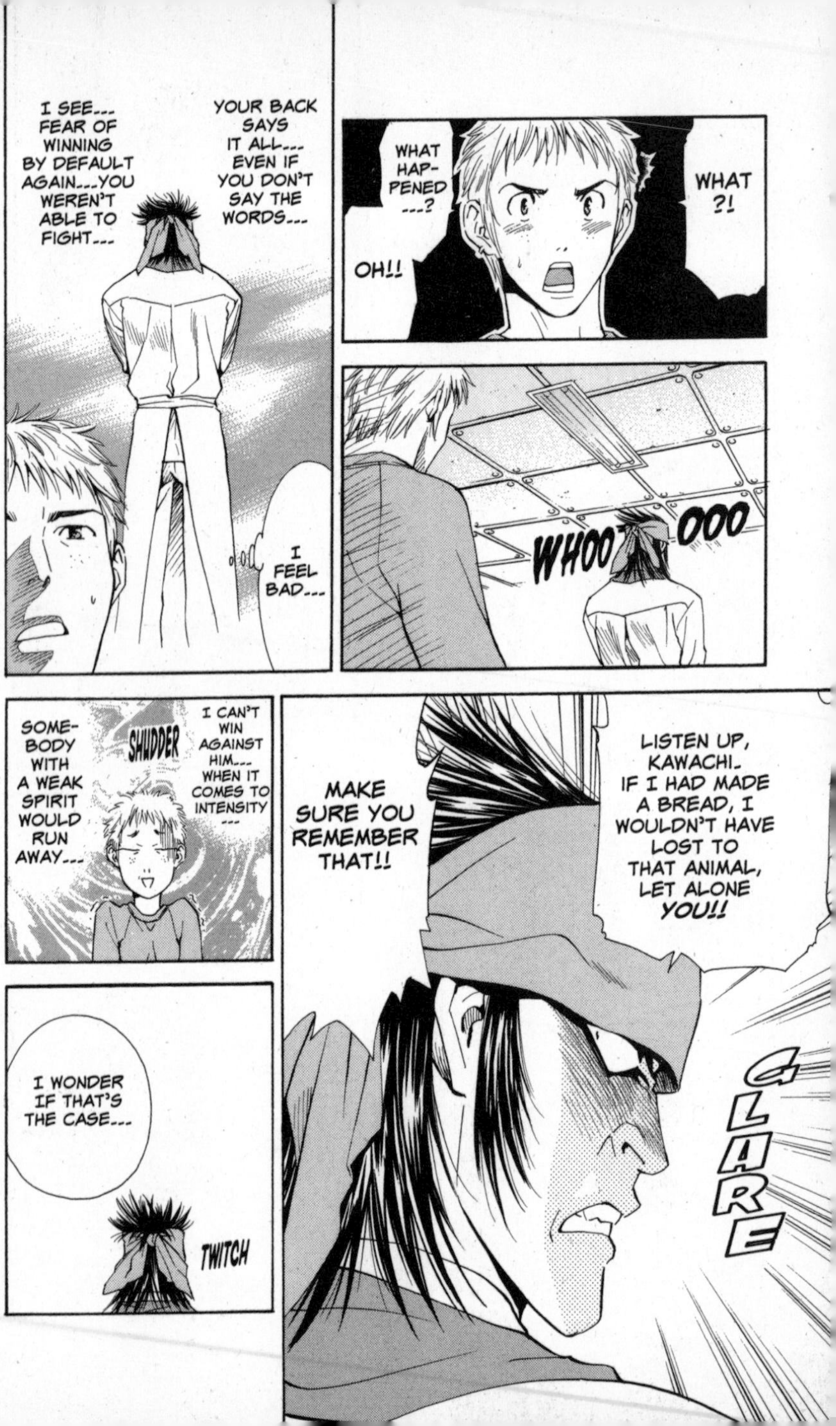
WHAT ?!
WHAT HAPPENED ...?
OH!!
WHOOOOO
YOUR BACK SAYS IT ALL... EVEN IF YOU DON'T SAY THE WORDS...
I SEE... FEAR OF WINNING BY DEFAULT AGAIN...YOU WEREN'T ABLE TO FIGHT...
I FEEL BAD...
LISTEN UP, KAWACHI. IF I HAD MADE A BREAD, I WOULDN'T HAVE LOST TO THAT ANIMAL, LET ALONE YOU!!
MAKE SURE YOU REMEMBER THAT!!
GLARE
I CAN'T WIN AGAINST HIM... WHEN IT COMES TO INTENSITY ...
SHUDDER
SOMEBODY WITH A WEAK SPIRIT WOULD RUN AWAY...
I WONDER IF THAT'S THE CASE...
TWITCH

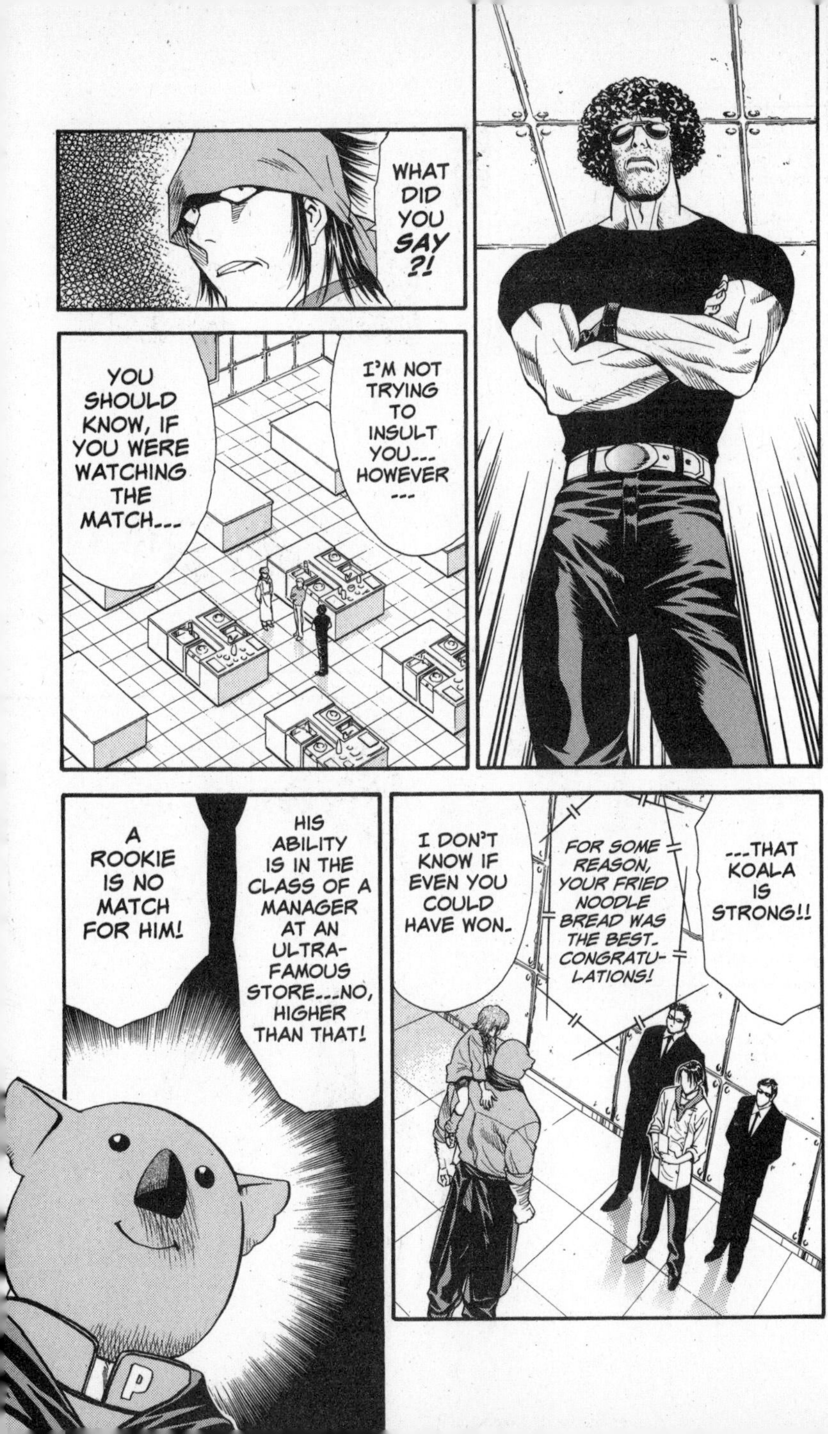
WHAT DID YOU SAY?!
I'M NOT TRYING TO INSULT YOU... HOWEVER ---
YOU SHOULD KNOW, IF YOU WERE WATCHING THE MATCH...
---THAT KOALA IS STRONG!!
FOR SOME REASON, YOUR FRIED NOODLE BREAD WAS THE BEST. CONGRATULATIONS!
I DON'T KNOW IF EVEN YOU COULD HAVE WON.
HIS ABILITY IS IN THE CLASS OF A MANAGER AT AN ULTRA-FAMOUS STORE...NO, HIGHER THAN THAT!
A ROOKIE IS NO MATCH FOR HIM!
P

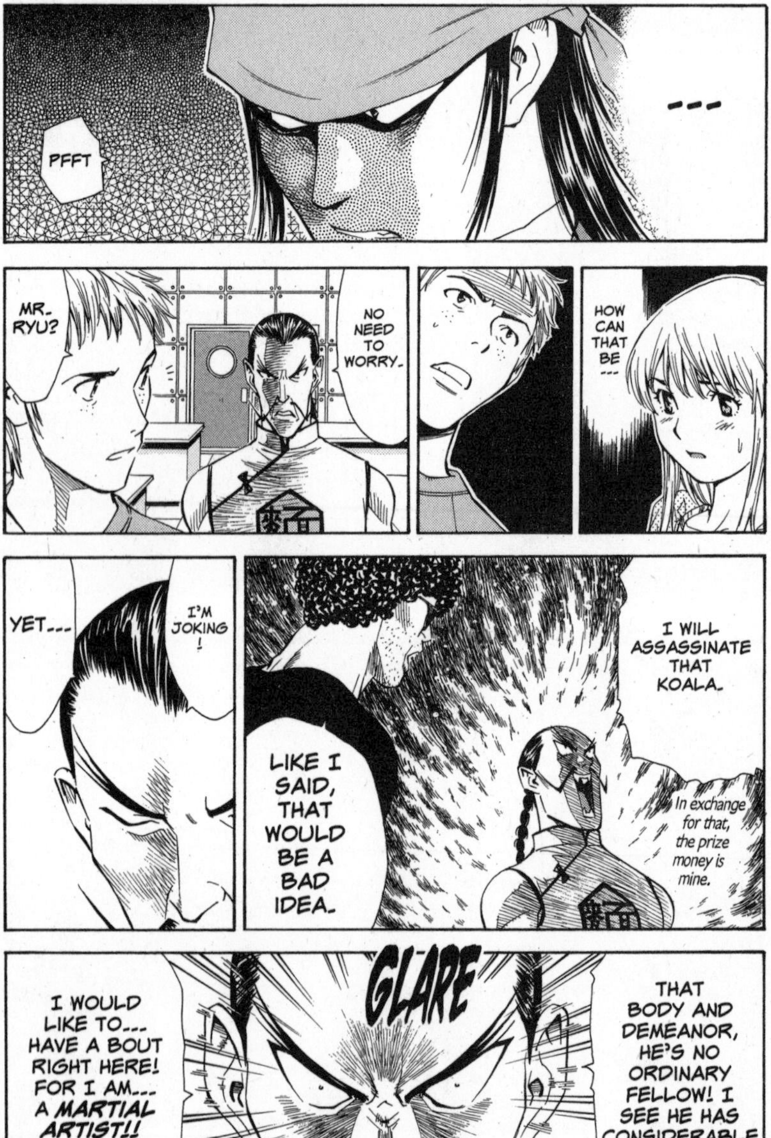

PFFT
HOW CAN THAT BE ---
NO NEED TO WORRY.
MR. RYU?
I WILL ASSASSINATE THAT KOALA.
In exchange for that, the prize money is mine.
LIKE I SAID, THAT WOULD BE A BAD IDEA.
I'M JOKING!
YET...
THAT BODY AND DEMEANOR, HE'S NO ORDINARY FELLOW! I SEE HE HAS CONSIDERABLE ABILITY!!
GLARE
I WOULD LIKE TO... HAVE A BOUT RIGHT HERE! FOR I AM... A MARTIAL ARTIST!!

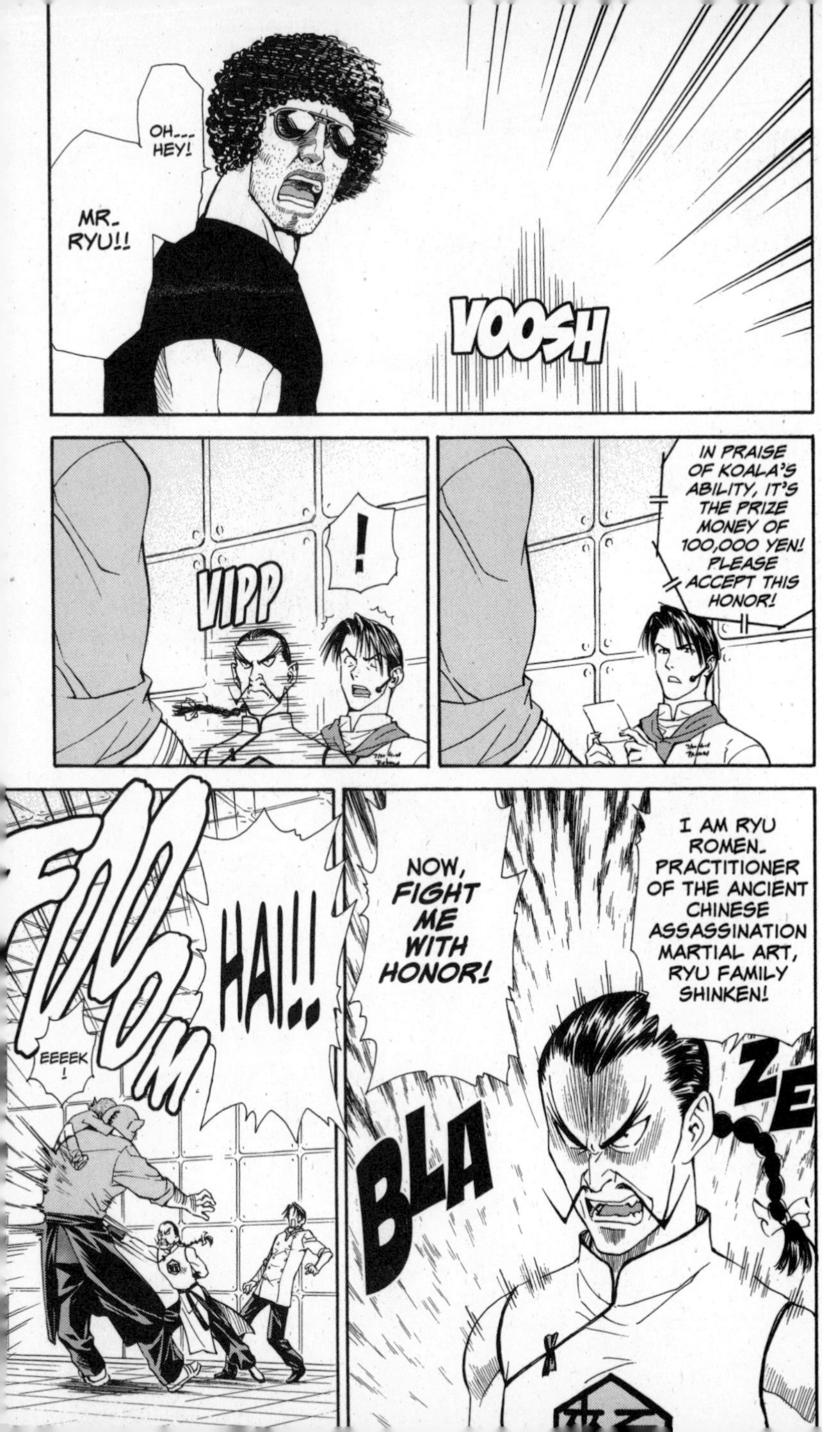
OH... HEY!
MR. RYU!!
VOOSH
IN PRAISE OF KOALA'S ABILITY, IT'S THE PRIZE MONEY OF 100,000 YEN! PLEASE ACCEPT THIS HONOR!
!
VIPP
I AM RYU ROMEN. PRACTITIONER OF THE ANCIENT CHINESE ASSASSINATION MARTIAL ART, RYU FAMILY SHINKEN!
NOW, FIGHT ME WITH HONOR!
ZE
BLA
HAI!!
EEEEK!

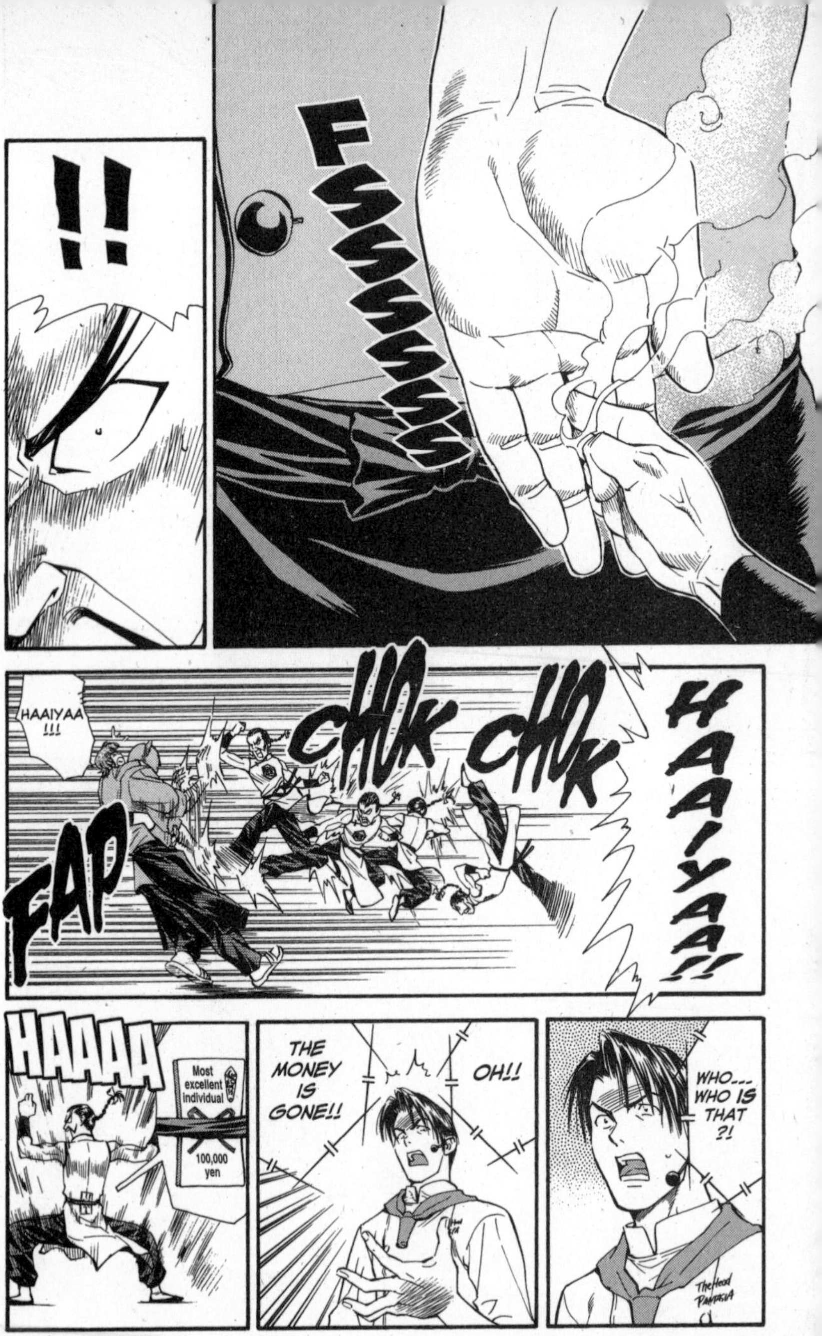
FSSSSSS
!!
HAAIYAA!!
CHOK CHOK
FAP
HAAIYAA!!!
WHO... WHO IS THAT?!
OH!!
THE MONEY IS GONE!!
HAAAA
Most excellent individual
100,000 yen

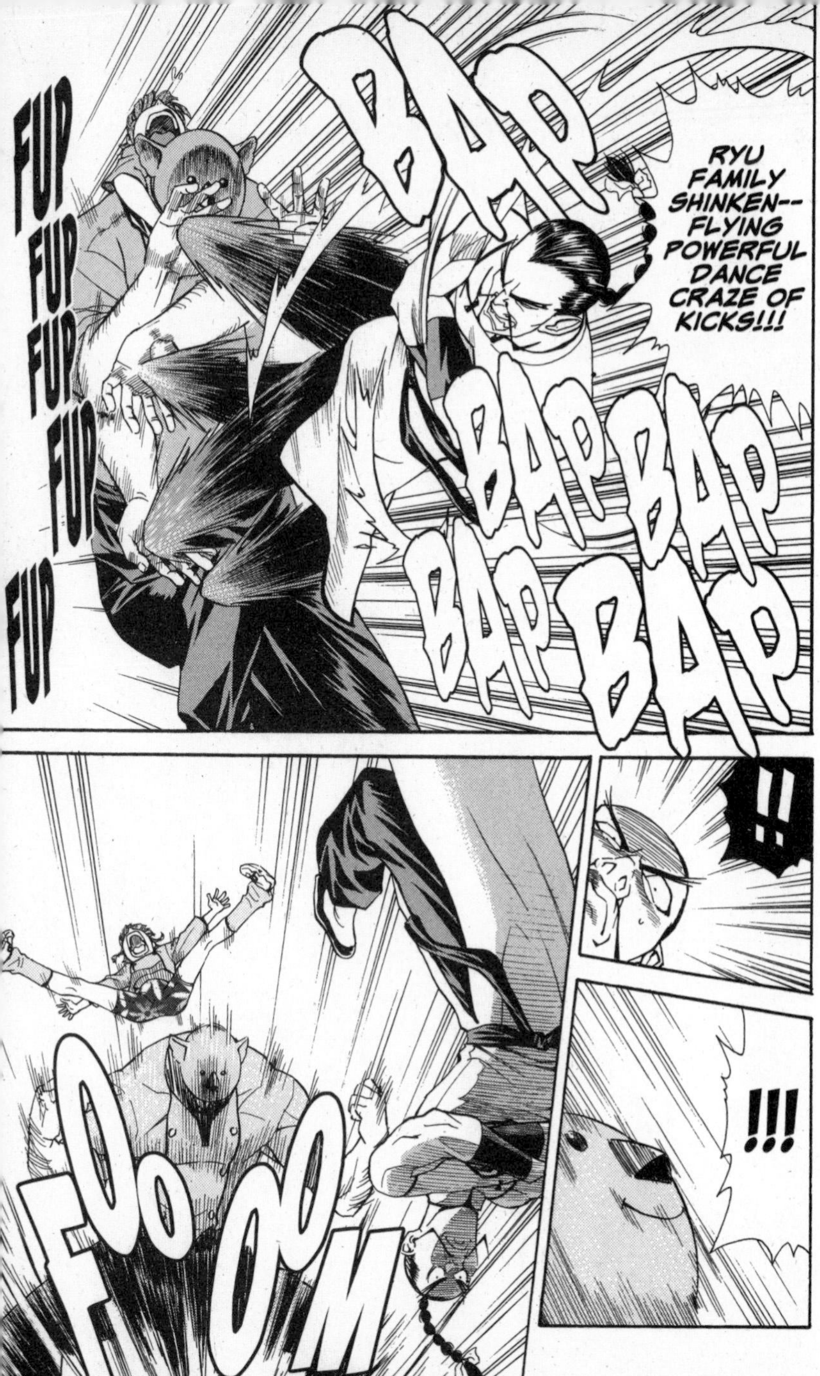
BAP
RYU FAMILY SHINKEN-- FLYING POWERFUL DANCE CRAZE OF KICKS!!!
BAP BAP BAP BAP
FUP FUP FUP FUP FUP FUP
!!
!!!
FOOOOM

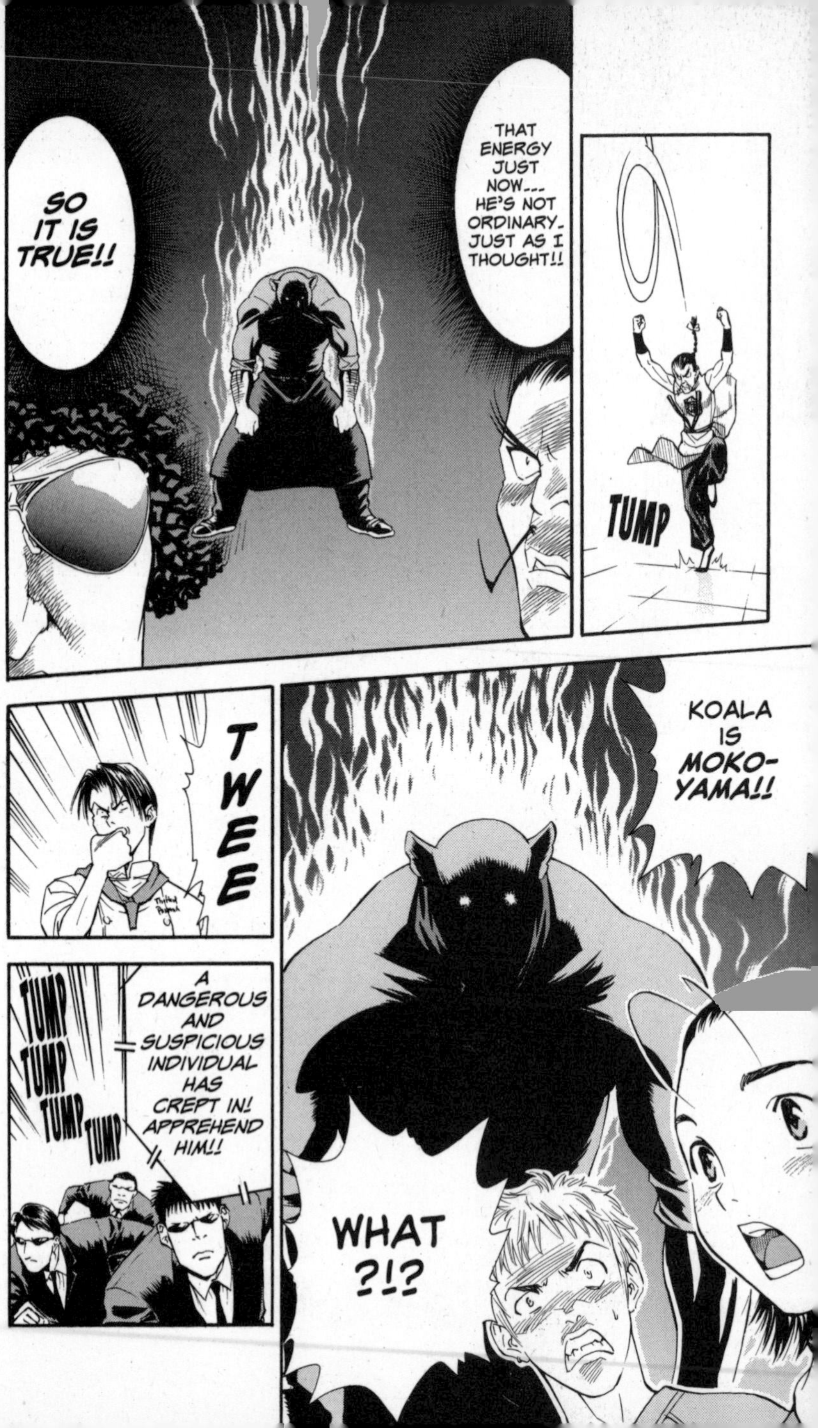
TUMP
THAT ENERGY JUST NOW... HE'S NOT ORDINARY. JUST AS I THOUGHT!!
SO IT IS TRUE!!
KOALA IS MOKO-YAMA!!
WHAT ?!?
TWEE
TUMP TUMP TUMP TUMP
A DANGEROUS AND SUSPICIOUS INDIVIDUAL HAS CREPT IN! APPREHEND HIM!!

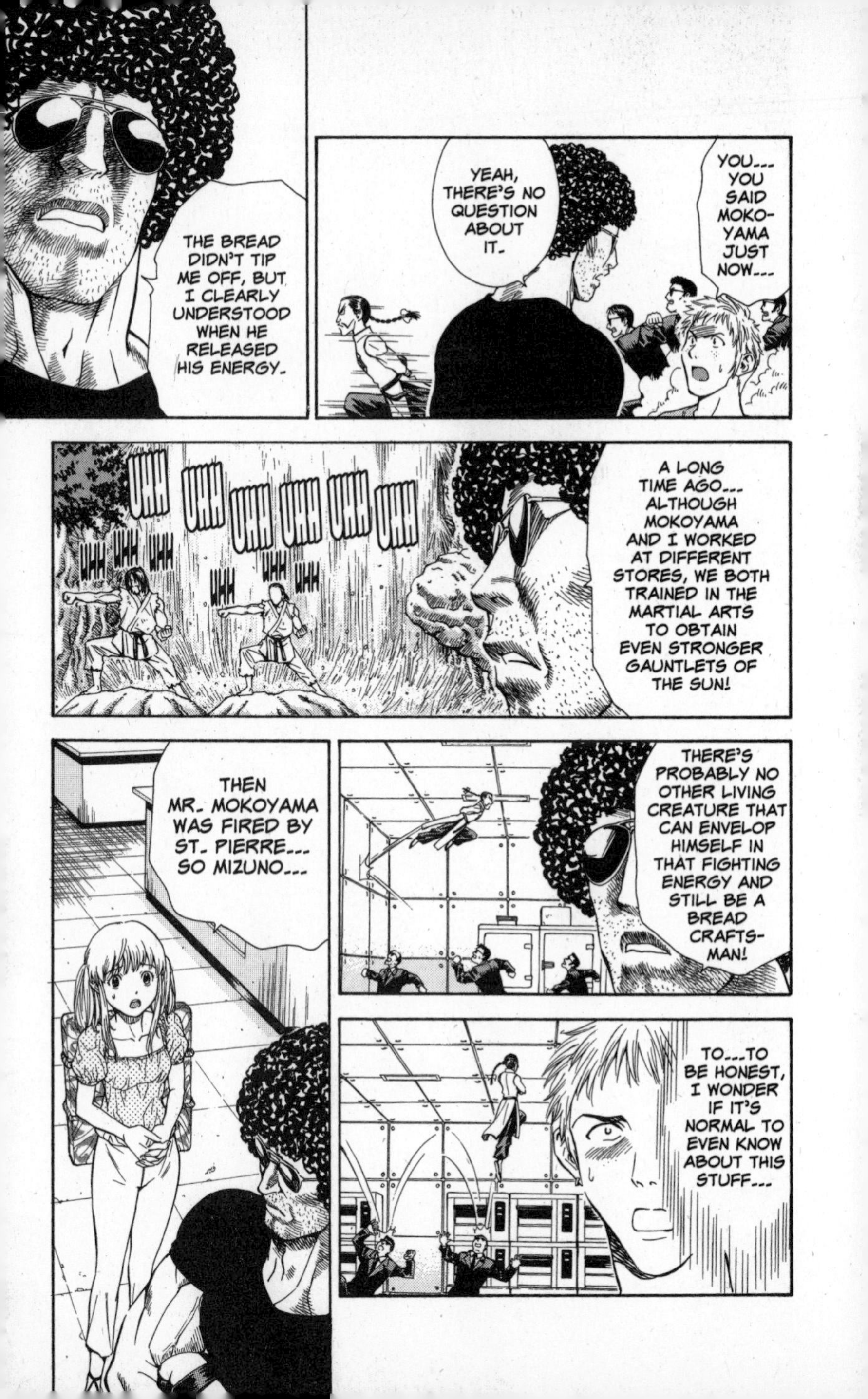
YOU... YOU SAID MOKOYAMA JUST NOW...
YEAH, THERE'S NO QUESTION ABOUT IT.
THE BREAD DIDN'T TIP ME OFF, BUT I CLEARLY UNDERSTOOD WHEN HE RELEASED HIS ENERGY.
A LONG TIME AGO... ALTHOUGH MOKOYAMA AND I WORKED AT DIFFERENT STORES, WE BOTH TRAINED IN THE MARTIAL ARTS TO OBTAIN EVEN STRONGER GAUNTLETS OF THE SUN!
UHH UHH UHH UHH UHH UHH
UHH UHH UHH UHH UHH UHH
THERE'S PROBABLY NO OTHER LIVING CREATURE THAT CAN ENVELOP HIMSELF IN THAT FIGHTING ENERGY AND STILL BE A BREAD CRAFTSMAN!
TO...TO BE HONEST, I WONDER IF IT'S NORMAL TO EVEN KNOW ABOUT THIS STUFF...
THEN MR. MOKOYAMA WAS FIRED BY ST. PIERRE... SO MIZUNO...

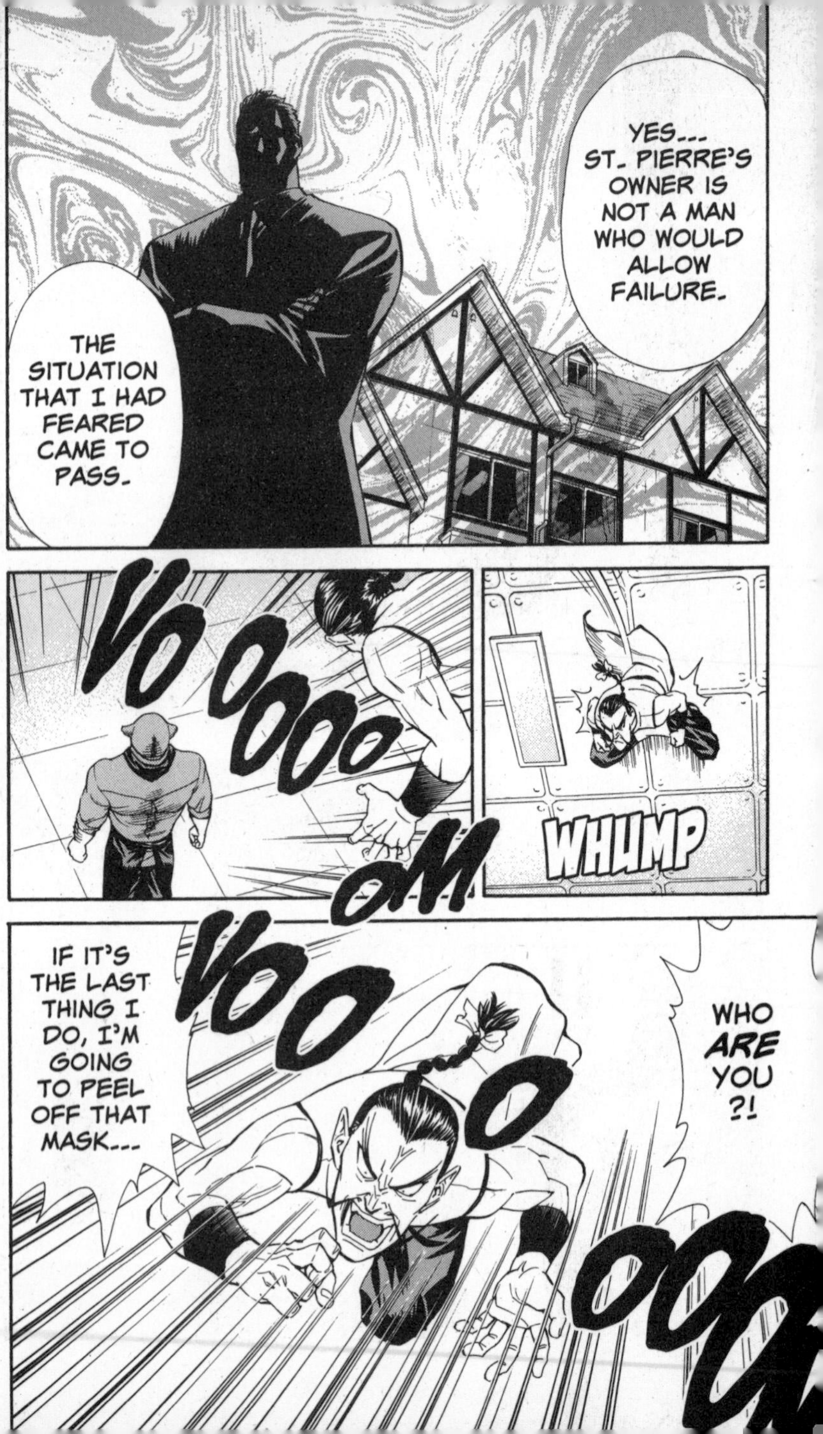
YES... ST. PIERRE'S OWNER IS NOT A MAN WHO WOULD ALLOW FAILURE.
THE SITUATION THAT I HAD FEARED CAME TO PASS.
WHUMP
VOOOOOOM
WHO ARE YOU?!
IF IT'S THE LAST THING I DO, I'M GOING TO PEEL OFF THAT MASK...
VOOOOOOOO

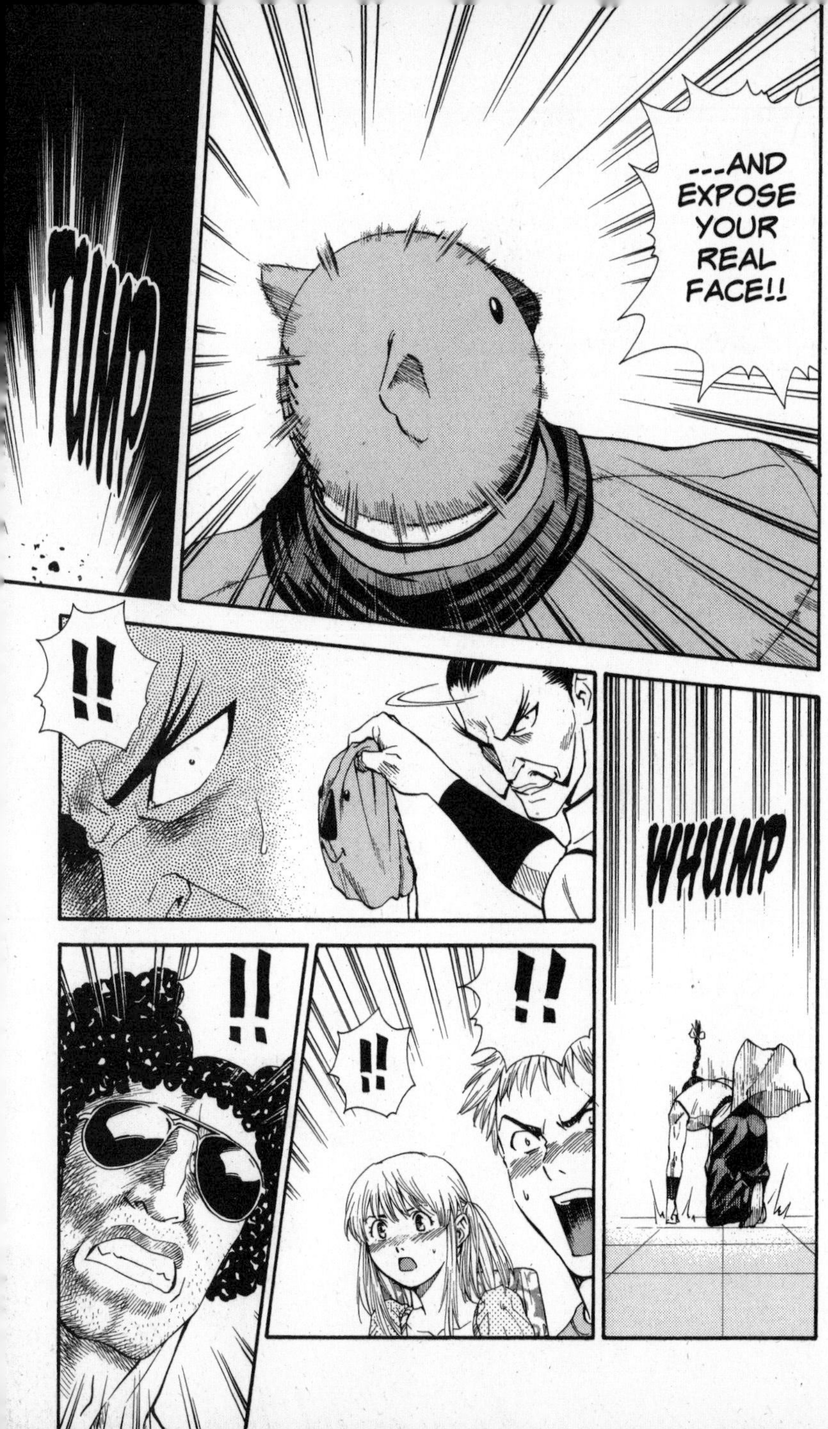
---AND EXPOSE YOUR REAL FACE!!
TUMP
WHUMP
!!
!!
!!
!!

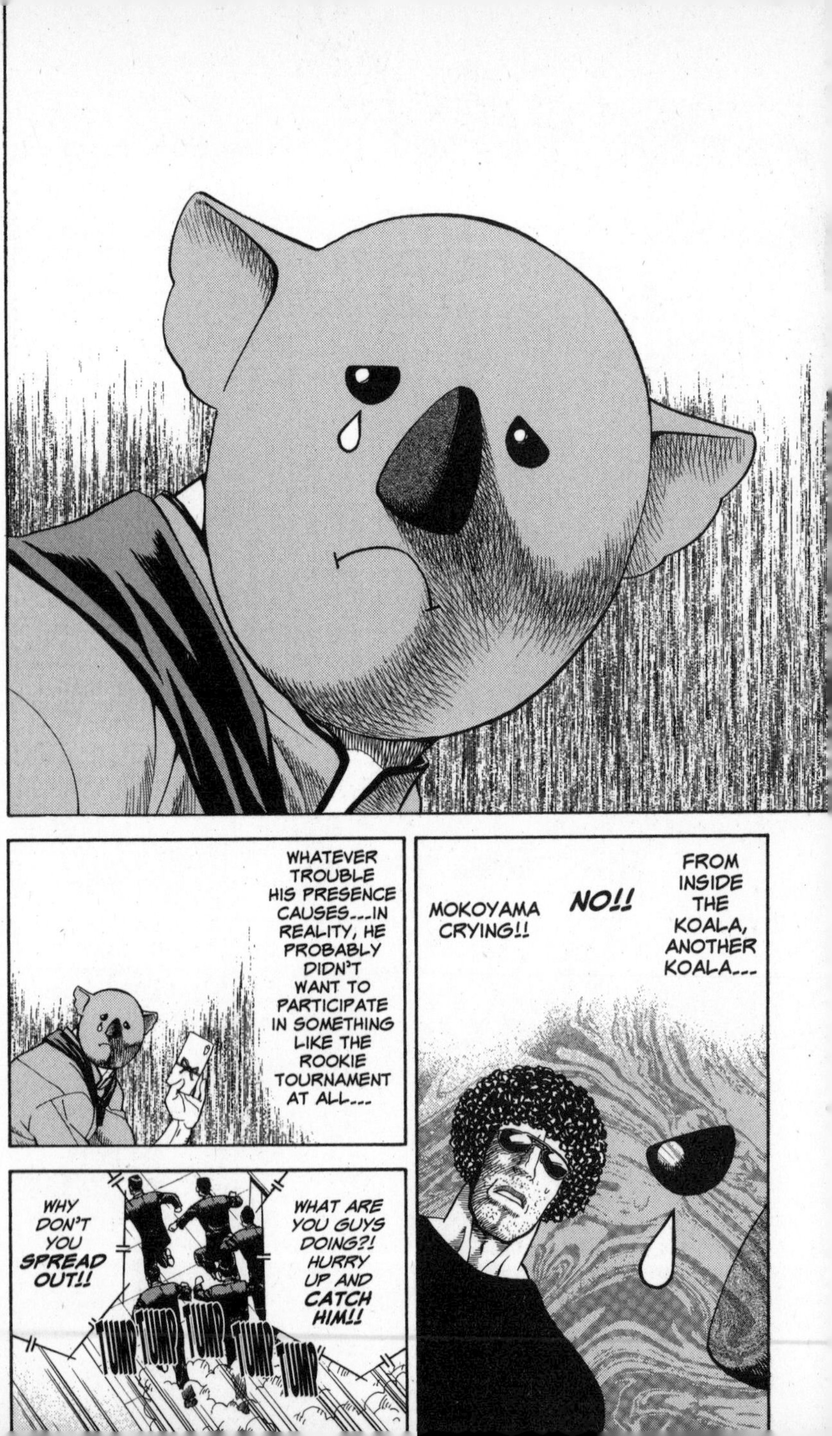
FROM INSIDE THE KOALA, ANOTHER KOALA...
NO!!
MOKOYAMA CRYING!!
WHATEVER TROUBLE HIS PRESENCE CAUSES...IN REALITY, HE PROBABLY DIDN'T WANT TO PARTICIPATE IN SOMETHING LIKE THE ROOKIE TOURNAMENT AT ALL...
WHAT ARE YOU GUYS DOING?! HURRY UP AND CATCH HIM!!
WHY DON'T YOU SPREAD OUT!!
TUMP TUMP TUMP TUMP TUMP

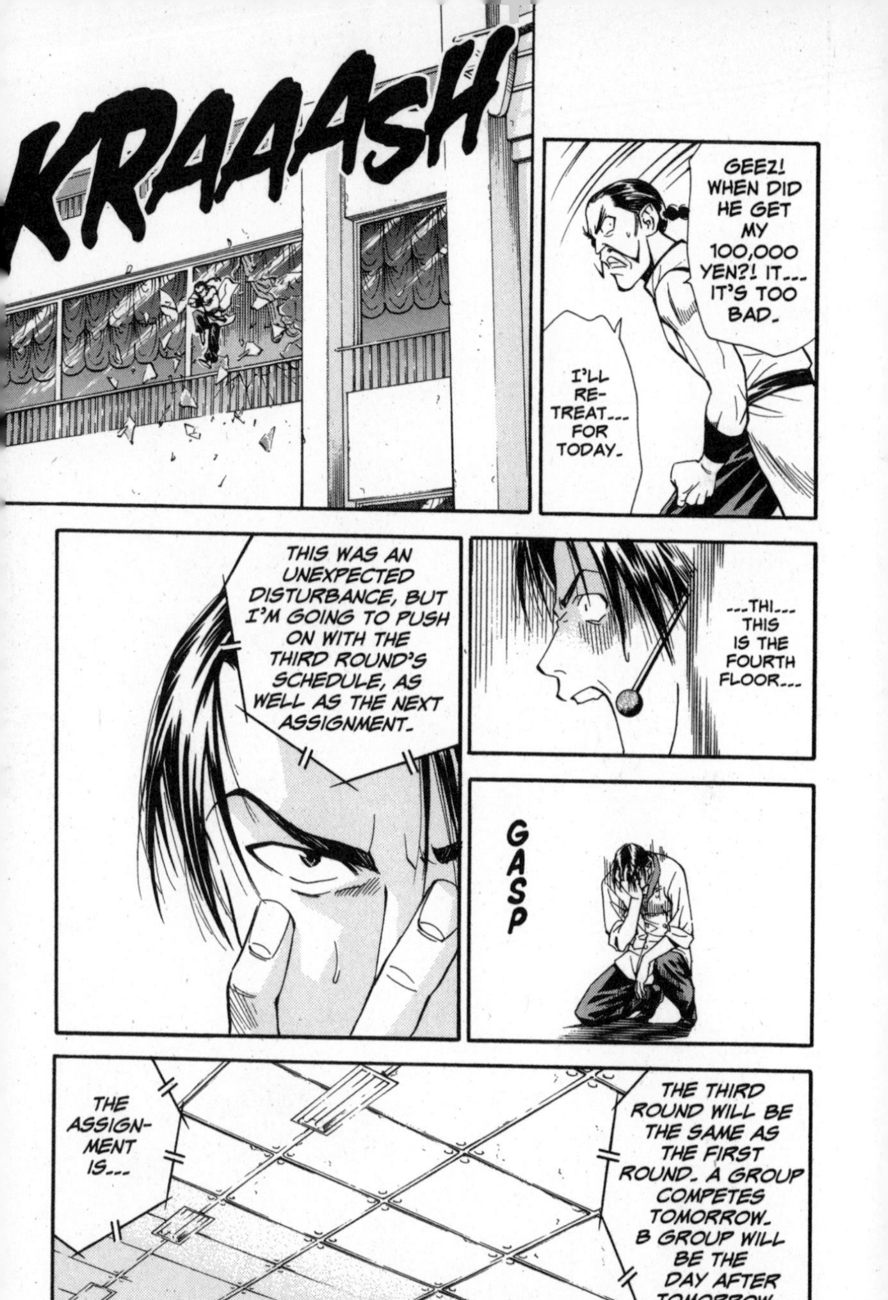
GEEZ! WHEN DID HE GET MY 100,000 YEN?! IT... IT'S TOO BAD.
I'LL RE-TREAT... FOR TODAY.
KRAAASH
...THI... THIS IS THE FOURTH FLOOR...
GASP
THIS WAS AN UNEXPECTED DISTURBANCE, BUT I'M GOING TO PUSH ON WITH THE THIRD ROUND'S SCHEDULE, AS WELL AS THE NEXT ASSIGNMENT.
THE THIRD ROUND WILL BE THE SAME AS THE FIRST ROUND. A GROUP COMPETES TOMORROW. B GROUP WILL BE THE DAY AFTER TOMORROW...
THE ASSIGN-MENT IS...

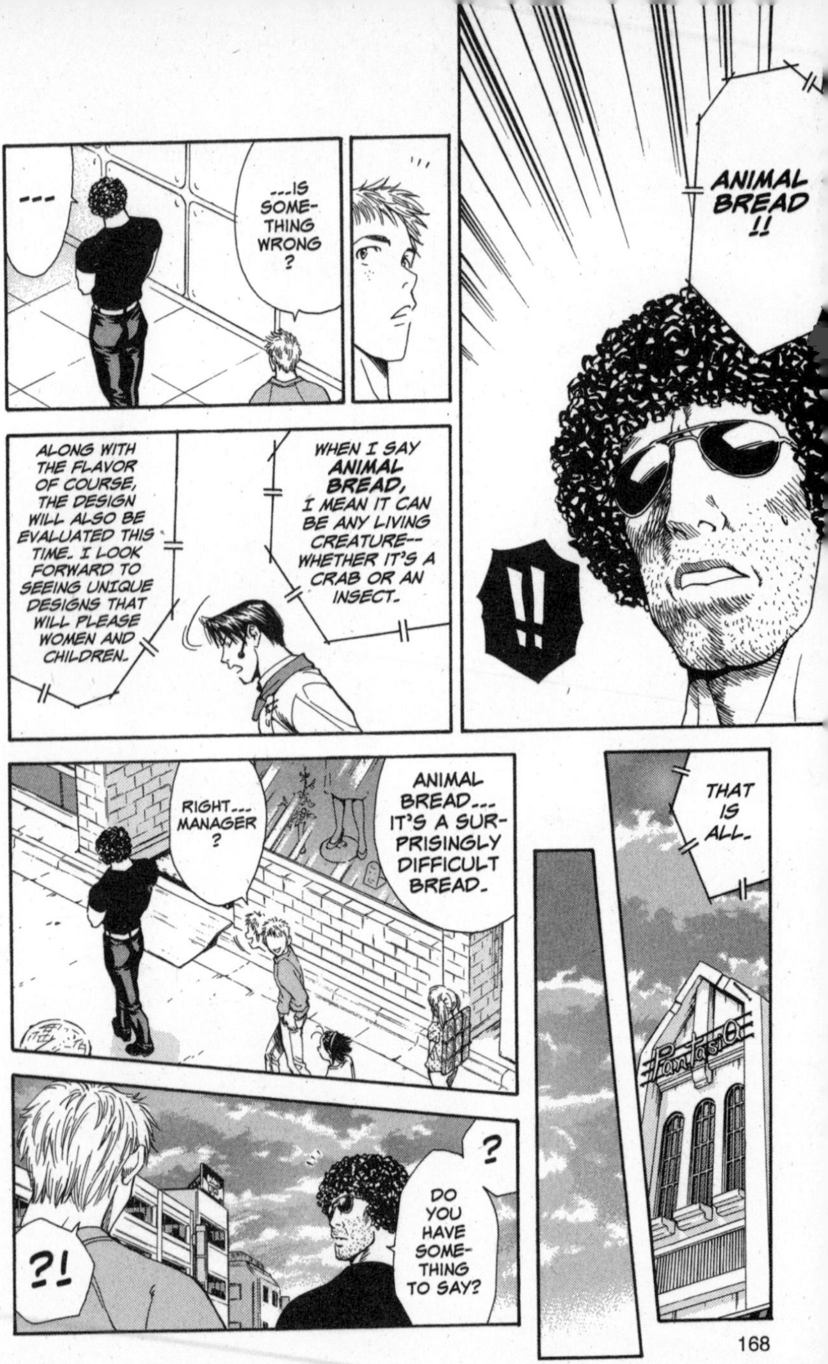
ANIMAL BREAD !!
!!
...IS SOMETHING WRONG?
...
WHEN I SAY ANIMAL BREAD, I MEAN IT CAN BE ANY LIVING CREATURE-- WHETHER IT'S A CRAB OR AN INSECT.
ALONG WITH THE FLAVOR OF COURSE, THE DESIGN WILL ALSO BE EVALUATED THIS TIME. I LOOK FORWARD TO SEEING UNIQUE DESIGNS THAT WILL PLEASE WOMEN AND CHILDREN.
THAT IS ALL.
Pantasia
ANIMAL BREAD... IT'S A SURPRISINGLY DIFFICULT BREAD.
RIGHT... MANAGER?
?
DO YOU HAVE SOMETHING TO SAY?
?!

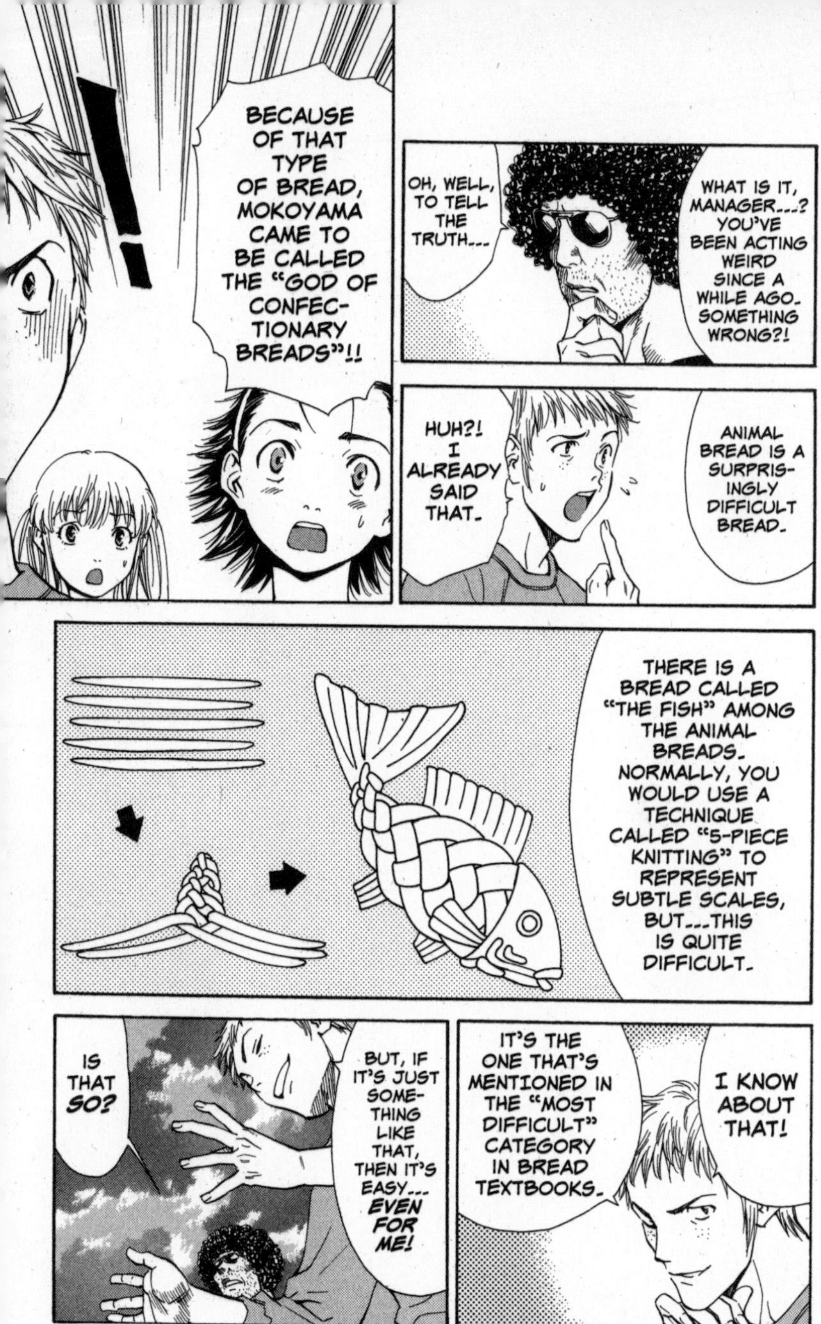
WHAT IS IT, MANAGER...? YOU'VE BEEN ACTING WEIRD SINCE A WHILE AGO. SOMETHING WRONG?!
OH, WELL, TO TELL THE TRUTH...
ANIMAL BREAD IS A SURPRISINGLY DIFFICULT BREAD.
HUH?! I ALREADY SAID THAT.
BECAUSE OF THAT TYPE OF BREAD, MOKOYAMA CAME TO BE CALLED THE "GOD OF CONFECTIONARY BREADS"!!
THERE IS A BREAD CALLED "THE FISH" AMONG THE ANIMAL BREADS. NORMALLY, YOU WOULD USE A TECHNIQUE CALLED "5-PIECE KNITTING" TO REPRESENT SUBTLE SCALES, BUT...THIS IS QUITE DIFFICULT.
I KNOW ABOUT THAT!
IT'S THE ONE THAT'S MENTIONED IN THE "MOST DIFFICULT" CATEGORY IN BREAD TEXTBOOKS.
BUT, IF IT'S JUST SOMETHING LIKE THAT, THEN IT'S EASY... *EVEN FOR ME!*
IS THAT *SO?*

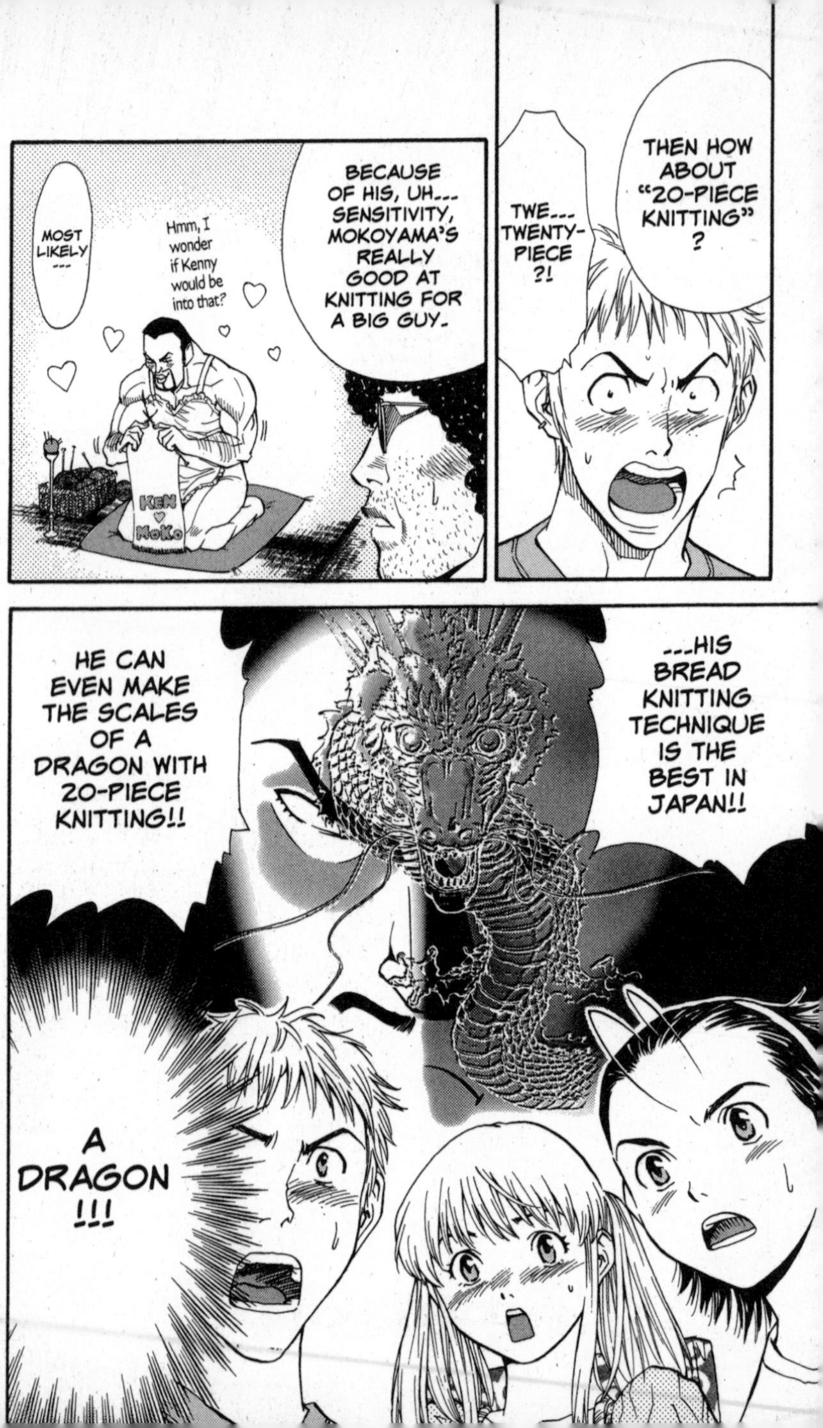
THEN HOW ABOUT "20-PIECE KNITTING"?
TWE... TWENTY-PIECE?!
BECAUSE OF HIS, UH... SENSITIVITY, MOKOYAMA'S REALLY GOOD AT KNITTING FOR A BIG GUY.
Hmm, I wonder if Kenny would be into that?
KEN ♥ MOKO
MOST LIKELY...
...HIS BREAD KNITTING TECHNIQUE IS THE BEST IN JAPAN!!
HE CAN EVEN MAKE THE SCALES OF A DRAGON WITH 20-PIECE KNITTING!!
A DRAGON!!!

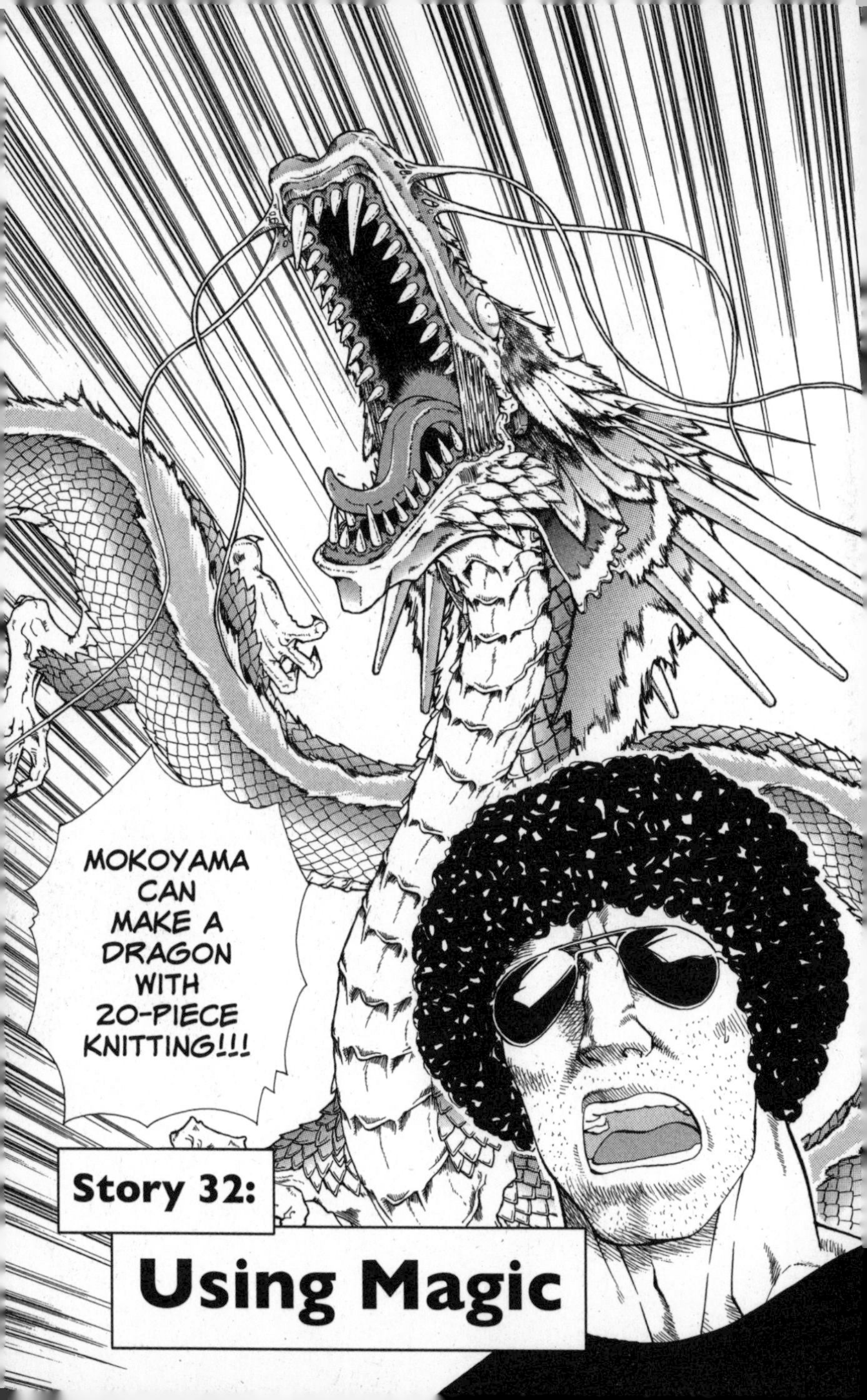
MOKOYAMA CAN MAKE A DRAGON WITH 20-PIECE KNITTING!!!
Story 32:
Using Magic

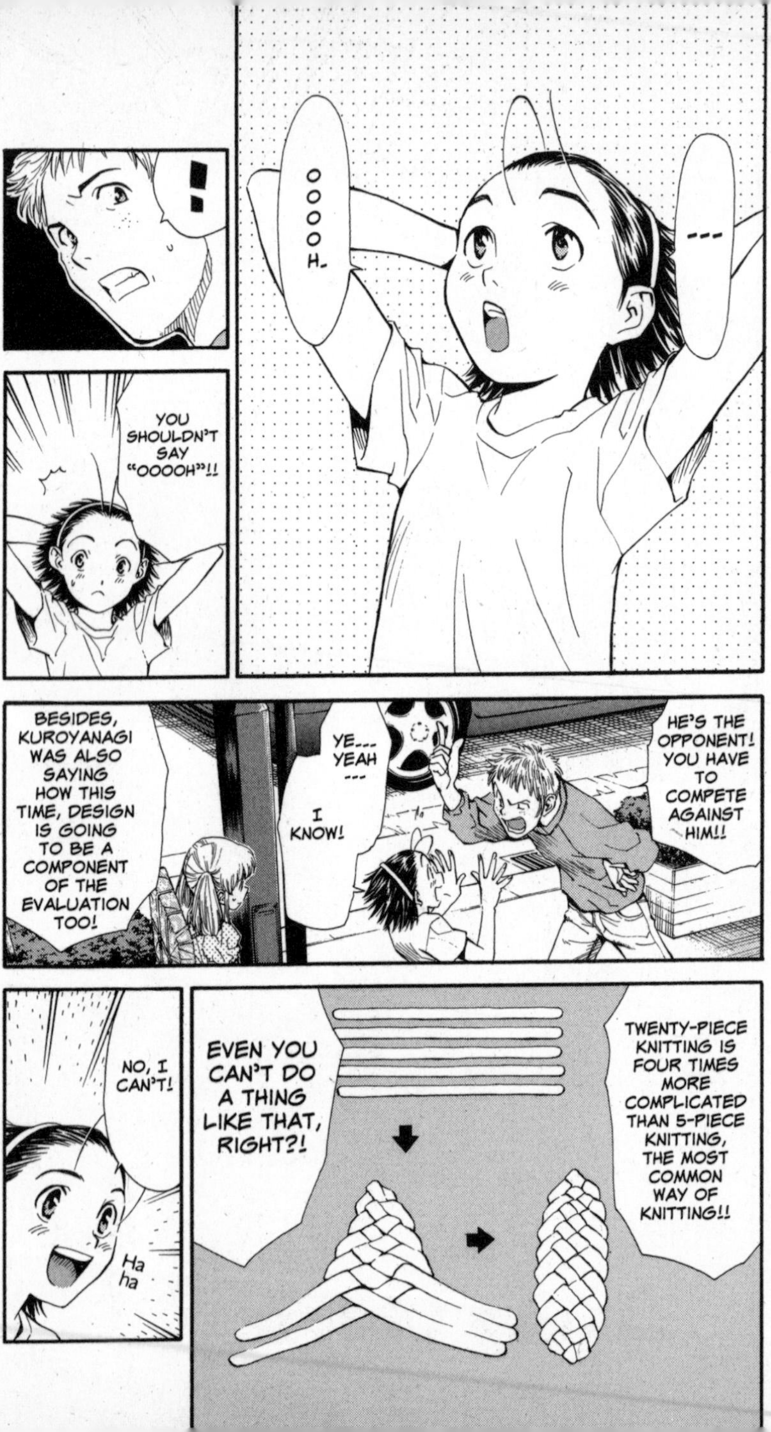
...
OOOOH.
!
YOU SHOULDN'T SAY "OOOOH"!!
HE'S THE OPPONENT! YOU HAVE TO COMPETE AGAINST HIM!!
YE... YEAH ...
I KNOW!
BESIDES, KUROYANAGI WAS ALSO SAYING HOW THIS TIME, DESIGN IS GOING TO BE A COMPONENT OF THE EVALUATION TOO!
TWENTY-PIECE KNITTING IS FOUR TIMES MORE COMPLICATED THAN 5-PIECE KNITTING, THE MOST COMMON WAY OF KNITTING!!
EVEN YOU CAN'T DO A THING LIKE THAT, RIGHT?!
NO, I CAN'T!
Ha ha

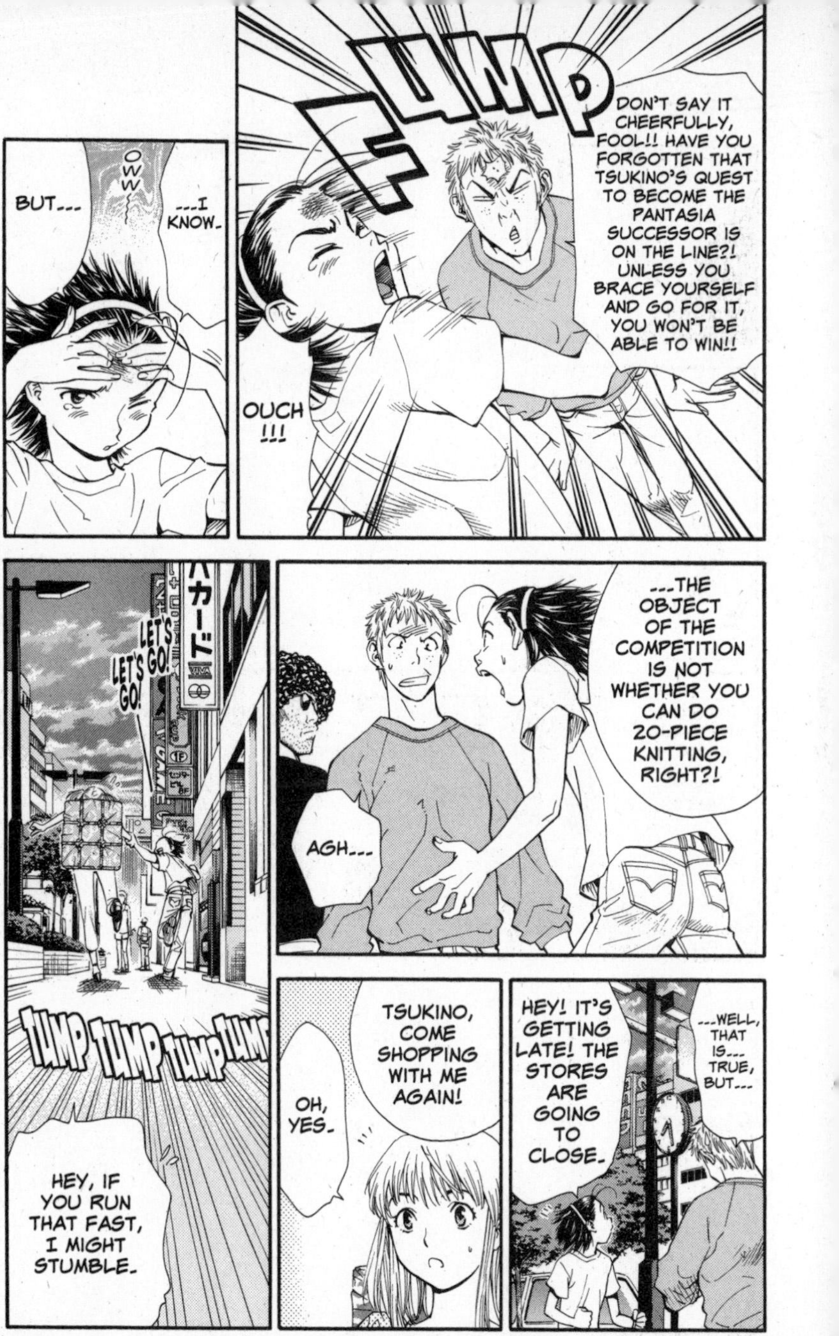
TUMP
DON'T SAY IT CHEERFULLY, FOOL!! HAVE YOU FORGOTTEN THAT TSUKINO'S QUEST TO BECOME THE PANTASIA SUCCESSOR IS ON THE LINE?! UNLESS YOU BRACE YOURSELF AND GO FOR IT, YOU WON'T BE ABLE TO WIN!!
OUCH !!!
OWW...
...I KNOW.
BUT...
...THE OBJECT OF THE COMPETITION IS NOT WHETHER YOU CAN DO 20-PIECE KNITTING, RIGHT?!
AGH...
...WELL, THAT IS... TRUE, BUT...
HEY! IT'S GETTING LATE! THE STORES ARE GOING TO CLOSE.
TSUKINO, COME SHOPPING WITH ME AGAIN!
OH, YES.
LET'S GO! LET'S GO!
TUMP TUMP TUMP TUMP
HEY, IF YOU RUN THAT FAST, I MIGHT STUMBLE.

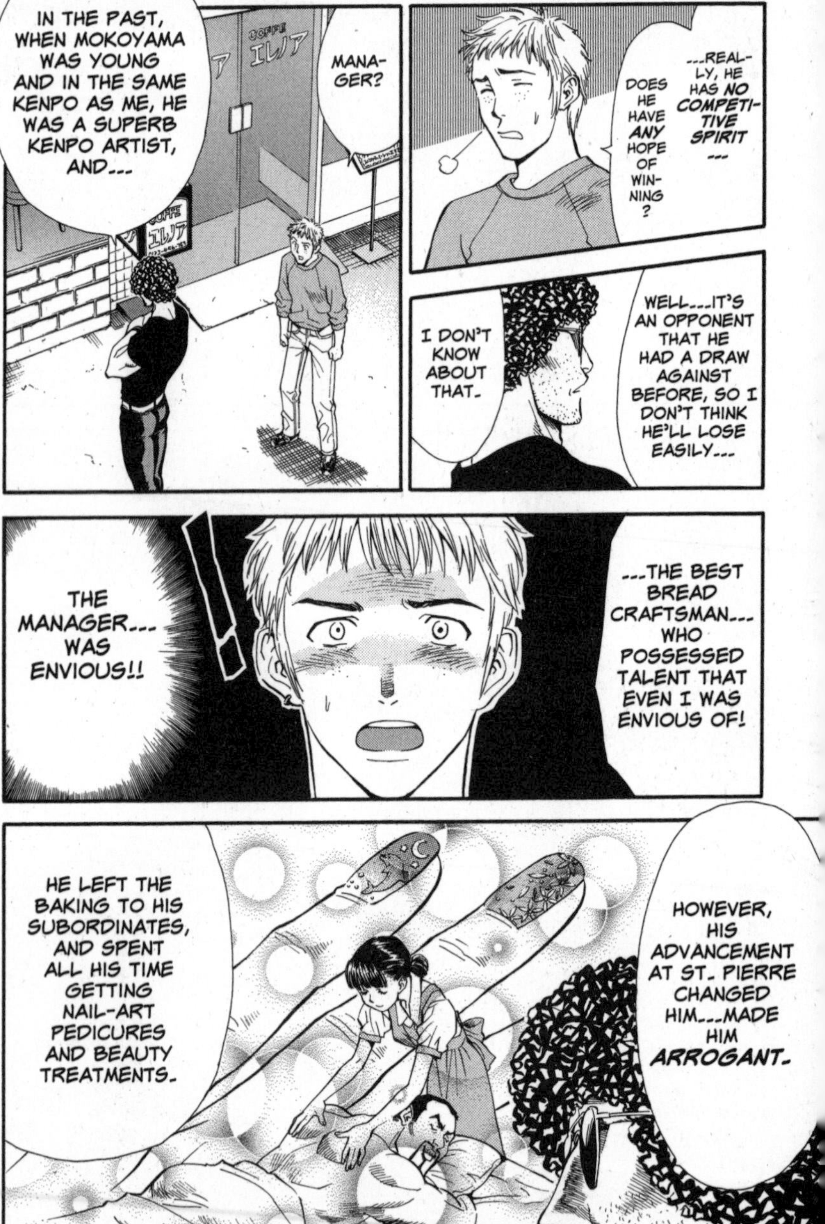

...REALLY, HE HAS NO COMPETITIVE SPIRIT...
DOES HE HAVE ANY HOPE OF WINNING?
WELL... IT'S AN OPPONENT THAT HE HAD A DRAW AGAINST BEFORE, SO I DON'T THINK HE'LL LOSE EASILY...
I DON'T KNOW ABOUT THAT.
MANAGER?
IN THE PAST, WHEN MOKOYAMA WAS YOUNG AND IN THE SAME KENPO AS ME, HE WAS A SUPERB KENPO ARTIST, AND...
...THE BEST BREAD CRAFTSMAN... WHO POSSESSED TALENT THAT EVEN I WAS ENVIOUS OF!
THE MANAGER... WAS ENVIOUS!!
HOWEVER, HIS ADVANCEMENT AT ST. PIERRE CHANGED HIM... MADE HIM ARROGANT.
HE LEFT THE BAKING TO HIS SUBORDINATES, AND SPENT ALL HIS TIME GETTING NAIL-ART PEDICURES AND BEAUTY TREATMENTS.

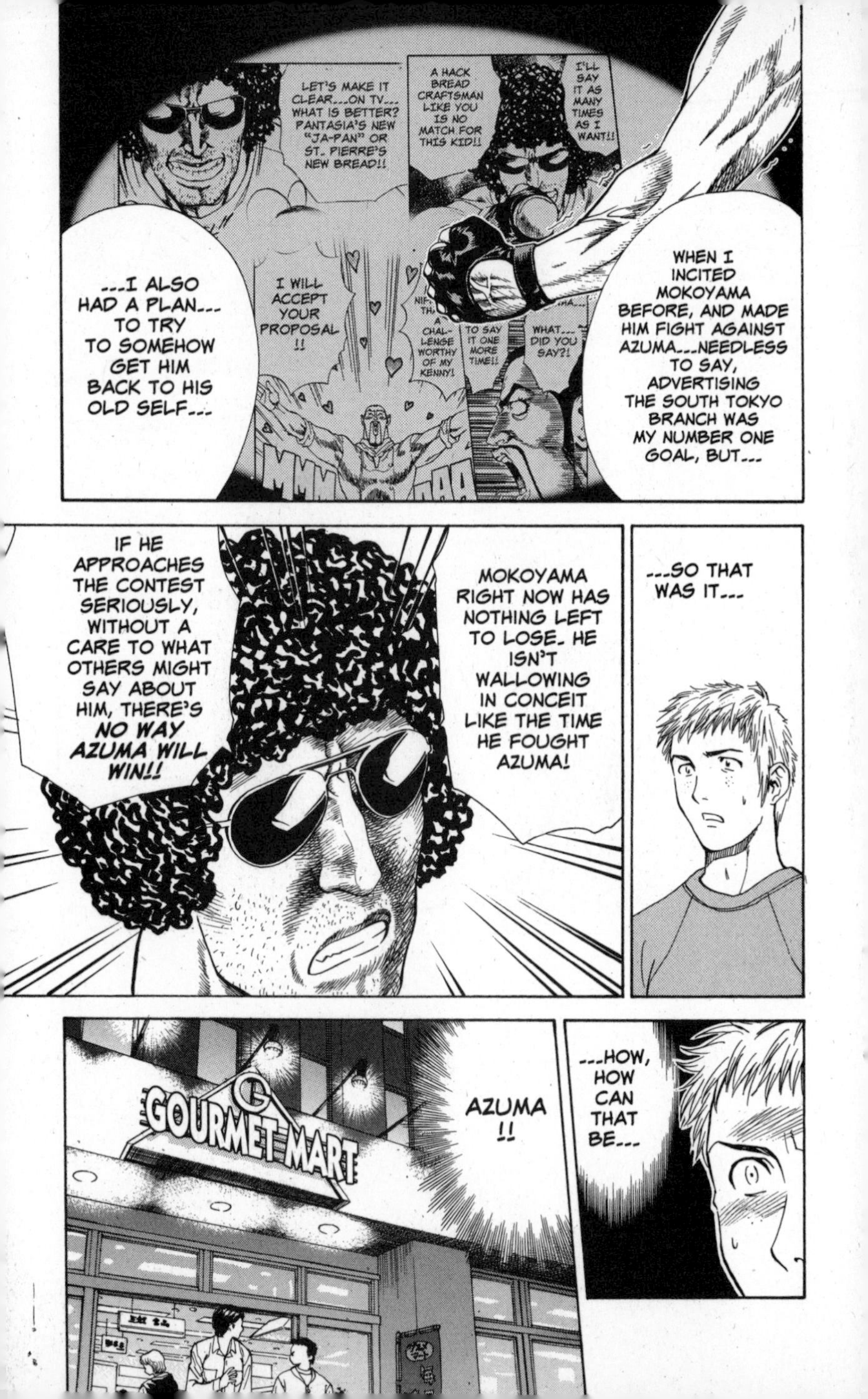
WHEN I INCITED MOKOYAMA BEFORE, AND MADE HIM FIGHT AGAINST AZUMA...NEEDLESS TO SAY, ADVERTISING THE SOUTH TOKYO BRANCH WAS MY NUMBER ONE GOAL, BUT...
I'LL SAY IT AS MANY TIMES AS I WANT!!
A HACK BREAD CRAFTSMAN LIKE YOU IS NO MATCH FOR THIS KID!!
LET'S MAKE IT CLEAR...ON TV... WHAT IS BETTER? PANTASIA'S NEW "JA-PAN" OR ST. PIERRE'S NEW BREAD!!
WHAT... DID YOU SAY?!
TO SAY IT ONE MORE TIME!!
A CHAL-LENGE WORTHY OF MY KENNY!
I WILL ACCEPT YOUR PROPOSAL !!
...I ALSO HAD A PLAN... TO TRY TO SOMEHOW GET HIM BACK TO HIS OLD SELF...
...SO THAT WAS IT...
MOKOYAMA RIGHT NOW HAS NOTHING LEFT TO LOSE. HE ISN'T WALLOWING IN CONCEIT LIKE THE TIME HE FOUGHT AZUMA!
IF HE APPROACHES THE CONTEST SERIOUSLY, WITHOUT A CARE TO WHAT OTHERS MIGHT SAY ABOUT HIM, THERE'S NO WAY AZUMA WILL WIN!!
...HOW, HOW CAN THAT BE...
AZUMA !!
GOURMET MART

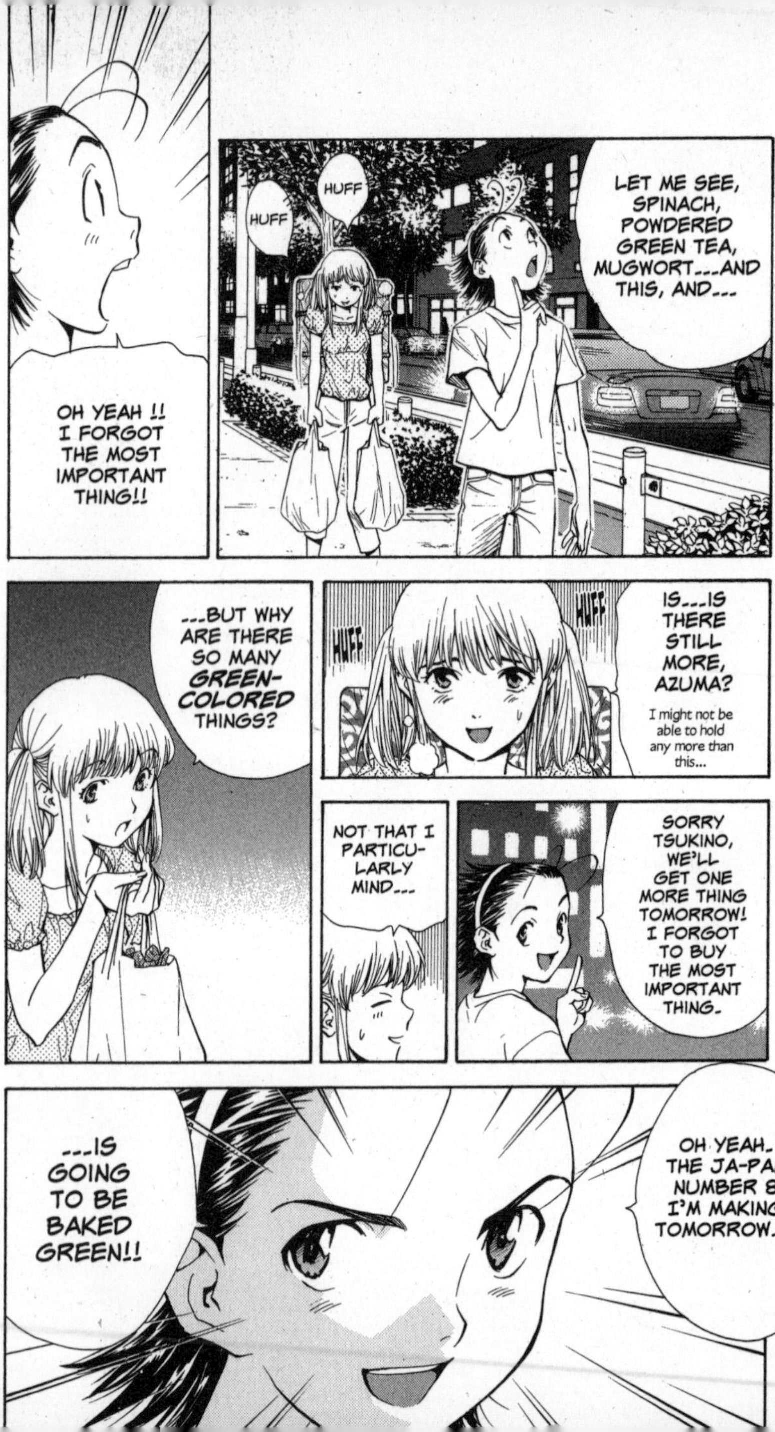
LET ME SEE, SPINACH, POWDERED GREEN TEA, MUGWORT...AND THIS, AND...
HUFF
HUFF
OH YEAH !! I FORGOT THE MOST IMPORTANT THING!!
HUFF
HUFF
IS...IS THERE STILL MORE, AZUMA?
I might not be able to hold any more than this...
SORRY TSUKINO, WE'LL GET ONE MORE THING TOMORROW! I FORGOT TO BUY THE MOST IMPORTANT THING.
NOT THAT I PARTICU-LARLY MIND...
...BUT WHY ARE THERE SO MANY GREEN-COLORED THINGS?
OH YEAH. THE JA-PAN NUMBER 8 I'M MAKING TOMORROW...
...IS GOING TO BE BAKED GREEN!!

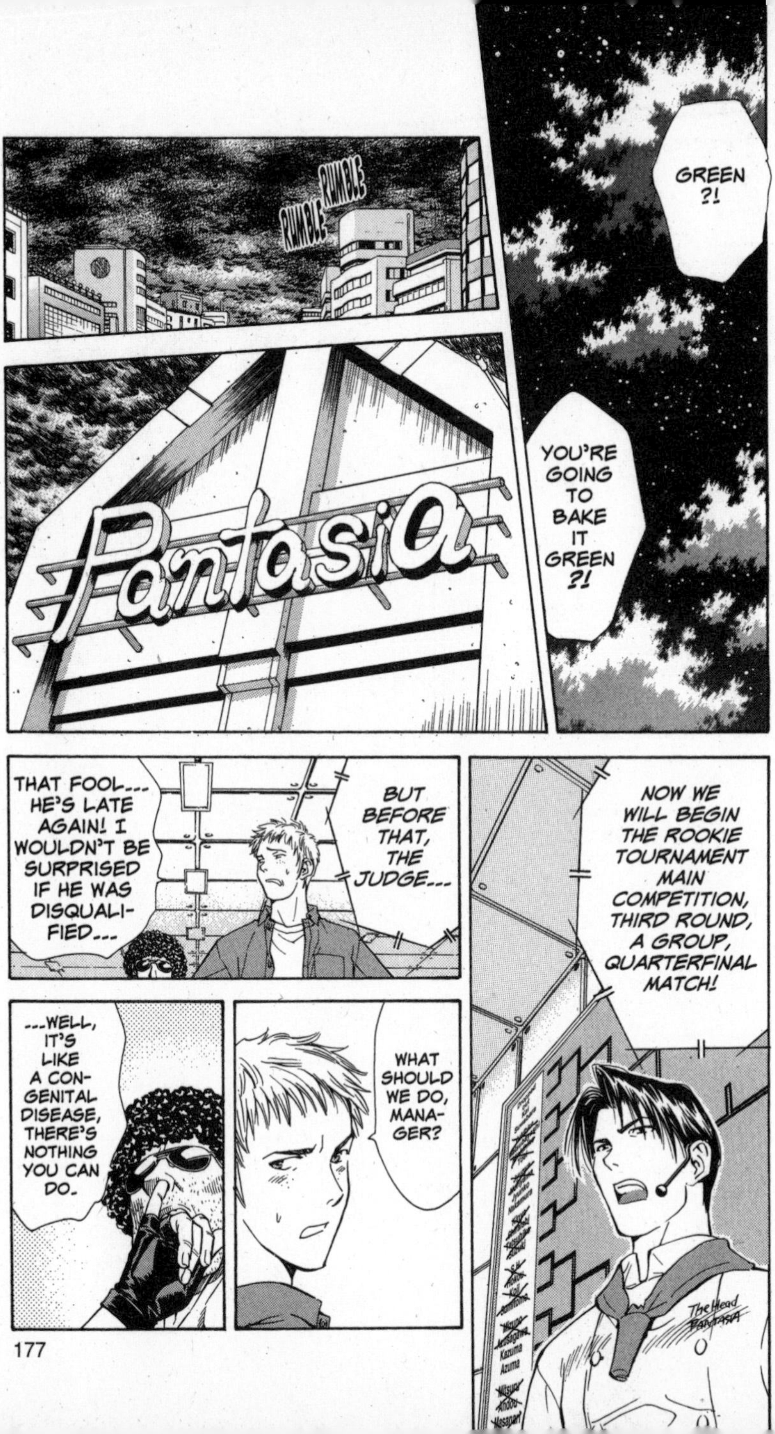
GREEN ?!
YOU'RE GOING TO BAKE IT GREEN ?!
RUMBLE RUMBLE
Pantasia
NOW WE WILL BEGIN THE ROOKIE TOURNAMENT MAIN COMPETITION, THIRD ROUND, A GROUP, QUARTERFINAL MATCH!
Kazuma Azuma
The Head PANTASIA
BUT BEFORE THAT, THE JUDGE...
THAT FOOL... HE'S LATE AGAIN! I WOULDN'T BE SURPRISED IF HE WAS DISQUALIFIED...
WHAT SHOULD WE DO, MANAGER?
...WELL, IT'S LIKE A CONGENITAL DISEASE, THERE'S NOTHING YOU CAN DO.

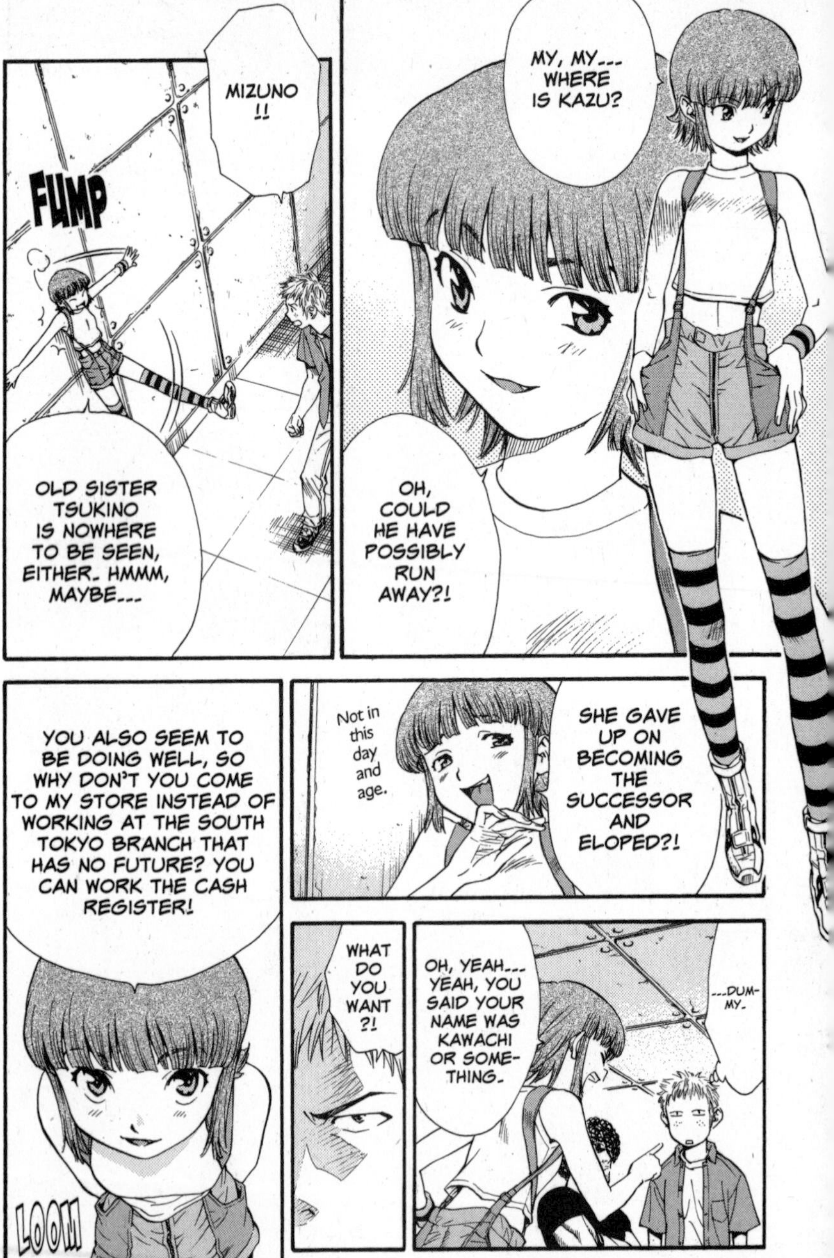
MY, MY... WHERE IS KAZU?
OH, COULD HE HAVE POSSIBLY RUN AWAY?!
MIZUNO !!
FUMP
OLD SISTER TSUKINO IS NOWHERE TO BE SEEN, EITHER. HMMM, MAYBE...
SHE GAVE UP ON BECOMING THE SUCCESSOR AND ELOPED?!
Not in this day and age.
OH, YEAH... YEAH, YOU SAID YOUR NAME WAS KAWACHI OR SOME-THING.
...DUM-MY.
WHAT DO YOU WANT ?!
YOU ALSO SEEM TO BE DOING WELL, SO WHY DON'T YOU COME TO MY STORE INSTEAD OF WORKING AT THE SOUTH TOKYO BRANCH THAT HAS NO FUTURE? YOU CAN WORK THE CASH REGISTER!
LOOM

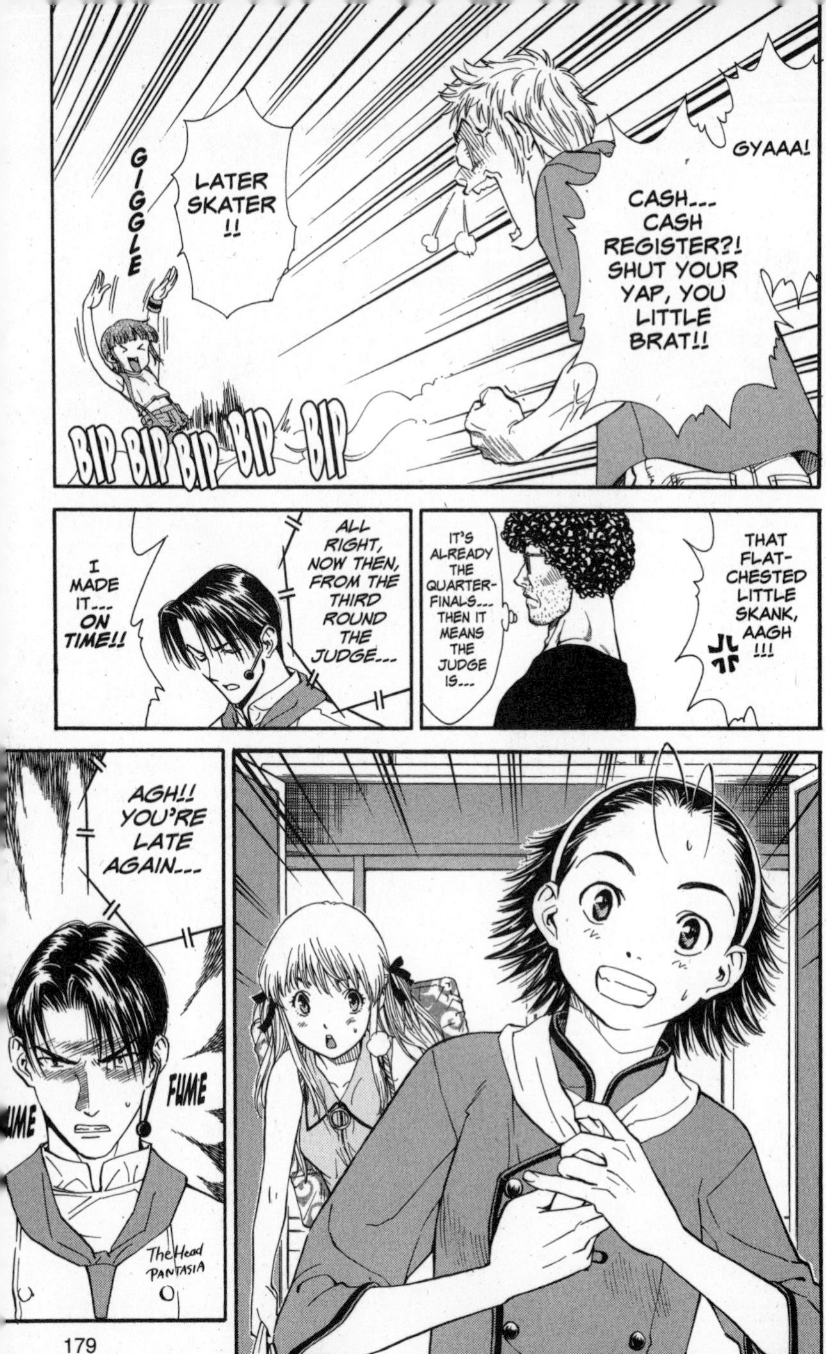
GYAAA!
CASH... CASH REGISTER?! SHUT YOUR YAP, YOU LITTLE BRAT!!
LATER SKATER!!
GIGGLE
BIP BIP BIP BIP BIP
THAT FLAT-CHESTED LITTLE SKANK, AAGH!!!
IT'S ALREADY THE QUARTER-FINALS... THEN IT MEANS THE JUDGE IS...
ALL RIGHT, NOW THEN, FROM THE THIRD ROUND THE JUDGE...
I MADE IT... ON TIME!!
AGH!! YOU'RE LATE AGAIN...
FUME
FUME
The Head PANTASIA

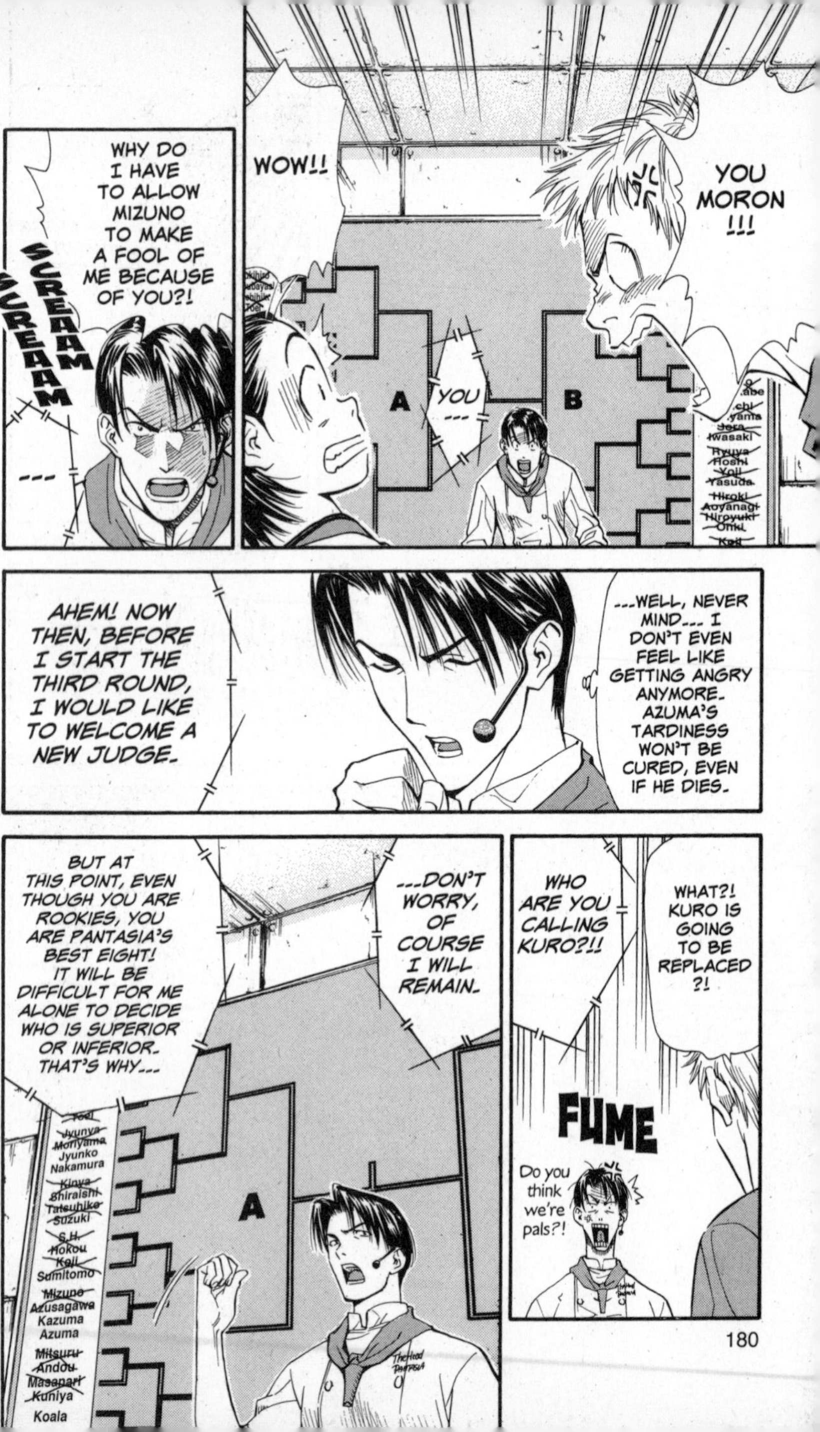
YOU MORON !!!
WOW!!
YOU ---
WHY DO I HAVE TO ALLOW MIZUNO TO MAKE A FOOL OF ME BECAUSE OF YOU?!
SCREAAM SCREAAM

---WELL, NEVER MIND--- I DON'T EVEN FEEL LIKE GETTING ANGRY ANYMORE. AZUMA'S TARDINESS WON'T BE CURED, EVEN IF HE DIES.
AHEM! NOW THEN, BEFORE I START THE THIRD ROUND, I WOULD LIKE TO WELCOME A NEW JUDGE.
WHAT?! KURO IS GOING TO BE REPLACED?!
WHO ARE YOU CALLING KURO?!!
FUME
Do you think we're pals?!
---DON'T WORRY, OF COURSE I WILL REMAIN.
BUT AT THIS POINT, EVEN THOUGH YOU ARE ROOKIES, YOU ARE PANTASIA'S BEST EIGHT! IT WILL BE DIFFICULT FOR ME ALONE TO DECIDE WHO IS SUPERIOR OR INFERIOR. THAT'S WHY---
Toei
Jyunya Moriyama
Jyunko Nakamura
Kinya Shiraishi
Tatsuhiko Suzuki
S.H. Hokou
Koji Sumitomo
Mizuno Azusagawa
Kazuma Azuma
Mitsuru Andou
Masanari Kuniya
Koala
A

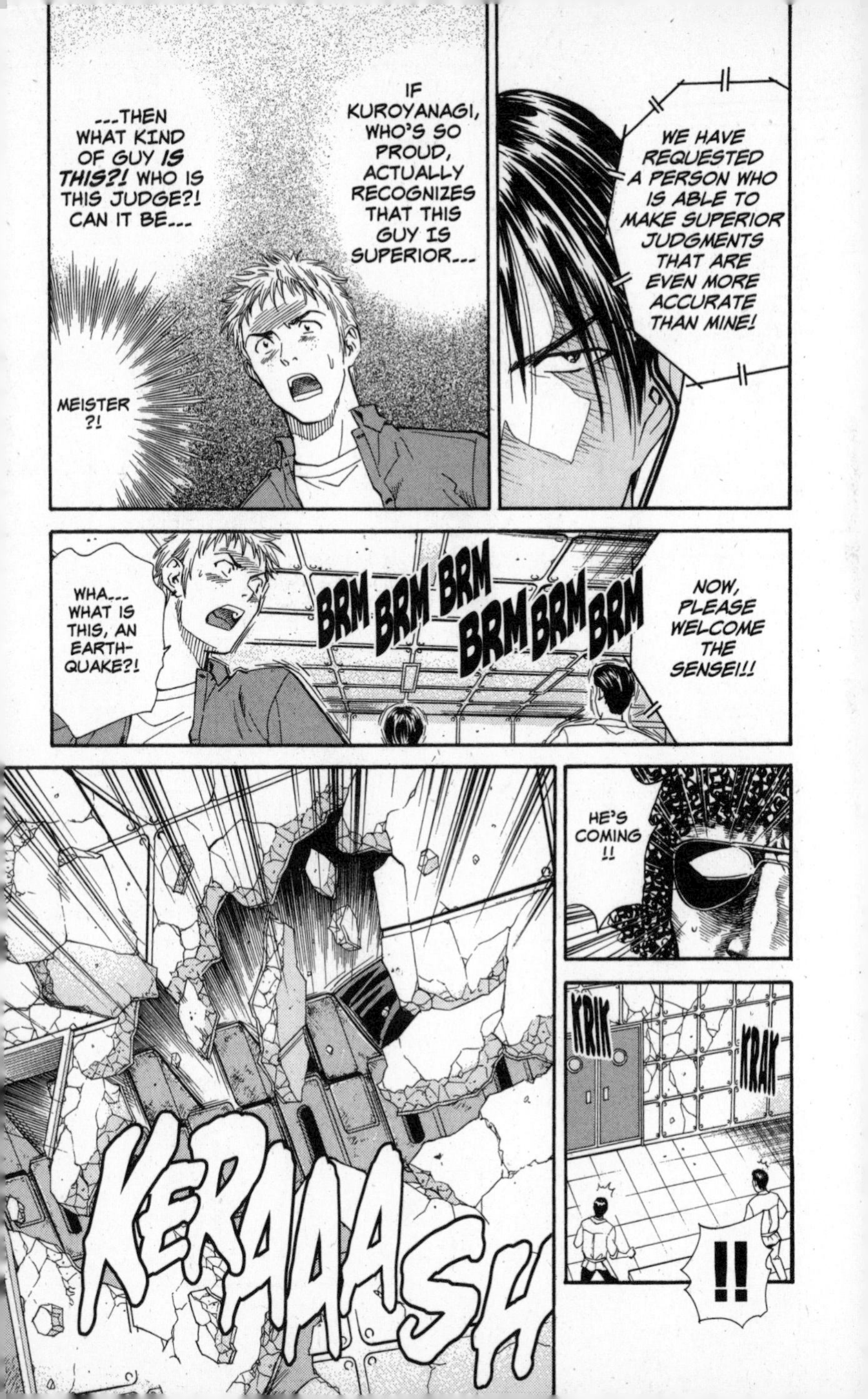
WE HAVE REQUESTED A PERSON WHO IS ABLE TO MAKE SUPERIOR JUDGMENTS THAT ARE EVEN MORE ACCURATE THAN MINE!
IF KUROYANAGI, WHO'S SO PROUD, ACTUALLY RECOGNIZES THAT THIS GUY IS SUPERIOR...
...THEN WHAT KIND OF GUY *IS THIS?!* WHO IS THIS JUDGE?! CAN IT BE...
MEISTER ?!
NOW, PLEASE WELCOME THE SENSEI!!
BRM BRM BRM BRM BRM BRM
WHA... WHAT IS THIS, AN EARTH-QUAKE?!
HE'S COMING !!
KRIK
KRAK
!!
KERAAASH

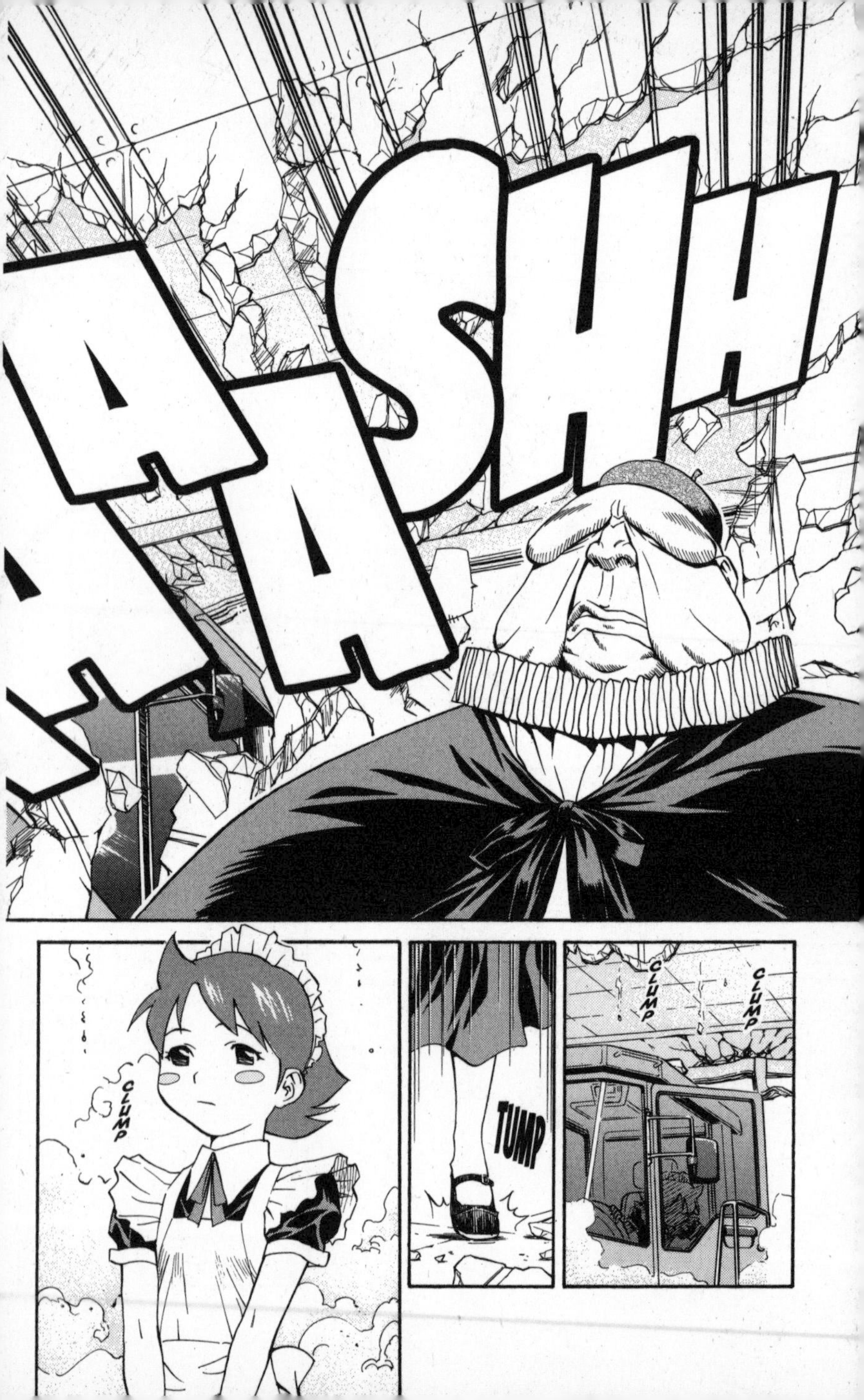
AASH!
CLUMP
CLUMP
TUMP
CLUMP

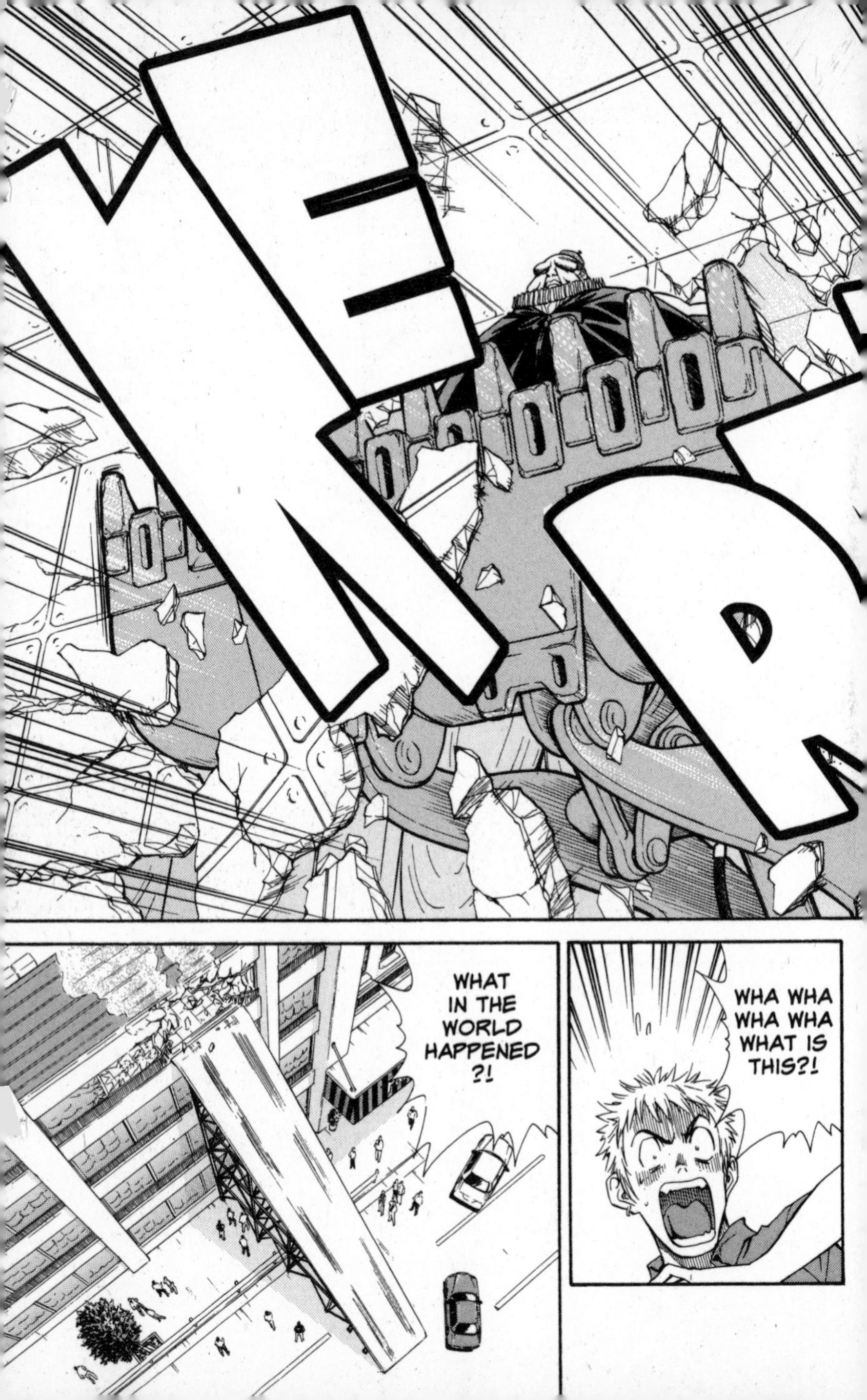
WHA WHA WHA WHA WHAT IS THIS?!
WHAT IN THE WORLD HAPPENED ?!

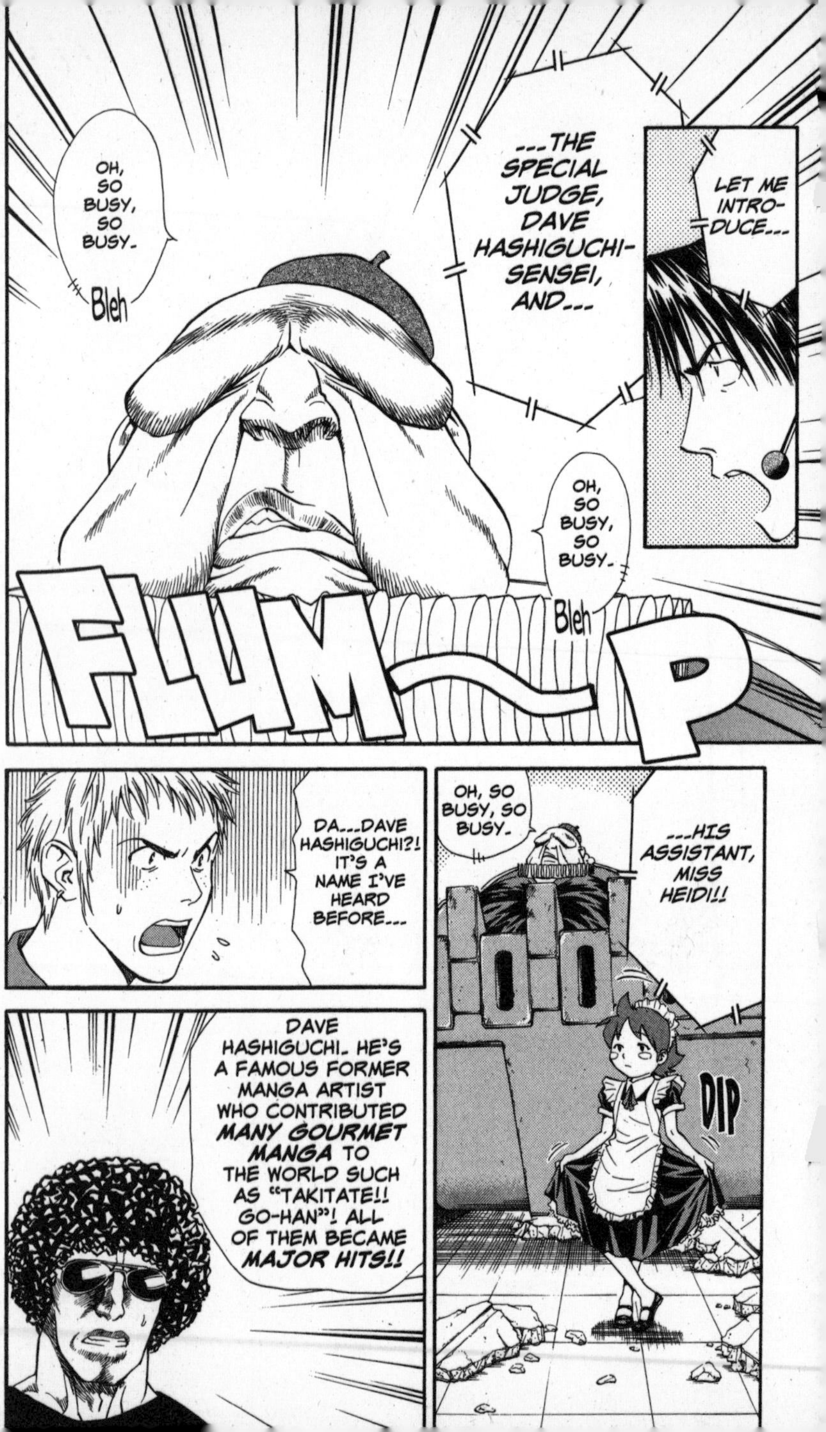
LET ME INTRODUCE...
...THE SPECIAL JUDGE, DAVE HASHIGUCHI-SENSEI, AND...
OH, SO BUSY, SO BUSY.
Bleh
OH, SO BUSY, SO BUSY.
Bleh
FLUM~P
...HIS ASSISTANT, MISS HEIDI!!
OH, SO BUSY, SO BUSY.
DIP
DA...DAVE HASHIGUCHI?! IT'S A NAME I'VE HEARD BEFORE...
DAVE HASHIGUCHI. HE'S A FAMOUS FORMER MANGA ARTIST WHO CONTRIBUTED ***MANY GOURMET MANGA*** TO THE WORLD SUCH AS "TAKITATE!! GO-HAN"! ALL OF THEM BECAME ***MAJOR HITS!!***

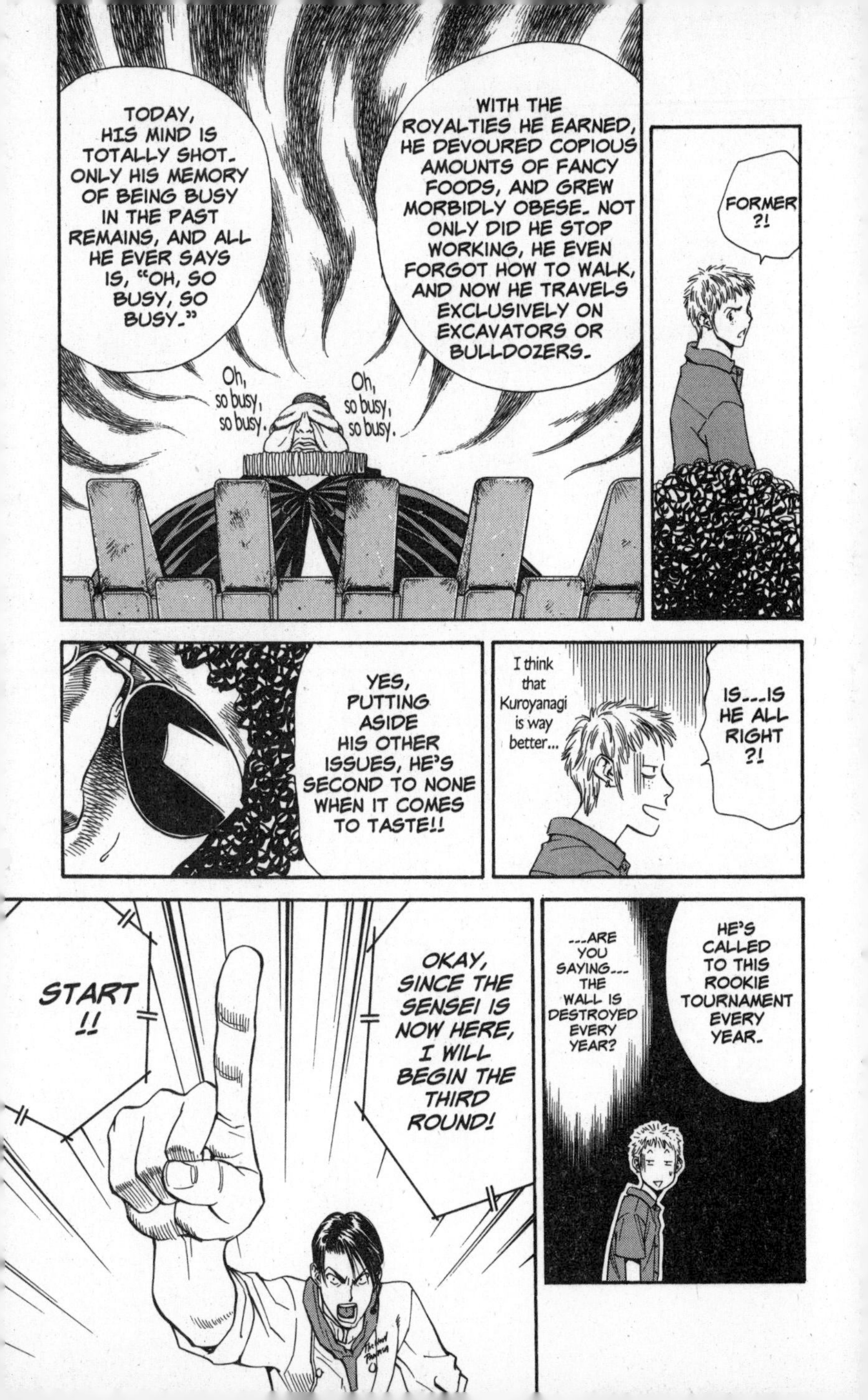
FORMER ?!
WITH THE ROYALTIES HE EARNED, HE DEVOURED COPIOUS AMOUNTS OF FANCY FOODS, AND GREW MORBIDLY OBESE. NOT ONLY DID HE STOP WORKING, HE EVEN FORGOT HOW TO WALK, AND NOW HE TRAVELS EXCLUSIVELY ON EXCAVATORS OR BULLDOZERS.
TODAY, HIS MIND IS TOTALLY SHOT. ONLY HIS MEMORY OF BEING BUSY IN THE PAST REMAINS, AND ALL HE EVER SAYS IS, "OH, SO BUSY, SO BUSY."
Oh, so busy, so busy.
Oh, so busy, so busy.
IS...IS HE ALL RIGHT ?!
I think that Kuroyanagi is way better...
YES, PUTTING ASIDE HIS OTHER ISSUES, HE'S SECOND TO NONE WHEN IT COMES TO TASTE!!
HE'S CALLED TO THIS ROOKIE TOURNAMENT EVERY YEAR.
...ARE YOU SAYING... THE WALL IS DESTROYED EVERY YEAR?
OKAY, SINCE THE SENSEI IS NOW HERE, I WILL BEGIN THE THIRD ROUND!
START !!

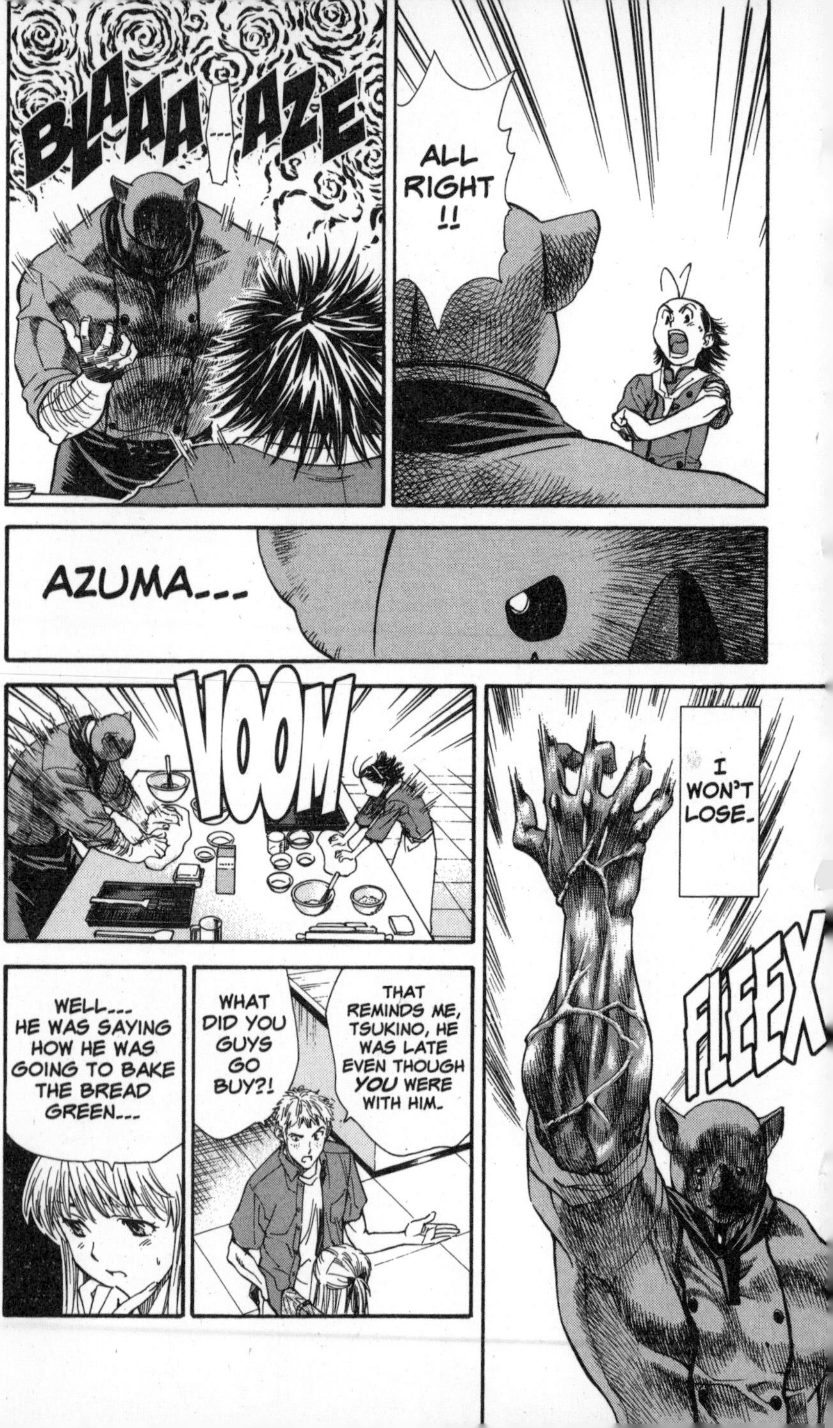
ALL RIGHT!!
BLAAAAZE
AZUMA...
I WON'T LOSE.
FLEEX
VOOM
THAT REMINDS ME, TSUKINO, HE WAS LATE EVEN THOUGH *YOU* WERE WITH HIM.
WHAT DID YOU GUYS GO BUY?!
WELL... HE WAS SAYING HOW HE WAS GOING TO BAKE THE BREAD GREEN...

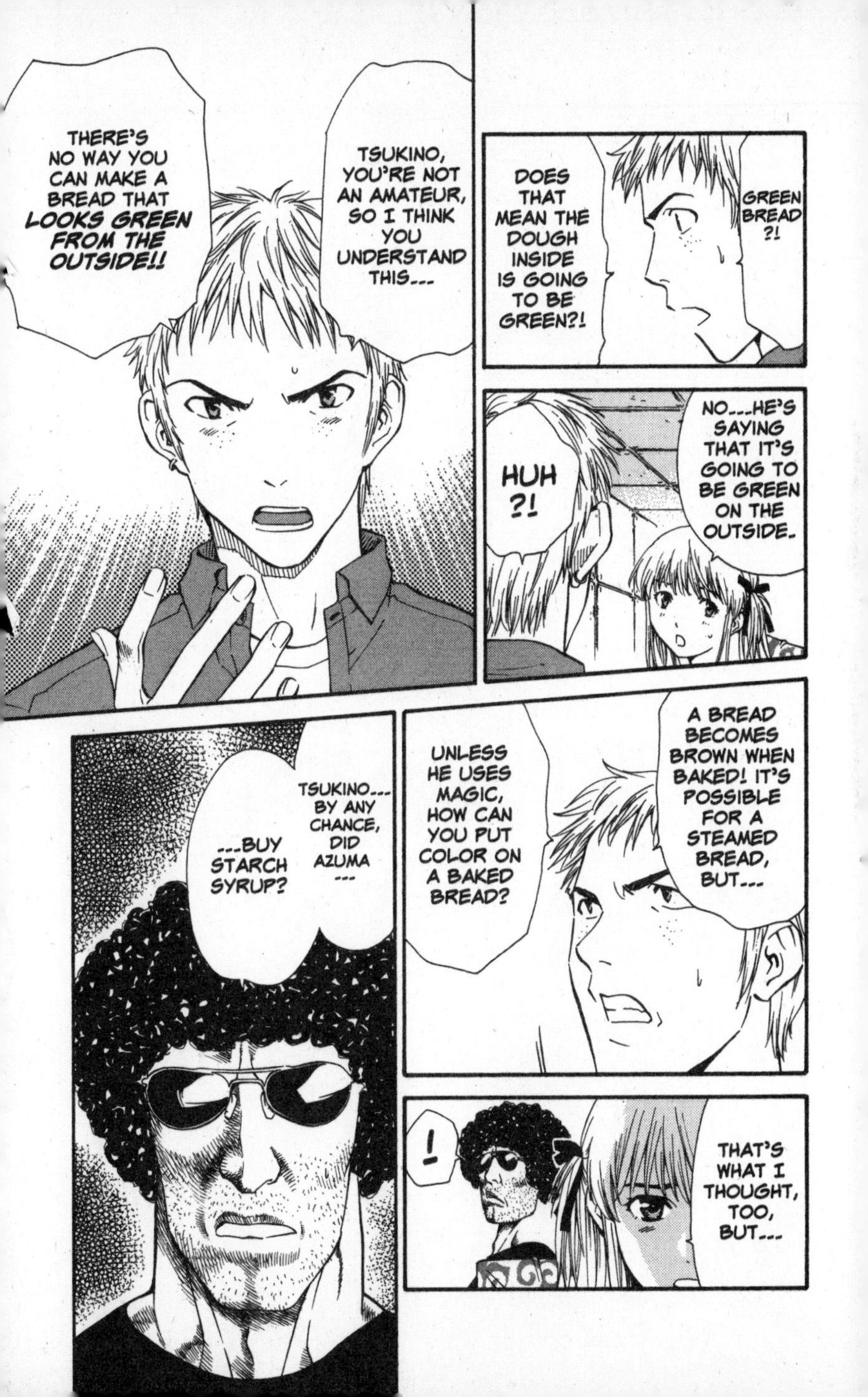
GREEN BREAD?!
DOES THAT MEAN THE DOUGH INSIDE IS GOING TO BE GREEN?!
NO---HE'S SAYING THAT IT'S GOING TO BE GREEN ON THE OUTSIDE.
HUH?!
TSUKINO, YOU'RE NOT AN AMATEUR, SO I THINK YOU UNDERSTAND THIS---
THERE'S NO WAY YOU CAN MAKE A BREAD THAT LOOKS GREEN FROM THE OUTSIDE!!
A BREAD BECOMES BROWN WHEN BAKED! IT'S POSSIBLE FOR A STEAMED BREAD, BUT---
UNLESS HE USES MAGIC, HOW CAN YOU PUT COLOR ON A BAKED BREAD?
THAT'S WHAT I THOUGHT, TOO, BUT---
!
TSUKINO--- BY ANY CHANCE, DID AZUMA ---
---BUY STARCH SYRUP?

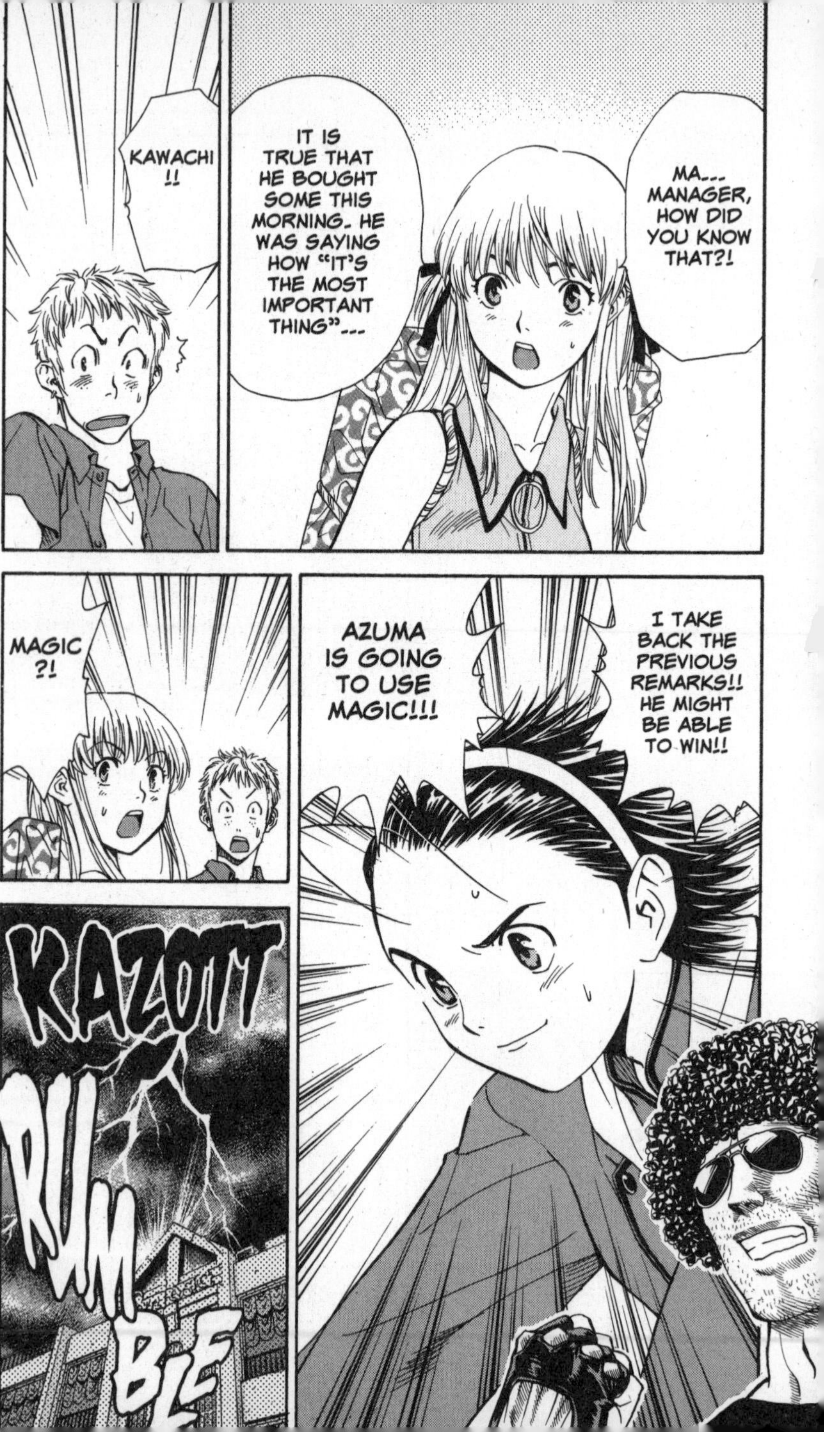
MA... MANAGER, HOW DID YOU KNOW THAT?!
IT IS TRUE THAT HE BOUGHT SOME THIS MORNING. HE WAS SAYING HOW "IT'S THE MOST IMPORTANT THING"...
KAWACHI !!
I TAKE BACK THE PREVIOUS REMARKS!! HE MIGHT BE ABLE TO WIN!!
AZUMA IS GOING TO USE MAGIC!!!
MAGIC ?!
KAZOTT
RUMBLE

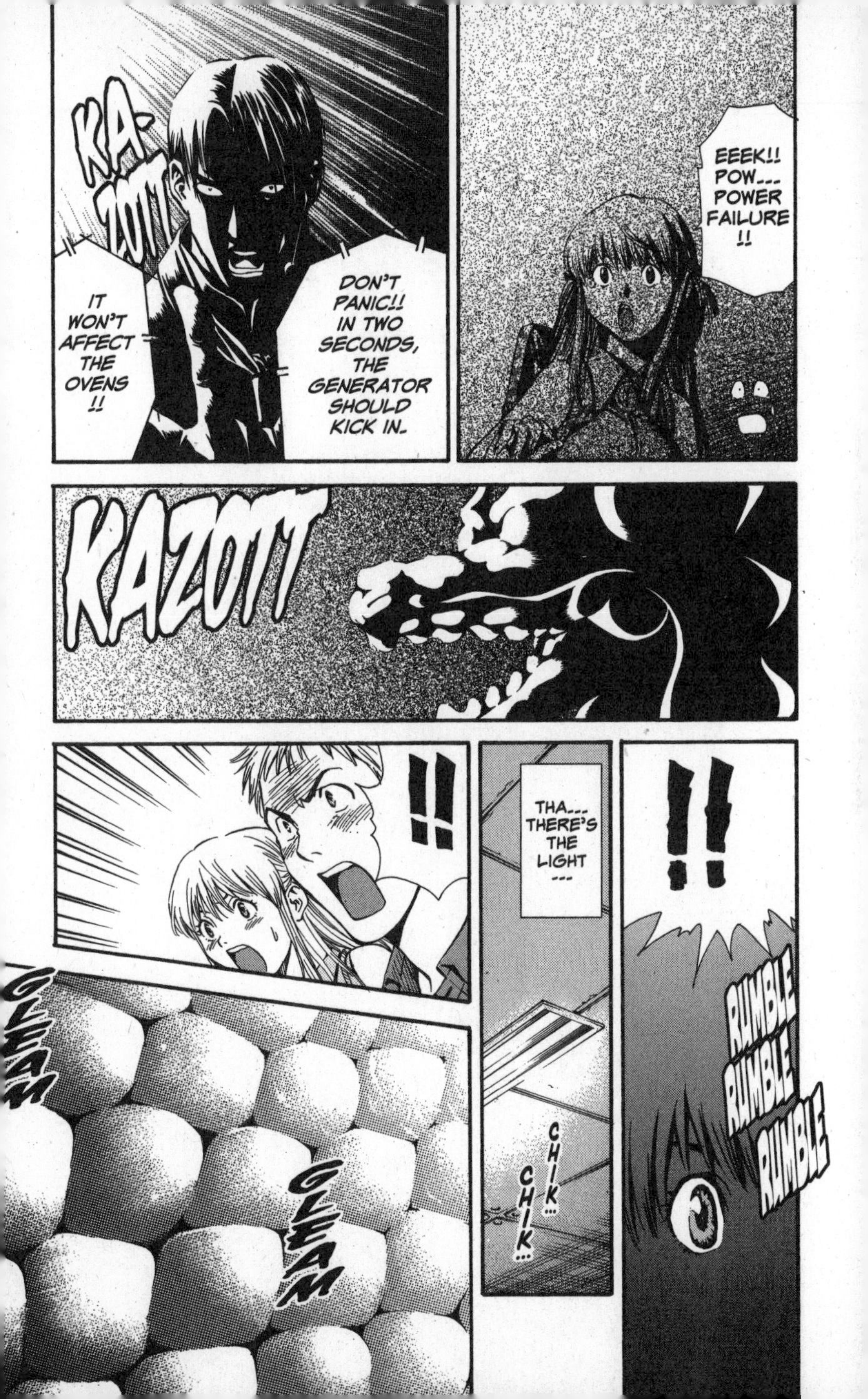
EEEK!! POW... POWER FAILURE !!
KA-ZOTT
DON'T PANIC!! IN TWO SECONDS, THE GENERATOR SHOULD KICK IN.
IT WON'T AFFECT THE OVENS !!
KAZOTT
!!
THA... THERE'S THE LIGHT ...
CHIK... CHIK...
!!
RUMBLE RUMBLE RUMBLE
GLEAM
GLEAM

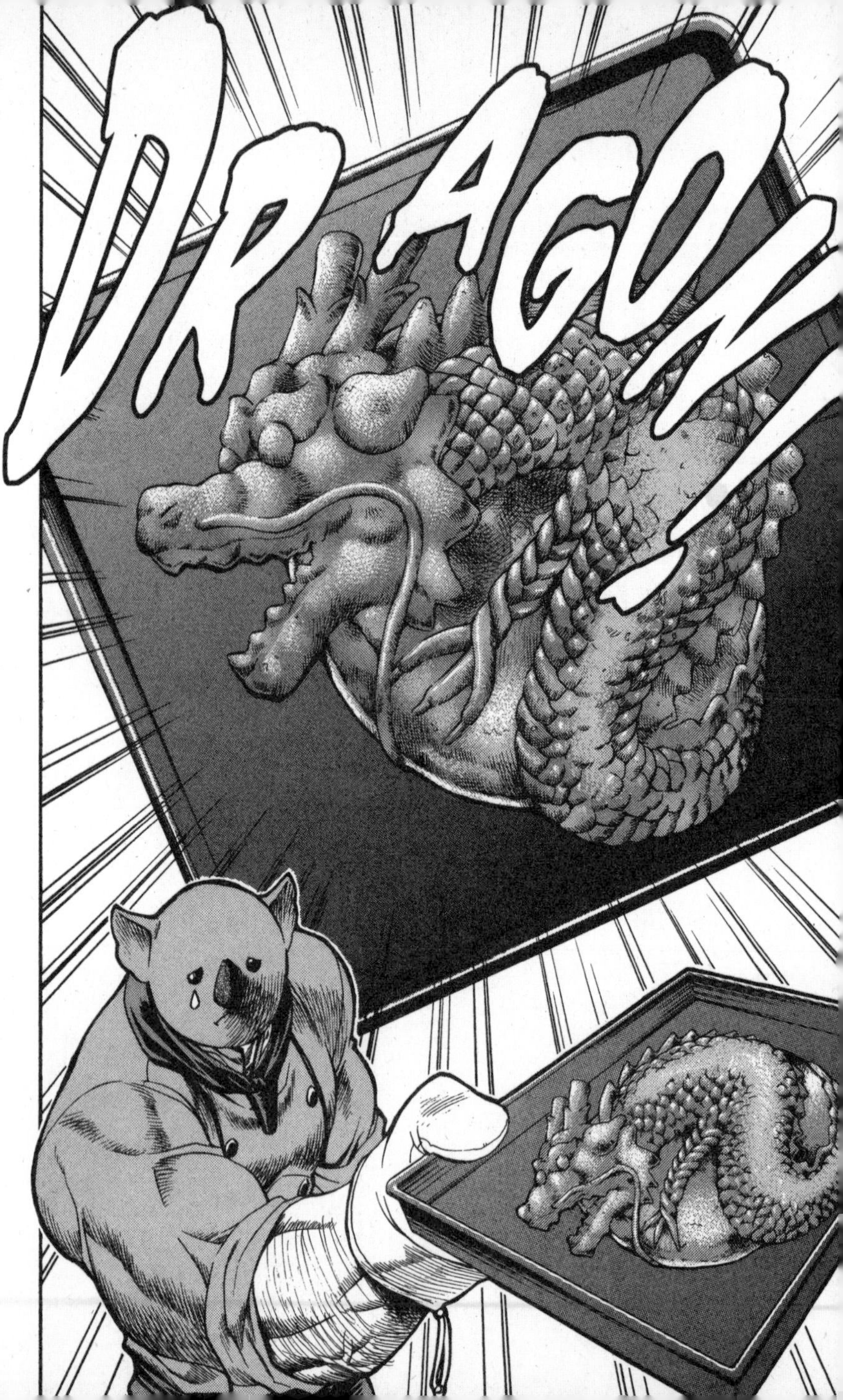
DRAGON!

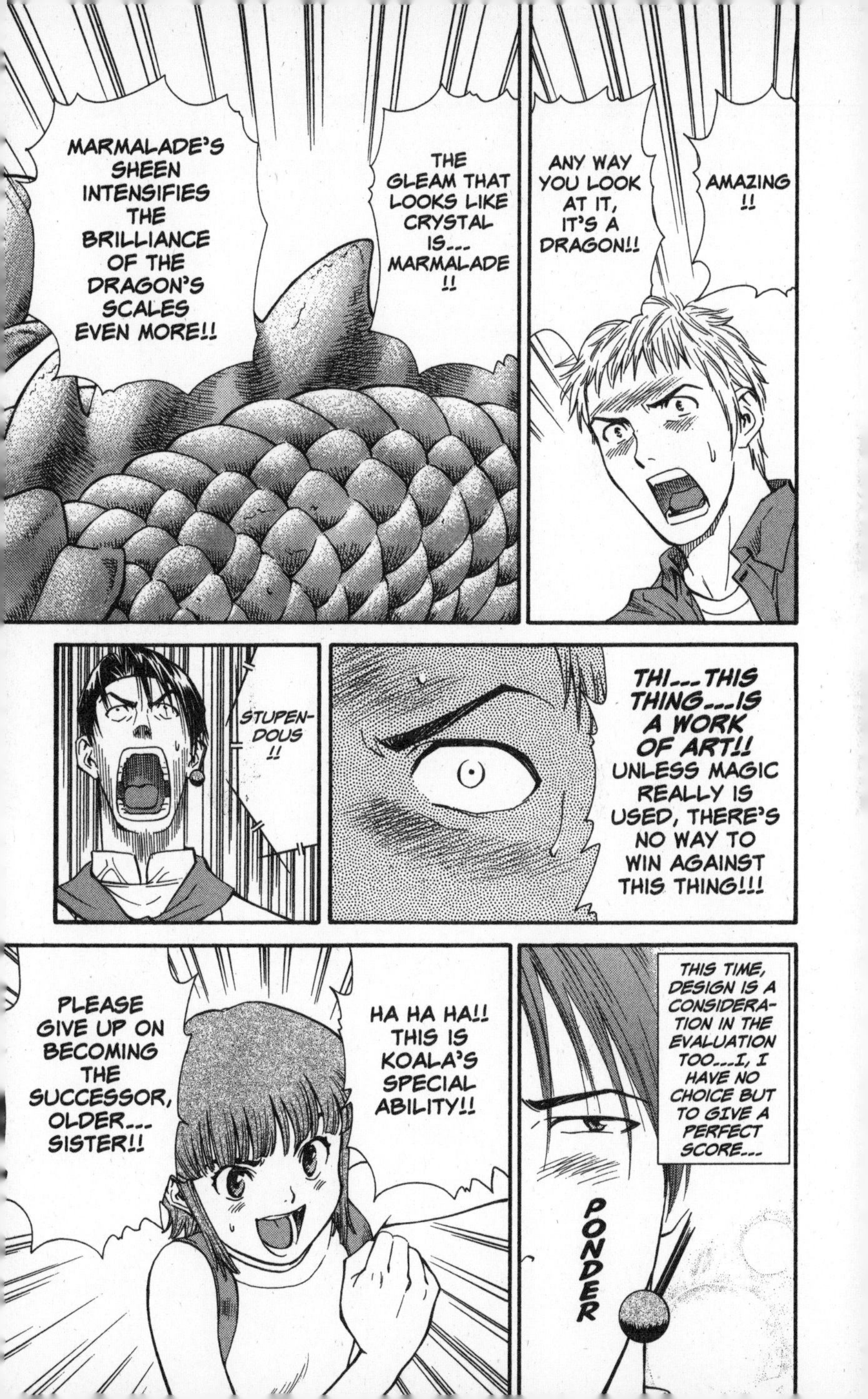
AMAZING!!
ANY WAY YOU LOOK AT IT, IT'S A DRAGON!!
THE GLEAM THAT LOOKS LIKE CRYSTAL IS... MARMALADE!!
MARMALADE'S SHEEN INTENSIFIES THE BRILLIANCE OF THE DRAGON'S SCALES EVEN MORE!!
THI... THIS THING... IS A WORK OF ART!! UNLESS MAGIC REALLY IS USED, THERE'S NO WAY TO WIN AGAINST THIS THING!!!
STUPENDOUS!!
THIS TIME, DESIGN IS A CONSIDERATION IN THE EVALUATION TOO... I, I HAVE NO CHOICE BUT TO GIVE A PERFECT SCORE...
PONDER
HA HA HA!! THIS IS KOALA'S SPECIAL ABILITY!!
PLEASE GIVE UP ON BECOMING THE SUCCESSOR, OLDER... SISTER!!

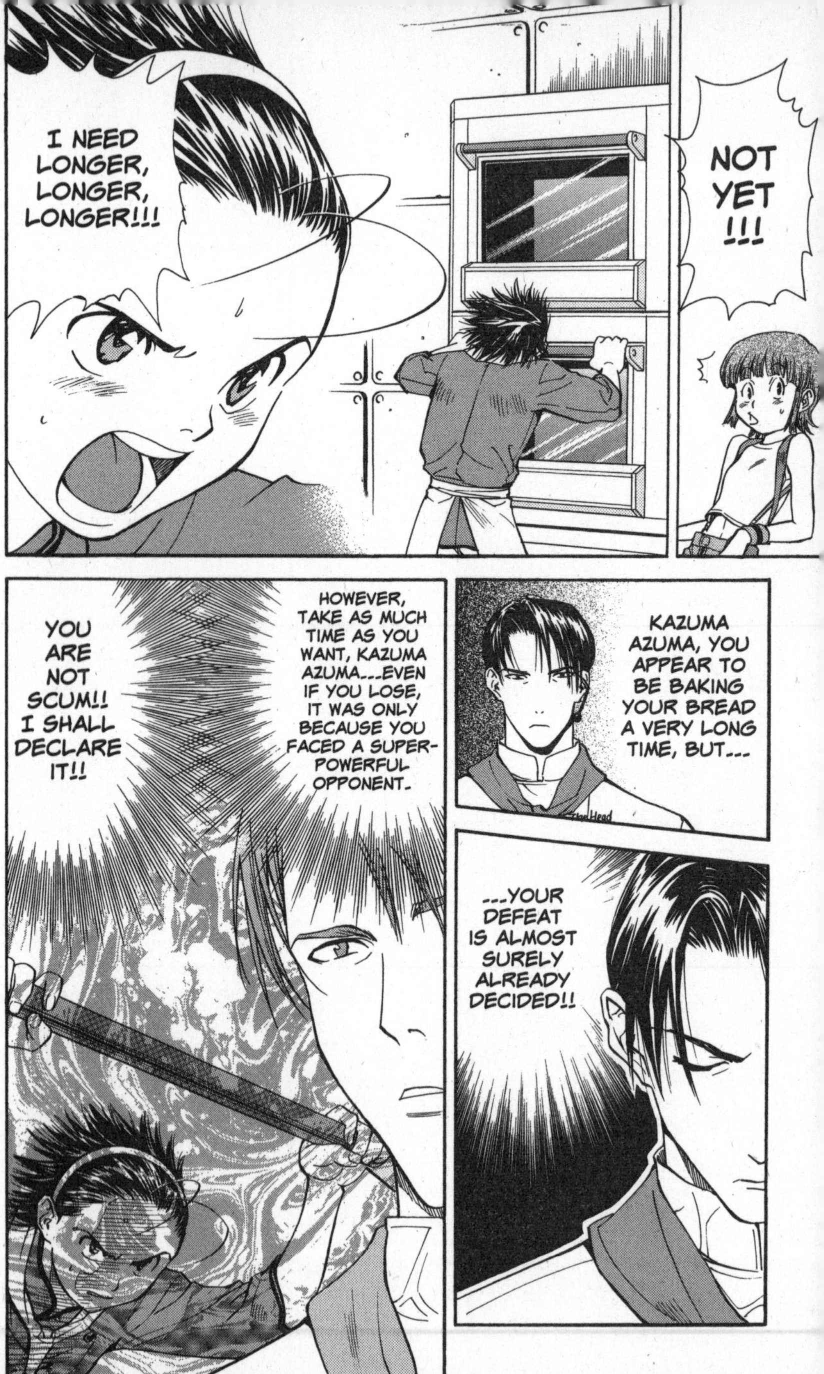
NOT YET!!!
I NEED LONGER, LONGER, LONGER!!!
KAZUMA AZUMA, YOU APPEAR TO BE BAKING YOUR BREAD A VERY LONG TIME, BUT...
...YOUR DEFEAT IS ALMOST SURELY ALREADY DECIDED!!
HOWEVER, TAKE AS MUCH TIME AS YOU WANT, KAZUMA AZUMA...EVEN IF YOU LOSE, IT WAS ONLY BECAUSE YOU FACED A SUPER-POWERFUL OPPONENT.
YOU ARE NOT SCUM!! I SHALL DECLARE IT!!

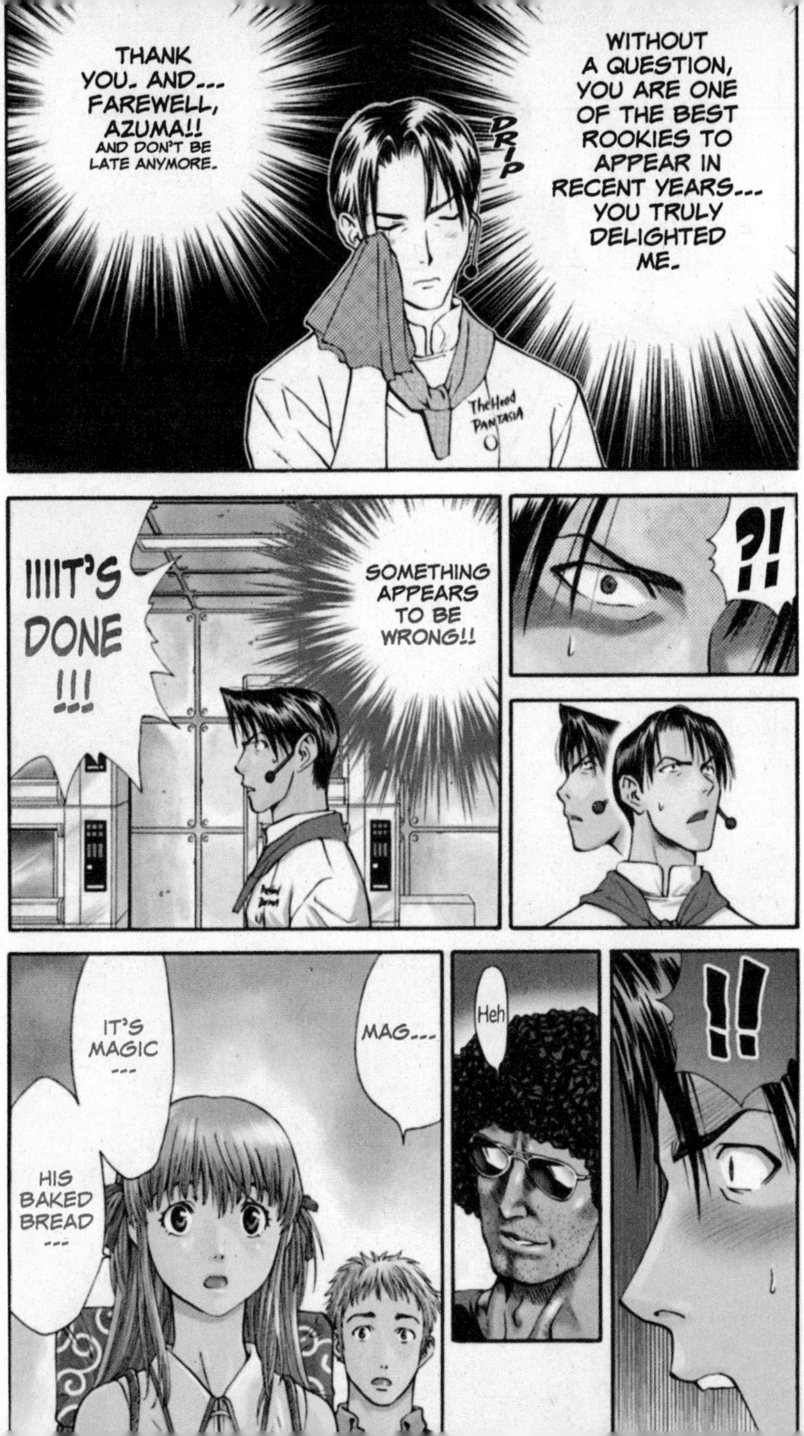
WITHOUT A QUESTION, YOU ARE ONE OF THE BEST ROOKIES TO APPEAR IN RECENT YEARS... YOU TRULY DELIGHTED ME.
DRIP
THANK YOU. AND... FAREWELL, AZUMA!! AND DON'T BE LATE ANYMORE.
TheHead PANTASIA
?!
SOMETHING APPEARS TO BE WRONG!!
IIIIT'S DONE!!!
!!
Heh
MAG...
IT'S MAGIC...
HIS BAKED BREAD...

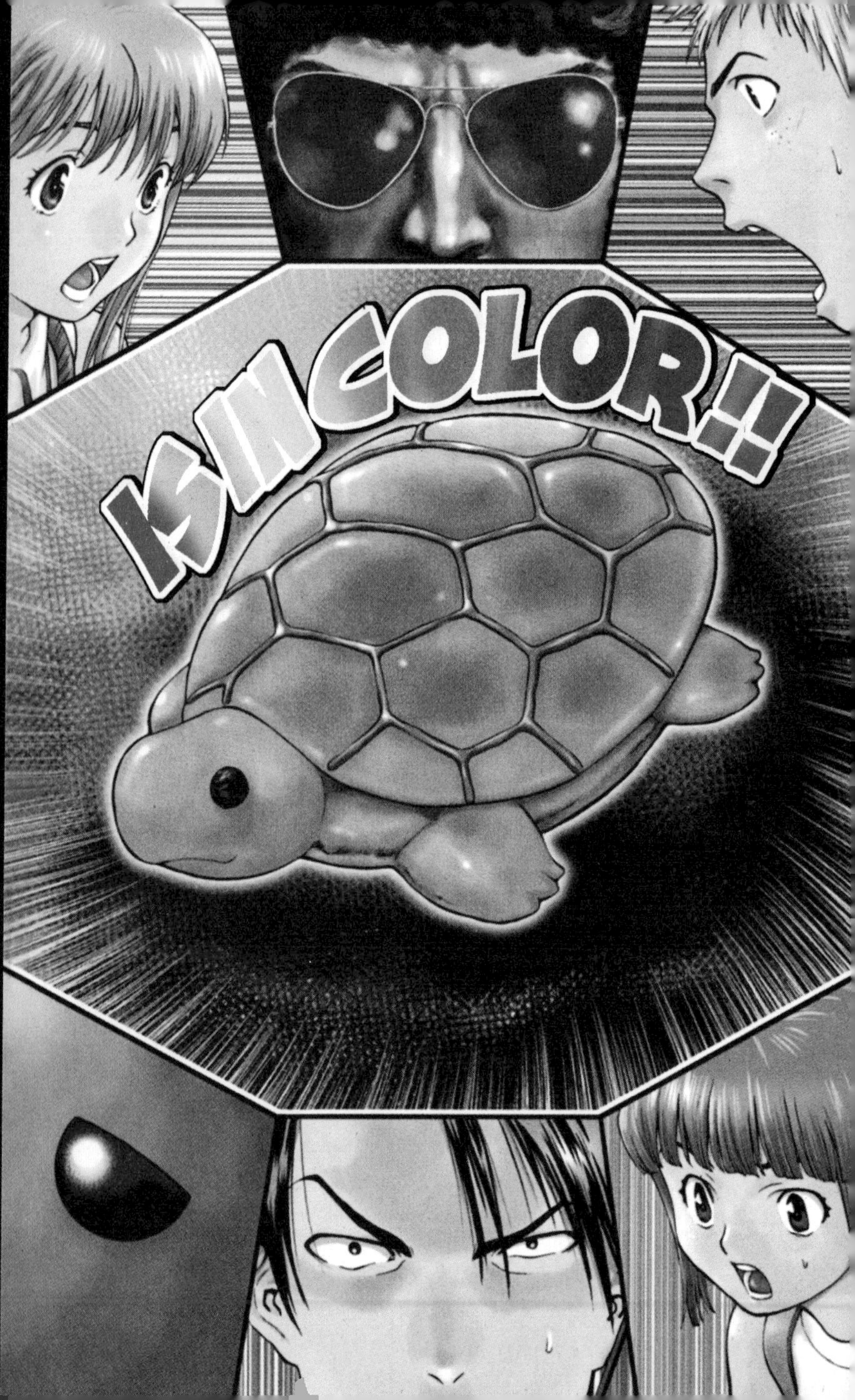
IS IN COLOR!!

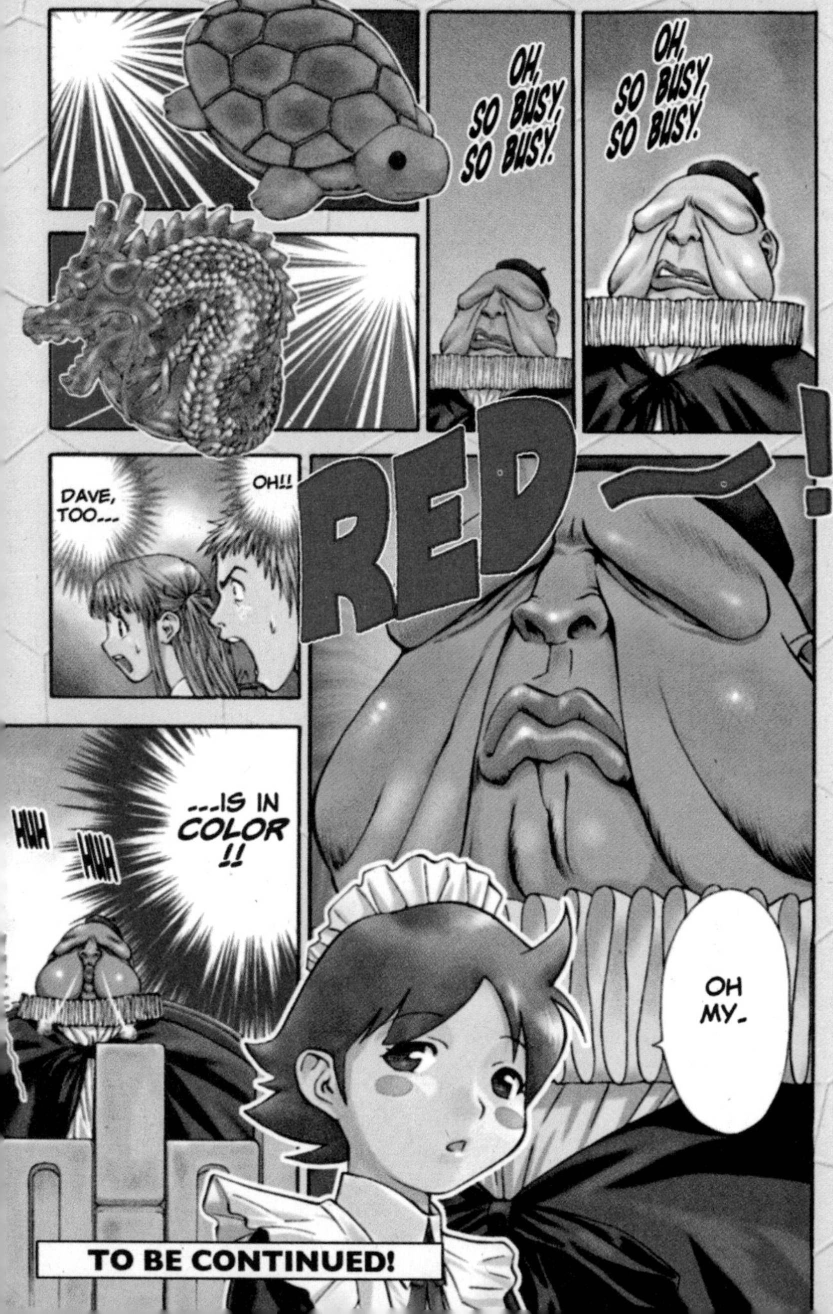
OH, SO BUSY, SO BUSY.
OH, SO BUSY, SO BUSY.
RED~!
OH MY.
OH!!
DAVE, TOO...
...IS IN COLOR!!
HUH
HUH
TO BE CONTINUED!

Since color was put on the last page (right), we also decided to include photographs.

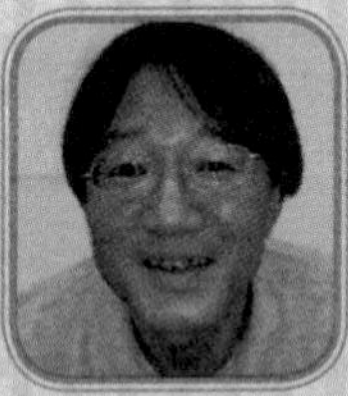

Person in charge of manga editing

Yoshihiro Iida

●45 years old

"A gentle person"

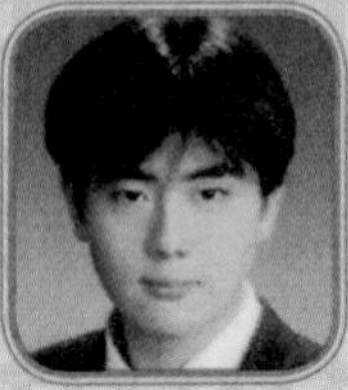

Person in charge of serialization as well as manga editing

Shigeru Kanmuri

●29 years old

"Only wears a suit occasionally"

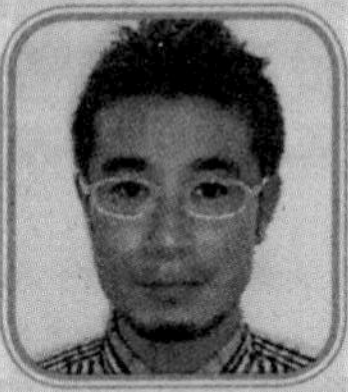

Manga Editing

Youtaro Yamamoto

●28 years old

"The person from Ai Production"

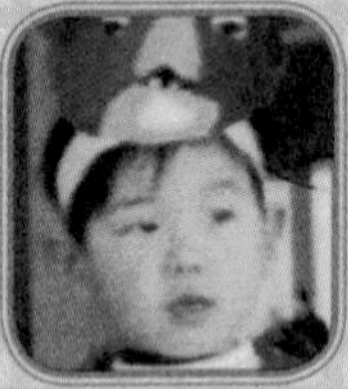

Author

Takashi Hashiguchi

●3 years old

"A kid"

* The printing is in order of the ages in the photos.

YAKITATE!! JAPAN
VOL. 4

STORY AND ART BY
TAKASHI HASHIGUCHI

English Adaptation/Drew Williams
Translation/Noritaka Minami
Touch-up Art & Lettering/Steve Dutro
Cover Design/Yukiko Whitley
Editor/Kit Fox

Managing Editor/Annette Roman
Editorial Director/Elizabeth Kawasaki
Editor in Chief/Alvin Lu
Sr. Director of Acquisitions/Rika Inouye
Sr. VP of Marketing/Liza Coppola
Exec. VP of Sales & Marketing/John Easum
Publisher/Hyoe Narita

Printed in the U.S.A.

Published by VIZ Media, LLC
P.O. Box 77010
San Francisco, CA 94107

10 9 8 7 6 5 4 3 2 1
First printing, March 2007

www.viz.com   store.viz.com

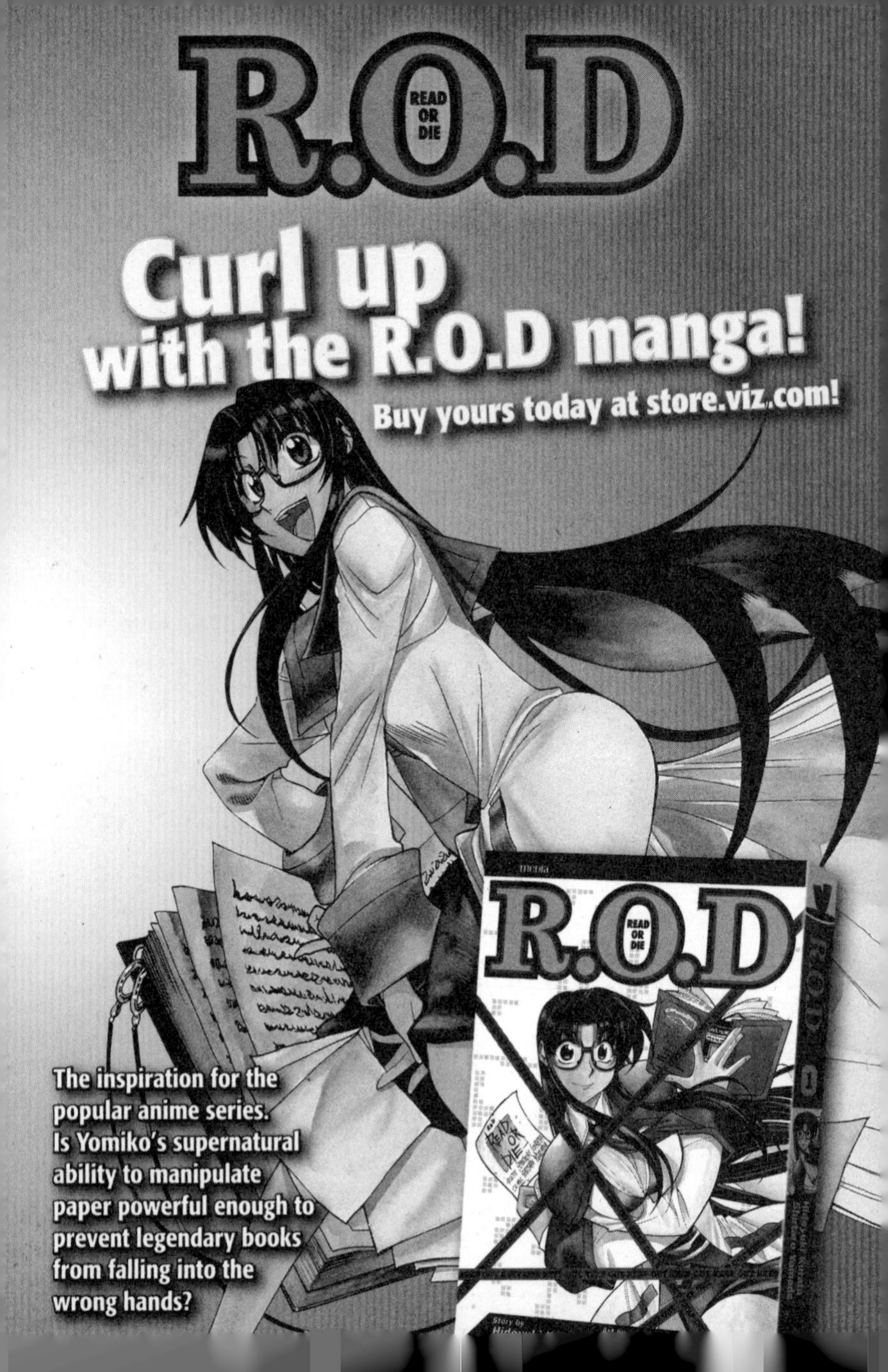
R.O.D
READ OR DIE
Curl up with the R.O.D manga!
Buy yours today at store.viz.com!
The inspiration for the popular anime series. Is Yomiko's supernatural ability to manipulate paper powerful enough to prevent legendary books from falling into the wrong hands?
R.O.D
READ OR DIE
READ OR DIE

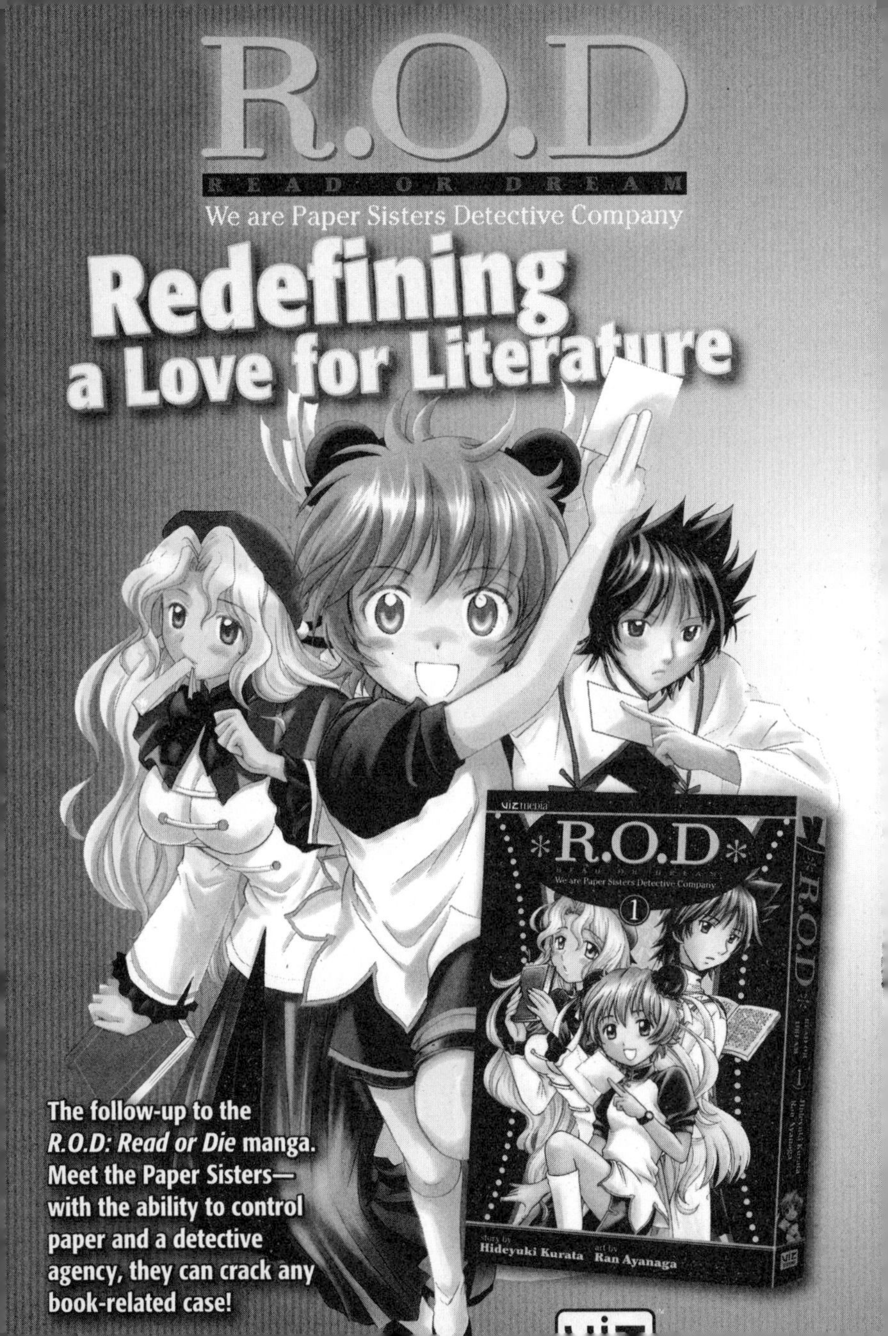

R.O.D
READ OR DREAM
We are Paper Sisters Detective Company
Redefining a Love for Literature
R.O.D
We are Paper Sisters Detective Company
1
story by Hideyuki Kurata
art by Ran Ayanaga
The follow-up to the *R.O.D: Read or Die* manga. Meet the Paper Sisters—with the ability to control paper and a detective agency, they can crack any book-related case!